The W... ...lon

History Workshop Series

General Editor
Raphael Samuel, *Ruskin College, Oxford*

Already published
Village Life and Labour
Miners, Quarrymen and Salt Workers
Rothschild Buildings
East End Underworld
People's History and Socialist Theory
Culture, Ideology and Politics
Sex and Class in Women's History
Living the Fishing
Fenwomen
Late Marx and the Russian Road
Theatres of the Left 1880–1935
Language, Gender and Childhood

Routledge & Kegan Paul
London, Boston and Henley

Jerry White

The Worst Street in North London

Campbell Bunk, Islington, between the Wars

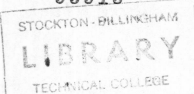
First published in 1986
by Routledge & Kegan Paul plc

14 Leicester Square, London WC2H 7PH, England

9 Park Street, Boston, Mass. 02108, USA and

Broadway House, Newtown Road,
Henley on Thames, Oxon RG9 1EN, England

Set in 11/12 Linotron Bembo
by Input Typesetting Ltd, London
and printed in Great Britain
by T. J. Press (Padstow) Ltd, Padstow, Cornwall

© *Jerry White 1986*

Library of Congress Cataloging in Publication Data

White, Jerry, 1949–
The worst street in North London.

(History workshop series)
Bibliography: p.
Includes Index.
1. London (England)—Social conditions—Case studies.
2. Islington (London, England)—Social conditions—Case
studies. 3. Slums—England—London—Case studies.
4. Campbell Road (London, England)—Case studies.
I. Title. II. Series.
HN398.L7W45   1986   306'.09421'4   85—14438

British Library CIP data also available
ISBN 0–7102–0700–X

for
Raphael Samuel

Contents

    Context   161
    Walter Spencer: The straight and narrow   167
    Billy Tagg: A chapter of accidents   172
    Harry James and the young thieves of Campbell Bunk   176

7   Young women and the new world outside   188
    Work, culture and marriage   188
    May Purslowe, Nancy Tiverton and the struggle with   199
        mothers
    Jane Munby and the delinquent solution   208
    Mavis Knight, Olive Tasker and a new world for   212
        women

8   The fall of Campbell Bunk   219
    Moving out   219
    The war   226
    Slum clearance   234
    Epitaph   236

    Figures and tables   238

    Notes   264

    Bibliography   295

    Index   309

Illustrations

Acknowledgments

I hope this book is easier to read than it was to write. It was put together largely between 9 p.m. and 1 a.m. in the dark hours left by an over-demanding, full-time, non-related job and a young family which managed to expand by three children during the process. No book should be written like that: and if this one sometimes appears a little ragged at the edges it is but the faintest indication that I am, too.

Any number of people have prevented me from coming apart completely at the seams. First, most important and generous, have been ex-residents of Campbell Bunk, without whom this study would have been impossible: Mrs Lily Abbott, Mrs Ellen Bartlett, Mr Alfred Bartlett, Mrs Rose Bennett, Mrs Fran Callum, Mr Tom Callum, Mrs Myra Keen, Mrs Clara Munger, Mrs Marguerite Thacker, Mrs Eileen Rossehill, Mrs Violet Carpenter, Mrs Florrie Maggs, Mrs Lil Mundy, Mrs Cissie Pollard, Mrs Kitty Smith, Mrs Annie Vyce, Mr Charles Aldridge, Mr James Beales, Mr 'Bob' Burchnall, Mr John Blake, Mr John Barrett, Mr Henry Corke, Mr James Day, Mr James Green, Mr Wally Jerrams, Mr Arthur King, Mr Fred Lawrence, Mr George Sailing, Mr Lenny Sailing. In the text, these names have been changed to maintain confidentiality of personal information. A number of other people gave me information about the street, in particular Mrs Hilda Hewitt, Mrs Ada Watkins, Miss Dorothy Harmer, ex-PC G. M. Hoyle, ex-PS Stan Costen, ex-PS S. C. Caplen, ex-PC E. Abrams, ex-PC Ernest Creed, ex-PC Jones. And some others have helped with general information about Islington between the wars, especially Mr Louis Gillain, Mr Bill Salisbury, Mrs Lily and Mr Albert Deane, and Mr Ken Weller. Taped interviews, transcripts and letters will eventually be held at the London History Workshop Centre. The Nuffield Foundation gave me a generous grant to help with transcription facilities and an extensive computer analysis of the New Survey of London household survey cards at the London School of Economics. The grant could not have been administered without the kind assistance of Noel Parry at the Polytechnic of North London, and of José Parry, who carried out the research with dedication, skill and patience. I would like to thank the staff at a variety of research libraries and institutions, especially the Library of Political and Economic Science at the London School of Economics, the British Library, the Greater London Record Office, and Islington Central Library; Mr William Stevenson, formerly Chief Environmental Health Officer to the London Borough of Islington, kindly loaned me photographs; and Rev. Short of St Mark's, Moray Road, gave me access to marriage registers. The Greater London Council gave permission to reproduce photographs nos 12 and 13; the Guildhall Library the photograph of Brand Street (no. 11); and Syndication International the 1935 street party (no. 2); others were kindly supplied by people from Campbell Road. The manuscript was typed by Lesley Muggeridge, and was read by Sally Alexander, Anna Davin, and Ruth Richardson, who gave invaluable advice. Needless to say, I am entirely responsible for any sins of omission or commission in what follows.

There is one other group without whom this book could not have been attempted. One burden (and delight) which the historian who is unattached to a teaching institution and library facilities has to bear is the accumulation of a personal library. My last thanks go to the secondhand booksellers of south-east England, especially John Hodgkins, B. L. Coombes, and Nick Spurrier, who have provided me with many treasures over the past eight years.

Jerry White
Stamford Hill, N16
February 1985

Map 1   Holloway, *c.* 1930

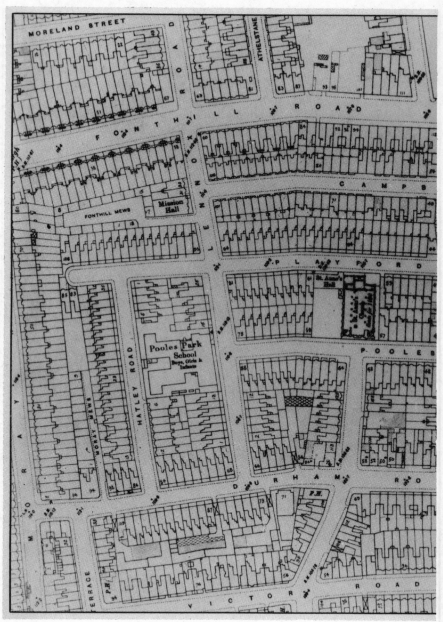

Map 2   Campbell Road, *c.* 1922

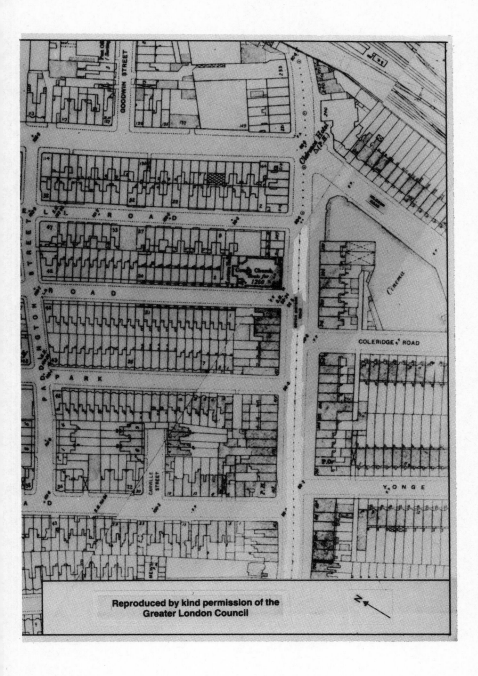

Introduction

I first heard of Campbell Bunk during the summer of 1971. At that time I was a health inspector for Islington Council, with a district to the south of Seven Sisters Road covering parts of Holloway and Finsbury Park. I didn't know it at the time but Campbell Road had lain immediately to the north, running out of Seven Sisters Road close to Finsbury Park underground station.

One day, during the course of my work, I met a Metropolitan Water Board inspector – wizened, bent and close to retirement – who had known Holloway and Finsbury Park all his life. Somehow we fell to talking of the terrors which might befall the unwary official in those parts, and about past terrors which I had luckily been spared. 'You should have known Campbell Bunk!' he told me, and recounted an incident which had happened to him there, I think just after the war. He had been walking through the street to attend to some supply defect when his peaked cap had been spotted from an upper window. He heard, 'Bleedin' Rozzers!' and simultaneously was soaked in kitchen slops. 'Water Board!' he replied, not inappropriately, and a woman appeared, apologised and took him indoors to dry him out and comfort him with a cup of tea. We laughed together over the story and went our separate ways; and although I saw him again many times we never, that I can recall, talked more about Campbell Bunk.

But, as often happens in other contexts, when once you hear a name you are struck by how often it appears subsequently. 'Campbell Bunk' did just that. It seemed to stand, in the popular memory of that sector of North London, as a sort of collective Artful Dodger. On the one hand the street was notorious as a terrible place – where the police only went in twos, where the inhabitants were violently hostile to respectable strangers, where the people were desperately poor: a corrective to the good old days vision of past and present. And on the other it was remembered for its vigorous street and community life, its spirited resistance to control by interfering outsiders, whether in blue serge or welfare workers' tweed: confirmation that in the good old days people were somehow more real, less conformist and stereotyped.

In the several conversations in which Campbell Bunk figured I was conscious that I was hearing only uninformed views – those of working-class neighbours or public officials or landlords' agents. So, on finishing my first book, *Rothschild Buildings*, I resolved to find some inside information by talking to people who had lived there. That proved fairly easy. A letter to the local newspaper in late 1977 provoked an eager response from a few ex-residents of Campbell Road: what proved to be an eight-year journey in search of the Bunk had begun.

The search was that long because I found the realities of life in Campbell Road so difficult to comprehend. Mine was a quest for understanding rather than description or narrative, but the contradictions exposed by life stories and other sources defied simple categorisation and left me bewildered afresh after each interview. In the end, of course, my search was incomplete and my understanding merely partial; but I felt that I had made some sense of the Bunk and had reached the point where I could reasonably share it with others.

Campbell Road was a peculiar place. Widely known as Campbell Bunk, or just 'the Bunk' by its habitués, it had a worse name than any other street in Islington. Each of London's working-class districts could claim its own 'worst street' but very few had a notoriety so indisputably black as Campbell Road's. It passed into local folklore, along with Bangor Street (Notting Dale), Litcham Street (Kentish Town), Rope Yard Rails (Woolwich), Baildon, Giffin and Hales Streets (Deptford), Essex Street and Wilmer Gardens (Hoxton), Perring Street (Bromley-by-Bow), Scott Street (West Ham) and a dozen more.

I suspect that Campbell Road held more than its reputation in common with streets like these. The Bunk was peculiar not only in name but in nature, and there is evidence that Bangor Street and the rest shared its distinctive characteristics. If Campbell Road can serve as a guide, these would have included a special place in the local housing market, catering for the very poor; a large number of men and women subsisting on the margins of wage labour, with many seeking a living through individual enterprise in London's street trades; 'backward-looking' traditions of popular culture at odds with the prevailing norms of working-class life; tendencies to living at least partly outside the law, with substantial minorities of men engaged in thieving and a smaller number of women who were casual or full-time prostitutes. Probably, too, a great deal of lived experience in Campbell Road was mirrored in these other places: extraordinarily high levels of domestic violence, predominantly against women and children; the puzzling contradiction of a close community where people were not always safe from neighbourly theft or communal attack; where worldviews militated against political allegiance and where loose ties to Labour might combine with fierce hostility to trade unionism; where women were the bearers of collective virtues but where struggles between mothers and daughters could be bitter and violent. In all this, Campbell Bunk might stand as representative of life in the toughest and poorest of the London 'slums' during the inter-war period.

A couple of years after beginning research I published an article in *History Workshop* which I intended to be my last word on Campbell Road. Although it included a side-swipe at sociology it was, in fact, flawed by the very thing I attacked. For the article was a snapshot in a vaguely-characterised time and place – 'inter-war London'. Some fascinating details of poverty, worklessness, violence and lawlessness were there, but though well enough dissected the street was anaesthetised in suspended animation, moving neither backwards nor forwards, surrounded by a vacuum. Slowly dawning appreciation of these inadequacies forced me into a book I never intended to write.

In the event, the book has had one organising principle in clear contrast to the article – understanding change in Campbell Road. I have focussed predominantly on the years after 1919, mainly because they were more accessible to oral history than the period before. But I needed to look at the street's origins to understand some of the underlying sources of change on which the 1920s built. No street is an island, and so to understand change I had to step far from Campbell Road – into its hinterland of Holloway (North Islington) and Finsbury Park, into the extraordinarily dynamic Greater London of the 1920s and 1930s, even into the changing social life of Britain as a whole.

In making sense of the contradictory community within Campbell Bunk, and its contradictory relations with the outside world, I have leant on what some might view as an outworn and tarnished prop – the Marxist analysis of class. This receives intrusive space to itself in Chapter 2 but not, I hope, so much as to make an obstacle to clarity or flow. Class analysis was one essential ingredient in understanding the complex weave of change in Campbell Road. But by itself it proved far from enough. The traditional Marxist focus on economic life and class relations helped explain how Campbell Bunk was created in the first place, identified some part of the cement which held it together for future generations to use, and illuminated a few important elements in the process of change which gradually dissolved it. But in none of these things could Marxism provide a complete explanation.

For example, one factor binding together the community of Campbell Bunk in the 1920s and 1930s was poverty and the collective servicing of needs which poverty inspired. But another was the psychic compensation for men with low status outside the street who created a hierarchy of masculinity in the Bunk and handed it down to their sons in turn.

That example concerns the traditions and continuities against which change had to struggle. Another might be cited from the process of dissolution which began to affect the street powerfully in the 1930s. Large processes in London as a whole helped wash away the economic base of Campbell Bunk – the street enterprises which men and older women entered in such large numbers. This undermined one element in communal solidarity – a common means of earning a living and the help and advice those similarly situated could contribute. But a far more important process (to which economics and class admittedly contributed) was the changing world for young women which affected their aspirations and expectations and weakened their ties with Campbell Road and the life chances it offered.

The changing social construction of gender – femininity and masculinity – and the very different worlds of men and women within Campbell Road, helped me fill the holes left by class analysis. For women, especially young women, seemed to me the vectors of change who were already transforming Campbell Bunk from within some years before the war and slum clearance worked out a final solution; whereas men, even young men, were self-conscious bearers of the Bunk's traditions and were a drag on change.

If I had been researching a more 'typical' London street – like Playford Road, perhaps, the street next door – I would have had immense difficulty in finding sources. But Campbell Road, because of its image but also its reality, drew comment and observation from all quarters. It receives dishonourable mention in social surveys and philanthropic records, and a reforming pamphlet to itself as late as 1943; its residents figure in 400 court reports in local newspapers between 1919 and 1939; it was the object of public complaint by sanitary inspectors, poor law officers, and police court magistrates. In all this, voices within Campbell Road are silent except when raised in self-defence.

The method open to the historian to break through this veil of class-imposed silence is, of course, oral history. Talking to people who lived in Campbell Road made this book possible, even though it is only in the last three chapters that life history is allowed power in its own right to elucidate change. But oral history could not be used uncritically. I found the reputation of the Bunk, even for insiders, sometimes too powerful to penetrate, imposing its own interpretation on events and obscuring day-to-day life altogether.

Partly because of that, I have not tried to make this book an insider's view of Campbell Bunk. I am gloomily conscious that its style and structure will not be immediately accessible, even though there will be much to strike sympathetic chords in people's memories. To avoid giving offence, I have changed virtually every name quoted by oral and written sources, rendering the text even more confusing to people who remember the street from the inside.

Nor, at the other extreme, have I sought to make the book especially relevant to an academic audience, although I have taken considerable care over verification and constructed a bibliography to help others into the largely uncharted waters of London between the wars. But I have not concerned myself with key debates in historical interpretation, and my excursions into theory take the reader down branch lines where many already see nothing but weeds and rust.

In the end I wrote this book for myself, because I wanted to understand better a street and a community which perplexed me beyond endurance. I hope there are grounds for feeling that others will find Campbell Bunk as fascinating as I did.

The structure of the book is simple enough. At front and back are two chapters which sketch in the history of the street before the First World War and during and after the Second. The first chapter deals with the formative period of 1865 to about 1885, when the street's character became socially and mentally fixed; and with the next two decades, which consolidated the street's class structure, culture and reputation.

The middle six chapters deal in more detail with aspects of social life and change in Campbell Road during the two very different decades of 'inter-war' London. The 1920s looked back more to pre-war Campbell Road and maintained greater continuity with it; whereas the 1930s saw the growth of that process of dissolution which was accelerated by the war and culminated in slum clearance during the early 1950s. Chapter 2 analyses Campbell Road's class structure between the wars, and the means of earning a subsistence for men, women and children there; it includes a brief exploration of the changing economy of Holloway and even Greater London as a whole. Succeeding chapters bring the focus down to ever smaller aggregates. Chapters 3 and 4 deal predominantly with the internal relations of the street – community life, politics, and views of the world. Chapter 5 describes family relationships and their impact on change within the street, and Chapters 6 and 7 come down to individual women and men and their life chances and choices in Campbell Road from about 1919 to 1940. Readers will not, I'm sure, allow themselves to be seduced too much by the appealing logic of this design. For in everything, I have been struck by the pervasive interaction between class, community, family and individual. They are truly *indivisible* elements of social life, and dissecting them one by one is merely an artificial device of analysis.

This will be the second book I have written with 'community' as a dominant theme. Community is a well-worn category in British social science, a trifle too threadbare to be fashionable at present. But this does not mean that community studies have exhausted the possibilities of the genre. For those studies which have focussed on a definable place – rather than on a more general-ised class culture – have, virtually without exception, been marred by an unhistorical approach in which the community appears as somehow timeless and unchanging. And when the 'traditional' working-class community, for example, *is* changed, it is by forces outside – like redevelopment or 'privatisation' – without any apparent dynamic from within.

Taking a longer view helps illuminate the dynamics – and thus the very nature – of communities. For communities never stay the same. They are always fluid, more agitated at some times than others and often for different reasons, but changing none the less. Besides the sociologist's one-moment-in-time approach, one other optic serves to obscure change when communities are studied. This is the dominant focus on unifying factors, exaggerating those elements of community life which people have in common and which are thus used to define a population as a community.

Change within communities, however, is sited in disunities, in the contradictions of social life which are as real within communi-ties as outside. Indeed, at one important level, community is defined by just such a contradiction – in the separateness of one population from another. Seen from that view, communities are made as much by people who leave as by those who choose to stay.

Within a community, the most important sites of change are in the ever-present inequalities of wealth, power and status, and in the struggle between collectivism and individualism (or the contra-dictions of class); in the separate spheres of men and women (or the contradictions of sex and gender); and in the struggle between youth and adults (or the contradictions of generation). The import-ance of each will depend on the changing circumstances of history. This book is about how those forces worked themselves through in 'the worst street in North London'. I hope it will convince some readers, by its example, that a community study is necessarily an historical venture.

1 The rise of Campbell Bunk

Campbell Road, Holloway

Holloway is an unexceptional London suburb.[1] Only the association of its name with a notorious prison distinguishes it from the
rest of that uneven ring of mid-Victorian London of which it is
part. It dissolves imperceptibly into Kentish and Camden Towns
in the west and Finsbury Park and Hornsey in the east, but it
would not look out of place next to Shepherds Bush or Clapton;
or even tucked in between Stockwell and Clapham North.

Today Holloway is unarguably an inner-city area. But sixty
years ago it lay on the edge of two Londons. It faced out to the
northern heights of Highgate and Hampstead and Muswell Hill,
as well as to the social foothills of Tottenham, Harringay and Noel
Park. But it also faced into the old city from which it had grown
like green wood round the heart of an oak; to the Angel Islington,
Clerkenwell, Hoxton and St Luke's.

From the outside there was nothing exceptional about Campbell
Road itself. It did not look like a typical London slum. Built
originally for clerks and artisans, it continued to bear some marks
of its first respectable pretensions. It was wide enough to balance
the height of buildings on either side. It opened confidently from
a premier shopping street, rather than hiding behind railway line
or gasworks. The railings which kept private a dusty apology for
a garden still clung to about half the houses. The street line was
marred, for the discerning, by the kink to the left at the far end
from Seven Sisters Road, an afterthought in the Victorian planning
process; and by the chaotic horizontals of parapets and window
openings, testifying to some anarchy during building. But there
was nothing to the passer-by which marked Campbell Road apart
from a thousand other streets in Holloway and neighbouring
districts of North London dating from the 1860s and 1870s.

When first built, Holloway was itself a suburb and Campbell
Road truly suburban. Yet the pace of building in the thirty years
after 1860 was such that the area quickly lost its edge-of-town

character. And for other reasons, Campbell Road lost it more quickly and completely than the rest of Holloway.

The relationship between Campbell Road, Holloway, and North London has its roots in the 1850s and 1860s. To unearth them is not merely of antiquarian concern, for patterns were laid down then which still shaped experience seventy and eighty years on – Campbell Road's place in the housing market, a reputation, links with sister streets, ownership and settlement amongst certain families, even tensions which artificially divided the street against itself. Some of this legacy will be dealt with more fully later. But in this opening chapter we see how Campbell Road, a street much of a piece with the rest of Holloway's suburban development, became transformed into Campbell Bunk – 'the worst street in North London'.

It 'never had a chance'[2]

Holloway was largely built between 1860 and 1880. But some important elements in its social makeup had already been established during the first half of the nineteenth century, on a haphazard foundation of scattered manorial hamlets and farms.

From Napoleonic times, Holloway's social structure and geography were at once plebeian and bourgeois in character, as indeed they still are. Its plebeian antecedents were rooted in the Sunday morning amusements of Copenhagen House, a popular out-of-town drinking resort from 1780 till about 1820. Copenhagen Fields, in which the House stood, were a meeting place for London radicals and Jacobins, but more often the site of a free and easy popular culture, with its

> Cricket-matches, foot-racing, boxing, wrestling, skittling, pigeon-shooting, games at fives and racquet, cock-fighting, and bull-baiting – the headquarters of what is generally known among the sporting fraternity as the 'fancy', with fustian-jackets, 'Newgate-knockers', and surly bull-dogs.[3]

It was around 1800, too, that the earliest of Holloway's manufacturing districts – Belle Isle, in the south-west corner – was planted with tile kilns, varnish makers and horse slaughterers, well away from London sensibilities. And the first plebeian housing was run up a few years after in George Place (later George's Road) and Eden Grove, near to where gallows had once stood at the Ring Cross.

Holloway's bourgeois pedigree was almost as long but sited more to the north of lower-class Lower Holloway. Handsome villas stretched themselves along the Holloway Road from the 1800s, and the first middle-class speculative estates were put down 20 and 30 years later along Hornsey and Hanley Roads and Tollington Park. Middle-class building development was aided by the two-horse bus to London from the 1830s, helping conquer the rising ground so favoured by social climbers of the period; 'The well-known salubrity of the air has long rendered the place the resort of valetudinarians from the metropolis.'[4]

By the 1840s, Holloway's divided character had been consolidated with more 'suburban gentility'[5] in the north (Hornsey Road and Archway), more slums in the south (the Brand Street area, where in 1849 '19 houses out of 68 have produced a convict'),[6] and open fields 'as pleasant as most in the neighbourhood of London' around and between them.[7] The Irish influx to Islington spread north in this period.[8] The 1850s were to see important urban developments, especially the Metropolitan Cattle Market (1855) on the site of Copenhagen House; Holloway Station on the Great Northern Railway from Kings Cross; wealthy villas in the western fields round Camden Road, lower-middle and skilled working-class terraces just north of Seven Sisters Road and in Lower Holloway; and an area of cheap and crowded tenement houses at Queen's (later Queensland) Road, close to the Brand Street area. Holloway's population more than doubled in the decade (see table 1).

It was also in the 1850s that much of the ground was laid for the speculative boom of the 1860s and 1870s. On surveyors' drawing boards, on bankers' balance sheets and in the calculating minds of a thousand petty investors, the fields of Holloway were already apportioned and dug and planted with brick. But it was a treacherous path which linked the fancy to its fulfilment; and none more so than in the strange case of Campbell Road.

Established by the local manor court in 1757, the title of the four fields later to form the Seven Sisters Road Estate passed by primogeniture and marriage settlement just five times in the following 94 years.[9] The fields were held by minor aristocrats and Anglican clergy until 1851 when they became pawns in the game of speculative gain fuelled by London's growth. Within five years they changed hands three times, and in 1856 part of the Estate was acquired by a group of five experienced gentlemen investors. These men were trustees of the St Pancras Benefit Building Society and directors of the St Pancras, Marylebone and Paddington Freehold Land Society.

Freehold Land Societies played a large part in the urban development of Holloway, as elsewhere.[10] The St Pancras had been active
in Holloway and other parts of London since the early 1850s, as
had the Birkbeck and the National. Their purpose was to sell
building plots on mortgage to society members. The society
prescribed the type of dwellings to be built, including their elev-
ations and annual rentals, and usually provided an infrastructure
of roads and sewerage. Individual investors then either built on
their plots, or leased them on to others who would build in their
place.

The St Pancras's Seven Sisters Road Estate comprised the
southern (and eventually larger) portions of what later became
Campbell Road and the west side of Fonthill Road, together with
the Seven Sisters Road frontage between them. The Estate was
divided into 134 building plots, and sold piecemeal to 89 members.
No member had more than two plots and none of those was
adjacent to one another, but some family holdings totalled four or
six.

Plots in Campbell Road large enough for a single house were
sold during 1857 and 1858 for about £32 on full building society
mortgages.[11] Yet for some reason – probably because the market
was glutted and rents were low – building did not begin until
1865, and then only in the most anarchic fashion.[12] By 1869, out
of 84 plots in the Estate's part of Campbell Road, just 56 had been
built on. The best part of the road consisted of 24 houses built in
1867–8 by Charles Gilliatt, and offset to the north-west from the
top of the Estate's section of Campbell Road and adjoining Lennox
Road. Only half the road was made up and a fraction of the
pavement laid.[13] Two years later, at the time of the 1871 Census,
there was no change. There were to be vacant sites in Campbell
Road until 1880.[14]

Just what went wrong is unclear. Fonthill Road was similarly
affected, at least until 1869, and undoubtedly the extreme individualism of this type of development had a natural tendency to chaos.
But whatever the cause, it was Campbell Road's bad start which
laid the ground for the development of Campbell Bunk. It struggled painfully into maturity and never recovered from its stunted
first years.

But the condition of the road does not fully explain its later
character. It might account for the difference in the roads immediately to the west – Palmerston Road and Pooles Park – which were
neatly laid out and occupied during the same period. But Fonthill
Road suffered the same muddy fate as Campbell Road without
following its subsequent career. The reason lay in the market

relations of which the Estate was part – especially in terms of its intended occupation.

Campbell Road was built for artisans and clerks (like R. Wilfer of Holloway in *Our Mutual Friend* (1865)) with sufficient means for its six rooms, scullery, outside WC and (in some cases) an attic for the skivvy. The street was wide enough to look comfortable; parapet walls hid the roofs from sight and iron railings guarded a small slip of ground before each front window. Fonthill Road was more showily petty-bourgeois (with balconies, parapet balustrades, blowsy stucco to the window heads, and arched doorways); it was able, at least for a time, to claim the tenants for whom it was designed, the smaller servant-keeping class of higher clerks, lower professionals and shopkeepers.

But the social structure of Holloway altered faster than brick-layers and carpenters could cover the ground. Between conception and completion the demand for houses in streets like Campbell Road changed from single-family occupation by clerks to prolet-arian tenants renting half a house or less. Property speculation supplied too much housing for the lower middle-class market which was already having second thoughts about Holloway and looking elsewhere for its suburban ideal. A local Wesleyan chapel complained that from the early 1870s 'circumstances changed with dramatic suddenness. The district began to lose its suburban character and families moved further out.'[15] But if the market for which the houses were built no longer existed, another was ready to take its place. This demand came especially from the workers needed to build Holloway and nearby suburbs; from railway workers, both uniformed servants and labouring navvies; and skilled workers in those London trades migrating for reasons of space from the inner city. Fonthill Road could still price such people out. Campbell Road, and streets similar to it, could not. But Campbell Road alone, through its disastrous beginnings, dropped rents low enough to let in anyone who wanted house room. In the class-rigid Victorian housing market caste was all. When one or two houses were let in lodgings, a street's market potential withered relentlessly, and the top hats and white collars sooner or later crept quietly elsewhere.

This uneven beginning shows in the 1871 census, when out of Campbell Road's 63 occupied houses, 26 were home to one house-hold and the rest to two or more; 5 houses contained 18 persons each (three per room) or over. Of 158 occupied males, 23 were labourers and 54 worked in the building trades; but about 20 households kept a servant, and lower middle-class occupiers included barristers' and solicitors' clerks, a music teacher, law

stationer, record keeper at Somerset House, and a writer at the
Board of Trade.[16]

Through the 1870s, the pressure on middle-class tenants to move
out was sustained by the perpetual bad condition of the road and
by the growing supply of better housing around. 'It was little
better than an open sewer,' remembered the local vicar; 'People
threw their slops and garbage out of the windows into the
streets. . . .'[17] In a memorandum called 'Campbell Road and its
Neighbourhood' submitted to Charles Booth's investigators, J. B.
Carnelly, a local brushmaker and missionary, also recalled the
1870s:

> About 25 years ago [1872] I resided in Lennox Road. The
> houses were cheap and the Neighbourhood was very
> respectable, consisting of well to do families of the middle
> class, Clerks, and artizans, but there was one dark spot, and
> that was half of Campbell Road between Seven Sisters Road
> and Paddington Street. . . . From the time I became
> acquainted with the Road there was a few vacant spaces of
> land. At this time the lads of the neighbourhood meet (sic)
> and gambled all day on Sunday. . . . I found one half of the
> Road different to the other half. Between Seven Sisters Road
> and Paddington Street consisted of labourers in the Building
> Class, Navvies etc. working for a low price in the jerry
> building line; most of the women had to work. The majority
> of them was of a low class with large families living in
> tenements of one and two rooms. . . . A few years after, the
> three Houses in the best part of the Road was let out to
> families living in one room. While at the corner of Paddington
> Street was a large House built for Public House but never got
> a license. A Mr. King took it and made a lodging house. From
> that time the respectable people began to migrate.[18]

John King, a lodging-house keeper from Eden Grove who had
similar ventures in other parts of North London, opened his
lodging house at 47 Campbell Road in 1880. It was licensed for
90 men.[19] As Carnelly claimed, this was indeed a turning point in
Campbell Road's career, a significant date in the making of the
Bunk.[20] For this was to be the first of many lodging houses in the
Road, giving it the largest number of doss-house beds for any
street in Islington by the 1890s.

It was during the 1880s that Campbell Road completed the
formation of its distinctive class and social structure. We can get
a picture of the street on the edge of its final transformation from

the 1881 Census. It reveals still a handful of middle-class occupations among the street's 1200 residents – 6 clerks (including the tenacious writer at the Board of Trade) out of 354 occupied males. But in comparison with the adjacent street – Palmerston (later Playford) Road, built about the same time, of similar house style and size – there are significant differences in occupation class, household structure and gender, and place of origin.

Campbell Road was distinctly more labouring-class in tone than Palmerston Road – 30.2 per cent of occupied males classed as one or other form of labourer against 7.8 per cent; there were more carmen, horsekeepers, sweeps, general dealers, porters and unemployed (17.8 per cent against 12.7 per cent); and more laundresses, washerwomen and charwomen (56 per cent of occupied women against 25 per cent). On the other hand, Palmerston Road had more clerks, shopworkers, other distributive workers and lower professionals (27.8 per cent to Campbell Road's 9.3 per cent) (see table 2).

Campbell Road was significantly more crowded than Palmerston Road, with more households per house (3.5 against 2.6), more persons per household (4.1 and 3.5), and more persons per house (13.0 and 9.1). Families with children were slightly larger in Campbell Road than in Palmerston – an average of 2.9 children under 14 compared with 2.4. And in keeping with other poor streets in London, more women were heads of households in Campbell Road than in Palmerston Road: 14.7 per cent (excluding the lodging house) against 9.8 per cent.[21]

Perhaps the most striking difference in the population of the two streets was their profile of geographical origins. Campbell Road's population was much more locally derived than Palmerston Road's, with 20.9 per cent of heads of households, spouses, boarders and lodgers having been born in Islington, against Palmerston Road's 7.5 per cent[22] (see table 3).

Campbell Road and the housing market

The class-stratified Victorian housing market had provided the context for the fall of Campbell Road and the rise of Campbell Bunk. Yet even within Campbell Road, the housing market was itself sharply differentiated, with each part having its own internal and largely specific relations. The importance of two particular types of housing tenure outweighed any other in fixing the character of the street during the 1880s and 1890s. These were common lodging houses and furnished rooms.

The oldest lodging houses in Holloway – some of the very first in England to be registered under the Common Lodging Houses Act of 1851 – were Willis's cottages at Gordon Place, Highgate Hill, on one of the busiest tramping routes into London. Common lodging houses had been subsequently established from time to time in the poorest streets of Holloway, especially Queensland Road and Brand Street, from about 1860.[23] Beds in shared dormitories were rented by the night or week (with Sunday free for six nights in advance) and lodgers prepared, cooked and ate their food in more or less convivial common kitchens. An indication of the numbers and location of lodging houses in Holloway and their change over time is given in table 4. By 1895 there were 31 for nearly 800 lodgers, mainly men; six of these, accommodating 251 persons, were in Campbell Road. They were licensed as shown in table 5.

Here as elsewhere, common lodging houses provided lodgings for the tramping artisan in search of work as well as the destitute wandering poor.[24] In Campbell Road it appears to have been the latter who predominated. It was these houses which contributed largely to the staggeringly high numbers of workhouse admissions from Campbell Road in the period 1890–1910 (see table 6). In 1890, the lodging houses were sending someone to the workhouse (or the infirmary via the workhouse) every three days throughout the year; those six houses provided 73 per cent of all such admissions from Campbell Road.[25]

We are given a glimpse of the place of these lodging houses, and thus of Campbell Road, in the shifting lives of their lodgers by some scattered poor law records which have survived unevenly for 1869 to 1890.[26] These records were taken for the purpose of establishing residential settlement to enable workhouse authorities to secure the removal of a pauper not the responsibility of their parish. They are consequently detailed on movements, but frustratingly less informative about occupation and other details.

A 78-year-old man, George Gazelly, was admitted to the workhouse from King's lodging house in August 1889. He had been there a week and before that had been 'moving about the Country past 50 years'.[27] A couple of months later a married couple were admitted from Arthur Norris's lodging house at 37 Campbell Road. They had been there about two months, previously at South Norwood for ten months. They had travelled around finding work – the husband was a blacksmith – for about ten or a dozen years. The husband was from Leicester and they had married in Brighton.[28]

There were casual labourers using the lodging houses for overwintering, working on farms and hopfields in the summer. And there was the London lodging-house habitué, like William Hawkins, 39 and single, admitted to the workhouse from 37 Campbell Road at Christmas 1889. He had been there one month. Two months before he had been admitted from 47 Campbell Road:

> Man states I had been there three weeks. Next before Crayford Kent six months. Next before Gordon Place 18 months *altogether*. Next before 39 Baildon Street, New Cross Road, about one year. Next before 31 St Clements Road, Notting Hill, three and a half years (Mrs Lamb). I had three Xmas's there. Next before Poplar fifteen months. I went to Mrs Lamb's just after Xmas left Summer 1886.[29]

The furnished rooms catered for a different sort of clientele – generally families who were too poor to sustain life in unfurnished rooms because they had no household equipment. Residence could be as short here as in the lodging houses, and some rooms were let to families by the night, rather than weekly. There was probably a marked growth of these houses during the 1880s and 1890s; 36 had been registered by the local sanitary authority by 1895.[30] By 1909, 45 houses in the road were let in furnished rooms, as against 34 in unfurnished rooms.[31]

Once more, in the 1890s patterns of mobility among the tenants of these tenement houses were nearly as diverse as in the lodging houses. Holloway continued to be a reception area for immigrants from the countryside and provinces, as well as from the central London districts. Campbell Road's furnished rooms provided convenient and cheap accommodation for the poorest and least settled of these migrants. From the workhouse records we hear of a Birmingham family who took in a 23-year-old woman who had tramped down from their home town;[32] of a 27-year-old woman with her son, destitute after being abandoned by her husband at their home in Wood Green;[33] of a widow and two children from Nottingham, with two other children in a Dr Barnardo's home, admitted to the workhouse from 25 Campbell Road – an address we shall meet with later.[34] And we hear also of fallen elements of the bourgeoisie in Campbell Road, like the son of a Tyneside shipbuilding employer 'come down through drink'.[35]

Campbell Road also began to develop in these years – in common with other lodging houses and streets of furnished rooms – a role of last resort for the poorest of Holloway's population; for Emma Atkins, 15, admitted to the workhouse schools when she was 8, left at 14 in the summer of 1889, went to service in

Crouch Hill, and then scrubbed doorsteps for coppers while living at 18 Campbell Road;[36] and for Louisa Rowlett, 19 and suffering from syphilis, who had lived with her mother in a court off George's Road for 13 or 14 years before finding a room in Campbell Road.[37]

These movements did not necessarily mean long-term settlement in the street – in fact this was probably rare until the later 1890s. There was considerable movement within Islington and Holloway, sometimes back and forth to the same street over time, and even considerable movement within a street. John Mills, crossing sweeper and watchman earning 7s a week, gave evidence in support of settlement when his wife was admitted to the workhouse as a lunatic in June 1890. They had been living in Alsen Road for a year; they had lived 'about this part of the Parish 40 years'; – at Campbell Road from 1878 to 1879, at Cornwallis Road from 1882 to 1885, back at number 35 Campbell Road in 1885–6, then to Cottenham Road for a year, and at 3 Campbell Road from 1887 to 1889.[38] And George Berridge, 62, in the parish 33 years, had stayed at 37 (twice), 54 (twice) and 100 Campbell Road between about 1886 and 1890.[39] Thus could extreme mobility disguise important subterranean patterns of settlement.[40]

Strangers to the area would find out about these rooms by asking around. 'It is a frequent occurrence', wrote the local sanitary inspector in 1908,

> to see a man and a woman dragging several children behind them down this Road looking for a furnished room, which they usually get for say three shillings, four shillings, or five shillings per week, according to the size. . . . Some of the keepers of these houses have to let the rooms at say from eight pence to one shilling per night. These rooms are of course very roughly furnished. In a large room there would be two bed-steads, palliasses, a flock bed and sometimes two sheets and a blanket.[41]

The daughter of one of the managers of these furnished rooms remembered an incident from about 1910. Her mother, who also was one of the street's moneylenders for a time, was born locally and had moved into Campbell Road around 1902 from Fonthill Mews:

> 'We were all sitting on the pavement at number 47, number 29 I should say. And we saw this little crowd coming, turn round from Seven Sisters Road. . . . And they came round the

corner with a pram and they got two children in a pram, a
big bundle, a heap in between these two kids, there was about
four of them trailing along behind. The father was pushing
the pram, and he'd got a club foot, and you know sort of
hopping along; and the mother, she looked like she'd just
drawn out of a rag bag, she looked a poor old thing. The old
man called out, "D'you know where we can get a room?"
So of course we just get up off the pavement and run in and
say, "Mum, there's somebody out 'ere wants a room!" And
when me mother looked she said, "Where the effin' 'ell 'ave
you lot come from then?" So they said, "Oh, well, we've
been travelling", they travelled all the way from Kent. . . .
Walking, mind you, with a baby in a pram. And they never
had not a stitch of anything. So mother gave them these two
rooms, and they lived next door, in number 27. She let 'em
have the middle floor in 27 and I think there was about eight
of them altogether in these here two rooms.'[42]

Campbell Road was not the only street in Holloway to provide
this sort of accommodation. There were isolated houses offering
furnished rooms probably scattered through most working-class
streets in the area. But there were similar concentrations, linked
with common lodging houses, in Queensland Road ('the Land' or,
from about 1915, 'Australian Avenue'); the George's Road area;
and numbers of furnished tenement houses in Wellington Road,
Brand Street, Hornsey Road, Brunswick Grove, and particularly
the Bemerton Street area to the south of Holloway in West
Islington.[43]

The similarity in housing markets between George's, Queensland and Campbell Roads gave them a special relationship. John
King had a lodging house in the George's Road area as well as at
47a Campbell Road, for example, and there were discernible
patterns of movement (and so settlement) between the three areas
from the 1880s on.[44] But connections were also established from
further afield – from the other lodging-house and furnished room
areas of London and Middlesex. Notting Hill, Whitechapel, the
tramping lodging-house street of Lorenco Road (Little Russia) on
the borders of Tottenham and Edmonton, all recur in family
histories or the workhouse records. It seems likely that these
patterns were affected by the demolition of similar areas to
Campbell Road in the older parts of inner London. Observers
certainly thought at the time that clearances around the Angel
Islington, Somers Town and the Old Nichol area of Shoreditch
and Bethnal Green had caused displaced slum dwellers to settle in

Campbell Road.[45] It may have been for this reason that Campbell Road was thought still to be 'going down' in the mid-1890s when streets like Queensland Road were stable, or even marginally 'improving'.[46] George's Road was said to have a special underworld relationship with Hoxton, 'the leading criminal quarter of London, and indeed of all England'.[47] Campbell Road, too, had its Hoxton connections, appearing from time to time in family histories. One man, born at 21 Campbell Road in 1902, his father a painter and street seller, his mother a doorstep cleaner, moved out three years later. The family then lived in Wilmer Gardens and Essex Street, both known at various times as the worst streets in Hoxton; then back to Holloway, in Brand Street and eventually Queensland Road before 1914.[48] It is likely, too, that Campbell Road's gypsy connections – undocumented apart from later oral evidence – dated from this time or even before,[49] and other examples will be found later.

Settling down

But the stratified housing market is not sufficient in itself to explain patterns of movement or settlement, or connections between areas. Economic and cultural opportunities also substantially explain why people come to a district, and why some move on and others stay. One reason for Campbell Road and similar streets attracting the poor was the availability of casual work locally for unskilled men and women. Without this labour market flexibility it is unlikely that the patterns of settlement which evolved during the 1890s and early 1900s would have taken their eventual forms.

Holloway was a dormitory area, always sending more people to work elsewhere than found work within its boundaries. But it was still an active manufacturing suburb of London, attracting additional industries from the crowded inner city – especially clothing, printing and book binding, engineering, furniture, musical instruments, toys and prepared foods. Its predominantly residential character, however, helped to create an important largely casualised labour market outside the manufacturing sector, and this was particularly important for unskilled labour, both men and women.

Like the housing market, there was not one labour market in Holloway but several, segregated from each other to a greater or lesser extent. They were defined by gender and age, producing male, female, and juvenile labour markets. The first (and, to a more limited extent the second) was further segmented by 'skill', or the value of labour-power workers could bring to the market. This division will be explored in more detail later, but one defining characteristic should be mentioned here. The skilled labour market was more or less specific to the skills involved: a cabinet maker might turn his hand to shop-fitting or even joinery at a pinch, but he could not become an engineer. Whereas the unskilled labour market traded in undifferentiated 'general' labour-power, with (for men) a value in building, dock work, road transport, portering and so on.

Large residential suburbs like Holloway needed a labour army to distribute the commodities to retail outlets and homes. This distributive function provided the basis for the unskilled male labour market in Holloway. First, there was employment at the wholesale perishable commodity markets of London. Holloway's own, of course, was the Metropolitan Cattle Market where a quarter of a million animals were slaughtered each year and where for one day a week, later two, it was transformed into the great Caledonian Market for secondhand goods. But Smithfield, Billingsgate, Spitalfields and Covent Garden needed similar workers and were all in easy reach. Second, road haulage demanded a considerable supply of labour-power locally; more road transport workers lived in Islington than in any other metropolitan borough before the First World War.[50] Movement of commodities in and out of Holloway's numerous railway goods yards provided much casual road work from the 1850s on. The King's Cross Potato Market, established in 1864, was one important source of this work, but probably the commodity which was handled most by local unskilled labour was coal. This was shifted from eight main sites in Holloway including the GNR Goods and Coal Depot at Finsbury Park (c. 1869),[51] and the Edgware branch of the GNR yards at Ashburton Grove and Drayton Park (c. 1875).

Apart from distribution there were two other major sources of unskilled male employment. The building industry was an important local sector since the boom of which Holloway was one physical manifestation, although it declined in importance from the First World War. And municipal enterprise needed unskilled labour for dust collection (the dust wharf and incinerator were immediately north of 'the Land'), road and sewerage building and maintenance, and electricity production (the Council's electric light station was built in Eden Grove during the 1890s).

Holloway's class structure and residential character also determined a large demand in the service sector for female employment, for the classes lived cheek by jowl in this area more than any other in London, according to Booth.[52] In 1911, female economic participation rates were significantly higher in Islington than in London (or indeed England) as a whole – 41.8 per cent of women aged 14 or over against the county of London's 34.3 per cent; 14.6 per cent of married women to 13.2 per cent.

The manufacturing sector was the largest employer of women's labour-power – 23.9 per cent of working women laboured in the tailoring trades, for instance – and there were substantial openings for the 'unskilled'. Button-hole hands and seamstresses in the tailoring; cardboard box making; jam and sweet and preserved meat factories around the Brewery Road area; show-card mounting in the printing trades, and paper bag making – all offered employment, much of it seasonal or casual, to Holloway women. So did the Vestries, who employed women dust sorters until about 1900. So did the locally important service industries, as waitresses in coffee shops, public houses and hotels; and most importantly in the large and small laundries serving the needs of Holloway's bourgeoisie. It was areas like Tufnell Park, Hillmarton Road, Highbury, and the adjoining middle-class districts of Stroud Green, Hornsey, and Finsbury Park which provided women with employment as domestic servants, living in or out. At the traditionally 'rougher' end of domestic service, day servants and charwomen (5.7 per cent of working women) were mainly widowed or married women, whereas laundresses were unmarried.[53]

The opportunities provided for men and women, together with complex patterns of economic individualism and the evolving cultural traditions of the street, were crucial supplements to Campbell Road's place in the housing market in attracting longer-term settlement there. Campbell Road never lost its function as a transient refuge for people passing through. But from the earliest years there were the long stayers who lived side by side with the ebb and flow of new or half-remembered faces past their street doors.

Although it inevitably took on its own peculiar character, this settlement was no different from that taking place in the 1890s over Holloway as a whole. The decades either side of 1900 were periods of consolidation, fixing for the next two generations the social geography of the district. The tendency for working-class colonisation of areas originally intended for the middle classes gained strength and met resistance only in the solid bourgeois neighbourhoods of Camden Road, Tufnell Park, and parts of Archway – although even in the wealthiest areas by the late 1890s it was lamented that, 'The best people are leaving.'[54] George

Gissing, ever watchful of London's nuances of class, cast Holloway in the mid-1880s as the place to which the newly-bourgeoisified Richard Mutimer aspires for a home with one servant; by the early 1890s, a Holloway connection is symbolic of the taint of the London poor.[55] Booth's poverty maps give an indication of the process between 1889 and 1897, with a tendency to change streets from 'fairly comfortable' to 'poverty and comfort mixed'.[56]

The decade either side of 1900 was also the period of Campbell Road's maximum growth. The number of households was to increase by 29 per cent to 440 from 1881 to 1909, and the population may have peaked in the late-1890s, but certainly from about 1913 the population entered into a secular decline until the street's eventual demolition.[57]

Yet within this general drift away, many stayed on. The earliest available reference to a long-staying family actually pre-dates this period. The Steed family first appear in the street directory in 1874, and there is other evidence that they lived there continuously from the 1860s to the 1940s, and owned properties in it until the end.[58] There is evidence also of at least one other family in the street from the 1870s to the 1920s.[59] The Catchpoles, a family of chimney sweeps for at least two generations, appear in the street lists from 1882 to 1941. It is likely that the Bests, who kept a grocer's shop at the bottom end from 1919 to 1941, had settled in the street around 1884. Walters's – the corner general shop at Paddington Street and Campbell Road – ran from 1898 to 1935. Bucknell's coal and general shop was in the same hands from 1901 until about 1937. Ernie Neal, the coal dealer at 42 Campbell Road, opened his shop around 1908 and still had property in the street in the 1950s. The Stevensons, coal sellers and greengrocers, who were there until the Second World War, opened a business in the street about 1909. And Burton's chandlers shop ran from 1913 to 1930.[60]

It is because of these families' business interests that they are documented in street lists and rate books, but other families, too, began to put down extensive roots in Campbell Road before the First World War. The Spencer family, for example, who had 40 relatives in Campbell Road in the 1930s, had been there since the 1890s if not before; the Steel and Anstey families also lived in the street from the 1890s to the 1930s; and we shall see other evidence later.[61]

Patterns of ownership also had much to do with the way the settled part of Campbell Road's population began to evolve in these years. Large landlords like Arthur Norris, a notable temperance leader and house screwer,[62] who had 15 properties in the street by 1919, had only a fleeting personal connection with

Campbell Road, although property stayed in his and his heirs' possession from the 1880s to the 1950s; and his manager, Tubby Nicholls, lived in Campbell Road almost certainly from before the First World War. A more significant development was the growth of property portfolios in the hands of people who also lived in the street. This seems mainly to have happened between 1905 and 1919. These resident owners included the Lovelaces (7 tenement houses), the Steeds (7 houses), and Gabriel Walters, the corner shop keeper (14); after the First World War they were to be joined by Ernie Neal (10 houses).[63] These local connections helped kinship networks grow among tenants well known to landlords who were also neighbours.

There were other patterns, too, which established themselves in these years. There was the growth of a tradition of living by one's wits, eking out a subsistence on the streets of North London. There were the traditions of public violence and street theatre, especially street gaming, dating from the 1870s according to Carnelly's testimony. And the road was probably playing important roles in the underworld by the 1890s, if not before.

There were two other significant contributions of that time. One was to establish for ever a reputation for Campbell Road as 'the worst street in North London'. And the other was to erect a structure of charitable resources and local state control adapted specifically to Campbell Road. Both contributions were, of course, intricately connected.

'The worst street in north London'

Campbell Road's reputation was established by the early 1890s, and probably before. In an advertisement for financial support, the Finsbury Park Working Lads' Institute (opened 1893 in Pooles Park) pointed to the value of its work

> in a *poor* and *crowded working class* neighbourhood . . . N.B. – one of the streets is considered by the Police as the 'worst in North London'. (*Vide* newspaper reports)[64]

This local wisdom was given academic respectability in Booth's *Life and Labour of the People in London* (1902–3) which accorded Campbell Road three pages to itself, a unique honour, and which again quoted 'the worst street in North London' tag:[65]

> A street fairly broad, with houses of three storeys, not ill-built,

many being occupied as common lodging-houses; broken
windows, dirty curtains, doors open, a litter of paper, old meat
tins, heads of fish and stalks of vegetables. It is a street where
thieves and prostitutes congregate. The thieves live in the
common lodging-houses, paying fourpence a night, and the
prostitutes, generally two together, in a single furnished room,
which they rent at four or five shillings a week. They are the
lowest class of back-street prostitute, and an hour or two after
midnight they may be seen returning home.[66]

The police, it was said, would not walk alone through it at night.[67]
And Carnelly wrote that Campbell Road had 'such a bad name
that no-one would live in it except those Persons that had large
families and could not live anywhere else.'[68]
   Small wonder, then, that this labelling had its effect on the lives
of people in Campbell Road. A local Salvationist reported that
women had difficulty obtaining domestic employment in the late-
1890s:

Does not think many do charing as people will not have them.
As one woman told her 'To say you come from Campbell
Road is quite enough.'[69]

From time to time, the scandal attaching to the street erupted
afresh. In 1896, for example, a smallbox outbreak leapt from
Queensland to Campbell Road, infecting 11 cases and requiring
extra sanitary staff to carry out house-to-house inspections in the
street.[70] And in early 1909, when complaints by the Board of
Guardians led to a special investigation by the Council. The
Islington Gazette – 'A Remarkable Report. Shocking Revelations'
– relayed the Poor Law medical officer's experiences of conditions
of furnished rooms in Campbell Road:coming away from confinements covered in fleas, number x is a disgrace to civilisation, eight
persons and a dead child found in the front room, and so on.[71] In
voluminous reports, and after six sanitary inspectors were detailed
to inspect living conditions, the Council tightened up its limited
control of housing in the street. The sanitary inspector responsible
for day-to-day supervision of Campbell Road concluded his report
as follows – a nice example of social observation, class bias, and
how comprehensively labelling was imbibed and propagated:

This road is the king of all roads. I have been in practically all
the slums in London; Notting Hill, Chelsea, Battersea,
Fulham, Nine Elms, and also the East End, but there is nothing

so lively as this road. Thieves, Prostitutes, cripples, Blind
People, Hawkers of all sorts of wares from boot laces to
watches and chains are to be found in this road, Pugilists,
Card Sharpers, Counter Jumpers, Purse Snatchers, street
singers, and Gamblers of all kinds, and things they call men
who live on the earnings of women, some of whom I saw
outside the Town Hall with the unemployed last week. I
could say a lot more about this road, but I think I have said
enough to prove to you the class of people who inhabit it.
Of course, there are a few who perhaps get an honest living,
but they want a lot of picking-out.[72]

To deal with the perceived problems of Campbell Road to
middle-class society, a philanthropic panoply was erected from the
1870s on. The road attracted zealots like holy relics on a pilgrims'
way. The New Court Congregationalists were first, taking a room
for their Home Mission at 48 Campbell Road in 1875, forming
the Campbell Road Institute and Sunday School at 89 in 1880,
and four years later establishing the Lennox Road Mission facing
Campbell Road and devoted entirely to its top end; Carnelly was
one of its workers from the 1870s until 1919.[73] For the bottom
end, the Palmerston Road Congregational Church had another
mission. The Salvation Army put much effort into the road,
especially with its common lodging house visiting, and later
opened a small citadel there for a time. And as we have seen, the
Finsbury Park Lads' Institute, two streets away, was built with
Campbell Road very much in mind.

Time and again the themes woven into the early years of Campbell
Road will sound out in the 1920s, 1930s and even later. In
important ways, the inter-war period was determined by what
happened to Campbell Road in the 1880s: not in the sense that it
made things happen 50 years later, but in that it constrained the
possibilities of change in certain crucial respects. The 1880s defined
Campbell Road's relative place in the Holloway housing market,
for example, even though the number of lodging-house beds fell
by 75 per cent between 1910 and 1920.[74] A template of ownership
and family settlement was constructed to which newcomers had
to adapt. A label was fixed to the street in the local popular and
bureaucratic imagination, a label which interacted with the daily
experience of people who lived there. The road became a focal
point of middle-class concern, ensuring that it would also be a
place of struggle over dominant values and patterns of behaviour.
Holloway's casual labour market had changed from the 1880s: but

in the 1920s it was still recognisably the same place. And the road's cultural traditions – most notoriously street gaming – held good from the 1870s to the 1950s. All of these factors combined to produce and reproduce the road's class makeup, and its place in Holloway's class structure. If one of the themes of this book is change, especially during the 1930s and 1940s, it must be seen in response to the traditions and continuities it was pulling against.

2 The dynamics of class: Campbell Bunk and the lumpenproletariat

Campbell Road's class structure

Some time in 1929, an interviewer from the New Survey of London Household Survey visited 25 Campbell Road. 'Slum property', he noted on some of the cards he made out for each of the seven households living there. In the ground floor front room he met Mr and Mrs Nixon; they had an income of 10s from Mr Nixon's disablement pension (he was 62 and didn't work) and a further 10s from the Poor Law. In the room behind them lived Henry Hallett and his wife; Hallett had been a 'butcher's assistant but now rag and bone merchant'. In the ground floor back addition lived Herbert Bennett and his wife; Bennett made 'wire baskets etc. for sale in streets and markets'. In the middle floor front room were the Drovers; George, the father, a 'jobbing sign writer', living with his wife and three children of 10 and under. Like Hallett and Bennett, he earned 30s in a good week: the poverty line for a family of that size was over 40s. In the room behind the Drovers lived Mr and Mrs Craft and their baby son; Mr Craft was a carman for a firm (probably Carter Paterson's) at Goswell Road, apparently in regular work. At the top of the house at the front lived Ernie Barnes, a knife grinder who 'travels all over north London', with his wife and five children 10 and under, all in one room. And in the top back were the Bakers; Henry a 'tiler's labourer but now on casual work', with his wife and three children under 10. 'Very poor family', noted the interviewer, 'but of the type who seldom seek relief.'[1]

We can get some insight here into the sort of people who lived in Campbell Road between the wars, but alone it is difficult to make much of it. How typical was number 25 of the other 100 or so houses in the Street? What was the class makeup of Campbell Road? How did its population compare with the class structure of Holloway in general?

'Class' is the most contested category in the whole lexicon of the social sciences. We all know class and classes exist, but it and they elude both scientific definition and enumeration. Whatever conceptual pigeon-holes we painstakingly build, the infinite variety of human experience spills messily over the crosswalls.

Nor is the task made easier when the framework is taken for granted. Class is as much an unsettled question in Marxism as in bourgeois sociology and historiography – apart from generalisations which take us not very far in understanding historical specificities and change within classes.

Yet a feeling of class – of sharing the same predicament, of being in a particular position within the social framework, and of being at odds with some other parts of society – was an important fact of life for people in Campbell Road, even though they would not all have felt or expressed it in quite that way. And it is clear from a variety of evidence that Campbell Road was especially occupied by certain groups as against others, even within the Holloway 'working class'.

But it is when we try to reconstruct the material base on which class feeling built that we meet our first problems. There are no comprehensive data on the class makeup of Campbell Road, even occupation class, for the inter-war years. Because of the 100-year ban we have the 1881 Census only, and then we have to glean hints from biased or small-scale sources thereafter. Before trying to analyse class further, or to assess its meaning for people in Campbell Road, it is worth laying out just what that evidence is.

Our first evidence comes from the self-descriptions of occupations given by people appearing at those inquests and court hearings during the inter-war period which were reported in the local newspapers. People from Campbell Road figure in over 400 such reports. I have divided details of occupations by decade for men and women, although the data for the 1920s are far fuller than for the 1930s. In this way, there is information on 230 men and 39 women. To this I have added the occupations of a further 23 men and two women who appear in Poor Law records during 1929, the only year available to me (see table 7).

This is obviously unsafe as a comprehensive source for Campbell Road's class structure and can only serve as an indication of it. There are biases in self-reporting before magistrates (for example one man, a street singer, whose son reported him never working for anyone in his life, described himself as a 'labourer' before a coroner's court, and there were other dubious cases); in the slanting of the material presumably towards the 'rougher' end of Campbell Road's class spectrum; and in the drastic under-reporting of women's labour (the many Campbell Road women described as 'married' in the newspaper reports could not all have been economically inactive even if not regularly or frequently earning).

But for what it is worth, then 'labourers' and street entrepreneurs account for 60.3 and 59 per cent of male earners in the 1920s and 1930s; and charwomen and street sellers are well represented among working women, at least in the 1920s.

For purposes of comparison, and also to add to the sample populations from those Holloway streets most nearly approaching Campbell Road's reputation, I have carried out a similar exercise on some 700 newspaper reports involving people from the George's Road, Queensland Road and Rupert Road areas. These give information on 405 men and 77 women. Here labourers and street sellers, street dealers, etc. account for 50.4 and 48.1 per cent of male occupations in the two decades. Even among reputedly similar communities, then, Campbell Road's population seems especially concentrated within these two groups.

The second source is the memory of people who lived in Campbell Road. An analysis of interviews has given occupations of 112 named men and 55 named women who were both economically active and resident in Campbell Road during some part of the period 1919 to 1940 (see table 8).

This is a better source for women's work, especially younger women, who (for reasons to be discussed later) appear infrequently in court notices. But it distorts in important ways. First, some jobs are more memorable than others, especially fifty years on when trades might have disappeared and are thus more remarkable today. Second, the extent of shifting employment among general labourers tends to be fixed in one period which the respondent remembers – A worked in a glass-blower's when B remembered him; but he might also have been a builder's labourer and dustman. These factors might tend to overestimate the numbers of street earners, but compensate for it by understating the extent of casual and general labour.

This source supports the first, in that 50.5 per cent of male earners were street sellers, etc., or casual or builders' labourers; and among women, charwomen and street sellers once more easily predominate.

The third source is not as inherently distorted as either the newspaper reports or the oral testimony, but its sample is too small to be of real value. It also relates to one year only, 1929. The New Survey of London Life and Labour's household surveyors visited three houses in Campbell Road. They thus surveyed 15 households out of perhaps 380 living there at the time.[2]

The survey gives information on 13 economically active men and 6 women (see table 9). These are striking figures. In the whole of Holloway, the New Survey of London surveyors only identified 32 men and women earning a living in the streets, and of those 5 lived in Campbell Road. Out of 32 'casual labourers' or 'labourers (unspecified)' in the whole of the Holloway sample, 4 lived in Campbell Road.[3] And the New Survey ignored the street's lodging-house population of 45 men, mostly employed casually or in street enterprises.[4]

In Islington as a whole in the Census year of 1931, the groups which massively dominated Campbell Road's class structure were numerically trivial. The 'unskilled' represented about one in five of Islington's economically active population, as against one in three who worked in non-manual clerking, shopworking and managerial, etc. (see table 10). And within the 'unskilled' categories, the general labour, cleaning and street earning groups totalled about 6 per cent of the occupied population (see table 11).

From all the evidence, Campbell Road stood Islington's class structure virtually on its head. At the bottom numerically – but not in power or influence – was a small number of real property owners, both men and women: ten or a dozen shopkeepers, landlords, coal dealers and building employers. Then a thin layer of the uniformed working class and a few others with secure incomes: railwaymen, postmen, busmen or tram-men, printers, male and female shop assistants, engineers and craftsmen in the building, furniture and clothing industries. Apart from the building trades, each group would have been represented by no more than a handful. Then a larger number of semi-skilled or unskilled workers in regular employment, like slaughterers, licensed porters at Smithfield, glass makers, engineering machine minders, lorry drivers, laundry workers, and an important group of young female factory hands, especially in the electrical engineering trades. Next a large number of unskilled workers in definite trades but always liable to insecurity of employment – labourers in glass works, foundries and machine shops and women in jam and other food factories; building labourers (both general and craftsmen's), porters in markets and warehouses, railway carriage and office cleaners, coal heavers at the railway yards and coal men delivering door to door. This group would merge to a greater or lesser extent with the general labourers, usually men who lived on odd jobs – trench digging, coal humping, hod carrying, scene shifting; and women who worked odd days at charing in houses or pubs, cinemas and offices. Both in turn tried their hand at any of the street trades which formed the main source of income for another large group. These were the finders and sellers (general dealers, totters, rag and bone and old clothes men and women), and buyers and sellers (costermongers, newsvendors, hawkers, pedlars), the makers and sellers (of football favours, sweetstuffs, baskets, children's windmills), the street repairers (tinkers, knife grinders, chair and umbrella makers), the entertainers (singers and dancers, organ grinders, one-man-band artistes), and even the beggars. The last three groups (the street earners, general labourers and unskilled workers in more or less vulnerable employment) characterised and dominated the class structure of Campbell Road. And it is probable that over 50 per cent of Campbell Road's economically active population was formed of groups representing merely 6 per cent of Islington's population as a whole.

All this should at least show that the perceived difference of Campbell Road to its neighbouring streets – a perception common to middle-class social scientist, working-class neighbour, and Campbell Road resident alike – had a material base. The street's class structure was radically at odds with Holloway's; it was an inversion of Islington's working class, with skilled workers drastically under-represented; and in one regard, its proportion of street traders and others subsisting by economic individualism, it could probably only be compared with five or six other streets among Islington's one thousand or so.

What were the forces which continued to reproduce in the 1920s and 1930s the effects of the rise of Campbell Bunk fifty years before? This question raises large issues, taking us far outside Campbell Road into the nature and dynamics of class itself, especially as they relate to an under-theorised class position or place in the class structure – that occupied by the lumpenproletariat.

The lumpenproletariat

Within theories of class, 'lumpenproletariat' is a more-than-usually contentious term in a taxonomic battlefield. It is an ugly word, more often one of political abuse than theoretical explication. It is un-English and, if further disqualification were needed, it is also tainted by a provenance within the Marxist tradition. Indeed, it was Marx himself who gave the fullest description of the lumpenproletariat and its politics in Paris around 1850:

> Alongside decayed *roués* with dubious means of subsistence and dubious origin, alongside ruined and adventurous off-shoots of the bourgeoisie, were vagabonds, discharged soldiers, discharged jailbirds, escaped galley slaves, swindlers, mountebanks, *lazzaroni*, pickpockets, tricksters, gamblers,

maquereaus [procurers], brothel keepers, porters, *literati*,
organ-grinders, rag-pickers, knife grinders, tinkers, beggars,
in short, the whole indefinite, disintegrated mass, thrown
hither and thither which the French term *la bohème*. . . . This
scum, offal, refuse of all classes.[5]

The political opposition of Marx and Engels to the lumpenproletariat is clear enough – although some of their earlier work was
less critical and concerned, for example, to stress the humanity of
individual thieves and prostitutes.[6] But their writings on class were
notoriously incomplete and apparently contradictory and so we
have no clear statement of how they conceived of the lumpenproletariat as a theoretical concept.[7]

Even so, there are hints. The lumpenproletariat was distanced
from the working class by both politics *and* by being outside the
social relations of wage labour.[8] Its historic source had been the
'reserve army of labour' or the potential working population
surplus to capital's requirements. It had been initially created by
the de-population of the countryside and the growth of towns.
Thus the lumpenproletariat had a history, taking various forms
between the sixteenth and nineteenth centuries.[9] And at times the
lumpenproletariat could act as a 'class for itself', initiating action
on behalf of its unique class interests, alone or in alliance with
other classes.[10]

Within the Marxist tradition, classes are defined by reference to
the rights and powers their members hold over a society's
productive forces.[11] These rights and powers are not always
synonymous with ownership, but for simplicity's sake they are
here construed as though they were. In capitalist society, for
example, ownership of the means of production – raw materials,
machinery, factory buildings – is in the hands of the bourgeoisie.
These productive forces are set in motion by using the capacity of
others for work, so gaining for the bourgeoisie the means of life.
These others are people who do not own any of the productive
forces sufficient to meet their own subsistence needs. They merely
own the capacity to work – their 'labour-power' – and so are
dependent on selling this capacity to the owners of the productive
forces. People in this position are 'proletarians' – more generally
'the working class'.

Apart from these major blocs, capitalist societies also reproduce
other class positions, the boundaries between which merge imperceptibly into their neighbours in real life but which can be separated
for the purpose of analysis. The 'traditional petty bourgeoisie',
for example, is a position occupied by economically independent

workers who own small-scale means of production but have still to labour themselves to attain a livelihood, even when hiring the labour-power of other workers.

The lumpenproletariat occupy a separate class position within capitalist relations. In setting the forces of production to work, there will be those people whose labour-power is useless to the bourgeoisie and so not worth buying (rejection by the labour market); and there will be others who, although possessing labour-power, do not offer it for sale (rejection of the labour market). Within these two extremes lie those for whom the sale of labour-power is so limited that it will not by itself provide the means of life. When people from all these groups own insufficient means of production to maintain their subsistence, they are lumpenproletarians. Historically, the ways they obtain a subsistence are varied but have included brief and irregular bouts of casual labour, economic enterprise, dependency on state aid or charity, or 'crime' – the appropriation of a subsistence from other people.

Within the economic structure, class positions are in contradiction, one with another. Members of the proletariat, for example, have an interest in selling their labour-power as expensively as they can, to provide them with more of the means of subsistence; members of the bourgeoisie, on the other hand, have an interest in buying labour-power as cheaply as possible, so that they in turn may secure more of the means of subsistence to themselves.

The lumpenproletariat is in contradiction with both proletariat and bourgeoisie. The interests of the lumpenproletariat lie outside labour market relations, seeking a subsistence without selling the capacity to work. They do so through charity, state benefits which are not the result of past labour (unlike pensions bought by workers' own contributions) and crime – all of which act as a social charge on both sellers and buyers of labour-power.

The class position of the lumpenproletariat is not an enviable one in capitalist class relations and there are many reasons why individuals in that position should seek a way out. One clear way is through wage labour, and so the interests of the lumpenproletariat may be served by the creation of more work for those who cannot, under present circumstances, sell their labour-power. This may involve accommodation with the working class (on a political level, for instance) or with the bourgeoisie (by blacklegging during strikes). Another is to seek ways of enhancing the possibilities of economic individualism, eventually acquiring means of production which can be utilised by the individual's own labour. The lumpenproletariat thus faces in two mutually opposing directions: to the working class and to the traditional petty bourgeoisie.

Class positions are relatively unchanging as long as a particular mode of production continues to exist. But the movement of individuals in and out of them is much more fluid, and nowhere more so than in structurally ambiguous class positions like the lumpenproletariat. Yet it is the occupants of class positions who create, by their lived experience, 'classes'. Classes are formed by the social relations between people occupying the same class position in an historically specific time and place. One of the most important limitations on, or determinants of, those relations will be the rate of change in the personnel occupying the position in question.

There are three main routes into the class position occupied by the lumpenproletariat. The first is by inheritance. Being born into any class position is not necessarily a life sentence, but it will have determining effects for a term of years uncertain. The two major dynamics – rejection by and rejection of the labour market – still apply but work themselves out in different ways. They are substantially influenced by parental and peer group experience and attitudes, especially to wage labour and the ideologies bearing on it. And they are also influenced by the reaction of society to the lumpenproletarian condition – a reaction which enforces class inheritance through educational and social interaction (social welfare policies, policing, labour market opportunities). These internal and external forces are strengthened by social relations between people occupying the same position. For classes exist not only in their own social space but in their own physical space too, separated by access to shelter in a class-structured housing market.

Second, there is the route which follows rejection by the labour market. Here is the structural connection between the lumpenproletariat and the working class, and the mechanics of rejection are geared with 'the reserve army of labour'. This is the proportion of surplus labourers in the population which the increasing efficiency of capital does not need to put to work. The reserve army is constantly in flux, as workers are thrown out of contracting areas of employment and sucked into areas of expansion. Thus a reserve of readily available labour-power is available at the beck and call of capitalist expansion in any sphere of production and at any time.

In this constantly shifting process of unemployment, part-time employment, and re-absorption into different areas of production, the reserve army becomes stratified. There will be those, for example, whose physical or mental incapacity for work useful to capital disqualifies them from being absorbed by the labour market in any but the most exceptional circumstances. There will be those whose labour-power is of relatively low value, with no special skills or strengths to make it attractive to the market buyers, and who are especially vulnerable to the vicissitudes of casual labour – 'the light infantry of capital', Marx called them, 'thrown by it according to its needs, now to this point, now to that'.[12]

None of these conditions is absolute. All are affected by the historically specific state of capitalist production in any society. For example, there will be times when the whole of the traditionally constituted reserve army of labour will be absorbed and new supplies have to be brought in – non-wage labouring married women, perhaps, or men from reserves in other societies. These periods of more or less rapid reconstruction of the reserve army have momentous consequences for the lumpenproletariat; although the class position remains unaltered, its personnel and social relations may be radically renewed.

Third, the labour process and the other power relations of wage labour are actively rejected by individuals. To this extent, lumpen-proletarians can make themselves, they are not just the helpless victims of blind social forces.

But even here, rejection is in response to the structural alienation of men and women in the very process of labour within capitalist relations. There are many ways in which people are alienated from their own human potential, but one is especially important within the Marxist tradition – what Marx called 'the alienation of labour':

> labour is *external* to the worker, i.e., it does not belong to his intrinsic nature; . . . in his work, therefore, he does not affirm himself but denies himself, does not feel content but unhappy, does not develop freely his physical and mental energy but mortifies his body and ruins his mind. . . . Its alien character emerges clearly in the fact that as soon as no physical or other compulsion exists, labour is shunned like the plague.[13]

We have here the central dialectic of class relations within the lumpenproletariat – rejected by the labour market and rejecting the labour market. In lived experience, the two were frequently difficult to distinguish one from the other. But the tension between them had tangible effects on most aspects of life in that class position.

This, then, is the theoretical base which underpins an under-standing of what happened in Campbell Bunk and why. We now need to uncover the ways in which this class position was filled and refilled in the real world of London in the 1920s and 1930s; and how the processes affected, and were affected by, Campbell Bunk in particular.

London's reserve army of labour

By 1930 the Victorian image of London as the very essence of moral and spiritual degeneration had been thoroughly redrawn. London was now the beacon illuminating the nation's path out of depression, the forcing ground of new ideas, new industries, new ways of living. The image had its material grounding in the glass and concrete industrial suburbs of the Lea Valley and West Middlesex.[14] London and its fattening satellite towns were home to the fastest growing industries of Britain, a growth at its most dramatic between 1925 and 1935:[15] radios, batteries, vacuum cleaners, electric lamps, radiant fires, extractor fans, meters and photographic equipment; motor cars, buses and vehicle parts; ladies' nylons, potato crisps, celluloid dopes, artificial limbs, pickles and eiderdowns – all made in London, now more than ever the capital of finished goods manufacture. Between 1920 and 1938, the number of factories using power in Greater London had risen from 25,177 to 32,779 (or by 23.2 per cent).[16] The beacon drew workers like gnats to a hurricane lamp – the growth in population between 1921 and 1931 in London's outer ring was equivalent to adding the total population of Birmingham to the Metropolis;[17] 36 per cent of the increase in Britain's insured population between 1923 and 1937 took place in Greater London alone (703,000);[18] and among them were many of the chronically unemployed from hard-hit regions like North-East England and South Wales. The growth of suburbs, industrial estates and offices gave London pride of place in the building boom which helped lift Britain out of the slump from 1933 on.[19] At the outset of his English Journey, J. B. Priestley found this modern world symbolised by the Great West Road: 'being new, it did not look English. We might have suddenly rolled into southern California.'[20]

Islington, including Holloway, played its part in this new age. 'The Borough is becoming more and more a factory and workshop area,' complained the Medical Officer of Health as early as 1922,' and Islington continued to attract jobs for another thirty years or so.[21] But situated as it was at the place where the old centre and the new suburbs met, it could play a supporting role only: the new enterprises established themselves but had little room to expand. The borough continued to take an important share of London's food processing, electrical engineering (especially radio and battery assembly), clothing, furniture making, printing, chemicals, toy and brush making – but there was a tendency for firms established in the 1920s to seek more or better or cheaper space in outer London during the 1930s (particularly in vehicles

and vehicle and aeroplane parts, and food and drink manufacture).[22] Even so, the street directories for Holloway list 49 engineering and metal part manufacturers in 1919, 80 in 1939; the figures
for electrical appliance manufacturers were 19 and 41.[23]

But in this picture of London's prosperity in the midst of the
slump – a prosperity in which Holloway shared – there were
patches of deep shadow. For although unemployment never
reached the proportions of the depressed areas, London's huge
workforce meant that unemployment in the capital was none the
less a mass problem. Compare Wales, the hardest hit region of
Great Britain, and Greater London, the least affected area apart
from South-East England outside London. The unemployment
rates in Wales never fell below 19 per cent between 1929 and 1939
and rose to 36.5 per cent in 1932; the rates in Greater London
never rose above 14 per cent (1932) and more typically averaged
6 per cent. Yet there were more unemployed people living in
Greater London during these years than in the whole of Wales.[24]
During the worst months of the slump, the total out of work in
Greater London reached 350,000; even in the LCC area, nearly
220,000 were unemployed in January 1933.[25]

Within London, the unemployment blackspots were
Bermondsey and Poplar, but Islington, with the largest workforce
living within its boundaries of any metropolitan borough, had
unemployment rates consistently higher than the county average
(13.7 per cent in 1932, the worst year, against 12.7 per cent). At any
time in 1932, some 16,500 people were out of work in Islington; the
number of unemployed in Jarrow at that time was 7,500.[26] Figure
1 shows the total unemployment trend for Islington Borough from
1929 to 1940.

Unemployment selects its victims differently, according to
whether they are young or old, men or women, skilled or
unskilled. Differentiation by gender will be discussed later,
especially for the young. But for both men and women, the crucial
component in determining the patterns of long-term unemployment – forcing the victims outside wage labour for a long period,
perhaps permanently – was skill. This is not to say that all of
the chronically unemployed were without skill, however defined.
Industrial restructuring threw many skill-holders permanently out
of their trades. But restrictive production inevitably hit unskilled
labour first and hardest. Skilled workers were generally the last to
be laid off and the first to be taken on, but generalised labour-
power was always dispensable and replaceable: 'a large, and
perhaps increasing, proportion of unemployment is accounted for
by a relative over supply of the more untrained types of labour.'[27]

Although London's reserve army of unemployed workers was constantly changing its composition and personnel – and the situation was markedly more dynamic in London than elsewhere in Britain – there was still a problem of long-term unemployment. About 8 per cent of the unemployed on the employment registers in London in 1937 had been out of work for more than a year – some 10,500 people;[28] and it is likely that the problem had been worse at the nadir of the depression.[29] And 'below' them were the long-term unemployed on poor relief who were not in receipt of the dole, estimated at another 10,000 in 1931.[30]

Living on a poor quality diet took its toll on physique and left workers unable to reproduce their capacity to labour.[31] This was especially significant where lack of a marketable skill left a worker access only to physically demanding general labouring jobs. The psychic experience of being out of work was harder to characterise, observers writing of the sense of being lost without a job, of rejection and degradation (at least among those used to regular labour). There was, too, a process of 'adjustment' to unemployment as a normal state among the long-term unemployed, and for some 'it would be hard to bring themselves to take work if it were available'.[32] Then there was the discrimination by employers against the long-term unemployed which gave the screw another twist.[33]

These factors all helped influence adversely the value of the labour-power long-unemployed workers could bring to the market.[34] When Islington Council organised relief works for the unemployed in the mid-1920s, for example, they had great difficulty recruiting labourers who could cope with the heavy demands of unskilled labour, partly because labouring does indeed demand skills and special strengths which cannot be developed overnight: 'the technique of the shovel, if one is to be a real artist with it, demands long practice.'[35] Out of 180 unemployed men taken on for one Holloway Road resurfacing scheme, 59 had to be sent home as physically incapable or insufficiently skilled: 'some have found the work quite beyond their strength.'[36] In a large reserve army, it was thus particularly difficult for men weakened by unemployment to recover their position. And demand for unskilled adult male labour remained relatively slack in London and elsewhere until 1940.[37]

It is often difficult to separate out the long-term unemployed men and women from those affected by disabilities of one sort or another,[38] and in Campbell Road the two seem to have gone together. A builders' labourer who died at number 93 in 1919 had not worked, according to his daughter's memory, for about 15 years following an accident at his last employment.[39] A man with a bad chest who came to Campbell Road after his hawking business failed around 1926 did not do a day's work until he went firewatching during the Blitz in 1940.[40] A 38-year-old labourer convicted of breaking and entering a Stoke Newington house had been unemployed for three years apart from 'a little window-cleaning'.[41] A Campbell Road painter, convicted of stealing milk from a doorstep to feed his hungry child in 1932, had done no work for 18 months.[42] It is likely that cases like these of no work at all over extensive periods were relatively unusual. More typical were those men and women on the fringes of casual employment, picking up a few weeks' work during the year at one of the many openings which London offered. For, as in the period before 1914, London continued to be the greatest reservoir of casual labour in the country.

The casual labour market in Holloway

Ronnie Drover left Industrial School when he was 16, in 1918. He had been born at Tottenham and when he was about 10 or 11 the family were evicted from a tenement house at Lorenco Road, the notorious 'Little Russia' with its tramps' lodging houses, on the Edmonton border. He and his mother slept for a time in a van before the family moved to 25 Campbell Road around 1912. After leaving the reformatory where he had been sent for chronic truancy, his first job was as errand boy in a greengrocer's, but he lost it through bad time-keeping. For the next seven years until 1925 he had a succession of casual short-term jobs; and when he returned from seven years' service in the army the old pattern continued. He dug trenches for new stands at the Arsenal football ground; he went out totting for metals; he drove a horse and van for Neal, a coal-dealer in Campbell Road; he worked a press in a battery factory at York Way; he scraped tar from wooden road blocks at a yard in Greenwich; he was a hod-carrier at Catford, a brush-hand for public works contractors, a general labourer at a building site in Victoria Street; he pushed a barrel organ around North London, and when he came out of the army in 1932 he stayed at a Salvation Army lodging house and took out a barrow collecting waste cardboard from shops; sometimes he would form a troupe with two other young unemployed men from Campbell Road and perform somersaults for pennies in Finsbury Park.[43] He might be out of work for half a year at a time,[44] and a full catalogue of his jobs, employed and self-employed, would be much longer than this, could it be compiled. Ronnie Drover's was a representative male experience of chronic underemployment in the London casual labour market between the wars.

London's casual labour market of the 1920s and 1930s bore many similarities to that of the 1880s and 1900s, but it was not the same. The brief period of full employment caused by the First World War, when new layers of the reserve army of labour (married women as well as the chronically underemployed) were sucked into the full-time labour market, had finished with a bang in 1920 and 1921. Although mechanical handling and efforts to de-casualise a major source of the demand for casual labour – the docks – had their effects on the margins, other countervailing tendencies (particularly mass-unemployment) combined to expand the casual labour supply, rather than diminish it. As before the war, the demands for short-term labour were at their greatest from London's insatiable appetites,[45] and Islington shared in them to the full.

The fluctuation of Islington's employment demand is plain from figure 1, where winter demand was frequently 25 per cent below the summer figure, and when every Christmas 2,000 Holloway workers could be taken off the dole queue to help sort and deliver mail at Mount Pleasant and elsewhere.[46] But in the structure of the under-employed casual fringe, certain industries were of far greater importance than others. The docks played hardly any part at all in the demand for casual labour in Holloway, although there is evidence of one or two dockers living in Campbell Road in the 1920s and 1930s.[47] But the building and civil engineering industries had always been London's other main source of the demand for casual labour, and Holloway was home to an important (though declining) reservoir of building workers. The building and road-making boom of the inter-war period resulted in the growth of casual labour in the industry, especially in London, as large numbers of the unemployed registered as building labourers in the search for work.[48] At any one time, and especially in the winter months, unemployment in the building industry was some 50 per cent higher than in other London trades.[49] Even in the *summer* of 1932, 2,000 building workers were registered as unemployed at the Holloway exchange.[50]

For the building labourers of Campbell Road, the general experience of short-term engagements and filling in between whiles was punctuated by prestige projects providing stable employment for some months – like the Arsenal Stadium improvements of the 1920s and 1930s; super-cinemas like the Finsbury Park Astoria, opposite the Bunk in Seven Sisters Road; even the West London exhibition centres of Olympia and Earl's Court and Wembley drew workers from Campbell Road.[51] The organisation of the local building industry was predominantly in small-scale enterprises (there were 139 building or decorating firms listed in the street directory for Holloway in 1929) with a small number of permanent tradesmen, hiring and firing general labour by the hour.[52] Campbell Road itself had a building firm – Ernie Neal's – and Tubby Nicholls, the deputy of 14 houses in the street, kept several Bunk men in work distempering rooms and carrying out repairs at the order of the sanitary authority.

In this vulnerable market, Walter Spencer's father was more out of work than in:

'Me father used to go into work and it rains, I've seen him come home sobbing, crying. Day in, day out, day home; day back again, go to work, back again.'[53]

And so was John Harper's father until he was made a foreman locally just before the Second World War.[54] Even when in work, the labour reserve kept wage rates for building labourers still notoriously low,[55] and they were but poorly unionised.[56]

Road transport was also an important industry for Islington's male casual labour between the wars, as it had been before 1914. Within the County of London, Islington was home to a dispro-portionately large number of road transport workers.[57] Apart from bus and tram work, which lost its casual fringe with mechanisation and the creation of the London General Omnibus Company monopoly in the late 1920s,[58] the largest demand for casual labour came from road haulage. Despite the importance of large firms like Carter Paterson's and Tillings, the organisation of the industry locally was overwhelmingly small-scale.[59] This type of haulage often depended on local short-term and seasonal demand – carrying small loads short distances, like furniture removals and laundry.[60] Carriers would often take on men, including many from Campbell Road,[61] by the day to suit the needs of the job, and as in other trades with a casual fringe, the workers proved extremely resistant to unionisation[62] (see chapter 4).

Coal carrying was the most seasonally affected end of the industry, and only favoured workers would be kept on in the summer months. Despite the poor conditions, coal carting could draw on a reserve of casual labour.[63] 'Coal carmen are a distinct and restricted class of men, who for that reason are more indepen-dent and enjoy more free-and-easy conditions than other transport workers,' it was said in 1934.[64] Most coal was moved by major contractors like Tyne Main, Charringtons or Rickett, Smith & Co., employing labour to heave the coal from railway wagons to bunkers and lorries and to deliver the coal to consumers. But this trade, too, offered opportunities of independence to individual workers who had access to a horse and van and who hired work-mates, often on a part-profit basis. One of Campbell Road's enter-prises – Neal's, who also employed boys and men from Campbell Road[65] – seems to have begun that way, and the road provided a ready supply of casual unskilled labour at the local coal yards. Indeed, Campbell Road appears to have supplied a casual fringe to a casual fringe: George Fletcher, defending a Poor Law charge at a local police court, described himself as a 'coal trouncer',

> a man who was allowed to accompany the regular carman of a coal van, and all the pay he received was what the carman chose to give him. The carman usually handed over the 'beer money' given by the householder who received the coal.

Eventually Fletcher secured a regular coal carman's position at 10s 6d a day.[66]

There were many other demands for casual labour in London between the wars, and Campbell Road men answered the call to varying degrees. There were London's great wholesale commodity markets, with casual demand particularly high at Billingsgate, Covent Garden, Spitalfields, the King's Cross Potato Market, and a little at Smithfield.[67] There was the Caledonian Market in Holloway, where men got two uneven days' work a week port-ering for stall holders or running for pitches.[68] Radio shops would pay for accumulators to be humped to generators for re-charging.[69] A day or two's gardening could be had for householders in Crouch End and Muswell Hill.[70] The London film industry needed scene shifters, crowd extras, and stunt men, and shows at the Finsbury Park Empire and exhibitions at Olympia and the Agricultural Hall demanded labourers by the day.[71] For the desperate, there was the sandwich board – 'advertising labourers' they might be called; they reportedly even had a London union in the early 1930s.[72] Within Campbell Road, apart from building and coal carting, there were other opportunities for a day's or half-day's work pushing a coster's barrow.

Lastly, municipal enterprise made large demands on the casual labour market, at least in the 1920s. Like road transport, Council services were widely affected by mechanisation around 1930 with a consequent reduction in the demand for casual labour. So the tendency here was to de-casualise as the 1920s wore on, providing regular employment for a part of the previously casual fringe and dispensing with the rest as much as possible.[73] Heavy snowfalls would still produce queues at the Vestry gates in the 1930s, but by then the regular early-morning hirings for dust collection and street cleaning were largely over. There was also progressive de-casualisation in the electricity supply industry during the 1920s; this mainly affected coal heavers.[74]

So far, we have considered the casual labour demand for men. Women were greatly exploited and underpaid in the London labour market and their work was frequently seasonal. But there were not the violent fluctuations in terms of short engagements with little control by the worker over hiring and firing which character-ised the casual labour market for men. Women had far fewer opportunities, and those were dominated by demands for domestic rather than industrial employment. In addition, the supply was in part formed by those needs, casual labourers among women being predominantly married or widowed, often with other large demands on their resources. Casual labour was not, generally, a young woman's fate.[75]

The female casual labourer was personified in the charwoman and the washerwoman. Again, one of the tendencies of the 1920s and 1930s was to decasualise charing, with agencies organising office and cinema and factory cleaning. But the majority of char-women depended on short-term arrangements with numerous clients; middle-class housewives contacted through the Lennox Road Mission,[76] or newsagents' windows, or by knocking on doors. And there were public institutions like hospitals and schools. The supply of charwomen from Campbell Road included old-stagers, spending their half-crown a day at the pub, having a meal at work, and otherwise doing without food and bothering little about home comforts – like Mrs Tiverton, whom we will meet again.[77] But it was also the resort of married women like Mrs Duncan, who chared until she found work in a radio factory (unusually for an older woman).[78] Several charwomen also took in laundry or went out washing in people's homes. Conditions for charwomen were poor and frequently degrading. Yet even so, the over-supply of women from Campbell Road was such that chars could come to blows over the competition for work:

> ' "Who told you to do that step, Mop?" She said, "Lady called me in to do it, said you wasn't coming." So I said, "Did she? Oh." I get hold of the rest of the water and chuck it right over her. . . . "Now, you've got that for doing my step, ain't

you?" I said, "You do any more of mine, you'll get some more." '[79]

Chronic underemployment in the casual labour market produced a double alienation from wage labour in the attitudes of mind which being casual fostered. Some valued the freedom not to work which casual work offered: 'but I couldn't get up in the mornings, honestly.'[80] The monotony or degradation of work at the lowest end of the market could be counteracted by job changing: away from the heat and smell of the annealing furnace for glassworks labourers, or away from the filth of a tar block cleaner's – 'we was like Newgate's Knocker. . . . Never seen a job like it in my *life!*'[81] Indulging a hot temper – normally the prerogative of the employing class – was simpler when jobs were easy come easy go: 'I ought to remember his name, I hit him with a shovel,'[82] recalled a Campbell Road labourer of one Holloway building employer; and it is easy to see how charwomen could have been similarly affected. For social scientists like Beveridge, these were symptoms of 'demoralisation'.[83] But for some casual labourers – especially those untrammelled by family responsibilities – they were proof of a limited personal independence. This was strengthened by poor unionisation, which militated against collective solidarity at work.

Collective solidarity out of work was weakened, too: large numbers of breadwinners in Campbell Road paid no national insurance contributions at all and so received no dole.[84] And in a culture like Campbell Road's, the gaps (frequently lengthy) between jobs could be turned to account in a variety of ways which strengthened independence even further. For these reasons, the experience of casual labour, and a position in the casual labour market from which (at least until 1940) it was hard to escape, strengthened the links with long-term unemployment. Of 48 chronically unemployed general labourers surveyed in Deptford in the late 1930s, only 8 had previously had 'good employment records . . . the great majority had drifted most of their lives.'[85]

So far, in analysing the ways in which the class position of the lumpenproletariat came to be filled in London during the 1920s and 1930s, attention has been paid to the forces of demand in the labour market – the structures of unemployment and underemployment. Intricately bound up with these were problems of supply – the quality of labour-power which individuals could bring to market.

'The unemployables'

One day, some time around the end of the First World War, the man downstairs at 21 Campbell Road showed little Lil Wilsdon how he earned his living. He had no arms. His brother, who lived with him, brought a stool, arranged some coloured chalks and took off one of his boots. The man with no arms picked up a chalk in his toes and began to draw a picture on the paving stones.[86] Annie Beer's father had been a carpenter's labourer but after an accident on the job, he never worked again. His sons were all in regular work and by the end of the First World War had moved away from the Bunk. All, that is, except Arthur who stayed on at Campbell Road, earning a living as a rag and bone man. 'He was a cripple. He had club feet.'[87] 1933 was a terrible year for the Mays at 52 Campbell Road. Ada, just 21, killed herself by eating rat poison.[88] People said she committed suicide because she had been jilted but the youth concerned, from George's Road, denied anything was wrong. This was a pitifully poor family. Her father 'was a very nice charming old gentleman but he was a bit weak-minded.' He sold salt, soda, vinegar, starch and so on from a barrow. At a time when the poverty line was about 40s for that size of family, he earned on average 10s a week, barely enough to pay the rent.[89] His son, Alfie, went to Romilly Road Special School. Alfie, too, was 'a bit weak-minded' and had trouble controlling his bowels: 'We used to call him Shit-Legs'.[90]

We must resist the temptation to see Campbell Road as some living backdrop to the Beggar's Opera, but it is worth noting that some outsiders did see it like that. The sanitary inspector's report on p. 25 above was echoed in 1933 by Dr F. C. Shrubsall, who had Mental Deficiency Act responsibilities in the LCC Public Health Department. In a report to the New Survey of London, he gave two examples of areas where 'mental defectives' – in the elegant bureaucratic language of the time – were concentrated. He supported the New Survey's findings that some districts, especially, the 'black' streets, had more than their fair share of people with mental disabilities:[91]

> Soap Suds Island in North Kensington used to be just such a centre with an undue proportion of MDs. [A marginal note adds] Or Campbell Road Islington where there is a PD, MD, or Blind, Deaf, or however person in practically every house.[92]

The good doctor exaggerated to push his point home. But none the less, if Campbell Road's class structure was predominantly lumpenproletarian then we should expect to find more people with physical or mental disabilities in that street than others. For in the labour market, it was an individual's capacity to work (as defined by the buyers) which determined whether a man or a woman would get wage labour or not. And those whose capacity was judged to be low or nil got work last or not at all. Rejected by employers, put on the 'dead man's register' at the labour exchange, they were officially classified as 'unemployable'.

Employability is, of course, a relative concept. The problem of the 'unemployables' virtually disappeared in periods of labour shortage, especially in the dramatic demands of total war: indeed, the first Disabled Persons Act of 1944 was designed specifically to utilise this potential source of labour for the war effort.[93] Mass unemployment between the wars created a critical climate for examining the value of labour-power which workers could bring to market, yet even here only 1 in 16 of the long-term unemployed was considered by the Pilgrim Trust as 'absolutely unemployable';[94] and in Ministry of Labour surveys of unemployment benefit cases in 1924 and 1928, only 3.6 per cent and 2.1 per cent of men were found to be 'verging on the unemployable'.

Yet if a large reserve of unemployed labour enabled employers to pick and choose between potential workers, discriminating against those considered to be less capable for work than others, one important feature of the labour market in County of London areas like Holloway encouraged that discrimination to a greater extent than elsewhere. This was the small-scale organisation of production. In Islington's manufacturing industry, the average number of workers per factory was 17.8 in 1938 (the figure for the LCC area was 20.1). In small-scale enterprises like these, those differences between workers which could be subsumed in a large factory took on exaggerated importance. So it became even more difficult for the worker with disabilities, however trivial in themselves, to compete for employment. In a buyer's market, low-value labour-power could quickly become unsellable; or sellable only at a price which could not afford the worker a subsistence. In those cases, the worker could not buy sufficient commodities to reproduce his capacity to labour, thus driving that capacity even further down.[95]

The largest group of potential workers rejected from the labour market in this way suffered some sort of physical disability, from general ill-health to missing limbs. Tom Tasker was invalided out of the army after being gassed at Hill 60. He had worked on his own account as a window cleaner until about 1926. Then he had a bad fall through a skylight and never worked again until he died in Campbell Road, twelve years later.[96] Mrs Knight would have supplemented her husband's earnings by charing, but she could go out only very irregularly through her chronic ill-health – psoriasis, rheumatoid arthritis, and malnutrition.[97] Her husband's earnings at the docks were made even more irregular by the terrible neuralgia he suffered, eventually revealing itself as a fatal nasal cancer: 'he used to bang his head against the wall'[98] with the pain. Ida Alexander's widowed mother was not able to seek cleaning work because she'd had some sort of stroke which gave her 'funny talk and a dribble with it'.[99] Lenny Chine's blind father stood outside Finsbury Park station selling matches.[100] Mr Drover, the one-legged jobbing signwriter at number 25, had lost a leg below the knee through an abscess at about the age of 11.[101] Harry Gough, a deaf mute of no occupation, was convicted of stealing a fellow lodger's boots at the Campbell Road lodging house 'so that he might have a better chance of getting work'.[102] And it is plain from other evidence that labour market discrimination could be prompted by 'social' handicaps – a bad stutter,[103] or ugliness,[104] or skin colour. 'Men of colour' were prominent among London's street entertainers, and a black father and son lived in Campbell Road in 1919.[105]

But throughout the 1920s, and even into the 1930s, the greatest source of physical disability continued to be the First World War: 1.7 million servicemen from Great Britain and Ireland had been wounded in the war, of whom 95 per cent were 'other ranks'. The repercussions echoed on for years. As late as 1933, St Dunstan's hospital reported frequent new cases of blindness from men whose eyes had been apparently only slightly damaged by active service; 39,000 men had lost limbs, and 42,000 had contracted TB.[106]

It had been the farm labourers and slum dwellers of England who had suffered first and most in the slaughter, and Campbell Road was prominent among them:

> Campbell Road is as patriotic a Road as any in Islington. 300 of its men have joined HM Forces, and over 30 have made the great sacrifice. Campbell Road decided to have a War Shrine, and on Friday this was unveiled by the Mayoress of Islington. It is a handsome and imposing memorial, and has been set up outside number 11, the residence of Mr. E [Steed], and where resided G. Elms of the Royal Engineers, the first Islington man to be awarded the D.C.M. The road was bright with flags and banners. . . . The Mayor [sic] said that the 300 men gone from Campbell Road was an inspiring testimony to

the whole-hearted, ready way in which the British working man had responded to the call and had gone forth to protect the hearths and homes of Old England.[107]

Henry Grant, of 19 Campbell Road, did no work for the eleven years following the Armistice: 'Has Army Pension for Gun Shot Wound.'[108] James Leary, a persistent Campbell Road beggar, claimed to have received a gun shot wound in the leg and so was unable to work.[109] A coal miner called George Thomas 'debarred from his work . . . owing to injuries to his hand received in the war' was convicted of peddling without a licence while living in Campbell Road in 1919.[110] Reginald Inskipp, blinded by a bayonet wound, was grinding an organ for a living in 1921.[111]

Then there were the physical effects of Campbell Road itself on the people who lived there. Appallingly overcrowded, its houses suffering from neglect and overuse, with facilities inconvenient or non-existent, Campbell Road provided living space which was inherently unhealthy and dangerous. As late as 1938, Campbell Road was ten times more overcrowded than the national average, and four times as bad as Islington as a whole: there were on average 1.9 persons per room or 11.2 persons per house.[112] Small wonder that TB, the disease most closely connected with overcrowded living conditions, should have been prevalent in Campbell Road between the wars.[113] All the houses were in more or less severe disrepair, through bad building and subsequent neglect. There was rising damp, leaking roofs and rotting woodwork; staircase balustrades had frequently been removed for fire wood even though stairs and passages were badly lit; the WC in the yard was sometimes shared by 30 people, the seat and pan fouled with 'Mr Brown';[114] one tap only was usually provided for the shared use of up to eight households; there was no gas for the vast majority of houses until about 1938, forty years after it had become the commonest fuel for cooking and lighting among the London working class.[115] Between the wars, and given the extent of Islington's housing problem, Campbell Road was not bad enough to be classed as a slum. But its combination of overcrowding, disrepair and poor amenities produced some of the most 'pitiful housing conditions' in North London.[116] They both undermined by stealth the constitutions of people living there and presented acute dangers as well. In July 1921, part of a roof coping collapsed onto a street party, causing severe head injuries to a 17-year-old girl.[117] Walter Spencer lost an eye on a rusty nail while playing in a neighbour's back yard.[118] And there were frequent scalds and fires due to the sheer impossibility of living safely in crowded rooms while using coal fires to cook on and candles and oil lamps to light your way.[119] Such were the hearths and homes the men of Campbell Road had gone forth to protect.

Living conditions like these took a psychological toll as well, unfitting men and women for regular work through various forms of nervous exhaustion or depression, and contributing to widespread alcohol abuse. Whether the cause was internal to Campbell Road or not, mental disability or illness of one sort or another were important sources of rejection from the labour market. Once more, categories of 'mental defect' are relative: in a reactionary report of 1929, still only 1.8 per cent of 'feeble-minded' men were 'unemployable'.[120] And a noted eugenicist was moved to write in 1937 that 'In a perfectly organised community which provided an appropriate environment and suitable work for all, there would probably be no chronic unemployed neurasthenics.'[121] But this was a time of authoritarianism in the definition and incarceration of 'defectives' which only deepened the alienation from wage labour of people so labelled.[122] The effects of institutionalisation, frequently for long periods, only made individuals less fitted for work in the eyes of potential employers. And again, the war's nightmarish reverberations – quite literally so in the case of shell-shock victims[123] – rumbled on well into the 1930s.[124]

'He was a neurotic,' claimed Mavis Knight of her father, who lived with his wife, step-daughter and his own seven children – ten persons in all – in two top-floor rooms at 91.[125] Jim Dunn remembers his father as diagnosed suffering from 'neurasthenia' – a popular psychiatric generalisation of the time: he'd had a bad war, but his condition couldn't have been helped by living seven in one room, as his family did when they first moved to Campbell Road around 1926.[126]

Drink dependence was a common problem in Campbell Road, perhaps at its worst amongst people living alone. Jane Alice Clapham, whose children were in the workhouse, and who was frequently arrested when drunk, claimed 'I suffer from fits and cannot work' in 1919.[127] In 1929, Jeremiah Taylor, a 53-year-old flower seller from Campbell Road, died of 'disease of the heart, liver and kidneys from chronic alcoholism'.[128] And Mrs Tiverton, the charwoman, must have reduced her capacity to work by her drinking habits; 'my mum was a boozer.'[129]

For young men and women, being categorised as 'mental defective' meant difficulties getting or keeping a job: failure to hold a job down meant running the risk of ending up in an institution. William D of 23 Campbell Road left special school aged 16 in 1929. He worked at a golf club for eight weeks or so and was then unemployed for six months; he got a job at a wallpaper factory, but was again soon out of work for more than half a year; when last visited by the LCC's follow-up service he was doing 'odd jobs'. And Elizabeth C, from 66 Campbell Road, had jobs lasting a few weeks only at a battery works, and factories making pickles, jam, sweets and artificial flowers before being committed to the Manor Hospital at Epsom.[130]

The power to make or break lives like Elizabeth C's lay substantially in the hands of local employers. The power was not wilfully abused, but wielded as market forces dictated. From 1919 to 1939, virtually without exception, those forces permitted, even demanded, discrimination against individuals whose capacity for work appeared smaller than average. But there were one or two more unusual ways in which the labour market discriminated against the people of Campbell Road.

The curse of Campbell Bunk

One, applying to individuals from the street and outside, was the barrier to employment of people who had served terms of imprisonment. It is one of the ironies of British social policy between the wars that imprisonment, which was seen by many magistrates and others as the surest cure for idleness, condemned ex-prisoners to a workless existence on their release. 'In despair', recalled Claud Mullins, the North London stipendiary during the 1930s, 'I sent GL to prison for a substantial time and could only hope that prison would teach him to work.'[131] And, indeed, the London prisons taught a variety of handicraft skills and rudiments of the engineering and building crafts.[132]

But on release this was all set at nought. The probation service and the discharged prisoners' aid societies all had an almost impossible task to place their clients in work.[133] There was active discrimination by employers at the point of entry to the labour market; discrimination by fellow workers whose suspicions of the ex-prisoner were sufficiently discomfiting to make him leave, or who actually hounded him out; and discrimination by the policeman with a grudge who alerted employers to a worker's 'character', as a 'favour'.[134]

That this affected the men (it related almost exclusively to men) of Campbell Road can be taken for granted. The court reports for 1928 and 1929, for example, tell of 15 Campbell Road men (no women) sent to prison for various terms, and the number of ex-prisoners in the street was many times that figure. And it was the street's connection with convicted thieves which provided one source of another labour market discrimination against men and women from Campbell Road: the social reaction to its reputation.[135]

There were many effects of being labelled a Bunkite, as we shall see. But probably the most widely-felt was the barrier to employment which labelling set up. It is quite possible that this feeling was more imagined than real. For example, it was said that the Ever Ready battery factory in Fonthill Road would not take girls from Campbell Road, but it did.[136] Yet there is no doubt that it was *felt* to be real, and that it was experienced as a direct and personal rejection by the labour market. 'I have written for hundreds of jobs,' complained 'A British Legionite' to the local newspaper in 1922, 'and when I mention Campbell Road it is all up, simply because the street has been given a bad name.'[137] Another wrote,

> I lived there five years [and] I could never obtain a berth from there. People said to me, you will never get anything while you live there. . . . It is like dynamite to mention the road. Why don't they alter the name? I wish, from the bottom of my heart, I had never known of its existence.[138]

There were ways of avoiding the stigma, like giving a false address: one youth from number 52 – on the Paddington Street corner – always gave his address as 52 Paddington Street.[139] And in 1924, a charwoman convicted of theft from an employer was said by the police to have 'lived in Campbell Road but gave another address'.[140]

Rejecting wage labour

The search for an alternative to wage labour is a constant feature of capitalist social relations and affects all levels of the working class. First-class engineers and compositors set up as their own masters;[141] 'painters, plumbers, gas-fitters, locksmiths, gardeners, electricians and people doing building repairs, make extras on their own, and this sometimes amounts to as much as 50% or more of their wages';[142] 'The ideal of many working men is a little business, a newsagent's or a fried fish shop.'[143] London's street sellers were constantly replenished by men and women acting out their escape from wage labour, 'independence [being] one of the chief attractions of street trading' according to the New Survey of London.[144]

But the tendencies to alienation from wage labour were strongest among those consigned to industry's most menial and undemanding tasks.

'We was all work-shy blokes', remembered Ronnie Drover of himself and the young men from Campbell Road he went about with in the 1920s and 1930s. There were many good reasons for not wanting to work at that time and in his place. The work offered to the unskilled was often dirty and dangerous. Its irregularity militated against loyalty to an employer or to work as an idea. It was boring and exhausting, over-taxing body at the expense of mind. It was low-status employment and more fortunate workers despised you for doing it. Discipline was harsher where employers knew other hands were ever eager to snatch up work for themselves. Worst of all, the wages never compensated for the burden of degradation.[145] It was apparent to all in this position that hard work reaped little reward, while insights into the relative riches of builders and factory owners, or the relative ease and security of Council overseers, were never hard to come by.

The 'alienation of labour' was immanent in the structure of wage relations and in the labour process. Just which individuals grew sufficiently alienated to reject wage labour altogether is a second order problem, though of the two it is the one which has given non-Marxist social science most cause for concern. It depended, certainly, on the individual psyche. But in matters like this the individual is socially constructed and many elements in socialisation could have nurtured, say, an abhorrence of discipline, or the low threshold of boredom which led to rapid job changing and eventually rejection of work itself. The only wage work which Bonar Thompson – the 'Hyde Park Orator' – accepted between 1909 and 1933 was apparently one week as a kitchen porter in a West End restaurant:[146]

My determination never to work unless I got a wage sufficient for the satisfaction of my modest requirements became so strong that it was almost an obsession. Hard work does not frighten me, but hard work at low wages and under conditions inconsistent with human dignity is unthinkable to a man of my temperament.[147]

Rejecting wage labour depended, clearly, on the expectations individuals had of their own potential. Inheriting a class position might normally make for resigned acceptance when confronted by those job opportunities which were part of the title-deed. But expectations and the potential for hope alter – as they did for youth in both the 1920s and 1930s. And the most talented of those frustrated by the gap might well react against the old conditions they remain forced to accept. There are many examples of the personal histories of individuals like this. Take John Worby, a self-styled 'spiv' before the term had earned its black-market notoriety:

> if I'd worked all my life, would I have been any further
> ahead? . . . what a mug I would have been. I began to look
> on these tramps and spivs in a different light. I began to see
> them as I now saw myself: rebels from everyday slavery. The
> others, respectable people, they were slaves to the clock. . . .
> What was the use of working for mere existence and nothing
> more? . . . I didn't object to work itself. Then what did I object
> to? Was it the wages, was it the conditions, was it the hours?
> Yes it was. It was all three. Was I born to work for thirty bob
> a week?[148]

An important factor in determining which individuals would reject wage labour at any particular point in their lives was the opportunity they saw for an alternative subsistence. Those opportunities were determined by economic structure, class and culture. They might be few, say, in a Durham pit village.[149] But in Campbell Road they were many, and individuals were conscious that they were so. The traditions formed by past generations of individuals sloughed off or withdrawing from the labour market, reproduced patterns which themselves became social forces, dragging men and women from under the grinding-wheel of capital. Street selling, scavenging and individual services, each with their own economic organisation, trade mysteries and language, still flourished during the 1920s. The alternative to wage labour of thieving and other forms of unlawful appropriations grew in potential and in reward, especially during the 1930s. It was easier for individuals, alienated from labour, to follow the logic of that alienation if alternatives were well-lit features of their everyday lives.

Growing up with poverty, in Campbell Bunk and elsewhere, gave many children an apprenticeship in economic individualism outside wage labour. The extent of the economic enterprise of London children before 1914 is documented in a wealth of evidence from Mayhew on. There had been a general falling off in the extent of children's self-employment since that time. In part this was attributable to LCC regulations made under the Employment

of Children Act 1903, the Education Acts of 1918 and 1921, and
the Children and Young Persons Act 1933.

Yet the forces which fostered economic enterprise among poor
children were stronger than even the LCC's tentacles could
restrain. Children's earnings remained an important source of
subsistence, especially in widows' families or where the male
breadwinner could or would not contribute adequately to the
family income. And at a time when children had never previously
had so much to spend their pocket money on, casual earnings
helped maintain their own standard of living. What limited
evidence exists supports the view that it was in the very poorest
families that children's economic enterprise was at its most varied,
ambitious and productive in terms of family subsistence.[150] It
amounted to a culture of independence which, if not moulding the
future adult's view of the world, gave him or her a consciousness
of a mode of existence outside wage labour or at its very margins.

Take, for instance, Tommy Short from 48 Campbell Road, a
widow's elder son who was 14 in 1934. The range of enterprises
he engaged in might have been wider than most but it testifies to
the vigour of this aspect of London's street life even in the 1930s.
He would 'mind' cars and motorbikes when the Arsenal football
team were at home; sing and do a few tumbles at the queues for
the Finsbury Park Astoria and the Empire music hall; beg for used
first-house programmes at the Empire and sell them to the second
house; pick up (technically steal) old tar blocks where wood-paved
roads were being repaired, chop them up and sell them for
firewood from a borrowed pram; use the same pram to go rag
and boning or totting, selling rags to a shop in Fonthill Road, and
the metals to a yard in Paddington Street; go snow shifting for the
big houses in Brownswood Road; do domestic work like brass
cleaning, and be a Jews' Poker on Saturdays round the Manor
House; steal coal from the wharves at Finsbury Park and boxes
from a local fishmonger and hawk them for firing; and collect and
sometimes steal bottles for the returnable deposit at pubs and
shops.[151] Walter Spencer collected jam jars and newspapers and
sold them in Fonthill Road and sold horse manure by the bucket
to local rose growers.[152]

Girls from poor families, too, had a share in this culture. It was
smaller than their brothers', even though they could have taken
part in most of the enterprises listed above. Girls also had their
own sphere. Marjie Drover, 14 in 1924, had to supplement her
father's small and irregular earnings. She went doorstep scrubbing,
knocking on the doors of 'posher houses' for her clients, and ran
regular errands within Campbell Road for a few pence each

week.[153] Mavis Knight, around 1930, sold her mother's surplus stock of salads from a basket on Sundays, went doorstep cleaning, and opened the doors for customers at Lyons's with her brother; and so on.[154]

Then there was street selling. The inherited tradition of London costermongering was still strong eighty years after Mayhew.[155] Family tradition was just one of the reasons for selling in the streets but it was a powerful distraction from wage labour for those born into it. Willie Knowles, from number 30, used to sell in the streets from time to time when his labouring jobs gave out. His mother, a famous drinker in Campbell Road, sold salads in the street. And her mother before her, granny Tibbs, who also lived in the road, had done the same.[156] Liza Harmer, a flower seller who died in Campbell Road in 1919, had originated from a travelling family who had settled in George's Road by the early 1870s. Her father, it was said, had been murdered on a country road for the gold coins he kept about him in a little bag.[157] The Stevensons were street sellers (both husband and wife) who had accumulated sufficient capital by the 1930s to hire out barrows and later to open a coal shop in the road; their children, too, became rag and bone men and street sellers, and one daughter became the 'Queen of Prostitutes' at Finsbury Park.[158]

The third important collective source of a tradition outside wage labour lay in various outsider groups, especially the gypsies. The connection between gypsies and London's most lawless communities has been well documented. Booth noted how in Notting Dale 'gypsy blood is very evident amongst the children in the schools, and noticeable even in the streets.'[159] There were other 'Metropolitan Gypsyries' in the Wandle valley at Wandsworth; at Mount Street in the notorious Old Nichol area of Bethnal Green;[160] at Hackney Wick and Battersea and other places.[161] Nearer Campbell Road, there had been gypsy camps north of Tollington Park in the 1870s and at Hermitage Road, close to the Manor House in the 1890s.[162]

There is no documentary evidence for a gypsy connection with Campbell Road, but the oral tradition is overwhelming (although not shared by the street as a whole). A gypsy – or 'pikie' in cockney slang – pedigree was claimed by Harry James and for a number of other families. There were the Brothertons, who moved into the street some time in the 1920s; Dolly Mills and his family put up in Campbell Road whenever they were in the neighbourhood; Gypsy Jack Hobbs sold manure from a horse and cart and later married a girl from the street; Liza Harmer and Mrs Knowles, the street sellers, both had 'Romaner' or pikie backgrounds.

The James family was headed by George, known as Dido. He was a tinker, repairing cane chairs and mats and sharpening scissors, knives, lawnmowers and so on from a richly-decorated barrow which he pushed over the streets of North London. He once fought Ernie Barnes, another knife grinder with a similar heritage, for the title of Campbell Road's 'King of the Pikies'. He went to Barnet Fair every September, a gathering place for gypsies, and he was said to have some sort of title to land there. He taught his son words which were not even in the varied London underworld cant of the 1930s – words like 'jas' for go, 'yog' for fire, 'chokkors' for boots. At least two of his boys never took to work, becoming professional thieves until after the Second World War.[163] And this alternative attraction of a criminal career for the young men of Campbell Bunk will be examined separately in chapter 6.

The lumpen economy of Campbell Bunk

So far we have looked at the sources of recruitment to the class position of the propertyless outside wage labour, and the links between that class position and Campbell Road. But once recruited to that class position, once a part of Campbell Bunk, how did people win a subsistence?

Street trading flourished in the spaces of a system of distribution reliant on small shopkeepers whose profit margins, though small, had still to account for high overheads including bad debts from credit arrangements. For working-class families with a little cash available, for whom quantity was more desirable than quality, street traders offered a potentially better deal than the corner shopkeepers. London's street markets more than doubled in size between 1893 and 1930–1, from 4,894 stalls to 10,492.[164] There had been a concentration of the trade in markets and away from 'perambulatory barrows', reflecting increased capitalisation and regulation of street selling. During the 1930s, the numbers of stalls fell,[165] partly due to dispersal of the working-class population on out-county estates and partly to the accelerating growth of multiple-retail outlets, department stores, giant co-ops, and eventually 'supermarkets'.

The opportunities for street services like chair, mat and saucepan menders, knife grinders, signwriters and so on, all depended on poor quality original articles and inadequate cash resources to replace them when outworn. The opportunities for street finders and collectors like rag and bone dealers, and bottle and glass

merchants, depended on the high cost of raw materials for manufacturers who saw a demand for low-quality reprocessed goods;
and a demand from the poor for secondhand goods. The opportunities for street entertainers like singers, musicians, female imperson-
ators, escapologists, and so on depended on a leisure culture which
was street- rather than home-based.

In the 1920s, none of these street trades had flourished as it had
done before the war, but they still survived in quantity and quality,
as any number of commentators testified.[166] All three sectors,
however, found a living harder to come by in the 1930s. Mass
production, greater commodity awareness, and a steady gain in
living standards for those in work made replacement rather than
repair an increasingly attractive and feasible option. The price of
waste clothing and metals fell as more were disposed of and the
demand from processors failed to rise;[167] and relative prosperity
after the depression virtually destroyed parts of the secondhand
market, in women's clothing especially.[168] The growth of wireless,
more indispensable than the kitchen sink by 1939; the unabated
popularity of the cinema; a desire for newness in virtually every
aspect of popular taste; rising standards of home comfort and a
reduction of overcrowding in inner city areas – all conspired by
the late 1930s to make street entertainers appear tedious and out-
of-date.

This falling social value of the street had other causes. Streets
formed the largest open space in London. They were traffic routes
for the distribution of commodities and the labour force. They
were still the most important sites of communal activity, as we
shall see in Campbell Road itself. They were a political platform.
And they were the factory and warehouse of the lumpen economy.
Ekeing a living from the pores of society, the lumpen economy
subsisted in the city's lacunae. But the streets of London increasingly became contested areas from the 1920s, with the needs of
commodity and passenger traffic winning virtually exclusive right
of way over other users, as we shall see in the chapter on 'Forms of
struggle' (chapter 4). And this constriction was once again squeezed
tighter from 1930 on.

It was one of the strengths of the lumpen economy of Campbell
Bunk that it could partly cushion its members from all these
tendencies. There was limited scope for co-operation within the
enforced or chosen individualism of lumpen enterprise, and
Campbell Bunk's class structure helped keep it alive. But subsistence was predominantly a matter for individual families to cope
with alone – even, indeed, in competition with one another on the
smooth-worn stones of London's streets.

Both Bill and Ada Dashett were costermongers. Every morning Bill went to Covent Garden to buy flowers, bringing them home in boxes on the tube. Later they would be delivered by lorry. Ada sold flowers and salads, cooking beetroots in the scullery copper shared with the other tenants of the house. Bill would resort to the common trick of dyeing his flowers, buying cheap white buttons, for example, and turning them mauve in a bucket of dye. Other poor street sellers would also buy the cheapest goods, virtually unsaleable elsewhere, like job lots of half-rotten chestnuts called 'fighting man's chestnuts' because of the response they elicited from customers; rotten walnuts would be soaked in water to make them swell so they would not appear empty; and so on.

Bill sold from a walking barrow in Blackstock Road, Stroud Green Road and all around. He held no Council licence. He hired his barrow by the day, and raised his stock money by getting credit from wholesalers: Ada would have raised hers by pawning household goods or by borrowing from the Bunk's several women moneylenders. From about 1934, Bill rented a shed at number 28 where he could store surplus produce. The Dashetts were thus at the lowest end of the street trading economic spectrum, owning no part of and having little control over the fixed or circulating capital required for their enterprise. That others were in similar straits is evidenced by the frequency of prosecutions for theft by Campbell Road street sellers of stock, barrows, scales or other trade necessaries.[169] The large Dashett family – Ada had 16 children – was never adequately supported by the parents' earnings. They were thrown many times on public assistance, especially during Bill's frequent brief desertions in favour of other women, unnecessarily lengthened by the prison sentences he received for leaving his family chargeable to the LCC.[170] In one court appearance, Bill claimed he could not earn enough to keep his family and they would be better 'on the Guardians'.[171]

The infrastructure of Campbell Bunk's lumpen economy was of some limited assistance to the poorest street sellers like the Dashetts. Barrows could be hired for tuppence a day from Neal's and later Stevenson's yards in Campbell Road and from Sheeny Clarke's stables in Fonthill Mews. Donkeys and ponies could be stabled in Andover Road and Lennox Mews. The cheapest of labour-power could be hired to pull barrows or set out a stall.

The Bunk's economic support system was of more value to the street finders and collectors like Pongo Blackman. He used to go out totting with a barrow, which his step-son frequently helped him pull. Capital of about five shillings was needed to set up as a rag and bone man, to hire a barrow and provide stock money to buy the larger items.[172] Again, this would be borrowed or raised by pawning. Iron and other metals would be taken to a dealer's in Hornsey Road, bottles to a publican dealer in New North Road, Islington. Rags he would bag up and sell to the rag shop in Fonthill Road or the rag-sorting factory which opened for a time at 47 Campbell Road during the 1930s. The better sort of secondhand clothing or furniture he put to one side and tried to sell in Campbell Road. On Sundays, the totters of Campbell Bunk would display their saleable goods on the railings and pavement in front of their houses, and some costers would do the same. There you would find iron bedsteads, chests of drawers, kitchen chairs, books, coats and hats and shoes and boots. The very best articles would be reserved for private sales in the street, Pongo sending a child to one of the prostitutes, for example, if any special items of clothing came along:

> 'say my father got some shoes . . . something like that you see. . . . Cos you knew that they had money, so they was the people liable to be able to afford a shilling or two. He'd say, "Take these shoes up to Margie. Ask her one and six for 'em." '[173]

Once more, Blackman's family was extremely poor. He doled out 2s 6d housekeeping a day, when he had it, for eight people: 'sometimes she got nothing, you see, so we had nothing. All depends on how he got on when he went out with the barrow.'[174] It was generally notorious how hard it was to get a living by totting, and frequently Campbell Road's rag and bone men were in trouble with the police for stealing what had not been thrown away.[175]

It was hard, too, to earn a subsistence by the variety of street services performed by those men and women who acted as entertainers, and the rarer forms of street sellers. The economy of the Bunk helped here as elsewhere, but the difficulties meant that no one could specialise in any one branch for long. It was a question of living on one's wits – all of them and all the time.

Jack Duncan's origins were obscure. He would have been born around 1875. He told his son he hailed from Norwich, the black sheep of a middle-class family with St John's Wood connections, but he was fond of making up stories about himself ('pitching the fork' he called it) and this might have been just one more. He claimed, too, to have slept in every lodging house in England on the travels he seems to have begun after leaving the army in the early 1900s. While passing through Reading he formed an attachment with a country labourer's daughter twenty years younger than himself, and it was with her and their two children that he settled at 52 Campbell Road in 1919 or 1920.

Jack Duncan had that heady mixture of bombast and talent sufficient to make him a relative success at living on his wits. He had a good voice and most of his earnings, in the 1920s at least, came from singing in the streets and pubs. As often as not he would go on his own to football grounds or other places where crowds assembled. Sometimes he would team up with men from the kip house to perform some piece of street theatre like the Corsican Brothers' dance – velvet knee breeches, clashing swords, ' 'ave at yers', all to the music of a barrel organ hired by the day from Alberici in Fonthill Mews. There was Dolly Mills of the gypsy stock, when he was in town; Nib Harper, who pulled the organ; and a falsetto singer whose name is lost to posterity. Routines would be planned in Jack's two first floor rooms, where Dolly, his wife and kids would be accommodated if they had nowhere else to stay, Jack's children sleeping on the floor until his guests left. Another acquaintance, Old Scotty from the lodging house, whose venerable white beard made him an easy touch for a soft-hearted punter, went singing in the streets with Jack's wife, whom he had taught some of the trade. Their repertoire – in this most demanding of street enterprises[176] – included 'Oh for the Wings of a Dove' and 'In the Wilds of Australia'.

Later, Jack worked more on his own, specialising in pubs. Those which refused him entry he termed 'sherricks'. In the rest he combined singing with little tricks to draw interest and free ale.

' " 'Ere, can you do this?" And he'd lie this bottle down. It was a bottle with a weighted bottom so it always stood upright until you got this piece of lead . . . graphite or whatever, put it in the hollow top – this was unseen of course. And he'd pick it up, give it to you like that so it fell into his hand, that sort of performance. [Without that] it wouldn't never lie down. "Do it *gently*!" he'd say.'[177]

His larger than life presence, his unblushing charm and gallantry, aided by a big waxed moustache – the 'Autocrat of the Boozer', his son called him – helped disarm the sceptics into giving.

Duncan also bought or made things for sale. He made brawn, for example, and sold it to Walters's, the corner grocer's in Campbell Road. But most of all, he made 'funkem'. He would invest in packets of small envelopes, a John Bull printing set, a pound or two of bran, and some lavender essence. The family would be conscripted to put the ingredients together:

'One of my father's enterprises was – funkem – was selling Panzene. And this Panzene – he'd knock on the doors of respectable homes and say, "Are you bothered at all with unpleasant smells or insects?" And this Panzene was bran – it was supposed to be lavender with a detergent capacity. And he'd make little envelopes, and he'd stamp those envelopes with an elliptical disc, and it had got, "Panzene – kills all known breeds of insects and animals" – it was only bran with a little bit of lavender essence thrown in.'[178]

Jack Duncan's theatrical talents were put to other uses, notably cadging from the relieving officer or larger charities, and we shall meet this again later.

This merges into one other Campbell Road street enterprise, closely akin to the lower forms of entertaining and selling – begging. Table 12 shows the large number of begging charges brought against residents of Campbell Road compared with Holloway's other 'rough' neighbourhoods. This was the last resort before the workhouse for the chronically sick and the blind, the deserted aged, the inebriates, and even the unemployed man or woman with a family to support. George and Kate Milton, both in their 40s, were convicted of begging and displaying their 4-year-old child for the purpose of begging in 1934. George, a street seller, had not had relief for ten months, and was not eligible for the dole. When arrested he said, ' "I would sooner beg in the street than have the House" . . . he only took his wife and child out to get enough money to buy food for the children when they came out of school, otherwise they would have had nothing for dinner.'[179] Some seem to have made a profession of begging over a number of years – James and Marion Leary in the late 1920s and early 1930s, for example,[180] and Arthur Boxer (in his late 60s) from 1936–8.[181] Once more, the lumpen economy of Campbell Bunk would have assisted with this type of economic enterprise, passing on the beggars' folklore of the best pitches and guises, the most generous (usually working-class) streets, the likely touches among the local clergymen.[182] Campbell Road itself was a source of support to the old who would beg openly from the young:

'Old Long Tom was one of 'em . . . used to wait for you to come round the corner. . . . " 'Ave you got a roaf?", that's

threepence like, or "You got a spranny?", a tanner. They never said in threepences or pennies or tuppences.'
Did you feel you'd have to give it to them otherwise you'd be thumped?
'No, no, no. You give it to 'em cos you know that you're in the same place as them they're gonna give it to you.'[183]

And there were old-fashioned examples of co-operation which were exceptional in post-1919 London but not unique. In September 1922, a 40-year-old charwoman from Campbell Road, 'very poorly dressed and miserable looking', was convicted of begging in Stoke Newington. She had with her the 4-month-old baby of a neighbour who had let her take the child in return for half-profits from begging. Both women received three months' hard labour.[184]

Begging was the final makeshift of economic enterprise. It required still some courage but was a long way from the resilience needed for thieving or prostitution, the most common alternatives to street selling and entertaining and totting. For the full-time beggars there was only one future, institutionalised in prison or workhouse. For the part-timers, it was a way of keeping going until something else turned up. And the something else was likely to be of a pattern, determined by the tendencies of economic opportunity flowing through the lumpen class position.

The dynamics of class

The economic tendencies of the lumpen class position were three-fold. The first, reflecting the processes of rejection from the labour market, was towards more regular wage labour. The second, reflecting the necessity of individual enterprise, whether rejected from the labour market or rejecting it in turn, was towards petty capital accumulation. And the third, for those unable to reproduce the capacity to work at all, was toward pauperization and dependence on non-contributory relief.

Even though the London reserve army of labour was not fundamentally restructured during the inter-war years it changed in important ways. Some of these changes, especially those affecting juveniles and women, will be discussed later. Some, affecting particular aspects of casual work, like road haulage and municipal labour, have already been described. But in general, the level of demand for labour-power did not reach its 1919–20 value until 1940, and this held as good in Islington as elsewhere. Yet a few local factors combined positively with the partial and uneven recovery from slump after 1933. The drift away from the outer ring of London county in the late-1930s was most notable among better-off workers.[185] Yet the local demand for labour-power increased not only due to the economic up-turn but also because Islington continued to attract jobs – both service and manufacturing.[186] This left room at the margin for enhanced opportunities for those previously rejected by the labour market.

With demand for labour-power still slack in absolute terms, little was done during these years to make the 'unemployable' more attractive to employers. Neither did the scales of unemployment benefit permit the unemployed to reproduce adequately their capacity to labour, especially in relation to food intake, clothing and fuel needs.[187] But by the late 1930s there was some improvement in housing conditions – slum clearance and rebuilding, a reduction of the worst overcrowding through the move away from the inner city areas, the almost universal availability of gas for cooking, heat and light – and even Campbell Road had been similarly advantaged by the end of the 1930s. Health care, too, had marginally improved due to the extension of LCC influence over London's hospitals from 1930,[188] and Islington's Labour Council's maternity and child welfare nursery and clinic schemes from 1934.[189] In addition, scales of relief had been revised upwards following a Labour victory in the LCC elections of 1934.[190] These benefits helped safeguard the value of labour-power, retarding in part the decline in work capacity through chronic unemployment.

These were small changes in themselves but significant in the aggregate, and served to strengthen the integument tying the lumpenproletariat to the working class. Mr Nesbitt the dustman, for instance, had interspersed pub and street singing with casual municipal and civil engineering jobs before becoming a full-timer on the dust around 1929.[191] Jack Harper was a three-day-a-week brush-hand who, during long stretches of unemployment, was tempted into small enterprises like 'penny-black knockers' – repainting front door knobs for a penny a go. He got more and more regular work as the 1930s wore on, eventually becoming a general foreman with a Hazelville Road builder just before the Second World War.[192]

The tendencies in capital accumulation from petty economic enterprise were rather more negative during the 1930s, as we have seen. Street entertainments and street services offered the barest subsistence at best. Only the hiring of labour-power could result in accumulation. Although this was possible in enterprises like totting, street selling offered a time-honoured method of hiring labour-power through the system of 'half-profits'.[193] A coster-

monger who had had a lucky break might try to capitalise on it
by buying extra stock and hiring an additional barrow. Someone
would then be hired to sell the stock, receiving half profits. It
relied on the acumen and honesty of the person hired, and was an
operation fraught with mistrust.

The quality of labour-power available to costers was one
important friction on accumulation. Frequently they had to resort
to those most desperate for any employment within the road; yet
street selling demanded self-confidence and a rapid grasp of figures
if it was to pay.

Even so, accumulation did take place. Musher Gates is a case in
point. He had been born in Campbell Road in 1902 but his family
left when he was about 3. They moved to Wilmer Gardens and
Essex Street, the two most notorious streets in Hoxton, and then
back to Holloway – at Albany Place, Brand Street, Hornsey Road,
and finally Queensland Road. He spent much time as a youth at
Campbell Road, but he considered himself out of 'the Land'.

He was a coalman in the winter, a costermonger selling fruit
and what he could get in the summer, and a thief for all seasons.
But through fruit selling and subcontracting at the Drayton Park
coal yards he had built up a lively business by the late 1930s.

> 'I know a fella what used to work as a clerk down the City.
> His money was three pounds a week. I said "How much!"
> That was before the war. . . . "Three pound a week? I give
> my old woman that! Some weeks. Give my old woman it." '
> *How much would you have earned a week, roughly, say in the*
> *summer?*
> 'In the summer? Sometimes about five or six pound or more.
> Or more. . . . Sometimes a tenner I've earnt in the summer
> with different barrows out. . . . I had about five or six barrows
> out I did. Different barrows I had out.'
> *How do you mean?*
> 'Well, people working for me, half profit, see? But they had
> the biggest half, which they know. I was satisfied if I copped
> a pound off one of them.'[194]

And this linked up with the winter coal business, which he had
begun by hiring a horse and van, taking out a load of coal on
credit, selling it door to door, and returning the price of the stock
to the merchant. By the late 1930s he had eight men working for
him in the winter, each taking out a horse and trolley. Musher
himself would use his motor lorry. Most of the horses were sold

at Barnet Fair in the summer for stock money in the fruit game, and bought in the winter at the Elephant and Castle horse markets.[195]

The links between lumpenproletariat and petty bourgeoisie were thus also strong. They were stronger still, perhaps, in the imaginations of those who had been pushed, or who had willingly launched themselves, into a life of economic independence without property. They were cemented, too, by the odd example of accumulation through 'criminal' enterprise, one of the sources of a thieving tradition among the young men of Campbell Bunk.

But those rising stars were in reality rare enough. And many an earth-bound astronomer found his feet dragged deeper into the clay as he watched. Ernest Willis, of Campbell Road, for instance, was charged in the summer of 1926 with attempting to commit suicide by swallowing carbolic. He had made a previous attempt two years before. Willis had been invalided from the army with malaria and amoebic dysentery after serving in Salonika. 'I am out of work, no dole, no pension, and they have stopped my relief. I have nothing coming in at all. . . . I was properly down on my luck and had nothing to do.' He was discharged from hospital and sent to the workhouse.[196] Thomas Minhinnick, of 61 Campbell Road, was charged in 1929 with stealing a pair of boots from outside a pawnbroker's in Blackstock Road. 'It was my birthday and I came out of a Poor Law institution on a day's pass. I met one or two friends, had a drink of beer and gave way to temptation.' He had given way before, and had eleven previous convictions from 1894, when he had first been sentenced for burglary. Minhinnick was one of the relatively few recidivists to receive preventive detention under the Prevention of Crimes Act.[197] Seven years before, and then of no fixed abode, he had again stolen boots, at that time from the workhouse itself.[198] In 1932, Alexander Parkinson, a 66-year-old organ grinder from Campbell Road, was convicted of stealing clothing from the workhouse.[199] He had been in and out of the workhouse for at least ten years – in the winter of 1922 he had been found wandering abroad, sleeping in a doorway at Campbell Road.[200]

The workhouse door had opened and closed on many people from Campbell Road, and often at different times in their lives. But the tendency appears to have been towards more frequent institutionalisation as individuals grew older, and table 13 is suggestive in this regard.

Bringing things together

There were, then, complex processes producing and reproducing rejection by or of the labour market in London during the 1920s and 1930s. In many cases, these processes were individualised, happening to people who might, under randomly ordered circumstances, have had no connection with one another even though they occupied the same class position in the social structure. But circumstances were not randomly ordered. There was the gravitational pull of Campbell Bunk itself, its history and reputation within North London making it known and available to those who needed or wanted it. And there was the housing market, which rationed living space by price and social value, tending to consign those who could afford little to a relatively small and geographically prescribed sector of the market, and of which Campbell Road was one prominent part.[201] Both factors were mutually reinforcing and were difficult to separate in real life.

The classic accommodation for the individual outcast from work and property was the common lodging house. Only one Bunk lodging house survived the First World War, John Jaffa's 10–12 Campbell Road for 45 men, which ran until 1934. The lodging house was supplemented by the single furnished rooms, and it is likely that there was some connection between the two, long-term lodgers eventually finding a room in the street. In 1938, 23.8 per cent of Campbell Road households were single persons (see table 14). These 70 people were mainly men (probably 49 to 21 women, 18 of whom were widowed or married women living alone and just three unmarried).[202] This was a notably higher proportion than in Holloway's other poor streets (15.4 per cent) and working-class streets with populations living above the New Survey of London's poverty line (16.6 per cent) (see tables 15 and 16).

Rents for single rooms in Campbell Road depended on whether they were nominally furnished or unfurnished. Furnished rents had not been frozen by the Rent and Mortgage Interest (Restriction) Act of 1915, and so there was every incentive for Campbell Road's important place in this sector of the local housing market to continue.[203] Most of the single rooms were probably let with a charge for furniture, and so rents were nearly double the average for an unskilled worker's single room in Holloway – about 9s against 5s 6d.[204] But for the single man without furniture these rooms, however sparsely fitted out, were the only alternative to the lodging house; and for a single woman or family similarly situated they were the last chance before the workhouse.[205] Campbell Road almost certainly continued to provide more of this accommodation until the Second World War than any other street in Islington.

The single furnished room in Campbell Road also provided a home for a few families, but generally the unit of family accommodation was two rooms. Of all three-person households and larger, 54.5 per cent lived in two rooms in 1938 (see table 14). Rents for two rooms paid by unskilled workers in Holloway averaged 10s 1d. For unfurnished rooms in Campbell Road, the rents were probably significantly lower, certainly as low as 7s 10d; two furnished rooms cost about 12s 6d.[206]

Apart from rent, one other characteristic of Campbell Road's housing market of great importance, especially in attracting poor families to the street, was its tolerance of overcrowding. Over-crowding in London's tenement houses had been nominally controlled by the Public Health (London) Act of 1891 and byelaws made under it. But not until the Housing Act 1935 were adequate bureaucratic checks constructed, and in Islington they were not in force until 1938. The 1891 Act standards were pathetically low and those of 1935 were a much-criticised bare minimum.[207] In reality, levels of crowding were set as much by local custom as by law, and in Campbell Road the custom erred on the side of generosity. In England and Wales in 1938, just 3.8 per cent of working-class households were officially 'overcrowded'; in Islington 7.5 per cent; in the Queensland Road area 18.6 per cent; in Campbell Road 30.6 per cent.[208]

In that rents were low, and in that overcrowding was tolerated to a remarkable degree by landlords, Campbell Road was attractive to large working-class families, who were especially vulnerable to life-cycle poverty where earnings were low and irregular.[209] Campbell Road had 14.7 per cent of its households in this large family category (7 members or more), compared with 8.6 per cent for Holloway's other poor streets, and 4.7 per cent for three nearby unskilled streets above the poverty line (see tables 14, 15 and 16).

We can see some of these processes in action through the experience of families who moved to the street during the 1920s. The Dunns lived during the First World War at George's Road. They appear to have been of Irish Cockney origin – Mrs Dunn, née McCarthy, was a catholic and had relations living in Campbell Road. Around 1918 the family moved to Cayley Street, Lime-house, where the father set up in a street selling business, hawking vinegar, salt and soda from a pony and cart. Mr Dunn's enterprise failed, and he was unable to work because of emphysema and neurasthenia contracted during war service. It is likely that the family's home, set up as the business had been by Mr Dunn's war gratuity, had to be sold around them as worklessness drove them further into debt and dependence. Cayley Street was not especially poor,[210] and Campbell Road offered the prospect of a cheap home among people with whom Mrs Dunn, at least, was familiar. In 1926, the Dunns, with their five children, the eldest of whom was 10, walked the 4 or 5 miles from Limehouse to Campbell Road to get a furnished room. Their belongings were few enough to be carried on the bassinet which held the newest baby, and the room, as Jimmy remembers it, cost 7s.[211]

In the same year as the Dunns came to Campbell Bunk, or just after, Albert and Eleanor Millgate and their baby also took a furnished room in the street. Albert, 31, described himself as a labourer, but in June 1927 he and Eleanor were charged with begging with a barrel organ in Hornsey Road and allowing their 11-week-old child to be used for that purpose. One week later Albert was also charged with bigamy. His real wife, by then living in Glamorgan, stated that they had been married at Tollington Park in 1921. In June 1923 Albert 'left home to go to work, and did not return. [He] took all the money she possessed – four shillings.' Eleanor said that they had met at a travelling fair in 1925, when she was 22, and were 'married' at Barking. 'Since then they had lived together at various furnished apartments', and Albert, at least, because of his local connection, would have known them to be available at Campbell Road.[212]

The Taskers were living in the King's Cross Road area around 1926, when Mr Tasker – a self-employed window cleaner, invalided from the army after war service – had a bad fall. He never fully recovered, and did no more work for the remaining 12 years of his life. In 1929, when there were four or five children in the family, they came to Campbell Road.

'*Do you know how or why they came to live in Campbell Road in the first place?*
'I think poverty brought them there, really, you know. They had nowhere to live. . . . As I say, mum had been in the workhouse two or three times and they had nowhere to live. So my dad came apparently down to here, Finsbury Park, and he saw – he'd been down: I can only remember what I've heard said: but when he was a younger man, he used to come down there, down that way; and he knew the street. And he knew the people there would help you, you know, if they could. And when they first came down, as far as I can remember, they were *furnished* rooms, you know, the 82 was furnished.'[213]

Whatever the route in of families like these, once in Campbell Road there were both reasons for staying put and for moving on. But once more the mechanics of the housing market displayed contradictory tendencies to mobility and stability. Mobility *within* Campbell Road was considerable. One of its primary motors was the search for more or better houseroom; and the transmission was oiled by ownership patterns which made the street's resident landlords readily accessible to home-hunting tenants. The Dunns, for example, in 1926 first occupied one room at number 67; then an additional room at 69 where the elder boys slept. They subsequently moved to 14 (three rooms), 88, 58, and 96 (where they had the whole house by 1944).[214] The Taskers had two middle-floor rooms at number 82 from 1929 to 1938. When Mr Tasker died, his wife became an invalid and her wheelchair demanded ground-floor accommodation. At first they could only find one room at number 94. Within a year, the family had moved to two rooms at 96, but these were in such a bad state that they had to move to two rooms and a scullery at 98 soon after.[215] And there are several similar examples.[216]

There were, of course, other reasons than the housing market for staying in Campbell Road. We have already seen how collectivities developed around the lumpen economy of Campbell Bunk, providing infrastructures for economic individualism and even for casual employment, which mirrored in scope if not complexity, those of the London craft districts.

But the most important collective experience of Campbell Road centred on the street itself – its popular culture, relations between neighbours, its self-identity in the face of a more or less hostile world outside. The experience was expressed not only in action but also in thought – shared values and worldviews, politics in the widest sense. And this will be explored more fully in the chapters which follow.

We will find, however, that the collective experience of Campbell Road was deeply fractured and contradictory. The source of those fractures lay in the contradictions immanent in the class position of the lumpenproletariat. But in reaching the surface they did not trace straight lines. The dialectics of class relations will explain much but not all. They interacted with the Bunk's own historically-formed traditions; with gender, which made experience of life in the street so different for men and women; with generational conflict in the family, which gave the young a view of the street other than that held by their parents.

Through it all, even so, the contradictory class relations of which Campbell Bunk was part affected at some level every aspect of life there. In all human society and in each human being, the struggle between collectivism and individualism grinds on without hope of resolution. In Campbell Road, that struggle was peculiarly intense. And the processes of rejection by and of wage labour were at its very heart.

3 Collective identities

Support networks

John Morley, 11 years old, was arrested for begging in November 1919. He had chronic conjunctivitis, 'fassy' eye or sticky eye, common enough in Campbell Road. 'He was in a filthy condition. It was a cold, wet day and he had no shirt. When food was offered to him he ate it ravenously.'[1] Daisy Booth, 19 years old in 1925, had a baby to keep: 'they were practically starving and without money. . . . "I had no milk and no fire at home, and not a penny coming in." '[2] When a Campbell Road painter was convicted of stealing milk from a doorstep in February 1932, the Court Missionary 'said there was no doubt [his] child was hungry'.[3] A police report in May 1933 on a 31-year-old labourer found he 'had no food in the house beyond a little bread'.[4] 'See, we was like animals, we was like animals at home, all of us hungry. . . . I used to sit eating cabbage stalks cos I was that hungry,' recalled Ronnie and Marjie Drover from number 25.[5] And Mavis Knight's mother suffered from psoriasis, rheumatoid arthritis and chronic under-feeding: 'She had to wear dark glasses cos her eyes was so affected by the malnutrition.'[6]

'I've been to school many times with women's shoes on, and women's stockings tied up in a knot there [for socks],' and so did other boys from Campbell Road.[7] 'No kids went to school in long trousers in them days. But they did from the Bunk because they were men's trousers cut down with your arse hanging down.'[8] The Tiverton girls, 14, 16 and 18 years old around 1920, shared one bed with their mother who came home drunk nearly every night.[9] The three Spencer boys slept on a wooden platform with a flock overlay as a mattress, built into the tiny attic at 86 Campbell Road. The makeshift bed was covered with war-surplus blankets and their Uncle Charlie's army greatcoat. There was a paraffin lamp on the wall, and the room was just big enough for the bed and little else:[10]

'And I remember up there Christmas time. One particular

Christmas . . . we used to hang our stocking over for
Christmas . . . I remember this particular year – my brother
remembers it, never forgot it. We woke up – I felt mine.
"Oh", I said, "we're all right . . . we got som'ink 'ere!" Cos
it felt . . . hard, like. We used to have orange, a penny, and
a few nuts and that. I thought, Oh it's all right, we got
something, cos the old man had had a bad year, that
Christmas. Oh, when we got up, you know, when it was light
in the morning, never looked at it until the morning, never
forget: it was cinders out the grate and hard bread. And my
brother ate that bloody bread! He really ate it – he was
crunching it.'[11]

We have here one basis for the support networks which the
people of Campbell Road established between the wars. The Bunk
was a place of desperate poverty. Its machinery of mutual aid was
fashioned out of sympathy for the plight of others; and from the
rational assumption that all might sooner or later need assistance
themselves.

There was one additional basis for systems of mutual aid. That
lay in the relations of Campbell Road with the world outside. For
the street's reputation was kept alive throughout the 1920s and
1930s, encouraging an attitude of collective self-defence against an
apparently hostile and uncaring environment. The Bunk continued
to be a source of ridicule, mistrust and fear:

CAMPBELL ROAD HOLLOWAY – 'one of the worst Roads
in North London' – '20 Fights Every Night'.[12]

A STREET OF ADVENTURE – DO YOU KNOW
CAMPBELL ROAD? Do you know where Campbell Road
is? You don't? No, but you've heard of it? Ah! We thought
so. There are few dwellers within the bounds of Islington
who have not heard of this thoroughfare. It possesses a
publicity service which is the envy of Los Angeles and the
French Riviera. Hundreds of our actors and actresses would
like to get into the news so consistently as does Campbell
Road. . . . Every day last week, one or more of Campbell
Road's residents occupied the dock at the [North London]
Court. The Magistrate asked 'Is Campbell Road a residential
place? Everybody smiles when I mention it.'[13]

That the smiles could turn to frowns we have already seen in
the process of labour-market discrimination against people from

Campbell Road, and there will be other examples affecting the lives of young men and women from the street. It should be no surprise that the embarassment and guilt which some felt at admitting they lived there was turned by others into a fierce collective pride demanding loyalty and support from neighbours.

But the networks of support were crosscut in important ways. The kinship networks put down since the 1890s and before gave a basis for special obligations between families, even though neighbouring in Campbell Road could not ignore the flow of people through the furnished rooms. Yet in constructing support networks, among kin and not, the most important divisions were based on gender. The largely separate spheres of men's and women's lives evolved largely separate systems of mutual aid, providing support specifically for women, boys and girls (to a certain extent 'children'), and men. But the first of these was so important that it was generally true that most of the realities of mutual aid within Campbell Road were created and sustained by women.[14]

Among the women of the Bunk, part of that network was organised, in that certain individuals had special functional responsibilities, or that certain features of women's collective life demanded planning and division of labour. For example, pudding-basin collections for bereavements were made at the top end of Campbell Road by Long Liz and at the bottom by Dolly Burt, usually on Sunday mornings when any male earners were at home.[15] Besides neighbourly help given at and after confinements, individual women specialised in housework, shopping, fixing meals for the family, all for a small payment.[16] The street's money-lenders were probably all women, usually house managers or the wives of shopkeepers and a few of the regular earners on the railway or bus services which Campbell Road could boast.[17] There is insufficient evidence for any earlier period, but certainly an abortionist who moved into the road around 1941 stated that during the 1940s and 1950s she operated on 'rough and ready' women from the Bunk free of charge: generally, she thought, for unwanted pregnancies by men who were not their husbands.[18] The women of the street organised an annual coach trip to Southend for women only on the first Monday of September: the men had their own trip two or three weeks later.[19] The lavish communal street parties – one for each end of the street – on Peace Day 1919, the Silver Jubilee of 1935 and the 1937 Coronation were all probably run by women.[20] Women from several families organised seasonal work and holiday combined in the hopfields, more usually the province of East End women at this period.[21] And women also organised neighbourhood-based 'diddlum' clubs for savings and credit.[22]

These organisational aspects of the Bunk women's support systems interacted with more spontaneous forms of assistance. There was extensive informal borrowing of household necessities like tea and sugar, or condensed milk. Borrowing money for rent, food or fuel, or fares to market or work, for example, was more formal but could have been arranged through neighbours or the moneylenders. Neighbours would have been first choice, because no interest was required, but it depended on the credit-worthiness of the borrower and the size of the advance. Matilda Purslowe would lend her upstairs neighbour clothes to pawn if she had no money;[23] Mrs Knight would send her daughter to women neighbours to borrow threepence for her husband's morning fare to the docks;[24] Mrs Spencer could send her son to a woman friend for even larger amounts:

> ' "Mum said, 'Don't be offended, can you lend her half a
> crown to see her through the week?' " Now, half a crown. I
> run up to the baker's I get threepennorth of stale bread, which
> come to anything up to twelve loaves. I get threepennorth of
> bacon bones, and a sixpenny hambone. . . . Now that last us
> two or three days. Inbetweentime, we get paraffin oil for a
> penny farthing, that's for our lighting. And a pennorth of tea,
> two ounces of tea for a penny. And probably ha'porth of jam.
> Now that half a crown see us through the week. Oh, and seven
> pound of coal. We'd pay it back the end of the week. . . .
> Soon as he got hold of a bit of money. He might do a day's
> work: back goes the half crown.'[25]

Going to the moneylender was a more serious business, not least because it could turn into a regular household commitment among women behind the backs of a male 'breadwinner'.[26] During the inter-war period there were at least six women who were recognised as moneylenders, although whether they were registered or not is impossible to tell. In three cases, these women also had responsibility for letting out rooms in the street and so frequently the money borrowed was to pay for the rent.

Whatever the negative aspects of this relationship, the gender-based mechanics of moneylending did enable women to secure some independence from men in organising the home economy, and there were other aspects of women's support networks which were similarly related: instructing women on how to take up street selling, for example;[27] finding clients for casual charing work; or finding factory work for other girls from Campbell Road to help beat labour-market discrimination.[28] These arrangements could become more explicitly oppositional to men: in protecting wives from violent husbands, for example,[29] or enforcing codes of male sexual conduct:

'We saw this Mr Leggatt. He came home one night and went in a house with one of the women from down there. And I thought to myself, That's funny, he don't live in there. So me not knowing any different, a bit dumb in the brain box, I rushed home to tell me mother. So she went up and told Mrs Leggatt, "My May's just seen your old man go down in a house down there.". . . So of course down comes mother with Mrs Leggatt and rooting this here woman and her old man out. She took this woman to bits because she was in bed with her husband.'
Did they fight?
'Oh yes.'[30]

Women's support networks in Campbell Road were not merely concerned with women's survival. They were concerned also with the protection of children and young adults. Women enforced codes of conduct against child abuse, reporting a violent father to the NSPCC, for instance.[31] A woman neighbour took in Walter Spencer for almost two years, letting him sleep with her family and giving him a breakfast before school: 'We had no room. Unless she thought they were knocking me about so much she thought, Well, I'll take him away, sort of thing.'[32]

Most often it was female kin who took on this protective role as an extension of family responsibilities and as a solution to family pathology. May Purslowe's aunt, who lived next door but one, was the first refuge when May's mother was on the warpath: ' "Will you hide me, cos Mum's looking for me?". . . And she said, "Well, go and get into bed with Polly and Lil." '[33] Emmie Froud's maternal grandmother provided food and sympathy and Walter Spencer's took him in when his mother was especially vicious towards him.[34]

But it was more generally the case that the women of Campbell Road – generally married women with children of their own – would offer a home to the young rootless casualties of family life, whether from Campbell Road or not. Rachel Grogan, a tough costermonger, took in 14-year-old Harry James when he left home; he was a friend of her boy's.[35] Lou Porter – herself prosecuted for child neglect by the NSPCC – took in a recently widowed young friend and drinking pal when she had nowhere to live.[36] A family took in Helen Sims, a Hoxton girl, who was making a morally precarious living cadging from men in pubs; she had left home because of her step-father's sexual advances towards her.[37] Another family offered casual lodgings to Albert Quinn, a young thief from the poor streets west of the Caledonian Road, when he was homeless and courting their daughter.[38]

Such generosity was no more than part of the pervasive culture of sharing among the women of the Bunk:

'This Mrs Cope, for instance, and Mrs Henrey and Mrs Gates, you know. . . . People used to march into your house with half a loaf of bread and say, "Here you are, we can't eat that, can you manage it?" Knowing full well that they didn't have it to spare, the family would accept the way it had been given and eat it. And would do the same back. Every time, as I say, when Mrs Cope got hold of a couple of bob and went out and bought a few pennorth of chips, she would always send up a few, enough to put between two slices of bread for the kids. This is really what people were like. The old brass downstairs. I mean, she would always, when she thought that mum was having it really hard – she knew mum had no time for her – she would give me a shilling and say, "Give it to your mum to buy you some sweets." Now she knew my mum wouldn't buy me sweets, but she knew it would be very helpful to my mum. And my mum could accept it, because it hadn't been given to her. But they were all like it. Ted Nesbitt was a horrible rough type of man but very kind to us. If he was on his rounds at any time and he'd pick up anything – a jacket that he thought would do the old man – he would bring it home and give it to him. You know, their tottings, as they used to call 'em.'[39]

The last point reminds us that support and sharing were not exclusive to women in Campbell Road. But among men there was none of the sophisticated division of labour based on the neighbourhood which characterised women's collective experience in the street. Men would find moneylenders at work or in the pub, rather than among neighbours.[40] Working men helped boys from Campbell Road get jobs.[41] Costers would lend each other money when they had it. Men with underworld connections expected to give and to receive when fellow grafters were short of money, or when they had just come out of prison or borstal.[42] Homeless men could pass round the hat for a night's kip at the street gaming assemblies so much a part of Campbell Road's male culture.[43] And the kip-house lodgers would have enlightened each other in the ways of street earning or begging or securing odd jobs.[44]

But given the alienation from workplace we should not be surprised to find male neighbourhood-based support networks on a small scale. Tom Tasker was the ex-window cleaner who did no work from 1929, when he came to the Bunk, until 1938 when he died. His best friend was Joe Ryan:

'He lived in the Bunk, too. I think he lost his wife . . . and he was left with two boys . . . Joey and Ben. . . . He was a bit down, really down when his wife – he didn't know which way to turn. And my dad became very close with him. He probably felt sorry for him a lot. . . . But they became very good friends. And Mr Ryan, he would often send Joey down, his boy, over to us on a Wednesday, and say to dad, you know, could he lend us a couple of bob, sort of thing, until he got his bit of money on Friday. Dad was always willing to lend him a couple of bob – he always got it back, there was no thought whatsoever of him not.'[45]

This sort of relationship would have been so much more common among women. The difference between men's and women's networks is illuminated by Nancy Tiverton's family circumstances. She lived with her mother in Campbell Road from 1917 to 1920; and with her father in George's Road from 1914 to 1917 and 1920 to 1925. Around those times each parent separately provided some sort of home for three of four of their eight children (four others had already married and moved away), so each was a single-parent family struggling with great poverty. Although Mr Tiverton did no work and was at home all day, and although the women's networks of George's Road would have been just as extensive as the Bunk's, Nancy's experience of the two streets was quite different:

'Up Campbell Road, people would help you up there. Like, if they thought you was ill – they'd got nothing themselves – they'd send you in a cup of tea and a bit of bread or something to eat, or a bit of dinner or something, and they would help you, see.'
Did they do that in George's Road?
'Well, I've never known it to happen, not meself. My father wasn't very sociable, see. My father wouldn't entertain no

one. If anyone brought anything up to him he'd say, "No, I've got me own," see.'[46]

To a great extent, Campbell Road's support systems – and with them its community – were split in two. There was a top end and a bottom end, meeting at the common ground of the Paddington Street junction, the most important space in Campbell Road. This reflected in part the separate histories of the two parts of the street – the early respectability of the top compared with the rougher bottom end and its lodging houses. These differences had been all but obliterated by the 1920s but still the old tradition lived on. 'The two ends of the Bunk were two different streets, although obviously, you know, we knew people from each half.'[47]

Each end was more or less self-sufficient with its own moneylenders and bookmakers, its own November Fifth bonfires, its own street parties, its own support networks among the women. The shops at each end largely duplicated each other.

These shops, too, were a necessary part of the Bunk's support networks. Just over half of them seem to have been run by women. Most, not all, were forced – as in any working-class street – to give credit: 'strapping' or 'on the strap' as it was known locally. They had to be ready to keep long hours to meet the needs of families who might earn coppers, and so buy provisions for immediate use, at any hour of the day or night. They had to stock the widest range of available goods and be prepared to sell in the tiniest quantities – 7 lb of coal, a ha'penny fag, a penny bundle of firewood, a pennorth of jam in the customer's cup, a penny packet of cocoa or paper screw of tea, margarine in 2 oz pats and so on. And they had also to exchange the food tickets given as out relief by the Board of Guardians and Public Assistance Committee. In 1919, the bottom end of Campbell Road furnished a beer retailer, grocer, greengrocer, two chandlers, and a coal dealer; the top end a chandler, grocer, and two greengrocers. In 1938 there were two chandlers and a beer retailer at the bottom; and a baker, grocer, chandler, and coal dealer at the top.[48] Each shop tended to take customers from close neighbours but there was frequently the need to cross the Paddington Street front line.

Who were your friends in Campbell Road?
'Everybody – at the top end. But not down the bottom – you wasn't allowed to walk down the bottom. If you went down the bottom they'd give you a good hiding. . . . They didn't like you down that end. If you went down there for an errand – we used to have to go to Burton's, the provisions shop. I

used to be frightened out of me life! They used to get hold
of you and give you a bleeding good hiding for nothing at all.
Actually, they done the same if they went up the other end.'[49]

The division between top and bottom end was thus real enough.
It was weakened by sharing some services, and by the mobility of
families between one end and another in the search for more
convenient living space (see p. 69 above). But at the level of day-
to-day relations the street was *lived* largely as two communities.
Yet it was *thought* as one, at least in relation to the outside world.

What about top end versus bottom end?
'We've had that. But that is between ourselves. That was
between ourselves. No one was allowed to interfere.'[50]

This view of the street as one united community facing a hostile
world took root in the collective culture of Campbell Road's children. Indeed, their own support networks were largely directed
towards making this thought a reality, at least as far as outsiders
were concerned. Even if, in practice, they mixed with school
friends from other streets, it was the separate identity peculiar to
the Bunk which children held to strongest and longest.

It is likely that the collective identity of belonging to the Bunk
was felt more strongly by boys than girls. More of children's
collective economic enterprise had been shouldered by boys,
although girls had played a part. It was generally boys who
indulged in the Bunk's street gaming; girls were not excluded, but
appear to have been less interested than their brothers. And it fitted
in well with the early gender formation of 'masculinity' that boys
should take on themselves the role of physical guardians of the
honour of Campbell Road and of any of its young citizens threatened by outsiders.[51]

Now this might not be much different from the acute sense of
territoriality found among working-class children of any generation and in any place.[52] But there were objective reasons why
feelings of rejection and isolation should be experienced by children
of the Bunk. In general the poorest of children in the local Council
schools, it was boys and girls of Campbell Road who were most
noticeable for shabby clothing or for body smells or vermin.[53] The
public reputation of the street, a byword throughout working-
class North London for its 'rough' behaviour, was enough in itself
to set its children apart; but its solitary position, surrounded by
'ordinary' respectable streets, set off its peculiar character and made
it seem even more special than it was. For boys and girls of the

Bunk, one reaction was to rationalise this specialness and make a
virtue of it, creating 'Bunk pride' as it were:[54]

> 'We are the Campbell Bunk boys [girls],
> We are the Campbell Bunk boys [girls],
> We know our manners,
> We can spend our tanners,
> We are respected wherever we go,
> Take a walk down Campbell Road,
> Doors and windows open wide,
> We can dance, we can sing,
> [We can hop and we can skip,]
> We can do most anything,
> [We can do all kinds of tricks,]
> We are the Campbell Bunk boys [girls].'

But there were other ways in which collective self-defence and
bravado – elicited in response to a hostile outside world – was
made manifest. One was antagonism to strangers which was a
strong feature of Bunk culture, but especially of children's support
networks. It waned with adulthood but did not disappear, and we
shall return to this when considering the politics of the Bunk.
Among children, it became a matter of pride that strangers,
representatives of a world which had rejected them, should be
rejected in their turn. And when this happened, it could only
strengthen and justify the reaction against Campbell Road.[55]

The only time Fred Brewster, from the Essex Road area, went
to Campbell Road was when he walked a girl home from a dance:
he was beaten insensible by a number of youths and ended up in
hospital with a dislocated jaw.[56] Another stranger was said to have
had his ear chopped off in a street gaming match.[57] A boy from
next-door Playford Road – 'Playford Road *was not the Bunk*, that's
just another road' – took liberties with a Campbell Road lad who
beat him in a street fight: 'But within a week they moved. It was
as simple as that. They knew they wasn't going to get no change
out of us, they knew who was shouting for who round there.'[58]
A man reputed to be the 'Terror of Deptford' was laid out by a
Bunkite wielding a heavy pair of fire tongs – 'he was a stranger
to me: I mean, I knew everybody who lived up that Bunk.'[59]

What about if a stranger walked through the street?
'Now don't try to tell me you'd walk up there! Because as
soon as you're spotted, mate, up goes the hand, the warning's
gone over, and if you walk up there you stand to be kicked all

round the Bunk. Because they would say, without asking questions, that you was a copper.'[60]

Now there is room for embellishment in recounting actual events. But the strength of feeling against strangers is clearly apparent. Of the outside world, only certain parts were not seen as hostile. These need not necessarily have been geographically defined, for the Bunk's special place in lumpen culture made particular outsiders always welcome. But as we have seen, there were other streets with a special relationship with Campbell Road, and those relationships were kept up through the 1920s with George's Road and Queensland Road; and through the 1930s with Queensland Road (George's Road was in part demolished and replaced by LCC dwellings around 1930).

We can glimpse some of the ways Campbell Road interacted with the outside world, at the same time as seeing the internal support networks in action, through the Finsbury Park Coal Yard tragedy. Around midday, on Friday 3 January 1930, at least ten boys aged six to ten years had gone to play in the coal yard of the LNER depot. The entrance was in Fonthill Road, nearly opposite Paddington Street, and had been a haunt of local boys for generations. They rolled some empty oil drums. One boy with a box of matches set light to some paper and pushed it inside a drum. It was filled with petrol vapour and exploded. One boy was killed outright, another two died shortly afterwards of terrible wounds, and six were hurt – one was permanently brain-damaged.[61] Nine of the ten boys came from Campbell Road, one from Playford Road.

Conscious that 'This tragedy has struck at some of the very poorest inhabitants of the Borough', the Mayor of Islington established a relief fund to defray funeral expenses for the grave at Highgate Cemetery which the dead boys would share. It also paid for a solicitor to represent the parents' interests at the inquest, where the LNER and the oil company which owned the drum also appeared. Thousands of people turned out for the funeral, which started off from 66 Campbell Road:

> As the wreaths arrived they were placed on two costers' barrows which stood in the roadway, and the big display included over a dozen floral tributes from the people in Campbell Road who had themselves collected a large sum for the purpose. There were also two from the Hornsey Road . . . Police Station, and a similar number from the workers at the Great Northern Laundry, Fonthill Road [where many

Campbell Road women worked]; neighbours in Hatley Road [a respectable turning at the top of the Bunk, mainly occupied by railwaymen and their families]; and Mrs Ross. Other floral tributes were sent by Poole's Park School, Blackstock Road School, the Holloway and Finsbury Park branch of the British Legion, Post Office workers at Goodwin Street [next to the coal yard], neighbours in Queensland Road, friends at White Hart Lane, Tottenham [either ex-residents of Campbell Road or people from the Lorenco Road area], Mrs Grogan, Rachel Grogan [both from Campbell Road], Bill and Sid Butrey, and others.'[62]

Within ten days, the Mayor's Fund had collected around £25, including Campbell Road collections (Mrs Wilson 11s 1d, George Bucknell, the shopkeeper, £3 16s 6d and possibly some others).[63]

This devastating additional burden to the lives of parents and children in Campbell Road had provoked the expected response from the street's internal support networks, as well as more complex reactions from significant outsiders. The reaction of the police was not unexpected, given the amount of work Campbell Road gave the local force; many policemen would have known the extent of poverty in the street. But human sympathy could not restrain the police from preferring charges of drunk and disorderly against the parents of one of the dead boys within a fortnight of the tragedy.[64] For the way people consoled themselves in Campbell Road was frequently unacceptable to outsiders and provided reasons for reaction against the street. And in turn, the Bunk's cultural forms strengthened the collective identities of those who lived there.

Mutual consolations

Out of desperate poverty and social stigmatism grew laughter as well as tears.[65] The people of Campbell Road sought consolation for their condition in the popular leisure forms of the time: and made their own consolations within the particular traditions of the Bunk. Although these traditions were powerfully determining in their own right – encouraging certain activities in certain places just because they had always been done that way – they would not have lived on unless they contained meaning to those who maintained them.[66] These meanings lay buried in the Bunk's alienation from the world around it. In its poverty, depriving people of leisure activities which had to be paid for, available to the large majority of outsiders. In the meanness of the restless search for subsistence, the scrimping and pinching which made extravagance such an essential orgiastic release, providing a memory to be feasted on if nothing else could; in its absence of decent living space, torturing human relationships already under stress through inadequate means; in the rejection of society which deprived people of legitimate sources of pride or self-respect, and which needed alternative sources to be created within the street itself; and in the boredom of being workless and penniless in an age when free time had never been so expensive to fill.[67]

The people of Campbell Bunk were not always alienated from the means of spending leisure-time commonly available to the great majority of contemporary Londoners. The cinema was cheap enough, at least the local flea-pit if not supercinemas like the Finsbury Park Astoria, a visit to which would have been an event. (From 1930, when the Astoria was opened, some Bunkites ironically re-named Campbell Road 'Astoria Avenue'.) The Finsbury Park Empire music hall had cheap seats, and neither did it cost much to get into the Arsenal on Saturday afternoons, although away matches were only for relatively well-off fans. Cafés, the twentieth-century version of the coffee-shop, where an afternoon could be spent over one cup of tea, were a great attraction to the Bunk's adolescents. But dancehalls were more of a problem, demanding clothes which could bear scrutiny under bright lights. And billiard halls, skating rinks, greyhound racing racks, speedway meetings, all took toll of a light pocket through the hidden extras charged inside. All these were collective enjoyments shared with neighbours outside the home, and bearing in mind the quality and quantity of the Campbell Road dwelling there were severe constraints on the potential for leisure time spent indoors. Even so, domestic parties were common enough, music provided by a concertina or hired piano, and bottled ale contributed by guests and hosts alike.

The 1930s' tendency to more home-based leisure was, however, fostered only with difficulty in Campbell Road. We can see this in the case of radio. The absence of electricity from the street meant that people had to rely on heavy accumulators to power the sets they had made, bought or hired. Accumulators were usually rented, and there were regular costs incurred by re-charging them at the wireless shop. There is evidence that one company tried to install a relay exchange in part of the street in the 1930s, linking a number of receivers on a common cable from one power source outside the street.[68] This reflected the growing indispensibility of the wireless, even in Campbell Road. But a crowded one-roomed

dwelling, with poor radio reception, did not encourage the dedi-
cated listening habits which by then kept men and women in
increasing numbers from other amusements.

The most important of these remained the pub, especially for
men of all ages and middle-aged or older women. The failed pub
designed for the Campbell Road/Paddington Street crossroads was
not missed. The quickest road out of Cambell Bunk lay through
the public bars of a dozen houses within five minutes' stagger –
the Pooles Park Tavern, the Durham Castle (called Dillinger's
House because of the number of fights there, and the Whore House
for more obvious reasons); the Duke of Clarence in Seven Sisters
Road; the Railway Hotel and the Earl of Essex, both in Wells
Terrace; Spralls's (or the Policeman's House) and the Duke (or the
Gentleman's Pub) both in Fonthill Road; the Crown in Lennox
Road and so on. And for home consumption there was the beer
off-licence at the bottom end of the Bunk.

Drunkenness was a common feature of life in Campbell Bunk, as
popular among women as men. The newspaper reports of charges
brought for drunkenness and related offences indicate that they
held up well in Campbell Road even during the 1930s (see table
12), despite the national decline in charges brought between the
wars.[69] And drunkenness accounted for 20 per cent and 33 per cent
of all charges reported against Campbell Road women in the 1920s
and 1930s respectively.

Most arrests were for outrageous behaviour by individuals. But
although getting arrested for drunkenness might have been a solitary activity, drinking was not. Alcohol provided consolations
unlike any other, building its own fantasy world which an unpalat-
able reality could not penetrate. It wiped away anxiety and physical
discomfort. For some it was the only way of escape, perhaps the
only way to sleep easily.[70] For others it was the only way they
could laugh at the world. In Campbell Road, drinking to excess
was a rational solution to insuperable problems.

Mrs Purslowe, the landlady-moneylender, used to drink regularly at the Duke in Fonthill Road 'with the lady upstairs. Because
it was always Irish Whiskey and it used to drive them crackers.'[71]
Mrs Tiverton used the Pooles Park Tavern: 'She had all her little
mates round there, so she'd trip round there and come back well
canned.'[72] Mrs Boycott 'took to drink' while living in Campbell
Road, and 'she used to go on them brake outings and all, what
they had.' She, too, went regularly to the Pooles Park, again with
a neighbour.[73] Pongo Blackman and other men from the road
would sing after closing time at the Paddington Street junction.[74]
Some costermongers, both men and women, kept the tradition of

St Monday alive, taking the day as the Costers' Holiday and spending much of it in the pub.[75]

Drinking, too, costs money – indeed the cost of getting drunk went up in the period[76] – and we shall look later at some of its financial and emotional implications for family life. Gambling, Campbell Road's other great collective 'vice' also cost money but not in the same way. The gambling habit grew nationally in the inter-war years, principally by the accretion of new outlets like the football pools, Sunday newspaper competitions, café fruit machines and pin-tables, and greyhound racing. These were grafted on to an already lively foundation of horse-race betting, in working-class areas through illegal street bookmakers and their runners.[77]

The pools and the *News of the World* puzzles were universal pleasures, Campbell Road included. The dogs attracted the 'hounds' of Campbell Road, its young men, especially those on the 'wide' side.[78] Street betting was classically the gambling outlet for married women and in Campbell Road, rare but not unique, one of the regular runners was a woman and so, less frequently, was another.[79] The sources of working-class gambling have been much commented upon – the excitement of risk-taking, the 'everyone has an equal chance' feeling so rarely indulged in a world where the odds were otherwise stacked against you, the use of skill in devising 'systems', the role of luck or fate in ordering the events of people's lives over which they felt they otherwise had no control.[80] There was one other source in Campbell Road deriving from the very economic insecurity which made the means of subsistence so frail. Street selling, finding, entertaining and the rest – and their alternatives outside the law – were themselves a gamble. Every costermonger who bought as cheaply as he or she could never knew how much the market would bring in return. Women street sellers would gamble the rent or bedclothes to 'turn over' the sum and add to it, or lose it in unsellable stock. The street singers and organ-grinders never knew how much their pockets would weigh at the end of the day, nor the totters just what they would find or be given. A casual labourer would hardly ever know on a Sunday night how much he would earn by next weekend. A gamble on the horses or pools or dogs was scarcely less certain than the daily roulette of economic enterprise: it became just one more way of earning a crust.

Campbell Road provided an exceptional outlet for this universal gambling urge. The tradition of street gaming with dice or cards or coins or crown and anchor board had begun in Campbell Road in the 1870s and was to last until it was demolished, eighty years later.[81] Although there were numerous gaming pitches elsewhere, gaming in Campbell Road was probably only matched in Holloway by Queensland Road, where courts running off 'the Land', itself a cul-de-sac, gave an exclusive privacy which the Bunk was denied. In Campbell Road, street gaming was uniquely brazen, in full view of foot passengers in Seven Sisters and Fonthill Roads, and of the police. This was at a time when gaming in the street was so rare that the social surveys ignored it altogether as a form of working-class gambling. In Campbell Road, it was organised with lookouts ('doggers out', frequently children), a 'croupier' for the complex dice games, regular pitches around gas-lamps (the most popular at the Paddington Street junction, against the flank wall of the old lodging house at number 47), and a reliable time-table in summer and winter (mainly Friday and Saturday nights, and Sunday lunchtimes). 'There's been *millions* of pounds down that [Campbell Road] over the years.'[82]

This was an arena where the men of Campbell Bunk could display the numeracy which was a more important skill than literacy in the life of the street entrepreneur.[83] It thus provided one route to acquire social value within Campbell Road. Pongo Blackman was one of the Bunk's favourite croupiers. A game might involve 40 players. Some would bet on the dice falling on certain numbers; some would bet on other numbers coming up first – a game called locally 'seven's and eleven's', a version of the American 'craps'. Stakes would be held by Pongo, who paid out to the winners on even money. There were no odds, but the demands on the croupier's memory during an exciting game were intense; 'you had to be the top notch to get that job, cos there was money . . . you had to be able to hold your own.'[84] Pongo did in more ways than one – he 'palmed' half-crowns from the stake money as an informal recompense for his labour-time.[85]

Gambling was a never-ending source of visual entertainment even for those who were not contenders. As such it was absorbed into the street theatre which was so much a part of the Bunk's collective identity and communal life. The street, the factory of Campbell Road's lumpen economy, was also the forum for its internal social relationships. The division between public and private spheres in Campbell Road was almost non-existent, partly because of the inadequacy of household living space, but partly also because the street exercised such a pull on people, providing a space for activity, even 'domestic' activity, of all kinds.

Centre-stage, quite literally, in Campbell Road's street theatre was the Paddington Street corner. Here the biggest gambling schools met. Here the 'hounds' had their meeting place and observation point against the flank wall of the old lodging house at 47, just waiting to see what would happen, or making their own amusements – like foot racing round the block for small bets;[86] 'shooting off the wall' with pennies or ha'pennies; swapping stories and jokes; horseplay and more ritualised fighting among themselves. It was, for instance, at the Paddington Street junction one Sunday morning (a favourite time for Bunk happenings) that Billy Tagg settled his score with Harry Tasker, some time around 1934.

Billy, Harry, Harry's brother Bert, and Tommy Stevenson had been playing cards one Friday night in a Fonthill Road café, as they and others often did. There was a row over cheating and Billy was persuaded by his step-father, Pongo Blackman, to fight Tommy in Paddington Street on their way home. Tommy retired with a cut eye, and they shook hands and were about to part when Harry caught Billy a heavy punch to the side of his jaw. It was broken and had to be wired up at the hospital casualty department; his gums and lip needed a dozen stitches:

> 'And I used to wait of a day for him, you know, thought to meself, Can't let it rest, like, I gotta – . So I still got me jaw done up, so I'm waiting there one afternoon . . . and he came along. So I said, "You're not going to get away with this, you know, Harry!" So he said, "Well, come and fight now!" I said, "Well, you're taking a bit of a liberty ain't you?" Because I had me jaw done up. So I said, "Make it Sunday.". . . So I was out of work at the time, but he was working, see. . . . Bigger feller than me, two stone bigger than me. But I was fit, I used to keep meself fit. So you used to get up early in the morning to have a run round the old park. Anyway, we arranged that we'd go over Hackney Marshes and have a fight to the finish, you know. So anyway, I'm ready, got no shirt on [just] a jacket and a scarf. So I come out in the morning and see all the brothers and their father on the corner, waiting, so I went in and said, "They're all on the corner, dad." "Pho!" he said [bustling into his clothes], "come on!" Down we go. All down the corner he said, "Well! Where is it?" I said, "Well, we'll go to the Marshes, like we said." See? So my old man, he said, "Oh, don't fuckin' fight there!" he said. "Have it here!" All right. So of course, you know what it was down the Bunk there, all the windows open like. . . . I get people coming up now and say, "Remember that fight you had?". . .'
> *How long did it last?*
> 'About twenty minutes, something like that.'

Were people round you watching?
'Oh yeah, oh yeah . . . they was on the streets, like. Corner of the Bunk and [Paddington] Street. . . .'
Who won?
'Oh, *I* did, naturally.'[87]

The roots of violence in Campbell Road are complex and will be exposed more carefully in a moment. But for the onlookers, tournaments like these helped satisfy the Bunk's love of spectacle, to be savoured at the time and to be talked over for years afterwards. Sometimes these moments of theatre were impromptu: Bert Lax and his pals, young troupers in khaki at the end of the First World War, appropriating costers' donkeys from the mews and racing them down Campbell Road;[88] Baccadust Smart's frightened pony stampeding out of his house, chased and caught to the delight of the Bunk's children;[89] The noisy late-night singsongs lubricated by bottles of beer or a kettlefull of tea and accompanied by harmonica or squeeze-box;[90] and the charwomen enjoying a knees-up to the wistful chords of a barrel organ. 'Dear! I've seen some happy times there!'[91]

The combination of excitement, opportunism, surprise and laughter blended together in Campbell Road's passion for the practical joke. London humour was full of verbal sparkle and that of the people of Campbell Road was no exception. The practical joke should not, therefore, he interpreted as compensation for an impoverished vocabulary. Rather, it exploited best the medium most available to the workless poor – time. It extended humour, injecting laughter into the joke's conception; the anticipation after the trap had been set; the successful conclusion; the unpredictable reaction of the victims; and the potential for oral embellishment when the joke was described to those not lucky enough to be there. It offered, too, psychological consolation for those who felt themselves rejected by the wider society: the practical joke created someone else to be laughed at, deflecting scorn on to other victims.

When a girl ran an errand to fetch a quartern of whiskey for an elderly woman, the empty bottle was returned filled with urine by the street corner boys.[92] One woman costermonger asked another to take a parcel to the pawn shop for beer money; when the pawnbroker unwrapped it he found a cod's head.[93] 'The old costers used to leave their barrows out in the road, and next morning they'd come and find them on the lamp post. . . . With the wheels off!' And the same could happen to young mothers' prams and pushchairs.[94] The occasional street singer might find himself half-stripped and tarred with axle grease and feathered from an old pillow. Many jokes were played on drunks – stripping and leaving them in ridiculous situations, or distempering them, and so on. And frequently, too, they involved some of the Bunk's disabled men in a way which at first might seem demeaning but which at least gave these individuals a role in the community, if only that of jester.[95] Simple-minded Tich Kinnock boasted he'd been stripped naked, painted in red, white and blue stripes and wheeled on a barrow up the road; 'he thought this was really the height of his career.'[96] Alec, 'he was a bit simple, like', could be persuaded to have public sparring matches with a partner who could emphasise his slowness, or who wore boots on his hands for comic effect.[97]

This spontaneous theatre drew on traditions of behaviour in Campbell Road, and so did one other important event in the Bunk's calender – Bonfire Night. November Fifth celebrations were extensive in London's poorer streets, and as late as 1931 it was reported that as many as 30 bonfires along the carriageway of a single street might be seen in Islington.[98] Campbell Road took Bonfire Night as far as it could, building mountainous pyres for days beforehand, and appropriating carts to collect extra fuelling on the night. Like the gambling, bonfires had been a feature of Campbell Road's open spaces in the 1870s.[99]

It was the form of the Bunk's mutual consolations, and the patterns of traditional behaviour there, which gave the road a special place in Holloway's lumpen culture as a whole. The street's reputation as a place where something was always happening was one attraction; so were the prostitutes who might take men back to their furnished rooms; so was the street's role as a hiding place from the police. It was a place which made the 'rough and ready' feel at home, perhaps more at home than in the respectable streets they haled from. Street gaming was probably the biggest draw for men living outside the street, and regular punters would have outlived the status of stranger.

One of these was Bert Lax, perhaps the most notorious local villain of his day. He lived for a short time in Campbell Road but was originally 'out of' Hurlock Street (a slum turning off Black-stock Road, cleared by the LCC in the early 1930s) and settled in Playford Road until the last war. Yet he was associated so much with Campbell Road that he was very much part of it, intimately involved with the street's internal feuding and its underworld connections. Street gambling provided one of the main attractions for Lax, who was a regular attender at the large weekend 'schools':

'There was Bert Lax . . . throwing up the pitch and toss with the coins. Right, so he'd had a bet. He said, "Plenty of money where this come from!" Never forget that, cos I thought, Well, I wish I had some of it! . . . And on the floor was about four or five quid, or six quid.'[100]

Internal tensions

Lax's boast, and the young lad's envy, remind us that the collective identity of Campbell Road disguised a world of sharp inequalities of wealth and power. We have already seen that the street's class structure was far from homogeneous and that some of the support networks actually depended on inequalities – in the ability of some women to become moneylenders, for example. We have also seen the tendency for the street to turn in on itself in the face of a hostile world outside. In that environment, the street's inequalities did not remain mutually isolated, interacting in separate spheres with social relations beyond Campbell Road. Rather, those possessed of relative wealth and power entered into exploitative relationships with their neighbours, deeply fracturing collective identities.

The resident landlords and house managers of Campbell Road possessed great power over the lives of their neighbours. They could and did evict them or distrain their few possessions for rent owed. They could and did inveigle them deeper into indebtedness by lending money at high interest to pay off arrears. A manager like Tubby Nicholls could and did exact labour-time or sexual favours to help wipe out a bad debt:

'Tubby Nichols, he used to come up our end for rents. I'll never forget it – I was only young, about 13. And he went to this Jessie Sweet for the rents. I heard him say, "It's twelve and sixpence now." And she lifted up her clothes: "Well, take it out of this!" And he went through and all, went in there, yeah!'[101]

Nicholls could also use violence to exact his dues, and was summonsed for assault on at least two occasions.[102] But for most landlords, the economic relationship was quite sufficient:

Was there ever any violence against Fred Neal?
'That's peculiar, no . . . if they was moneylenders or landlords, you got a bit scared in case they slung you out. It was only about five bob a week, four and six a week. Well if they slung you out and you went round Playford Road they might not

have you in there. That's what it was all about. They had the whip on you. They knew what they was doing of.'[103]

Moneylenders were similarly placed to the house managers and, indeed, were frequently the same people. But the tensions they provoked were more complex because of the gender complications. As we have seen they were almost exclusively women dealing with an entirely female clientele. Debt collection could again be enforced with violence – Matilda Purslowe would fight with debtors to make them pay up; or by blacklisting among the other moneylenders; or by the threat of informing to the husband who was usually ignorant of the deal. The whole arrangement weakened male authority within the family and could lead to violent efforts to regain it; and this violence was not always confined to husbands and wives. In October 1927 Frank Gillam, a 26-year-old labourer of 21 Campbell Road, was charged with assaulting Gypsy Jim Hobbs, pedlar, of 42 Campbell Road. Hobbs

said that on Saturday night he was sitting at home playing draughts with friends, when he heard the noise of someone moving in the passage. A member of the party opened the door, when prisoner walked in, and, without saying anything, struck him in the face. He had known Gillam for 18 months, and there had never previously been any trouble. Witness's wife was a registered moneylender, and accused's wife owed her money – this was the only reason he could give for his conduct.[104]

Relations with shopkeepers were more complicated still. Fred Neal was a shopkeeper and a landlord and his sister was Gypsy Jim Hobbs's wife, the moneylender. The Steeds were landlords and shopkeepers and moneylenders, and Gabriel Walters and George Bucknell ran shops and owned houses. The financial dependence of customer on shopkeeper, fostered by accumulated debt, weekly credit and outrelief tickets, was always open to abuse, even if not every advantage was always taken:

Where would you cash your food tickets in?
'Right opposite where we lived, a man named Secretan. . . . Not supposed to have no fags or baccer out of it but Mr Secretan used to be very good and let the old man have a bit of baccer, like a bit of Boar's Head, they nearly all used to smoke shag.'[105]

But even these good turns, which could not be repaid, merely emphasised the inequalities of power which the shopkeepers wielded – the petty oppressions as much imagined as real; the doubts over credit which always fell in the shopkeepers' favour; the short change or short weight, adulteration or poor quality goods; the power to call time on a debt overdue, and the public shame of a request for credit refused.

This economic power had its psychic manifestations, forming for some a positive image and for others a negative one. But both accorded the shopkeeper a primary place in the social and mental worlds of the Bunk:

> 'Yet in my child's eye the bewildering and dazzling variety of all the world's fruits stored in the vast cornucopia which Walters' shop represented, would account for the automatic response which sprung to one's lips when asked what you would like to be on achieving majority – a fervently whispered "To own a shop!" represented the wildest dreams of the answer to the permanent state of hardupness which permeated the street.'[106]

> 'To be born healthy and to live in vermin and filth, and the Council knew it was happening, the doctors knew it was happening, and the police knew it was happening, and no one was bothered. They just let the people take the money, make themselves fatter and richer – they've all got out to Canvey Island these Neals. . . . And all they was doing . . . was fleecing the bloody [poor people].[107]

It was not just 'the rich ones'[108] who were set apart within the collective identities of Campbell Road. There was a certain amount of outcasting against individuals or groups, much as in any other community. There was probably less of this than elsewhere because the Bunk itself suffered more than most from outcasting by the wider society. Certainly, people with mental disabilities were accepted more within Campbell Road than appears to have been the case among London's ordinary working-class streets in this period.[109] We have already seen their part in street theatre, many people recalled individual acts of kindness to mentally handicapped children, and one local policeman remembered a 'mongol-type of woman' who collected parcels in a battered push cart for pawning on Monday mornings from other Bunk women.[110] Inevitably, there were isolated individuals, perhaps especially men, who slipped through Campbell Road's neighbouring, like the 56-

year-old found dead in his room in 1932. He had lain there for two days and his eyes had been eaten by rats. He had no relatives, was reported always to have been in a dirty condition, and had a growth on his tongue.[111]

Sexual deviance probably attracted most opprobrium within Campbell Road. Male heterosexual promiscuity before and after marriage appears to have been treated with considerable tolerance, although this did not necessarily mean that youngsters were promiscuous. There was less freedom for girls, where sexual expression could be vigilantly guarded against by parents. We will hear more on both in subsequent chapters. I have almost no evidence on homosexuality, although Musher Gates treated one homosexual man to some rough horseplay involving threats of sexual abuse.[112] At least two male exhibitionists (or 'flashers') lived in the road for a time, but one of them was avoided more because he was a tough and violent man than for any other reason.[113]

It was the street's prostitutes who were cast most of all in the role of out-group. This casting was again a construct of the women of Campbell Road and it was widespread. To a certain extent this is surprising, because prostitutes had lived there since the earliest days and were present in sufficient numbers to avoid the stigmatism attaching to an individual deviant. In addition, the line dividing 'prostitute' from, say, 'charwoman' or 'waitress' was not always easy to draw, as some women were 'half and half if you know what I mean'.[114] There were young and middle-aged prostitutes in the street, mostly living alone but some lived two together in a furnished room. This combination could give a house, deservedly or not, a reputation as a brothel.[115] There were also at least three male protectors or ponces living in the road, one of whose careers will be traced in more detail later, who also received some of the antagonism provoked by the prostitutes. It was the wives and mothers of Campbell Road who felt this antagonism most fiercely – unmarried girls seemed to have bothered little about what their friends' mothers, or their friends, got up to: 'Actually, the Stevensons, the girls of them, they turned out the prostitutes. But they were nice girls and that.'[116]

'We didn't have nothing to do with them. My mother wouldn't let us go in a house where there was a prostitute.'
Were there prostitutes in the street?
'Yeah, opposite me, Mrs Brittan. And her boy was my mate. If I was to go in that house, my mother would kill me. "Keep out of there!" I didn't know what it was all about then. But

as I got older and I seen the woman in Fonthill Road with blokes and that, up against the wall, I knew straight away.'[117]

Likewise Mrs Harper 'wouldn't have anything to do with the old brass downstairs' at number 38.[118] And children's nicknames for individual prostitutes included 'Ole Muvver Woodbine' and 'Dust'ole Kate', unflattering references to the way these particular women conducted their business.[119]

That these tensions could lead to more than name-calling is clear from the case of Mrs Brittan, who was born around 1884 and was a prostitute in Campbell Road during the 1920s at least. In 1924 ('CAMPBELL ROAD SUNDAY NIGHT SCENE – Sequel at North London Court') she was charged with assaulting Alfred Baron, the 18-year-old son of her neighbour in the same house. Mrs Brittan admitted the assault but claimed it was self-defence. 'Seven hooligans, together with the prosecutor, had entered her room and saturated her with water and given her a black eye and bruises.' Thirty shillings had been taken from underneath a vase and the room turned upside-down. A PC 'said he was called to the house and prisoner's dress was wet. There were blood stains on the floor outside the room, which was in a state of disorder.' Both were bound over for twelve months.[120]

Five years later she was in trouble again, quarrelling with another family in the same house. She had some words with a woman and her husband about their children. The husband 'called her filthy names, and she said, "I am a woman, but I will fight you" ', challenging him to fight in the road. He was charged with grievous bodily harm, having bruised her face and broken her tooth and her wrist. He was fined £2, the police having confirmed he was a 'respectable married man . . . in regular employment since leaving the army.'[121]

There might have been special reasons for Mrs Brittan's proneness to this sort of incident, but there is other evidence of assaults on prostitutes, or alleged prostitutes, in the street.[122] The source of this particular tension seems rooted both in the threat which prostitutes posed to the relationship of husband and wife; and, perhaps more curiously, in the protective culture of the Bunk's women. It is significant that the incidents of hostility quoted above involved mothers of sons. Prostitutes were the potential corruptors of boys as well as girls. It might mould a young boy's sexuality into the forms all too visible in their weak-minded fathers who could not be trusted to avoid the temptations of Campbell Road's 'loose women'. And in protecting their sons, they were thus protecting also the young women they would choose for their own wives in years to come.

But inequalities of wealth and the construction of outcasts provided merely some of the roots of tensions and violence within Campbell Road. Much, perhaps most, of this violence began within the family and will be considered later. But a good deal was between neighbours, and for its explanation we must return to some of the contradictions of life in the Bunk.

For men, the condition of worklessness (both chronic un- and under-employment) had major implications for gender identity. Work, usually through hard physical labour, provided a large part of a man's own concept of masculinity. This was strengthened by the overlays attending the role of male worker as provider and protector of his dependents, the earner of the 'family wage'. Rejection from the labour market deprived men of that source of male identity.[123] On the other hand, rejection *of* the labour market did not imply a rejection of masculine identity. In both cases, men sought ways of compensating for worklessness and the threat to gender it implied.

For individuals alienated from their gender identity in this way there were few ways to recover male self-esteem. Youths and men in Campbell Road were relatively untouched by formal schooling and any intellectual ambition it might have produced. Their opportunities for entrepreneurial expansion were curtailed by structural restrictions on capital accumulation. Their poverty would not permit them to emulate the masculine heroes of the time in dress, or leisure habits, or success with women.[124] Campbell Bunk did provide one route out of these problems for young men – through the underworld, as we shall see below. But for all those men who had not been disabled by war or poverty or accident of birth there was one other way – through physical culture and the development of 'masculine' body skills, strength and bravado.

It was no accident that 'the cult of the body', as it was called at the time, received its most fervent adherents among the young male unemployed.[125] In Campbell Road it was actively encouraged by the missions, lads' clubs, industrial schools and borstals with which its young men came in contact. But it had internal dynamics which these more formal roots merely facilitated. Physical strength became the touchstone of masculinity because any other test was biased against the men of Campbell Road. It was an immanent quality which most were born with, not like those other indicators of value which were less evenly distributed by society – especially education and wealth. It was also largely eschewed by those with power over the lives of people in the Bunk, providing a separate and potentially oppositional structure of social esteem. Aggressive 'masculinity' became a class weapon, and we shall see more of this in a moment.

But if the culture of physical strength is to compensate fully for the loss of masculinity through worklessness and low status it has to be used and must be seen by others. These others do not have to be other men, and within the family this is plainly not the case. But in the wider community of the Bunk, contests of strength between men provided a hierarchy of esteem which no other value-structure offered, an ascending ladder of masculine credit. Not all, of course, chose even to step on the first rung. Yet those who did quite consciously saw it in that way:[126]

> *Was the top end better, slightly?*
> 'I would say yes, they had the more hardest men at the top end of the Bunk as against the bottom end of the Bunk.'[127]

Remember Dido James and Ernie Barnes who fought for the title of king of Campbell Road's pikies. And when Billy Penton kicked Bert Lax senseless at the Paddington Street junction in 1938, then 'he was king at the finish' of the Bunk's masculine world as a whole.[128]

The construction of gender can also help us explain the frequency of violence among women in Campbell Road. But it is not 'femininity' to which we should look. The vulnerable economic and psychic position of men in Campbell Road encouraged a struggle for power within the family. This was heightened by women's economic power which stimulated a feeling of egalitarianism with men, justified by a wife's frequently greater earning power. And many women, through war-widowhood or desertion, were sole providers in their own right. Power in the family was, as we shall see, equated with masculinity. When men and women fought for power they also fought for that gender identity. Men who used violence to assert the power and authority they had lost or felt in danger of losing could provoke a violent response from their female companions, and not all women were losers in these physical struggles. And among those women who engaged in battle there grew their own hierarchy of violence, much like the men's. Some adopted the full regalia of the masculine role – like Mrs Brittan challenging her male neighbour to fight it out in the street; or like Mrs Purslowe who 'used to fight Jim Knowles who lived downstairs. She broke his nose once with a poker';[129] or like Mary Ann Dunn, Long Liz, Mrs James and the rest who would take their blouses off, stand toe to toe and slug it out on the stones like men: 'Then next thing you know, my mother and Kate Murphy. . . . They stripped to the fuckin' waist.'[130]

Inequalities of wealth and status, and struggles over gender identity, interacted with each other and with the third major component of violence in Campbell Road – its traditions. The traditions of Campbell Bunk tell us much about female violence, as they do for men. There was the tradition of heavy drinking; the competition for clients among casual charwomen and for pitches among street sellers; the tradition which held that Campbell Bunk was a place where you had to stand up for yourself, whether man or woman, or someone else would push you under. 'You had to hold your own.'[131] 'There was a lot of conflict about in your association with [other children] and kids were always gonna whack you.'[132] Violence in settling disputes among children could also be actively encouraged by parents, directly transmitting the Bunk tradition from one generation to another. Tough children became a source of parental self-esteem. We have seen this already in the case of Billy Tagg, egged on by his step-father in his fight with Harry Tasker. But it might be the same for girls, too, as in this example from around 1935:

'I used to wear glasses, as I'm wearing now, and one girl said to me, "Lucky Look!" And I said, "I'll give you bleeding lucky look!" and I give her such a bleeding hiding. And her mother went round to my dad, "Look what your Nora's done to my Nellie!" So he said, "Well, what do you expect me to do? Fetch Nellie down at ten o'clock tomorrow morning, I'll have Nora round and we'll have them in the road together!" But Nellie never come. I had to stay in for nothing.'[133]

The taunt of 'Lucky Look!' reminds us that the immediate causes of violence within the street bore no necessary mechanical identity with the structures which underpinned them. Structural causes in class, gender and tradition were mediated through the day-to-day realities of living in Campbell Road. Certainly there were patterns – tensions over cramped living space, courage bolstered by drink, arguments between rivals or partners. Occasionally there were family feuds; more rarely there was victimisation and terrorism. But in general the violence was easy come easy go, clustered around peaks like closing time on Friday and Saturday nights, or around Sunday lunchtimes; it was expected that some trouble would occur and the expectation fuelled the trouble itself:

'I tell you what it used to be mostly. Half past ten at night, the pubs would shut, Saturday night. They all come up the road singing "Nellie Dean". Somebody'd say, "Why don't you shut that effin' noise up?" That's how it used to start. "What the 'ell's the matter with you?" "I'll soon show you!" Down they come, that's how it goes. That is exactly how it used to go.'[134]

Among women neighbours, children were a frequent immediate cause of quarrels which elsewhere might have provoked a shrug of the shoulders or a week's icy silence but which in Campbell Road might easily end more seriously. Louise Denly received a black eye from Lizzie Knowles because Louise had 'called her attention' to her baby left crying outside a pub.[135] Annie Sutton blacked the eye of Emma Weston because she had 'interfered with her children and insulted her'.[136] There were rows, too, over money owed.[137] But most of all, fights revolved around the use of equipment or living space in the home, or about the habits of the lodgers in the next room, or the rooms above and below. Annie Wareham, appearing in court with her eyes blacked and head bandaged, stated that when she arrived home on a Saturday night she 'heard a row on the stairs. She opened her door whereupon accused [Alice Carver] threw an enamel jug of water over her, saying, "Take that you – ." Florence Islip said that Carver had then ' "bashed" ' Wareham about the head with the jug and Carver was accordingly charged with grievous bodily harm. In her defence, Carver said it was all Islip's fault: ' "She has been nagging me about the man who has been living with me." ' A man, in Carver's defence, claimed to have seen Mrs Wareham hit her, and Mrs Islip with her sleeves rolled up. The police commented: ' "This is the result of a series of quarrels between a number of persons living in the same house." '[138]

Among men neighbours, immediate causes included quarrels 'over a woman', name-calling and insults, and just accidental circumstances, with or without a previous history. Henry Arnold, 35, in hospital to have a leg amputated for gangrene, was charged with assault on Alfred May in August 1922. May had a broken rib and was also in hospital. He had allegedly called Arnold's son ' "a ginger-headed – " '.[139] Alfred London, 59, labourer, was charged with assaulting John Sands, a general dealer, by punching him in the mouth. Sands said that London had asked him for money for beer and when he refused he was struck. The two men were related. They had been drinking in the Pooles Park Tavern where Sands ordered two bottles of beer and asked London to come back to his house for a drink. 'When they arrived the beer was missing and prosecutor threatened Mrs London with violence, alleging that she had taken the beers. It was subsequently found that the bottles had been left at the Public House.'[140]

There could be more serious incidents than these and we should remind ourselves that one consequence of the hierarchy of physical strength and courage displayed through violence in Campbell Road was a tendency to terrorism by the strongest. There were many people who were avoided because they might, for no reason, demonstrate their power to hurt. These few could dominate the majority by fear. Gypsy Jim Hobbs had, it was alleged, 'a big lump of leather with chains on it' which he would use in defence and attack: 'All the people in Campbell Road were afraid of him.'[141] When Bert Lax and some cronies had a row with Baccadust Smart, they kicked out some iron railings, commonly used as weapons in street fights, and threw them through his windows while his wife was indoors. She and the landlady refused to give evidence against Lax and a detective inspector commented that 'He was afraid that they had been "got at" and that they were in a state of fear. "There has been a good deal of this window smashing going on, but people are afraid to come forward and prosecute". . . .'[142] There was a similar incident involving the same men two years later, in 1931.[143] And we will never know what lay behind the terrifying attacks on the Hume family in the summer of 1920. Two Pentons, Sonny Smithson (the kip-house deputy), and another man giving an address outside the Bunk but who lived there on and off for some years, were all charged with grievous bodily harm on James Hume 'by striking him on the head with an iron bar', and on Ethel Hume 'by striking her on the forehead with a brick'. James Hume alleged the men attacked him with iron bars, a hot poker and a brick. There was a 'terrible struggle' and Hume admitted using one of the iron bars on the elder Penton in self-defence, injuring him badly. Smithson threatened to burn out Hume's eyes with the poker. At the third court hearing the police reported that the Humes had fled and could not be traced. Dismissing the charges, the magistrate commented, ' "That may be the result of two things; one, the prisoners or their friends may have put the fear of God into these people, or they may think themselves in the wrong." '[144]

These more serious incidents may well have had underworld implications and we shall come back to them in chapter 6. Some, too, might have had the added complication of family rivalry, and often the two went together. It was said, for example, that the Chines and the Shorters were enemies, and the Chines and the

Hawses, who were related by marriage. There was a famous fight at a party when choppers were used and a woman, hit by accident, received serious head wounds.[145] But there were no real vendettas lasting years in Campbell Road, although old scars became inflamed from time to time.

It would be wrong to see violence as necessarily destructive of community consciousness or collective identity.[146] At one level it actively reinforced the feeling of proud exclusivity, that Campbell Road set higher standards of toughness than elsewhere. 'It was the survival of the fittest', is used frequently to explain life in Campbell Road by those who lived there, and it is said with at least a hint of self-satisfaction.[147] Violence helped bolster the image of an identifiable community for the benefit of outsiders.

Its role in the internal cohesiveness of the Bunk was more contradictory. For individuals – the Humes would be a good example – violence might be a cause for moving from Campbell Road, and so it was one small motor of change and mobility. For others, who knew they could hold their own, it provided stimulation and status: they were 'a big splash in a small pool'.[148] This is perhaps confirmed by the number of occasions on which fights ended with a handshake, cementing public-bar friendships rather than otherwise.[149] It thus provided fighting men and women with a reason for staying put. This tension obviously had its own dynamic, twisting the spiral towards yet more violence.

There was one other way in which the internal tensions of life in Campbell Bunk worked themselves through, the effects of which on collective identities were almost wholly negative. This was theft among neighbours. The amount of theft within working-class communities has been romanticised away in recent years,[150] whereas any superficial examination of court reports from the inter-war period will reveal it as a common fact of life. Within Campbell Road the risk of property stolen from households who already had little enough to their names was a serious problem.

Some cases from the late 1920s can give a flavour of the difficulties people might encounter. William Bennett, a 27-year-old costermonger, received six months hard labour for stealing five shillings by means of a trick from a Campbell Road news-vendor: he had given the paper-seller a note, purporting to be from his employers, instructing him to give Bennett the money.[151] Sonny Smithson was charged with stealing a tradesman's bicycle from outside a house in Campbell Road: he said, ' "As a rule they borrow one another's bicycles in Campbell Road to go for a ride".'[152] John Fitch, a 21-year-old labourer, admitted stealing three pairs of combinations and a costume from the washing line of the house next door: ' "I was starving at the time".' The owner of the clothes, who took out a barrel organ for a living, said, ' "Other people have lost things, and it is not safe to put your washing out in our street." '[153] And 'On Saturday, in a case of larceny at North London Police Court, a detective mentioned that in a certain house in Campbell Road there were padlocks on the doors of the rooms, because the tenants did not trust each other!'[154]

We will need to look more closely at the reasons for thieving by some people in Campbell Road before we can understand how they could so readily steal from their neighbours and yet maintain a close and supportive community at the same time. For this might serve as the quintessence of the tension between individualism and collectivism in Campbell Bunk, a tension which permeated political life and the various struggles against those whom the people of the Bunk saw as their enemies.

4 Ideology, politics and forms of struggle

The politics of Campbell Bunk

The ideologies – or the values and views of the world – which shaped political action in Campbell Bunk grew out of its lived experience of class, tradition, and collective culture. We should not be surprised to find those worldviews complex and contradictory, holding apparently mutually opposed ideas in precarious balance. But in all this there were key elements which would have been understood by the people of Campbell Bunk, even if they did not espouse each and every component. The same seed could nurture contrasting progeny – hot republicanism next to loyal monarchism, for instance; or deference to authority with aversion to discipline. Yet these strong opposites were all logical positions for people to reach. The conditions of life, and the possibilities of the time, predisposed towards a range of political attitudes: just which any individual chose to adopt was finally and unpredictably determined by personal psychology. It will be the construction of those political probabilities, and their effects on struggle with forces perceived as antagonistic, which will concern us here. And the four pillars of that construction were *egalitarianism*, or a feeling of equality with others and a rejection of the value attached to a 'higher' status or class; *individualism*, or a belief that the needs or ambitions of the individual should take priority over those of others; *libertarianism*, or the toleration of behaviour and attitudes which were outside society's normally approved moral codes; and *chauvinism*, or an aggressive dislike of people (and things) who were not English.

> *Did your father ever talk politics?*
> 'Only to the extent of saying to me he didn't agree [with] . . . he was jealous, probably, jealous of the fact that the Royal Family was up there. . . . On one occasion he said, "Well, what did you do in school?" I said, "Well, we say prayers, and then we sing 'God Save The King' – ". "*You* don't, do yer?" "Well, – ." He said, "Well you're not to!" I thought

[laughs] – I arrived at some compromise of mouthing the words without saying them and that sort of thing, not to get meself talked about and satisfy the old man. But he was manifestly against the toffs, that was one of his favourite expressions of them, "the toffs", was people [who were] parasites. I suppose in his way he was as much of a parasite, but none the less he was there by force of circumstances. He disapproved strongly of privilege, and that's rubbed off a bit on me. . . . He in his conversation tried to indicate that he was as good as *them*.'[1]

In a street which made so much of its 'Poor But Loyal' banner on days of national rejoicing, Jack Duncan's republicanism may come as a surprise. But he was by no means alone. Bill Dashett 'didn't believe in Royalty', and Thomas Knight 'walloped' his daughter for singing the national anthem: 'You talked about the King or the Queen, you'd had it.'[2] There were other symbols of privilege which were targets of this egalitarian impulse, like state bureaucrats and the impositions of employers, and we will return to this in the following sections.

We have already uncovered the roots of Campbell Road's egalitarianism. They lay in the process of rejection from the labour market and the outcasting which went with living in the Bunk; both of which in turn provoked a defensive rationalisation of that position, an alternative structure of self-esteem. This averred that Bunkites were as good as other people. When the young Walter Spencer wanted to leave a lunchtime gaming school in Campbell Road to return to work and his 'Guvnor', another punter exclaimed, 'Do what? You *got* no Guvnor!' No one owned you in that way, no one was your better, you were 'all equal'.[3] Equality was reinforced by the collective practice of mutual aid among women and by the construction of 'masculinity' which relied on inherent physical qualities rather than those acquired through privilege.

Individualism took root in similar ground. This time rejection *of* the labour market encouraged a feeling of 'looking out for number one'. The economic competition between the street earners, competing for pitches and customers; the violent intra-communal conflicts; the strong sense of having to 'hold your own' in Campbell Bunk – all contributed to a feeling that one's own interests were, at the last ditch, paramount:

'I remember when we were playing dice on the floor, you know, for money . . . outside in the street. And I won some old boy's rent. And he went round to my dad, he said, "Your

Nora's won my rent!" So my dad turned round and said,
"What the effin hell you think you want me to do, give it to
yer back!?" He said, "It's your bloody fault for playing with a
kid." And he come home and said, "Where's this bloke's
rent?". . . So I had to give it to him. And he give it to her
[my mother]. He said, "Now go up the road," to Ma, cos the
shops were open Sundays then: "Go up the road tomorrow,
Ada," he said, "get her two drill sets and two jumpers." Cos
they were only one and eleven pence each them, up Hornsey
Road. And I got two jumpers and two drill [sets] and then he
said, "Well, here you are, here's the money now, she's paid
for them, buy her a pair of shoes," they were two and six.'[4]

Individualism co-existed with egalitarianism and was constrained
by it. There was no legitimation within Campbell Bunk for the
creation of a hierarchy of privilege based on wealth – as against
physical strength or cunning. Remember the mistrust of, and
equivocal hostility to, shopkeepers, moneylenders, and rentiers
within the street. Individualism should not gain too much. It must
be kept within decent bounds. Certainly the fruits of individual
labour could be kept by the individual – the point of the practical
instruction to Bill Dashett's daughter in the example above. When
the odds were evens then good luck to the winner: the loser had
no right to complain. But there was no time for those who had
the odds stacked in their favour, and who could thus manipulate
and control the game's final outcome.

Individualism and egalitarianism combined to foster libertarianism. Rejection from and of wage labour did not necessarily
imply a rejection of dominant social values and ideologies. But at
the collective level of life in the street we have seen how the most
meaningful consolations were at odds with approved standards of
behaviour. The collective rejection of the dominant social code is
plainly implied in the Bunk's culture – its street theatre involving
violence, rowdiness, open gaming, some public nakedness and so
on. In this culture, oddness was not only tolerated it was encouraged, and we have glimpsed examples of this above. It was
summed up in the frequent self-description of people from the
Bunk as 'rough and ready'; and the internal labelling of streets like
it as 'do-as-you-please'.[5] There were, in fact, deep contradictions
in this libertarianism between the public sphere of the street and
the private sphere of the family, and we shall look at this again in
the next chapter. But libertarianism commonly manifested itself in
one other public and private phenomenon which was an important
determinant of behaviour in the street – a resistance to discipline.

This was more a reaction against authority, the forces of rejection, than a resistance to self-discipline. This is one of the oft-voiced criticisms of the 'slum' community, but there are many examples of self-discipline in Campbell Bunk – from the development of numeracy skills of the gaming croupier, the self-training of the street seller or professional thief, the legitimate scrimping and saving of the factory girl for her first 'costume', and so on. Rather, it was a feeling that no one had the right to order you about, at least in a way which threatened a dignity already over-sensitive from the processes of outcasting. The right was denied authority-figures as diverse as employers, policemen, school and local authorities, and even army officers and NCOs, as we shall see.

The fourth and final pillar of political consciousness in Campbell Road was chauvinism. This was less an English nationalism than mistrust, fear, even hatred of foreign people and things. It is not hard to see its origins in the intense parochialism which outcasting had spawned. But chauvinism could help rationalise that outcasting for those who lived it, making foreigners an easy object of blame. It was they who manipulated the system in un-English, over-competitive and unequal ways. They could symbolise the hidden interference which left people from the Bunk in such a hopeless situation. If there were no foreigners then there might be more chance for people like those in Campbell Road – good English people who surely had the first right to the benefits of their own country. Anti-Irish sentiment was common, even though many Campbell Road families could have claimed Irish descent: 'You never get no Irishmen round there. . . . They've give the Paddies all the pubs – but *you* try and get one.'[6] Anti-semitism was real enough ('I know the Jews run the country and they run everything')[7] although a very few Jewish individuals or families lived in the street from time to time. A couple of anecdotes tell of how black men were run out of Campbell Road in the 1930s after exemplary beatings from residents.[8] The immigration from Cyprus, which began in the 1930s, probably fuelled the anti-foreign impulse, but in general discrimination was indiscriminate. Musher Gates got the sack from a coal merchant's because a Belgian woman reported him for some misdemeanour: ' "Wha'dyer mean, you old cow!? . . . wha'ssamatter with yer? . . . Get back to your fuckin country where you belong to," I said. Belgians they was!'[9]

It was chauvinism, an essentially negative response rather than a positive espousal of an idealised English 'nation', which underpinned the Bunk's patriotism.[10] The 'Poor But Loyal'[11] banner and the faded Union Jacks hung out on Empire Day or Armistice Day or on Peace Day in 1919, and the national junkets of 1935 and 1937, expressed a two-fold desire for belonging. There was belonging in the internal sense of all being 'Poor', but defiant, not bowed down by it, capable still of spirit in their own community. And then there was the external sense of belonging ('Loyal') to a homeland, even though (and here the 'But' is significant) they had been effectively outcast from it. People in the Bunk did not *owe* loyalty, they gave it of their own collective free will.[12] Both of these internal and external relations were sources of pride, a much needed self-valorization in the face of comprehensive rejection. The consolatory sources of pride within the Bunk have already been dealt with. The external source of pride lay in England's achievements: not domestic progress, which had touched the Bunk hardly at all, but rather the domination over foreign competitors in the struggle for Empire. The ready volunteers which the First World War elicited from the Bunk would, in part, have derived moral justification from just this source. They gave loyalty to preserve the homeland more against the claims of foreigners from without than to preserve the monarchy or social hierarchy within. There was no stratum of British society that remained unblemished by the imperialist taint.[13]

No political party could hope to be the natural home for these contradictory ideological elements. Even where political allegiance was given to a party or movement, the worldviews of the Bunk cut across party loyalty. From the oral testimony I found not one person who claimed membership of any political party at any time of his or her life, and similarly for any parent of a person interviewed. To find the reasons why, we need to look at what political parties and movements could offer people from the Bunk, as well as what views people from the Bunk brought to politics.

In many ways it was the Labour Party which offered most, and to which the Bunk responded most warmly. This, after all, was the party with the interests of the poor apparently most at heart, promising the best deal for the unemployed, the sick and disabled, for those on poor relief and pensions, for those in slums or crowded housing:

> 'He always voted Labour, the old man. Well, you couldn't do nothing else, could you? . . . Well, you couldn't vote Tory if you never had nothing, could you, really?'[14]

Besides Jimmy Dunn's father, there was Jack Harper:

'He wasn't a political animal, really, but if he voted he would vote Labour. I mean, on the grounds that the others belonged to the other lot: like, the capitalists.'[15]

Tom Tasker was similarly disposed and Jack Duncan's son remembers him reading the *Daily Herald*, at least for a time.[16] And of the children's election songs it appears only to be the Labour ones which live on in the collective memory.

But there were good reasons why the affiliation to Labour should not rouse more passion than the quotes above imply. Stratification within the British working class has long been remarked and puzzled over. The major divisions have been by skill and regularity of employment, by sex, nationality and geographical region, in some areas by religion, and most recently by race and ethnic background. To date, the most important has been the first. For the past 150 years, there is hardly an aspect of working-class life which has not been marked by this divide, especially politics. The Labour Party, both nationally and locally, was a product of the skilled working class, in relatively high-paid, relatively secure employment, with a literate, organised and strongly-disciplined culture. From the very beginning, its leaders and activists had consciously distanced themselves from the unrespectable poor, with their drink, violence, dirt and licence. Nor was this merely a matter of diverging tastes. There was an acute consciousness among skilled workers, organised for defence in trade unions, of the enemy within – the casual workers of the reserve army of labour whose historical function for capital had been to keep wages low and to undermine collective industrial action. As late as 1944, George Orwell noted that

> Even in Socialist literature it is common to find contemptuous references to slum-dwellers (the German word *Lumpenproletariat* is much used), and imported labourers with low standards of living, such as the Irish, are greatly looked down on.[17]

This process of rejection from the labour movement was felt more or less strongly by individuals in Campbell Road. The Islington Labour Party was dominated between the wars by printers (especially compositors) and the uniformed working class. The Labour Party was strongest in South Islington and only gained lasting control of Tollington ward (in which the Bunk lay) in local elections from 1937.[18] The only Campbell Road resident recorded as being politically active was Ernest Steed, who stood unsuccessfully for election as a Labour Guardian in Lower Holloway ward in 1922: it will be remembered that Steed was a landlord and shopkeeper, and his wife was a moneylender (although he was described as a 'painter' on the candidates' list).[19] This candidature would not necessarily have endeared locals to the Islington Labour Party. Nor would the association of Labour with large local bureaucracies, which affronted both the Bunk's anti-authoritarianism and its class feeling against higher strata. And nor, necessarily, would the Labour opposition on Islington Council, who called publicly for the demolition of the street in 1930 and 1931.[20] It was rumoured, too, that the Finsbury Park Railway Club, affiliated to the Working Men's Club and Institute Union, discriminated against men from Campbell Road.[21] Standards of literacy were low in Campbell Road and its most popular newspaper, the *News of the World*, was rabidly anti-socialist. The lack of national insurance among many of the unemployed alienated men from the dole queue and the National Unemployed Workers' Committee Movement. The Islington Communist Party, whose leading cadres were busmen, railwaymen and above, canvassed Campbell Road vigorously but alienated residents through insensitivity to the outcasting processes suffered by the Bunk – they labelled it 'lousy' in the *Daily Worker;* in 1934 their top candidate in Tollington ward out of six polled 164 votes against the Municipal Reformers' 1,989.[22] And in important ways the common worldviews of the people of Campbell Road were inherently resistant to socialist propaganda: the reaction against discipline, anti-internationalism,[23] and most of all, individualism.

It was this individualism which justified the labour movement's fears on the one hand; and which was contributed to by the outcasting traditions of British socialism on the other. There was considerable hostility within Campbell Road to trade unions. Thomas Knight, the republican casual docker, 'wouldn't join a union. He was against the union.'[24] Jack Harper, a life-long Labour voter who worked in the building line, was 'anti-trade union'.[25] Both men were, at least for a time, on the very casual fringe of both industries. The resistance to trade unionism among such men was well known and had at its back fears of 'decasualisation' and its effects on employment chances for those on the industrial margins; and a resentment of the power wielded over workers by trade union officials who seemed to wax fat on members' contributions.[26]

We can get a glimpse into the effects of these attitudes from the General Strike of 1926. A 26-year-old, ' "more out of work than in it", who had been a casual carman and rag and bone dealer,

sold newspapers at Finsbury Park during the nine days' strike.[27]
And a 31-year-old labourer, arrested for begging in the summer
of 1927, had even enrolled as a special constable according to police
evidence.[28] It was at that time, too, that Musher Gates hired himself
out wherever he was needed for blacklegging, laying a running
track at the Arsenal Stadium; taking out a 'pirate' bus with the
'Sabini mob' and getting a bloody nose in the process from a
stone-throwing crowd of strikers and sympathisers; and carrying
coal for a merchant in Gillespie Road:

' "You blackleggin' – you blackleg, you fucking blackleg!" I
said, "Get out of it or I'll sling the fucking coal at yer! You
think my horse is gonna starve!? . . . Get out the way, you
cunts!" '[29]

Now, when Musher Gates voted, which was not always, he
voted Labour. And if it is starkly clear that political allegiance to
the cause of labour was selective in its application, then there was
no ideology or political practice from the right which was able to
hold the Bunk's worldviews in balance. Liberalism can be shortly
dismissed, although Lill Wilsdon's father, the regularly-employed
french polisher, was a Liberal and took the *Daily Chronicle*.[30]
Conservative Party ideology did coincide with that of the Bunk at
a couple of crucial points and so understandably had some loyal
followers there. Bill Dashett, the anti-royalist street seller, was a
staunch Tory, even in 1945.[31] It would probably have been the
Party's ideological concern for the small businessman and for
minimal municipal expenditure which attracted him most. The
Party of Empire, too, could not fail to harmonise, if only quietly,
with popular chauvinism. For others, deference – the feeling that
if there had to be leaders then it was these men who, by inheritance,
were most fitted to lead – combined with a calculating individualism quite in accord with the views of many in the Bunk who
need not have reached the same conclusions as did Walter Spencer's
father:

'He always reckoned Conservatives – he's right as well – they're
the ones who've got the money, they're the ones who can
employ you. That's what he used to say to me. He said, "If
you haven't got the Conservative," he said, "you got no
work." Yet there was about two million unemployed his
days.'[32]

On the other hand, of course, certain aspects of Conservatism were too disabling to make the party a natural political home for more than a minority of people in the Bunk. Some of these were the mirror image of the attractions of socialism and the Labour movement. But part of the common worldviews found no real expression in any party. This was especially so in the case of anti-authoritarianism. And neither could this be comfortably accommodated within the alternative political movement of the right – fascism.

Common wisdom would presume that support for the British Union of Fascists was strong in Campbell Road. Membership of the BUF is an under-researched area, but connections have been found with 'roughs' and 'ragamuffins', at least in the north of England.[33] And London's political folklore, if nothing more, would bear that out. The BUF's chauvinism and anti-semitism, its connection with violent political action, its concern for the petty bourgeoisie and its ostensible antagonism to big capital should all have fostered pro-fascist sympathy in the Bunk. In fact, this appears not to have been the case. Collective memory could not recall one blackshirt ever living in the street. In the frequent fights between fascists and their political enemies at open-air speaking pitches in Finsbury Park and Hornsey Road, not one person from Campbell Road gets his or her name in the ensuing court reports. In sum, there is no evidence whatsoever for a connection between Campbell Bunk and the fascist movement. Defying all received knowledge, this calls for some explanation.

It might merely be that people were reluctant to talk about a part of their past they now feel they should consider shameful. But that would not match the frequent if not universal readiness to talk about criminal careers, or the ease with which racist opinions are voiced. So if we accept that the collective memory is not wilfully or unconsciously repressing reality we must look for explanations in the relation between fascist ideology and the popular mentalities of Campbell Road's population.

At first sight, fascism's ultra-nationalism coincided with chauvinism within the Bunk.[34] In fact, the strength of this chauvinism represented fascism itself as an alien ideology. The people of Campbell Road had suffered too much in the Great War to align themselves readily with a creed which owed so much to a German Messiah. The anti-German riots of 1915 and 1917, including the stoning for four successive nights of an internment camp at the Cornwallis Road overspill workhouse, took place on the Bunk's doorstep:[35] it would have been astonishing, given Campbell Road's war record, if people from it had not made up some of the protagonists, and if some of that feeling were not still alive in the inter-war period. For example, Armistice Day wreaths were laid regularly on the Campbell Road war memorial outside Ernest Steed's house for many years after 1918. Italians were no more loved in Campbell Road than any other foreigners, and the relationship of British fascism with the 'Ities' was enough to condemn it in the eyes of Tom Nesbitt.[36] Then again, the importance among fascist cadres of shopkeepers and small employers[37] would not have endeared itself to the particular egalitarianism which had most currency in Campbell Road. The only fascists recalled by Musher Gates were a café proprietor and his wife from Hornsey Road, and two policemen.[38] These last remind us of the strong authoritarianism of fascism which was out of sympathy with the collective spirit prevalent in the Bunk's public sphere. The blackshirt uniform looked too much like a policeman's; and the law and order rhetoric sounded too much like a recruiting campaign for the unpopular men in blue.

All this is not to say that the people of Campbell Road were untouched by Mosley and the BUF. But participation was absorbed within traditions of street theatre – like the election-night jamborees at the Astoria, where the results were illuminated[39] – and betrayed no evidence of party political allegiance:

'They used to go up there [Finsbury Park], listen to him [Mosley], to get in with the fights, with the bricks – I used to meself. [A friend from the Bunk] got bashed up cos he wore a black shirt, but he wasn't in the blackshirt movement. . . . They used to like to hear old Mosley, he used to come round there now and again, didn't he? Round the Bunk . . . down the bottom of the Bunk – he had a couple of speeches down there. But he was always up Finsbury Park here.
Were there fights then?
Always fights, yeah, bricks and everything. You didn't care, you just threw 'em at anybody – didn't care who it was! They come your way you just throw 'em back.'[40]

As the inter-war period wore on, it is likely that the uneven attachment to Labour hardened somewhat. Labour in London won improvements in public assistance and welfare, especially after 1934. The continuing emigration of the middle classes from North Islington would have weakened the local Conservative propaganda. Structural changes in local industry, the waning stigma attaching to poor relief, the declining cultural traditions of violence, drunkenness and street theatre, all contributed to a reduction in alienation from society in general and working-class culture in particular. Even so, relations with political parties and ideologies remained vague and tenuous. Party allegiance was not significant in deciding how choices should be made or lives should be lived. It did not materially affect the way people viewed the world from within Campbell Road. Nor did it provide a defence against poverty or against attack on the Bunk's cultural institutions.

The last point was the most important. For the way of life in Campbell Road was under increasing attack from outside in the two decades after 1919. This was a war of attrition on both public and private fronts. And as 'legitimate' political forms of self-defence and retaliation were no part of the popular culture within Campbell Road, other forms had to be developed.

Collective self-defence

Slums . . . and the isolation of slum life, which encourages interbreeding and intensifies towards mental deficiency, may arise from racial, 'cultural' or other causes as well as from physical obstruction. However it may be caused, the more or less self-contained community of the poor and degraded which often constitutes the slum is undoubtedly a favourable breeding ground of 'mental deficiency', and a policy of dispersion of these foci of infection which is called for on other and more general grounds, should incidentally help in abating this evil.[41]

Thus the New Survey of London in 1934 resurrected the old arguments from eighty years before in the pseudo-scientific language of hereditarian psychology. The period between the wars was the dark age of British social science. From the middle-1920s to the Second World War, sociology was dominated by an extreme authoritarianism based on crude genetic theorising. The widely influential Wood Committee Report of 1929 claimed to identify a 'social problem group' of families containing 'mental defectives', who were also responsible for inordinately high levels of 'insane persons, epileptics, paupers, criminals (especially recidivists), unemployables, habitual slum dwellers, prostitutes, inebriates and other social inefficients', comprising 'approximately the lowest ten per cent in the social scale'.[42] This Committee wrote of 'the racial disaster of mental deficiency': 'the first nation to arrive at a solution of it will have an appreciable advantage.'[43]

The compulsory sterilisation of the 'unfit' was a question which fascinated the social scientists of the time and which prompted a

Departmental Committee Report in 1933 (the Brock Committee). It looked at comparable legislation in Nazi Germany and California but decided against compulsory sterilisation in Britain because of the uncertainty of predicting the outcome of procreation.[44] This was not the fantasy cult of some marginal minority. The mainstream of respectable academic sociology and social psychology could not shake itself free from this obsession until Hitler showed what the logical conclusion could be. The New Survey of London, the Social Survey of Merseyside, Carr-Saunders's and Caradog Jones's classic analysis of Britain's social structure, all made more than a genuflexion to genetic determinism.[45] Cyril Burt's enormously influential work on the educational abilities of London schoolchildren was moulded into a shape which justified his faith in inherited factors.[46] And there is considerable evidence that these views penetrated to all levels of administration of criminal justice, of sanitary and housing regulation, and of the organisation of moral reform.[47] Even the magistrate who heard many of Campbell Road's cases at the North London Police Court in the 1930s was a noted eugenicist.[48]

There is no doubt, too, that streets like Campbell Road were the very object of much of this theorising. The New Survey of London took pains to specify the role of the 'black' streets in propagating 'mental deficiency': Campbell Road, 'one of the worst streets in London', was among just 18 or so entirely 'black' streets in the 1929 poverty maps.[49] Dr Shrubsall's comment on Campbell Road has already been noted (p. 45): besides his work at the LCC he was also a member of the Wood Committee.

There is no denying the strong passions – both fear and loathing – which 'the social problem group' and its localised concentrations in 'degraded slums' provoked. But the ways in which social theory worked itself out through policy and practice are more obscure. The ground rules had been laid out before the First World War, and social policy during the next generation set itself only the task of refining them. Even so, there was hardly an aspect of life in Campbell Bunk which these refinements did not actually or potentially affect.

At the economic level, there were the ever-tightening restrictions on individual enterprise for adults and children, which have already been explored in chapter 2. The place of Campbell Road in North London's housing market was potentially affected by the Housing Act 1930, with its slum clearance and improvement area provisions, and by the Housing Act 1935, which attempted to control overcrowding (see chapter 8 below). Probably the major impact was in the policing of family life, especially in relation to juveniles. The object of much of the inter-war 'welfare' legislation was to increase the power of the state over children and adolescents, thereby weakening the rights and powers of parents. The improved state machinery intervened frequently in the family life of Campbell Road in a way which physically removed individuals from the street and its influences. This was not the 'policy of dispersion' the New Survey's author had in mind, but it sought similar objectives by more stealthy backdoor methods. Family policing filled the vacuum caused by lack of a policy initiative (like sterilisation or the clearance of areas on moral rather than sanitary grounds) to deal with 'the social problem group', and was to create its own theoretical object during the Second World War – the 'problem family'.[50] We shall return to family policing – and the struggle against it – in the next chapter.

The most significant state intervention in the life of Campbell Bunk, however, was effected by the police. The police had many hostile contacts with the people of Campbell Bunk. Street traders risked summonses for trading without a licence or for obstruction. Totters were wide open to charges of stealing by finding. Street singers and barrel organ players might be arrested for begging. All these were risks incurred daily on the streets of London.

But the home front of Campbell Road itself was a battleground. For the collective consolations of the Bunk – its street life – formed a bitterly contested issue between police and people.

It should by now be clear that the mutual consolations of Campbell Road were a perpetual affront to bourgeois society in general and to the forces of law and order in particular. There was no new legal intervention in this area between the wars. The old laws governing behaviour in the streets, most of them dating from the first twenty-five years of the Metropolitan Police, were considered good enough: it was merely a question of enforcement. Yet enforcement continued to be a contentious issue throughout the whole of Campbell Bunk's career.

It is worth stressing at this point that relations between police and people in Campbell Road were more ambivalent and complex than any slogan of the oppression of the propertyless might lead us to believe. People needed the police – to protect the weak against the strong (we have already seen some examples); to protect wives against husbands and children against parents (we shall see both in the next chapter); at times of tragedy and crisis (remember the coal-yard explosion). The London poor were as fiercely litigious as cheap police court justice would allow. They might think twice before involving police in their private and public lives; but still they did so on a massive scale.[51] And where a policeman took pains to enter into the spirit of Campbell Road then by all accounts he could become an honorary member of the community. Like Ginger ('Mister' to his face) Mullins, 'of great physique and as strong as an ox', who would put his helmet and belt on his neatly-folded jacket before interfering in a street fight 'with fist and boot'. Remarkably, 'no one would ever think of stealing [his uniform] whilst he was restoring law and order'.[52] So even where police interfered with the enjoyments of Campbell Bunk, the meaning of these interventions might be equivocal, depending on whom was most affected and how: like this example, from a street gaming school around 1930:

> 'And Crackers [a policeman] just put his head round the corner.
> But they wasn't pitching up then, they was throwing dice.
> He put his head round the corner, and I see him. And a relation
> of mine, Mrs Spencer . . . she was always hard up. She's just
> going down the shop to get a bit on the tick. Funny this is. . . .
> Anyrate, so he sees this woman coming down the road with
> somebody else, and he made a dart. Course, they left the
> money on the floor. He got up to my relation: "Help yerself!"
> And to the other woman: "Got yer rent?" "No." "Help
> yerself!" Sort of police they were. Very good. . . . And that's
> why I used to like the police.'[53]

Now whether or not it happened just like that is not as important as the internal meanings the incident had for Walter Spencer, the witness. It was Bert Lax's and other 'rich' gamblers' money on the ground. The policeman thus defends the poorest against the relatively well-off. He does not – as he might have done – pocket the money himself, but acts like a Robin Hood in blue. Yet the final judgment is inconsistent with a more sinister contact with the police which Walter later experienced, to be recounted in its place.

So even here, among one of the beliefs most strongly held to within Campbell Road, there were contradictions. But in general public opinion was clear: the police were to be avoided always, assisted never, inconvenienced where possible. 'You wasn't allowed to talk to a policeman, you know, *I* wasn't, even if I was young.'[54] Fred Neal, the builder, used to complain to the police about the gambling schools under his window: 'proper copper, proper copper's boy, Fred Neal.'[55] 'They didn't like police people. The police used to come round in twos and threes and stand on the corner there.'[56]

The origins of this avoidance are plain enough to understand. There was the general feeling that the police were not on your side, that they were there to protect other people against the likes of you: 'the hired enforcers of authority headed by the hated, yes really hated, bullying fat cozpots who strutted arrogantly upon our turf,' as Jack Duncan's son recalled them.[57] There was deep mistrust of the police, their elephantine intelligence systems and their almost limitless powers. This feeling of powerlessness against police authority was widespread – the police had to make seven arrests a week, and it might as well be you as anyone else;[58] they needed no authority to make a search other than their warrant cards.[59] These abuses were more imagined than real, fuelled by a wide-spread ignorance of civil rights, but there is no doubt that unlawful exercise of police power against people in Campbell Road gave genuine cause for mistrust and fear: 'fitting up' young men under the 'suspected person' laws or for street gaming; illegal detention in cells for a few hours, ostensibly as a practical joke; physical violence in the street and, more especially, in the police station after arrest.[60]

All this was true even when the individual policeman was known to, and even respected by, the people of the Bunk. That a policeman was known by his nickname – Crackers, Snakey, Three Twos, Shuffles, Nancy, Treacle, Slippery, or Fire-engine Jack – did not save him from abuse or even assault if the time was right. And for the local police force, Campbell Bunk was not a safe place to go alone:

it was an unwritten law that in the dark the road was patrolled in pairs. No special instructions were issued to this effect, it was done solely because of the notoriety of the inhabitants.[61]

The reputation of the Bunk was thus a source of fear for the local police and it was part of police-station folklore – as it was of the Bunk itself and those outside who knew of it – that at some time in the past a policeman had been stuffed down a drain in Campbell Road, later dying from his injuries.[62] Myth or reality, police fears were not without cause. For although policemen would walk through the streets in daylight on their own, when they tried to do so at night they would not always reach the other end:

P.C. Mills, 1057Y, deposed that at 10.40 on Friday night he was on duty in Campbell Road, when he saw the accused and two other men. Frinton came up behind him and said, 'I can lift you'. He replied, 'What is the game?' and requested him to go away, whereupon he was struck in the face. Frinton was closed with and arrested, when the other men came to his rescue, threw witness to the ground and kicked him. After a struggle witness succeeded in blowing his whistle for assistance, when one of the crowd snatched the whistle and broke the chain. Frinton was taken out of police custody and all the men got away.

In sentencing to hard labour two of the men who were later arrested at their Campbell Road homes, the magistrate commented:

'I am not going to have the police in this district assaulted, especially when they are alone.'[63]

Now it is quite conceivable that there was a cycle of violence, bred of mistrust and fear on both sides. It is likely that the police, because of their vulnerability, over-reacted. Crackers Pollard had a reputation for using his stick wildly whenever he felt himself threatened.[64] And in 1913, a labourer of no fixed abode, complained of being beaten by police in the Bunk: 'I don't know how I got to Campbell Road. I had not been there for twelve months, and whenever I do go the police are down on me. I never get locked up in any other neighbourhood.'[65]

On the other hand, there were men in the street who had a reputation for taking no nonsense from the police. There was James Murphy, a costermonger in his late 30s, whose wife Kate later took up with Freddie Creed and was one of the fighting women mentioned in the last chapter; he had lived in Queensland Road and seems to have been in the Bunk from about 1921 to 1925. Georgey Manning, a meat porter who was 24 in 1928; Sidney Shapland, a carman, a year or so older than Manning; Bill Traviss; Bill Bones, a 29-year-old labourer in 1930; Harry James, whom we will meet again; and, of course, Bert Lax, all had numerous tussles with the police, frequently in Campbell Road, at various times in their careers: 'I helped Cecil Pollard to bring in Lax, frog-marched, head cut to ribbons with truncheon cuts, still fighting.'[66] Another difficult man for the police to handle was Pongo Blackman, as in this case when he was arrested for an assault on a PC at 1.30 a.m. on a Sunday at Campbell Road:

The constable explained there had been a disturbance in which another officer had been seriously injured. The prisoner was very violent, and the witness fearing that he might be injured, took out his truncheon to defend himself. With the assistance of another constable, he got the prisoner to the station.

Detective Mountfield said that the prisoner was a violent man and had been convicted of assaulting the police, and had had five years' penal servitude.[67]

The occasion for this assault, remembering Blackman's moonlight trade of gaming croupier, was probably interference with one of the Bunk's time-honoured pleasures. For it was intervention of this kind which risked provoking collective self-defence by residents on a grand scale.

Police suppression of gaming, street betting and other unlawful behaviour in Campbell Road was difficult for a variety of reasons. As far as many in the Bunk were concerned, there was nothing wrong with these activities in the first place, and so the police were enforcers of an entirely alien moral code. This applied in many other streets to the enforcement of the Street Betting Act 1906, which accounted, it was said, for much of the unpopularity of the police force in working-class areas.[68] Betting and gambling were illegal not merely because of the obstruction of the carriageway and pavement – interfering in theory with the free passage of commodities and labour-power – but also because of the drain on working-class incomes they allegedly caused. Gambling, like drink, produced pauperism. Yet we have seen how gambling was a perfectly rational response to the daily struggle for subsistence shared by so many in the Bunk. And the fight against boredom, together with the cultivation of a style of behaviour which symbolically rejected the society which had rejected the Bunk, combined in a fierce resistance to interference in collective pleasures and consolations by the killjoys in blue.

Interference was watched for and guarded against. For the gambling schools there were the 'doggers-out', usually children or youths, posted at corners: 'they could smell a policeman.'[69] Street bookies or 'runners' were protected by a network of touts who would perform the same function, 'showing out' with hand-signals, or shouting to the bookie if time was short: touts could be arrested for warning bookies in this way.[70]

When a raid did take place, usually on Sunday afternoons but sometimes late at night, the first response was to run rather than stand and fight. Running was facilitated by the Campbell Road custom of allowing anyone fleeing the police in these circumstances into rooms, pretending they were one of the family or a visiting friend. Open front doors and broken backyard walls helped the passage from one house to another. 'It was very difficult to catch them, as all the street doors were open in that road,' complained a PC in 1927.[71]

When arrests *were* made, then all hell might break loose. There were collective assaults on police in Campbell Road reported in the local press in 1920, 1927, 1928, 1930 (twice), and 1938 (in Seven Sisters Road, when a Bunk character had been arrested). Many other occasions never reached the local press, but the 1928 case might serve as an example of those which did. Early on a Sunday morning in August a large gambling school had been in progress under a street lamp at the Paddington Street junction. It is not clear whether the police raided, or whether two PCs on duty interfered. Pongo Blackman and a 27-year-old coster called William Bennett were arrested. 'Blackman immediately became very violent and a hostile crowd gathered round.' The PC who arrested Blackman alleged in court that

> after he arrested Blackman the crowd attacked him from all quarters. Three times he fell to the ground and twice the man got away. On the second occasion he had to release him because he was in agony as the result of a kick he received in the stomach whilst on the ground. He lost his whistle, his tunic and his trousers were torn and he was bitten on the hand. . . . 'I was punched about by people in the crowd whom I don't know.'

George Bucknell, the shopkeeper, tried to get Blackman away from the PC and was truncheoned for his trouble. A PC still had hold of Bennett.

> but the circumstances were such that when Bennett gave his word of honour that he would surrender himself at the police station and get out of the trouble, witness released him and went to the assistance

of the PC who had Blackman. Bennett had only been out of prison three weeks. Blackman claimed he was set about in the police station: ' "They all got on to me and knocked me to the ground, and knocked my teeth out." '[72]

According to Bennett, 'The crowd referred to by the police consisted of "old women, girls and kids" '; the police put it at 250-strong and only men were arrested. The role of women in these disturbances is nowhere evidenced in the reported police prosecutions, yet other evidence reveals that they did, indeed, play a large part in the collective self-defence of Campbell Road. In many ways it is likely that police found the women hard to deal with, possibly being reluctant to arrest them, and face an embarassing public parade for the half-mile or so to the station. And possibly, too, the women played on this reluctance, protecting their more vulnerable male partners and neighbours:

> One of our boys [i.e. a policeman] . . . had been called to an internal dispute in one of the houses between man and woman, I won't say man and wife, that's doubtful. He must have had some difficulty in squaring it up and taken some time. As he came out of the house there was a gambling school right on the pavement outside. Jack cheerfully grabbed one of them, but for some reason or other the local women folk objected and tried to release him. He had a really rough time under a pile of women and came out with uniform all torn and face scratched, but still had his man.[73]

Some women, however, devised other means of insulting the police. One PC, walking through the street on an afternoon during the early 1930s, heard a shout of ' "Hi, copper." ' He looked round to see a woman offering him one of her breasts through an open window, to the loud laughter of her friends, until one said: ' "Put it away you daft cow. Do you want to get us knocked off?" '[74]

Interference with street theatre – fights, drunken behaviour, and bonfires – provoked more collective resistance:

> Bonfires in the street were a daily occurrence. One Police Superintendent, passing the street one day about mid-day, saw a big bonfire in the middle of the street. He marched up to the crowd round the fire and demanded they extinguish it. He had forgotten he was dressed in plain clothes, not uniform, and was unknown to the crowd. They became hostile to him and threatened to put him on the fire. He wisely beat a hasty retreat to Holloway Police Station where he blew 'his top' to the Station Officer. For weeks after a P.C. had to patrol it all the time to keep constant law and order.[75]

And Guy Fawkes night continued to be a major event in the street's calendar until the Second World War:

> I remember Bonfire night in 1937. The street was alight from one end to the other, doors, window frames, sofas blazing away and the Fire Brigade were unable to do anything. Hoses were cut and Police had to stand by in case of incidents. The next year arrangements were made for a number of P.C.s, myself and Inspector to patrol the road from about 4.p.m.

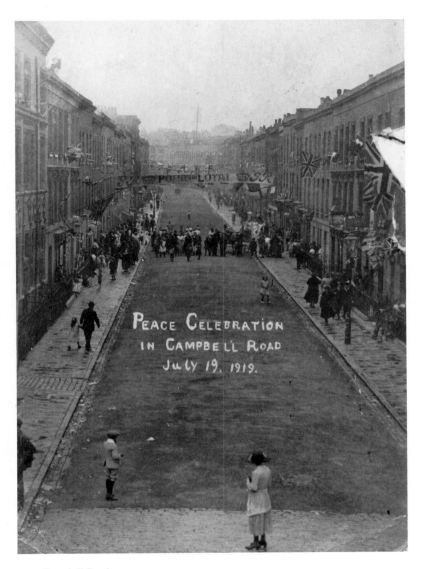

PEACE CELEBRATION
IN CAMPBELL ROAD
July 19, 1919.

1 Campbell Road, 1919
Campbell Road from Seven Sisters Road, taken at the start of the Peace Day
celebrations of 19 July 1919. The Poor But Loyal bedsheet banner, Union
Jacks and bunting are much in evidence at this bottom end. On the right,
the lodging-house lamp of 10–12 Campbell Road can just be made out,
advertising beds for men at 5*d* a night. It is a wet day but a small boy on
the left has no shoes. The little crowd under the banner probably surround
a barrel organ.

2 Campbell Road, May 1935
The bedsheet banner is out again, this time for the Silver Jubilee of King George V. The *Daily Mirror* used this photograph to exemplify patriotic enthusiasm in even the poorest areas. The children are turned out in their best clothes: none is barefoot, in contrast to the Peace Celebrations just 16 years before.

3 Musher Gates selling with a donkey, c.1919
The 17-year-old Musher is in front of his donkey cart, selling veg in Andover Road. He had been born in the Bunk, considered himself 'out of' Queensland Road or 'the Land', but was living alone in a room at Nailour Street, a poor street by the Caledonian Road market, when this was taken. The man at the donkey's head, a Pearly King's son from Slaney Place, Brand Street, was an army deserter and was arrested within minutes of the photo being taken.

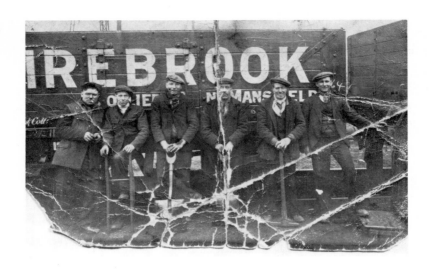

4 *Coal heavers*, c.*1930*
Coal shifting from rail trucks to waggons and lorries was a major source of
winter employment for the casual unskilled labour reserve in Holloway. This
is Musher Gates's (far right) crew at Drayton Park coal yards.

5 *'We are the Campbell Bunk Girls!'*, *1935*
Five Bunk girls, three of them sisters, at the top end of the road during the
Silver Jubilee celebrations. Honey jars with candles in them stand in for fairy
lights. The girl on the right is 16.

6 *'The Hounds'*, c.*1936*
Teenage boys used to gather at the corner of Paddington Street and Campbell Road, outside the old kip house at 47a. It was here, too, that the largest gambling 'schools would be held, but here the youths are waiting for something to turn up. Walters's grocer's shop is on the corner behind them.

7 *Campbell Road mother:* c.*1930*
A street bookmaker with her 9-year-old daughter, the last of 11 by two marriages. The girl had deformed feet through having been burned during an accident as a baby, when her mother was drunk.

*8 Campbell Road
daughters : 1   c.1918*
Three factory girls from
Turners' engineering
factory (Blackstock
Road) at the end of the
First World War. The
two standing are from
Campbell Road, the
other from Fonthill
Road.

*9 Campbell Road
daughters : 2   c.1920*
A 16-year-old factory
hand at the Star Brush
factory in Eden Grove,
taken shortly before
she left her mother's
Campbell Road home for
good.

10 Fathers and sons, c.1938
Campbell Road men on a beano to Southend. Like many other communities, men and women had separate one-day annual holidays, mothers and daughters taking theirs around the same time of year (early September).

11 Brand Street, c.1924
Built 30–40 years before Campbell Road, Brand Street was typical of London slums cleared between the wars. The contrast in appearance is plain enough, but the populations of Brand Street and Campbell Road were very similar, with some movement between the two streets. Brand Street was demolished during the late 1920s.

12 Queensland Road, 1956
29–41 Queensland Road, shortly before clearance by the LCC. The Land's
larger tenement houses were neighbours to less pretentious two-storey
terraces, especially in the blind courts to the north of Queensland Road. Like
Campbell Road, these 1850s houses reveal their first respectable origins.

13 George's Road, 1962
The oldest part of George's Road, dating from Napoleonic times, was cleared
by the LCC at the same time as Brand Street. These tenement houses, built
in the 1880s, were intended for letting by the floor or by the room.

14 Campbell Road back room, 1955
The first floor back room at 27 Campbell Road. In 1938 this room was the
kitchen of a three-roomed dwelling occupied by 2 adults and 4 children. Its
dilapidated state and antiquated furniture point to a long history as a
furnished room.

15 Demolition, 1956
The bottom end during slum clearance, August 1946. The top end went the
same way a year later.

We were able to assist the local authority dustmen to remove
any rubbish that was being prepared for a bonfire and the
Firemen to put out any fires that started. About 10 p.m. the
rain came down, and as all was quiet we decided to withdraw
but the residents had the last laugh, for suddenly the Inspector
in Charge was struck full in the chest with a bag of flour
which burst, and one can imagine the laughter that caused to
the residents.[76]

Campbell Road was not unique in playing host to incidents like
that, but as so often it was exceptional. 'Hostile crowds' preventing
arrests were common features of London's lower-working-class
areas in the 1920s, less so in the 1930s.[77] But generally they
occurred in the main roads of the poorer areas than the backstreets
– Holloway Road, Upper Street, Essex Road, Caledonian Road.
Isolated incidents from residential streets did occur – one thousand
people attacked police raiding a betting house at Half Moon Cres-
cent, Islington, in 1920, for example[78] – but reports over several
years of hostile crowds in the same street were rare. In Holloway,
only Queensland Road rivalled the Bunk, but it appears not to
have matched it.[79] And although anti-police struggles within the
Bunk fell off during the 1930s – as did assaults on police by
Campbell Road residents generally – it is clear from the evidence
above that the street was still a lively and threatening place for
policemen until the last war at least.

But policemen were not the only people to attempt to impose
an alien and unacceptable code of behaviour on the Bunk's way of
life and to be resisted in the process. Organised religion, through
churches, missions, and youth clubs sought to penetrate the lives
of Campbell Road's residents in a variety of ways. Once more,
we shall return to the most significant aspects of this process in
the following three chapters. We will see there that, in many cases,
this penetration was allowed to take place, indeed welcomed in
significant ways. Even so, interference with the public pleasures
of the Bunk, either by preaching publicly a conflicting morality or
by imposing a different behavioural code in return for material or
cultural benefits – was a contested area.

Perhaps the Lennox Road Mission entered most into the life of
Campbell Road. It appears to have been treated with almost
universal respect. Its old-fashioned evangelising, weekly summer-
time street services in Campbell Road (twice a year only in the
other streets in its catchment area), was tolerated with general
good humour.[80] Its youth leaders inspired loyalty, affection, even
reverence. Yet someone, it was said, stole a watch from Henry

Speller, the most loved of them all, some time around 1930.[81] Nothing was sacred.

Even less so was the anglican church of St Anne's, at Pooles Park. The Church of England was less useful to the people of Campbell Road than the Congregationalists, Salvation Army, or Roman Catholics. The building itself was a haunt for young children who used its grounds as a battlefield for gang fights.[82] In 1927, children and youths seem to have waged a battle against the building itself, breaking over 150 panes of glass in a three or four week summer period:

> The damage caused to St. Anne's Church, Pooles Park, by children throwing stones at the windows and in other ways mutilating the church, has become so extensive that the Rural Dean of Islington . . . has applied to . . . New Scotland yard for special protection. . . . About a week ago a large iron gate at the west entrance was removed from its hinges and badly broken. This is thought to be the work of a gang of youths.[83]

The YMCA Red Triangle Club in Pooles Park – remember its objectives regarding Campbell Road in the 1890s – also came in for trouble. It seems to have been a little more discriminating in its membership requirements than Lennox Road Mission, although some boys from Campbell Road went there for boxing and other sports. Others plainly felt excluded by accident of residence:

> 'And that's when we tried to join the club, we couldn't join the club and it gave us the needle, you know, and we felt like smashing their windows in.'
> *Why wouldn't they let you join?*
> 'Because we used to be down the Bunk, you see, they'd think you were all trouble.'[84]

Elsewhere many boys did smash club windows in and it would be surprising if the YMCA failed to suffer in the same way.[85] But the only incident which has come down to us involved a more subtle retribution. In June 1933 four young men from Campbell Road (aged 18 to 22), broke into the club and stole a silver cup, drum-major's staff, a safe and cash, worth in all £65. When they were arrested they had broken the cup down for melting. Only one of the boys had been a member – Charles Snell, the 18-year-old, who

was a good sportsman. He apparently left because he fell out of work. It was an unwritten law that those in work had a levy amongst themselves to pay the fares of their fellow football players who were out of work. Snell apparently dropped out because he did not like accepting the levy.[86]

Whatever the precise reasons behind this incident, in tactical terms it turned defence into attack. It would be difficult to disentangle the motive of material gain from the other overlaying objectives of a foray like this − retaliation for rejection, taking the more favoured down a peg by stealing their symbols of pride and achievement. But given Campbell Road's traditions and reputation, and the worldviews of many who lived there, it would be surprising if those motives were entirely absent.

Not all crime, not even all thefts, need be attended by this complexity of motives. Yet theft could fit well within the politics and practice of rejection. It could become a form of struggle − inarticulate and inchoate, no doubt; but a form which provided the only way of hitting back hard at those who were vaguely felt to be the oppressors.

Crime as struggle

This is a highly contentious area, so it might be best to begin with a less disputable area of struggle where unlawful means were used by those without legitimate power. This was the grinding subterranean war between landlord and tenant, waged for generations in Campbell Road with weapons assigned, as it were, with the right to occupy.[87] Moonlight flits to avoid arrears of rent were common.[88] Thefts of bedding from furnished rooms had to be guarded against by marking sheets and blankets with the proprietor's name in indelible ink. Even the furniture was not safe from these depredations: when Tubby Nicholls gave a tenant of two year's standing notice to quit in 1938 the tenant retaliated by taking with him 'a bedstead, spring, overlay, pillow, chair, table, washstand and fender' to new rooms in Isledon Road.[89] Property could be vandalised, with the object of annoying the landlord or for subsistence or even for enlivening a Guy Fawkes night:

> I have heard of persons draw the shavings and straw out of the palliasses and break an old chair up to make a fire in the grate and I have also known them to break up W.C. and room doors for the fire, flooring in passages, stairs, hand rails, doors off cupboards, or anything in the shape of wood that will burn. I

have also known closet pans and traps, water waste
preventors, lead piping, zinc gutters, and even iron stoves to
have been stolen from houses [in Campbell Road].[90]

That was 1908, but there were many similar occurrences between
the wars.[91]

Then there were assaults on rent collectors, kept to a minimum
by the large numbers of rentiers or agents in the street, but occur-
ring none the less. In 1920, a 34-year-old 'carboniser' from
Campbell Road was charged with assaulting the elderly Arthur
Norris. Norris

said he went to the house to collect rents, when the prisoner
refused to pay unless his room was done up. He was told that
the repairs would be executed in due course. Subsequently the
prisoner attacked him in the street, and striking him about
the face and head rendered him unconscious.[92]

Action like this could lead to properties being abandoned by landlords. Ted Nesbitt told his son that some houses had been abandoned in this way at the end of the First World War and had
been taken over by the Bunk's resident landlords.[93] There is no
corroborating evidence but it was not an implausible tale. It was
also apparently difficult to collect rates from Campbell Road. Jane
Munby's stepfather, a burly coal heaver originally from the Caledonian Road area, went to prison 'two or three times' for failure
to pay rates on the rooms he lived in.[94] And Bill Dashett was
another who had little truck with the local bureaucracy, as much
through wanting to be awkward as inability to pay: once paying
in halfpennies and once sprinkling the collector with the mauve
dye he used to colour his flowers.[95] Dashett was a coster, and we
have seen already how close to the pinching winds of 'justice' the
street people of Campbell Road had always to sail. All were more
vulnerable if they happened to be adolescents. And all were marked
by the curse of Campbell Bunk, the stigma of living in 'the worst
street in North London'.

The battle for subsistence took place in an arena where the
barriers between legal and illegal were hard to discern. In the
struggle between landlord and tenant, the vulnerability of the landlord's property was used to strike back at an otherwise unassailable
power. The role of the police as aggressor against Campbell Road's
street culture did not foster respect for their other duties as protectors of property. The ownership of property, in any event, did
not endear the poor to the possessors, if widely-held views on

shopkeepers and moneylenders in Campbell Road are anything to go by. And other popularly held ideals of a right to equality, the oppressiveness of regulations, and looking after your own interests first, could all encourage an unconcern for legality and the niceties of its forms.

It was in this context that some crime, especially theft, became a weapon of struggle, for serving the interests of members of one class position against members of others. It need not have been articulated in this way but that does not mean that theft was always an unconscious weapon. For it was a way of hitting back, not so much at an individual, but at the very structure which created the position of powerful and powerless, richer and poorer, in the first place.

Even within the lumpenproletariat, theft need not necessarily take on this particular element of struggle against opposing class positions. Some professional thieves may start out this way, stealing as much from a sense of resentment about their own disadvantages and the relative advantages of others as from motives of calculated gain. But although they may continue to use class inequalities to justify their depredations – like George Smithson, 'Raffles in Real Life'[96] – the only reason they steal from the rich is because they gain most from the theft.

So just when was this oppositional element of struggle most apparent in thefts and other crimes against property committed by people from Campbell Road? First we could cite the collective endeavours which were as much a practical joke on the propertied classes – and how well that fitted in to Bunk culture – as a means of financial gain. As when ten or a dozen youths from Campbell Road stripped an empty house in Highgate of its furnishings, bringing everything portable on barrows back to the Bunk over a number of days. When the police raided houses they retrieved carpets from floors which had never before touched even lino.[97] Then take the following example from the mid-1930s:

One day a well-dressed man drove a new expensive car out of Seven Sisters Road into the Bunk and parked it. Standing nearby was about half a dozen Bunkites who specialised in collecting car spares for a living. . . . "Will my car be safe here for an hour whilst I do some business in Finsbury Park?". . . "Yes, guv," said one, "We'll look after it for you," said another. "Oh thank you very much," he said and went away. No sooner had he gone than the Bunkites set to work on the car, an open tourer. When he returned over an hour later, as he turned the corner into the Bunk and looked towards his car he staggered with shock. The Bunkites had looked after it all right. All four wheels were missing and the chassis was resting on piles of bricks and boxes. For the rest of the car everything on it that was moveable had been taken leaving virtually just a chassis and body. Naturally when Police investigated no one knew anything and the [remains] were removed by a breakdown crane loading it onto a lorry.'[98]

I suspect that this oppositional motive attached itself to much of the stealing from shops which was such a distinctive feature of theft by young men (and to a much lesser extent young women) from Campbell Road. Some of this will be dealt with in detail in the chapter on young men's lives, but it might be noted here that many of the victims were local small shopkeepers. In early 1929 the police reported that Finsbury Park shopkeepers had written to the Commissioner seeking protection from youths snatching money from tills.[99] And that summer, in prosecuting men from Campbell Road and Pooles Park, police claimed that the

> Prisoners were two of a gang which infested Holloway, and had broken into shops owned by very poor people who could ill afford to lose what they had and who did not prosecute because they were in fear of their lives.[100]

Now getting their own back on shopkeepers might only have been a small part of the motives of thefts like these. But the antagonism towards shopkeepers provided an internal legitimation. And for the majority of people from Campbell Road, the concept of 'very poor' shopkeepers 'who could ill afford to lose what they had' would have been an incredible contradiction in terms.[101]

Occasionally, thefts from shopkeepers had a communal value and were done in a way which made them seem less like stealing and more like 'fiddling'. Walter Spencer's brother served in a Campbell Road corner shop as a lad:

> 'When people come in, he knew they had nothing, he'd give 'em say change for half a crown for a penny, that sort of thing. He's not catching nobody but he used to give them extra food.'

His other brother did the same for people from the Bunk when he worked for a bigger provision dealer's in Seven Sisters Road.[102] And so did Musher Gates for people queueing outside the 'grubber', a relieving station near King's Cross, handing out boxes of kippers from his employer's van.[103]

These last cases involved thefts from employers, and here too, in general, motives were clearly more complicated than mere need or greed. Legitimation was provided by the feeling that the employer could afford it relative to the employee; that theft was a means of getting your own back for injustices suffered, especially for getting less than a fair day's pay for a fair day's work; and that certain perquisites were yours as of right anyway.[104] Like the 63-year-old railway porter sentenced to one month's imprisonment for stealing a bottle of port, property of the Great Northern Railway Co.: ' "it was the first time and hard luck to be caught so near Christmas." '[105] Like the several coalmen caught embezzling their employers of cash or coal.[106] And, perhaps most of all, like the charwomen of Campbell Bunk.

In few jobs can the direct comparison of life-styles between the comfortably-off and the poor have been more easily apparent. The differences would not have been made less noticeable by the mistress-servant relationship, which provided a pointed contrast between the life-chances of women (especially mothers) in the Bunk and married women and their families outside. It was a contrast which must have been hard to bear. These richer homes undoubtedly tempted women in need: but it would have been difficult to detach from such thefts a feeling that the victims could afford it – almost, deserved it. Lou Porter pleaded guilty to stealing a pair of lace curtains from her employer's house at Roseleigh Avenue, Highbury ('middle-class and wealthy' according to the 1929 New Survey).[107] She stole the curtains on her third visit. Investigations during her remand in custody revealed that her 'home conditions were terrible, and she had been doing charing for two shillings a day. The Magistrate – two shillings! That's about the pre-war rate.'[108] A year later in 1924, Mary Eleanor Baron, 52, was charged with stealing clothes worth £6 from 5 Adolphus Road, Finsbury Park ('middle-class and wealthy' too).[109] Her employer had recently returned from India and when Mary got the job (two days a week at 5s a day plus dinner and tea) she had not given Campbell Road as her address. Within a month some sheets and a nightdress had gone missing but Mrs Baron denied any knowledge of their whereabouts. When the other clothes disappeared, about a month later, the police were called. Her daughter, single and pregnant, was charged with receiving the clothes and pawning them for 14s. While Mary was remanded, she was also charged with the theft of a ring worth £10 from a bank clerk in Barnet, almost certainly another employer. On this charge she was sentenced to three weeks' hard labour.[110] And there were similar cases reported during the 1920s.[111]

If there was a subjective oppositional motive in thefts like these it was based predominantly on class – retaliation for the injuries of inequality of wealth and power. Later we shall meet with similar motives overlaid by gender in the culture of young male thieves. But whether subjectively motivated in class terms or not, some crime was objectively part of a struggle for subsistence, a struggle necessitated by, and part of, class relations. The material deprivation caused by unemployment or poverty was not necessarily sufficient in itself for sufferers to take a way out through theft. It was the lumpen blend of egalitarianism and individualism which forged the pass key. For some who desperately sought a subsistence within the lumpen class position, the politics and ideologies of the Bunk provided a legitimation for casual theft (and some other crimes) as a natural ally to casual labour or irregular economic enterprise.[112]

In effect, the ideologies of individualism and egalitarianism could provide a rationalisation for actions condemned by prevailing morality. Albert Quinn, a young thief from the Caledonian Road area who lodged in Campbell Road on and off for a few months around 1933, justified his criminal career like this:

'Why should I be singled out to walk the places – nowhere to go, nothing to eat? Mother at home crying, Dad's out of work, and you see all these people with lovely horses coming down Holloway Road there, and always going out shopping with bags of servants – never used to seem right to me, somehow. Something seemed to be wrong, something's missing, you know, something's gotta be put right. I used to rebel against this. I used to take things as a right. If my brothers and sisters were at home crying, they got nothing to eat, and there's a baker's shop just round the corner full of bread!? *Course* I'm gonna nick some bread. It's mine! I want some.'[113]

How much this is all a rationalisation achieved long after the event is frankly unclear. There are similar examples from the autobiographies of English thieves, but then they might all serve that same function.[114] We can only guess what went through the heads of Campbell Road's street people when, on their travels, they spotted an opportunity for unlawful gain and seized it. Like the totters who raided empty houses and builders' sites in particular.[115] Or like George James, the travelling knife grinder, who dabbled in stolen property which he hid under the floor boards, Fagin-like, from his light-fingered sons.[116]

Perhaps the best way of capturing the flavour of the Bunk's combination of poverty, worklessness, economic individualism, and criminal enterprise is to examine some of the theft cases reported in just one year. I have chosen 1925, if anything a rather quiet year but one which leaves the later period free for consideration in the chapter on young men. It gives us, too, an indication of the way the lumpen economy of the Bunk, described in chapter 2, extended into the collective organisation of thieving among neighbours.

Two young women, one 19 and married with a baby, the other pregnant, were convicted of shoplifting, stealing a handbag. They and another girl from Campbell Road had all been convicted of a similar offence the year before. By now the woman who was pregnant had moved from the Bunk and lived in Upper Holloway. The police investigated the home conditions of the married woman and confirmed they were 'very, very poor. She lives in one of the worst streets in North London.'[117] A 44-year-old labourer, who 'had done no work for some time and had been convicted of larceny on three occasions', got three months' hard labour for stealing 20s 6d from his son's employer by means of a trick.[118] He was to get a similar sentence 18 months later for stealing £3 5s he had collected for his employer.[119] A 22-year-old costermonger, and the girl he was courting from Cumberland Street, a rough turning in Lower Holloway, were charged with stealing a gold watch and ring from a servant's bedroom at Roman Road, and with robbing a gas meter at the girlfriend's house.[120] A year before he had been convicted of stealing a bicycle with two other Campbell Road youths, and of stealing a watch and chain from a room in Fonthill Road; three years later he would be convicted of stealing a violin, clothes and other articles; and a year after that of stealing 5s by means of a trick from a Campbell Road paperseller. The magistrate asked of the police: ' "Can you say anything good of him? Witness: I am afraid it is an impossibility. . . . Even lodging-house keepers had turned him out because nothing could be left about where he was." '[121] Whatever 'oppositional' character this man's thieving might originally have contained had obviously been subsumed in a habit which did not discriminate in its victims. Finally, three Campbell Road youths, 18 and 19 years old, were charged with assaulting and attempting to rob a Tottenham Lane tobacconist and for robbing a gas meter elsewhere.[122]

There was another way to struggle for subsistence outside the amalgam of casual labour, economic enterprise and casual theft. It could still be illegal but it was less dangerous and there were no tangible victims. This was the manipulation of dependence on state benefits or organised charity. With skill and care, almost artistry, dependence on others could be turned into another form of economic independence.

This was not so, of course, for even the majority of those who took advantage, from time to time, of state or Poor Law benefits to which they were not legally entitled. The court cases reported in the local press were few and far between, just four in 21 years. In practice, these fiddles were more common than this would suggest, as other evidence makes plain.[123] Even so, the reported cases concern the smallest of small beer – 9s benefit unlawfully obtained by a man selling newspapers for his uncle; an old man failing to state an employer's pension in claiming out relief;[124] and there is no reason to think that large frauds were carried on over a number of years.

There was the odd case of assault on a relieving officer,[125] but those who struggled successfully against the regulation of state allowances had to use more subtle methods. They had also to spread their nets more widely to cover the range of benefits offered in return for humility and humbug by religious organisations. As for the London working class as a whole, organised religion touched the souls of Campbell Bunk hardly at all: but the Bunk touched clerical coffers frequently and without shame. Jack Duncan, though typical of no one, might represent here the more accomplished of Campbell Road's charity performers:

'And this is where my old man displayed both his contempt for the higher-ups – the *toffs* as he used to call them – and his natural con-artist's appreciation for the suitable stage-setting. . . . Shabby-genteel was my old man's *forte*: impoverished rather than hard-up; cheerful courage in the face of adversity. . . . [My] old man organised my mother to scrub and scour, to create the general image of poverty, hunger, and sparkling cleanliness – to show that Jack's little brood had no intention of succumbing to the squalor and lethargic helplessness abounding on all sides of this little oasis of culture. To emphasise the cultural angle, Poppa had painstakingly cherished the dozen or so reminders of our former happy state of affluence before falling from grace in the shape of his library, from which he stoutly refused to be parted. Odd titles which the old villain had culled discriminately from totters' Sunday markets in which they displayed the gems and plums of their weekly gleanings from

the totting with their barrows. They'd put them on the
pavements outside their houses. Titles like *The Mill on the Floss*,
Tom Hardy's *Tess of the D'Urbervilles*, Blackmoor's *Lorna
Doone*, *Cricket on the Hearth*, Marie Corelli's *The Sorrows of
Satan*, Hall Caine's *The Christian*, *The Manxman* and *The
Bondman*, etc. Predominance of place in our library was given
to titles more obviously with biblical connotations – *The Way
of the Transgressor* would have been most appropriate. The
book-case itself had been painstakingly crafted from an
eggbox, lovingly finished in two pennorth of mahogony-stain
varnish. . . . When old Goodrum [the Relieving Officer]
knocked at the street door, two knocks for us on the first floor,
not for him the bald invitation to "Come on up!" No, the old
man went down in person, to escort this distinguished
visitor. . . . Short of pinning a poster with "Down With
Drink!" on the door, old Jack went through the card. His
quiet, well-behaved kids – which we were, incidentally – and
attractive wife who knew her place well in the background, a
tidy home, and the *pièce de resistance*, Jack himself. Respectful,
without the nauseating obsequiousness which Goodrum
generally encountered; well-spoken, and cheerful and
optimistic, and paying lip-service to all the things which he
had no use for. Old Jack was the archetype of what the smug,
sanctimonious, Christian Board of Guardians – as a satellite of
the larger world of respectable society – stood for. He *was*
the deserving poor. For days after such an encounter Jack, to
our unalloyed delight, . . . was in high good humour. No
kicks and cuffs, and he was even civil to our mother. Well,
whether he took greater pleasure from the few bob he milked
the Guardians for or, more feasibly, as I'm inclined to suppose,
it was his artist's appreciation for his polished performance
. . . I'll never know, but old Jack was born to the
greasepaint. . . . You see, apart from that, I've always called
myself a Catholic. Until one time, fairly recently, "How did I
get this silly nom-de-plume of a Catholic?" And I realised it
was cos me father – at that time churches – the [Society] of
Saint Vincent de Paul, they were all very active in going
around among the deserving poor. And my father was creating
these little images, for any religion – it could have been the
Muslims or whatever – but it happened to be in this instance
the [Catholics]. The run of the mill was . . . each of the
churches around Christmas time used to run treats and so on,
and the old man used to steer us into them, not aggressively
– in fact we missed quite a few that other kids got – but

nonetheless he was always manipulating according to his own particular designs, and the Catholic Church was one he decided was about the most benevolent or beneficent. And he encouraged me to join the Catholic Scouts for *that* reason – well he didn't encourage me, he said, "Get in that lot!" and that was it. He was a survivor.'[126]

There is some evidence of how successful the wily Jack could be at these games. His wife was arrested whilst singing in the streets, convicted of begging and put on probation. Jack, the Autocrat of the Boozer, was also ruthless at his own hearth, capable of beating his wife mercilessly. Once – and it might have been at this time – he broke her ribs and on another occasion his son remembered him dragging her around the room by her hair. Because of this or similar ill-treatment, she left home, consequently breaking the terms of her probation order, and was arrested and imprisoned in Holloway. The three children were sent to the workhouse and then, because of the 'Catholic' connection, the two boys were sent off to a home run by the Sisters of Charity of Saint Vincent de Paul. There they stayed for just over twelve months. The debt owed to the Guardians for this stay was £17 19s 6d – a very heavy sum indeed for the time. Yet the Guardians wrote it off without making Duncan pay the customary 2s 6d a week.[127]

Jack Duncan has appeared more than once so far, and he might seem to be at odds through and through with the society he preyed on so cavalierly. We have glimpsed his economic enterprises, his little deceits, his hatred for the toffs, his delight in outwitting charities and the Poor Law. Yet how uncompromising was he in his monolithic opposition to society's norms? For, almost as an aside, we hear how he and his dreamy son stood timidly outside the Post Office Stores Department in Studd Street while Jack plucked up courage to enter and recommend his boy for a career as a postal clerk.[128]

George (Dido) James has been another character the spotlight has illuminated from time to time – here the King of the Pikies, there the enterprising knife grinder, and here again as a furtive dabbler in stolen jewellery: a man, we might think, as far removed from the wider society's moral codes as we could expect to find, even in Campbell Road. Yet James, when he discovered that two of his sons were becoming thieves, attempted to deter them with all the means in his power. He once strapped the younger to a bed and beat his bare back with the buckle end of his leather belt and the thick plaited straw from orange boxes; 'and my eldest brother

– he heard about my eldest brother thieving – he put his two hands in the fire.'[129]

How do we explain these inconsistencies? And why, in both cases, did these fathers' aspirations for their sons come to nothing? The answer to this last question will become clearer during chapter 6. But the first takes us into the contradiction between the public sphere of Campbell Bunk – relations between neighbours and the outside world – and the more private sphere of the family.

5 The family and social change

The Campbell Road 'family'

At first sight, there is only a very limited sense in which we can speak of a private sphere in Campbell Road. The separation of private and public – home and family from work and neighbours – had been growing within certain strata of the London working class since the 1880s at least.[1] And between the wars, the fetishisation of home-based privacy helped reconstruct the social and physical geography of London. Even Campbell Road was to feel the pull of this other world being created outside the county boundary, in the LCC estates at Becontree or Watling or White Hart Lane, and in the older private-renting areas of Tottenham and Wood Green and Walthamstow.

But all its life Campbell Road remained one of the least private streets in London. As overcrowded as any road in Islington, people lived 3.1 households to a house, 2.8 persons to a room as late as 1938.[2] The cultural importance of Campbell Road's open space – the street – meant that domestic concerns were necessarily public, including especially 'private' matters like family conflict, child discipline, even sleeping arrangements during hot summer nights when adults would sleep on pavements, doorsteps, or costers' barrows.[3] And in many families, the home was frequently invaded by lodgers or long-term guests, or young casualties of other families seeking sanctuary for a time.[4] There was, then, very little space within which the 'private' world of personal relations could work itself out. Everywhere socially constructed, the private sphere within Campbell Road was tightly constrained by the public world of the street.[5]

But at an important level personal relations did have relative autonomy and were socially constructing in their own right. The family in Campbell Road was at once the *site* of change – where outside influences brought about decisions and actions: and the *stimulus* of change – where the internal dynamics of family relationships were powerfully productive of decisions and actions in their turn. Take, for example, the decision to leave Campbell Road. It might be externally induced by a combination, say, of better work opportunities for an adult son elsewhere in London; the fear of bad influences on a growing daughter by mixing with boys and girls in the street; and the stigma, affecting all family members, of living in the Bunk. In such a case the family might decide to leave as a whole, and sooner or later would probably be able to do so. Alternatively, the decision to go might be stimulated entirely by, say, family tensions involving intolerable violence towards wife or child. In such a case the family might break up or a member might leave prematurely. In neither example is the family passively acted upon. Even in the first, social forces are mediated by personal relations within the family, even amplified by involving more people than the influence nominally affected. Yet neither need relationships be accorded complete autonomy: for there might be social influences within Campbell Road predisposing to domestic violence and other forms of family tension.

This chapter will focus on the determining and determined role of the family in changing Campbell Road from within. In chapters 2 and 3, the contrast between the 'settled' or rooted families and the 'mobile' households passing through the furnished rooms and lodging houses was pointed up as an important contradiction in the collective culture of the Bunk. Now we shall find that 'family' is also replete with its structural fractures, clustered widest and longest around gender and generation. But first, just what did 'family' mean in the complex reality of Campbell Bunk?

Nancy Tiverton was born in February 1905 at 9 Victoria Place, a small blind court of sixteen houses off Queensland Road.[6] About three years later, the family moved to Bratton Street, another narrow turning of tiny houses off George's Road, cleared as a slum just after the First World War. In 1911, the family struck a crisis, the origins and dynamics of which are quite obscure. Mrs Tiverton, whom we have already met as a hard-working and hard-drinking charwoman, seems to have walked out after one too many of the tempestuous rows – 'he gave her some good hidings' – which Nancy remembered from her earliest days. The family then broke up. An older sister, Minnie, then 12, was sent to a home for begging, and was never seen by Nancy again. There were four older children, aged about 16 to 22, who fended for themselves and subsequently had merely the most tenuous relations with the younger siblings like Nancy. The father, who worked only for a handful of short spells as a coal heaver during the whole of his adult life, went into the workhouse with his four youngest daughters, ages 1, 6, 8 and 10.

The four girls lived in the workhouse schools for three years. During that time, Mrs Tiverton (who had moved to a first floor slip room at 62 Campbell Road) came once to see the children, and was ordered out of the workhouse because she was drunk. Mr Tiverton was eventually discharged and applied to have the children released when he thought the eldest, Ada, was 14 and old enough to work. In fact she was 13, and he had to support them all for a time in one room at 114 George's Road.

John Tiverton proved a remote and repressive father though a competent housekeeper with what he could get from poor relief and, after 1916, a war pension for a dead son. As the girls reached their early teens they one by one reacted against his severe over-protectiveness, which hardly allowed them to leave the single room except to run errands and attend school. When Ada, then 15, began seeing too much of a 23-year-old man living in the same house 'there was terrible ructions' and she left to stay with her mother at Campbell Road. A month or two later, Mabel, nearly 14, took the same escape route, leaving Nancy and the youngest of all, Mary. When Nancy was 12½ (and Mary 7), Ada had been gone about eighteen months. One summer afternoon, instead of going home from school to George's Road, Nancy walked to Campbell Road, saw her mother in the street, and asked if she could live with her. She had seen her mother only once, on that abbreviated workhouse visit, in six years.

From 1917 to about 1919, Mrs Tiverton and her three teenage daughters lived, sharing one bed, in a single room 11 ft by 8 ft 3 ins at 62 Campbell Road. And then, as the girls grew more financially independent and found themselves having to keep their mother in drink, they began to drift back to their father in the order they had originally left – Ada, then Mabel, then Nancy in 1920. By now they were too old to live with their father in a single room, so he rented a bed for the four girls in a neighbour's house a few doors away, and eventually obtained a whole room for them at 123 George's Road; but they took meals, a daily tea and a Sunday dinner, in his room at 118 (to which he had moved from 114). Mrs Tiverton lived on at 62 Campbell Road from 1911 to 1944. The written records of Campbell Road – registers of electors, overcrowding survey – list her as a woman living alone. An apparently continuous thread of 'settlement' hides everything of this Campbell Road family drama in which she played a leading role from about 1915 to 1920, and which had other repercussions in the street: Mabel married one of the more difficult of the Bunk's young men in 1922. We shall look at these young women's lives more fully in chapter 7.

What can 'family' mean in circumstances like these? The four eldest children were virtual strangers to their younger siblings but seem to have maintained contact separately with both parents. The youngest child never knew her mother. A middle child permanently lost contact with eight siblings and both parents at the age of 12. And three daughters formed and re-formed family units with one or other parent over a ten-year period.

Like many another social category, in Campbell Road 'the family' is difficult to get 'formulated, sprawling on a pin'. It becomes a complex and fluid source of both individual and family-based households. Ties between parent and child still had, in most cases but not all, power to shape the lives of both. It is this household-forming based on and effected by family relationships which is so important in describing and explaining change in Campbell Road and yet which is so inadequately revealed by statistics from head-counts as final as the guillotine.

Table 17 compares household size in Campbell Road with Holloway's other 'rough' streets and a group of streets occupied by unskilled workers and others on similar incomes, including Playford Road, all in 1938. The most significant differences are the strikingly greater proportion in Campbell Road of single-person households and 'large young families'; and the comparatively low proportion of 'adult households'. The tendencies in Campbell Road's housing market which favoured the poor have already been discussed at the end of chapter 2. Among the single-person households would probably have been many long-stay elderly, living out their days as far as possible outside the workhouse. Compared with these, the large families with children were by their very nature the most potentially dynamic group. Large working-class families are not always poor, but they generally are when children are too young to earn a subsistence. This life-cycle poverty and its connection with Campbell Road's housing market seems borne out by the over-representation of large families (seven members or more) with some children under 10, and the under-representation of large families with several members of working age. It would be possible to construct a satisfying interpretation of the dynamics of family and household movement through the street on this sort of comparison: young families tend to move to the street only when they are largest and poorest; when children begin to earn, families tend to move away.

But once more, the real patterns appear to be more complex. In the Dashett family for instance, out of fifteen children, three died, one was born before Mrs Dashett's marriage to Bill and never lived with them, and one was informally adopted when small by a Lennox Road family: 'when he was a baby he kept having fits. And I couldn't cope with him.' In addition, Nora, the eldest daughter, left home at 14 to lodge with a married woman who had befriended her. When Nora married she provided a similar service for her 15-year-old sister some years later.[7] There was a marked tendency for young earners to leave home early in Campbell Road, at first lodging with friends and neighbours but soon finding their own furnished room. Frequently, rooms were found in Campbell Road itself, and these youngsters would have contributed to the over-representation of single-person households in the street. But this early household formation also accounted for some of the decline in the number of adult and larger adult households; the families need not have moved on – they just got smaller.

These protean families, so productive of change, lived side by side with families who presented traditional patterns of household formation – mature sons and daughters leaving home for work or marriage. We shall see some narrative examples in the chapters on young men and young women. Families like these which, in spite of all the tensions, kept intact or virtually intact, probably formed a large proportion of Campbell Road families. Of thirteen families, each resident many years in the street, for whom I was able to collect reasonably complete family histories, six seem to have followed this 'normal' trajectory. Departures from this ideal norm were children leaving home before 16 (three), children taken away by public authorities (two), and separation of parents (two). Of eighteen long-stay families for whom there are details of parents and siblings of informants, six included step-parents and/or half-siblings from another relationship, but these hybrid families were not necessarily more productive of change than those of first-time marriages. And of the remaining twelve sets of parents, the death of a partner left a widow and a widower with dependent children in two cases.

The large number of protean families in Campbell Road had many causes, some of which lay largely outside intra-family relationships. The First World War – of great importance to the street, as we have seen – was directly and indirectly productive of family break-up and re-formation through casualties and soldier romances. Most of the step-parent relationships identified above seem to have had war-time origins. Infant mortality, unequally concentrated among the poorest unskilled families, was also productive of family break-up: when Bubbles Dashett died of meningitis at the age of 4, her parents rowed so furiously over assigning blame for her death that they walked out on their remaining two children who had to be sent to the workhouse.[8] Then again, overcrowding expelled adolescents from one- or two-room dwellings where there was literally no space for another full-grown family member. On the other hand, the collective culture of the Bunk might provide a pull factor, drawing young men (particularly) away from family dependence and dependents. And there was the role of the state in family policing, taking children away from 'bad associations' and 'unfit' parents.

But other external factors – worklessness and poverty, for example – fused with internal family dynamics until there was no distinction between the two. And with that we enter the world of relationships between men and women in the Campbell Road family, and their impact on the street as a whole.

Men and women

'But another thing, if he was rowing with a woman he'd hit a woman the same as he [would a man], cos he always thought a woman was taking liberties by arguing with a man. . . . I've seen him pay my mother, and that, that's what used to, you know, really turn me against him. He'd set about her as if [she] was a man, you know.'[9]

The views of Pongo Blackman might have been more clearly expressed than most, but he was by no means alone in the way he used violence against his second wife. Out of fourteen long-stay families from whom there is evidence on parental relationships, thirteen reported fighting between husband and wife. In eleven cases, levels of violence were significant and in at least seven the men could reasonably be called wife-beaters. In some of these, the shadow of domestic violence has darkened forever all the memories of childhood:

'It's many years back. I can see, only being a child and getting in front of the pair of them, fighting and oh – I don't want to think of it, it's terrible when I think of it. . . . Oh, it was murder. I've seen my mother hit my father, me step-father, with a lamp, lighting fire, they've got to get it out they had. That was my mother done that. But my father had a chopper. . . . But I don't think of them memories – only when I'm asked to know anything.'[10]

'He got hold of her – did he hit her! I can see it now. He threw her from the top of the stairs down the first flight; he went down after her, threw her down the next flight.'[11]

Newspaper reports give some indication of the injuries women could receive at the hands and feet of their husbands in Campbell Road. Over a 20-month period, Annie Tibbs summonsed her husband four times for assault. He had punched her in the face, hit her on the head with a basin causing a cut which needed stitches, kicked her on the head, and punched her head once more: 'he threatened to take my life.'[12] A 40-year-old flower seller hit his co-habitee on the head with an enamel jug: 'The injury had suppurated and needed an operation.'[13] A 40-year-old labourer was sent to prison for assaulting his wife, a war-widow when she'd married him: he had punched her and banged her head on the floor.[14]

The court reports are concerned mainly with violence by men against women and there is only one recorded charge against a woman who attacked her co-habitee with a hatpin.[15] Yet the oral evidence makes plain that physical resistance – even aggression – by women was also extremely common.[16] Time after time we hear that 'she used to stand up and fight with me dad like hell'; 'she hit him first, apparently, and he retaliated'; 'she'd stand up to him'; or 'the old woman and old Till [a neighbour] used to knock the fuckin' life out of him!'[17]

The most noticeable manifestation of this physical resistance was the frequency with which women brought domestic disputes to the notice of neighbours. It appears to have been the woman who generally caused a fight which began indoors to be dragged into the street. Sometimes, of course, this will have been simply an attempt to escape an attacker or secure assistance.[18] But often it seems more like a way of shaming the man, of hampering any 'unmanly' excesses on his part, and of demonstrating the woman's own toughness in giving as good as she got. And resistance could be demonstrated in other ways, like the songs of solidarity and bits of motherly advice passed on to daughters:

'They made up a song about it, I think. It was

> "Sally roll your sleeves up,
> Take your mother's part,
> Father's come home drunk again
> And he's broke your mother's heart.
> They're fighting one another
> And he's give her two black eyes,
> But he'll tell her he still loves her in the morning."

They used to sing that quite a lot down there, you know.'[19]

'She always warned me, my mother did: "If ever you marry a man", she said. . . . "who knocks you about, always wait until he get in bed, and get the chopper or the hammer, and break his legs. He can't run after you and pay you no more." '[20]

It is not clear just how uncommon, compared with working-class London, the remembered and reported levels of male violence and female resistance were at the time. Table 12 shows the numbers of men from Campbell Road summonsed for assaulting their partners as against the other 'rough' areas of Holloway combined: 10 against 12 in the 1920s, and 2 from each in the 1930s. There are no published figures for domestic assault between the wars, either nationally or for London. The 1920s and 1930s saw the continuation of a secular decline in summonses for all assaults and it is not unreasonable to assume that actions for domestic assault declined as well. Cecil Chapman, a London magistrate from 1899, noted a decline in cases coming before his court by the mid-1920s, and it seems likely that the reduction in court proceedings reflects the reduction in assaults as well.[21] Although it is impossible to be sure, what evidence there is supports the contention that levels of domestic violence in Campbell Road were extraordinarily high for inter-war working-class London. Why should that have been so?

The character of family violence in Campbell Road demands that the question be broken in two. What were the particular roots of male aggression within the Campbell Road family? And what were the roots of a peculiarly strong female aggressiveness and resistance to male violence?

The special class and cultural position of Campbell Road men might help us understand better the first of these. The collective compensations outside the family for worklessness and low status among men have already been glimpsed in chapter 3. There the quest for self-esteem showed itself in the hierarchy of violence among male neighbours in the Bunk. But the family was the first battleground which a man had to master before he could legitimately claim victories in the world outside. This collective context impinged on the way men felt they had to behave in the family, reinforcing male assertiveness and demonstrating one more way in which the 'social' arena of the Bunk permeated the 'private' life of the family. In this world the henpecked husband, orally and physically humiliated in public by his wife, is a popular caricature of Bunk anecdotes, especially remembered by men.[22]

These social pressures acted on family relationships already under great strain. The effects of unemployment on internal relations of families is well documented for the inter-war years.[23] Men became variously depressed and nervous in the home, uncertain about their proper role when that of male breadwinner and provider was removed from them, some of them even becoming sexually impotent.[24] 'Phantasies of revenge struggle with a sense of impotence; phantasies of power with the loss of real ability. Desire and reality are constantly at odds.'[25] One way out of that contradiction was to create a self-image of powerfulness which could be reflected in reality – domination over other family members, if necessary enforced by physical violence. In other cases, problems for masculinity were offered not so much by worklessness as by low social status. This was probably felt most of all by men who had some talent and who were sufficiently aware of this to feel frustrated and bitter at their social rejection. Pongo Blackman was the fierce rag and bone man who had done penal servitude for assaulting the police and who had sufficient accounting talents to act as the Bunk's chief croupier. Jack Duncan – who broke his wife's ribs and pulled her round the room by her hair – could merely use his considerable social skills to scrape a living by street singing, confidence tricking, and so on. Exercising physical power over family dependents might have been one way of recovering a sense of value which such men felt was their due yet which was denied them everywhere outside the Bunk.[26]

The widespread resistance and aggression of women in the Campbell Road family shows that this construction of male self-esteem at the female's expense was a sharply contested area. Again, this has also been touched on in chapter 3, where some women in Campbell Road were shown to have built up their own hierarchy of violence among neighbours. But there is a small theoretical point to be made here which might help explain the frequency of tension in Campbell Road, including the vigorous female resistance to male violence, and even family breakdown. One function of the working-class family organised around a male breadwinner earning 'the family wage' is to reproduce that earner's labour-power, or capacity to work.[27] That reproductive role falls entirely on a woman more or less economically dependent on the labour-power she restores through her own domestic labour. Within the lumpenproletariat, this reproductive role is less clearly defined. When the male does not earn and appears unlikely to fulfil that role in the forseeable future, then that function of the family disappears. With it goes one of the ties which holds the working-class family together. For now the woman's first necessity is to reproduce her own labour-power, not that of a dependent man. A 'skilled engineer' in *Memoirs of the Unemployed* found this out the hard way:

> Eventually, after the most heartbreaking period of my life, both my wife and son, who had just commenced to earn a few shillings, told me to get out, as I was living on them and taking the food they needed.[28]

We have already uncovered the importance of women as earners in Campbell Road. And in at least two cases – Mrs Tiverton and Mrs Dunn – the husband failed to provide, the wives were hardworking, the husbands were violent, and the wives eventually left.[29]

The class-based weakness of men, with its implications for the construction of gender and 'manliness'; the aggressive assertion of male power in the family, frequently the only arena in which a man could force others to respect his artificially defiant self-esteem; the relatively strong position of women, based on male workless-ness and the importance of female earnings; the physical resistance to male aggression; all conspired to foster a prolonged struggle over who should fulfill the traditional 'masculine' role within the family. This was a struggle over the power to earn the family subsistence, control the budget, define the legitimate sphere for sexual activity, dominate decision-making and discipline chil-dren.[30] The struggle was waged on many levels within the family and exploited many weapons, including (but not necessitating) physical violence. Rows might need a catalyst, like drink, before the tensions provoked an assault, and it is clear from the oral evidence that heavy drinking on Friday and Saturday nights or Sunday lunchtime frequently precipitated violence on both sides.[31] Drink might explain how tensions could be exacerbated beyond endurance, but it does not explain the tensions themselves. For that we should look to the content of arguments themselves.

The causes of rows where the male was aggressor and which might lead to physical violence by him seem to have revolved around the wife paying too little attention to the 'female' role within the family, like housekeeping; or impinging on 'masculine' areas like implicitly questioning the adequacy of his earning power by borrowing money or pawning his clothes; or fears about her sexual life with other men.

An interesting example of the latter comes from a 1935 incident involving Ronnie Drover and his wife. Ronnie was the 'workshy' casual labourer, the eldest son of the one-legged signwriter. In one spell of unemployment he had been out of work for six months, but his wife was in work. She summonsed him for assault two weeks after having left him because of his behaviour:

> it appeared that he spent his time supervising his wife as to what time she went to work and what time she came home. It seemed that he had accused her of adultery with every person who had been employed by the firm at which she was employed.

Here Ronnie's equation of his wife's economic and sexual independence and power is very clear, and his fantasies evoked paranoia and fear in both departments: 'Her wages were one hour short and he wanted to know why it was,' he explained to the magistrate in mitigation of one of the assaults of which she accused him.[32]

The causes of rows where women were the aggressors were probably very similar. There were rows over husbands' complaints of wives inadequately fulfilling their 'female' role as housekeeper, rows based on sexual jealousy of the husband or of the sexual demands he was making of her.[33] And there was female aggression over even mild cases of a husband's laying unwarranted claim to the 'masculine' family role. 'Who wears the trousers?' pithily sums up the contested function of 'masculinity' in the family. It shows up plainly in this domestic drama from the mid-1930s, witnessed by a passing policeman:

> On Sunday afternoon I was walking up the Bunk when a little girl came out of the house crying and said to me, 'Come in our house and see what mummy's done to dad.' I went with the child and on the living room floor lying unconscious and spread-eagled on his back was the bald-headed husband, his head covered in blood. Standing over him, holding by the handle the remains of a chamber-pot, was a grim faced wife. The remainder of the pot was shattered round his head on the floor. 'What's happened here?' I asked. She looked at me for a moment, then said, 'I had just emptied this when he came in as usual, pissed. His first words were, "I'm the King of the Castle", so I f-ing crowned him.' He came to a short time after but he refused to charge her for assault.[34]

But it was rows over money which probably provoked most outrage and violence and psychic drama. Poverty at near-starvation level could breed an obsession with money, the tiniest amounts having the greatest significance. Money was a tremendous source of suspicion within the family, men and women even hiding and stealing it from each other. Mr Drover, the one-legged signwriter, hid money from his wife in his paintpots, the lavatory cistern, even his wooden leg. His wife, 'very cagey with her money', knew his hiding places well. 'I've seen her get a stick, she's got the pot of paint down and she's stirred it and there's half a crown at the bottom: she's got it.'[35] And the following example, from a family who had just moved from the Bunk to Fonthill Road, was a major trauma for the eldest son, who could never see his father in the same light again:

What would they mainly row about?
Money. Alway money. . . . There was one terrible incident in my life, actually, over money. She belonged to a loan club. I think they're still in existence, but at that time nearly everybody paid into a loan club. And I was perhaps 15 or 16, and she'd drawn the loan club out near Christmas. And my mother used to borrow against the loan club when it was due. And she used to really enjoy putting the money out on the kitchen table – it was only a few quid. . . . And then she had a lot of little pieces of paper that she owed to various people and she would do all her business on the table. Well, on this particular year, I was going out. And I went upstairs to get a tie. My father was in the room with her. Apparently my mother left the room to go to get some more pieces of paper. I came downstairs, I was tying my tie in front of the mirror in the kitchen – my father had left the room as well, apparently. When my mother returned to the room, my father behind her looked over her shoulder and said, "Where's your money, Liz?" And the money had gone. Now I never touched that money. Oh, there was a godawful row; everything got smashed in the room, and I stormed out of the house. And years after, I found out that my father did have the money. . . . And then my mother told me that she'd always known it was my father – not at the time, but at that Christmas they went down to her brothers' for the Christmas, and my father had plenty of money to pay for booze, you know. Oh it was a terrible incident in my life, believe me. The old man never admitted it to me – honestly – he wouldn't, I suppose.'[36]

This struggle for power within the family was waged with no holds barred. Men and women separated with extraordinary frequency, many (like the Dashetts) coming back together again many times. From the court reports, desertion by the husband was the most common phenomenon, but this may be an illusion due to the state's interest in finding a man who could be made to pay the cost of Poor Law relief or workhouse maintenance. The court appearances of Campbell Road wives demanding restitution for assault or a separation order (usually on grounds of cruelty), and of Campbell Road husbands sent to prison for running away and not maintaining their families, kept magistrates busy at North London and Clerkenwell courts for the whole inter-war period. Apart from legal enforcement of gender-based responsibilities, the state also spent much time in trying to keep men and women together. This action of the court missionary might at one level have been motivated by fear of public indebtedness through a husband's failure to maintain; but also, and perhaps primarily, through the state-nurtured ideology of the sanctity of the marriage contract. But the state's attempts to regularise relations between husband and wife could not hope to cater for the complexities of co-habiting and marital arrangements within the street. Some Campbell Road children might bear two surnames, and their father and step-father (or mother and step-mother) might both live in the street:

> It is quite natural for a woman to live with a man who is not her husband, and for the husband, himself living in the same street with another woman, to drop in once a week to pay for the children, or spend the week-end with his wife and her temporary partner.[37]

The relations between men and women in the Campbell Road family were plainly an important determinant of social change in the street. This was acted out most clearly at the level of demography. The rate of turnover of families passing through the street was quickened by family break-up and by rapid household formation.

The production of new households impinges directly, of course, on relations between parents and children. But the tensions between husbands and wives had their own effect on adolescents who wanted to escape a home life over-full of anger, peacelessness, and anxiety. Perhaps this was more so for young women, who could see in their mothers an object more of pity than of envy. For even in a struggle which women might wholeheartedly join, it was usually the woman who came off worse. It was she who was hospitalised through a husband's violence, not the other way round. It was she who suffered most from inadequate family subsistence rather than husband or children. And it was she, more often than her husband, who found a bitter refuge in asylums for the mentally ill.[38]

At some time of their lives, children will see their parents as an image of their own future: most often, it was the young women of Campbell Road who had cause to view that image as warning rather than promise.

Parents, children and the state

It is by no means the totality of relations between parents and children which need concern us here. Only the factors which had a bearing on change will be considered in any depth, especially as they divided according to gender. Here, even more strongly than before, the realm of the private becomes yet harder to isolate. For relations between parents and children in Campbell Road were peculiarly susceptible to manipulation from without. State enforcement agencies – police, school attendance and child welfare officers, mental health authorities – actively intervened in family life in ways which could be directly productive of change. Family contradictions helped alter Campbell Road from within; the state, the external force *par excellence*, consciously nurtured that internal transformation.

The sphere of state intervention was also the arena of parental intervention in the lives of children: the process subsumed under the generic title of 'socialization'. We should not be surprised to find in Campbell Road that socialization – the transmission of values, worldviews, ambitions, and attitudes – was more complex and contradictory than our uncritical categories usually allow room for.

Socialization will have to stand here for two analytically separate aspects of the regulation of children's behaviour by their parents. There was the regulation of behaviour in accordance with the dominant values, beliefs, etc. of the Bunk. And there was socialization in the normally accepted sense of transmitting society's dominant values from parent to child. Although separate, both these processes were connected – in that one tended to be the negation of the other; and in that both processes went on at the same time in most parent–child relationships in Campbell Road. But the processes of regulating behaviour had to vie with two other important elements in parent–child relationships; neglect and exploitation.

In only a few cases did neglect push aside entirely the other elements, resulting in the non-exercise of parental power over a child or children:

> 'And all the time I was with her, I'm not telling you a word of a lie, she never bought me a pair of stockings, a dress, coat or anything. She didn't care whether I had a bath or not . . . all the time I was with her I really kept meself.'[39]

That was Nancy Tiverton who, it will be remembered, stayed with her mother for the second time between the ages of 12½ and 15½. Yet even here, the mother's neglect of her daughter's needs competed from the start with exploitation of her daughter's earning power. Neglect, then, was partial.

None the less, it could be devastating in its effects. The court cases from the 'cruelty man' prosecutions tell us only one side of neglect, usually material deprivation largely connected with family poverty. In these cases, the family as a whole must have suffered. Lou and George Porter were prosecuted by the NSPCC in November 1919 for neglecting Mary (7½) and Clara (6). Their one room

> was in a filthy condition. There was one bedstead with a stinking mattress covered with an old coat. There was a general appearance of destitution. Both the children were very dirty, and had sores on the hands and face. Clara had no boots.

George claimed that Lou 'had brought him to this and had sold his home while he was in the army.' Lou, who was pregnant, blamed George for spending most of his 38s unemployment donation on the horses. He was bound over and she was sent to prison for one month.[40] Six months later, Lou's four-week-old baby daughter was accidentally suffocated in the family's common bed.[41]

The material neglect imposed by destitution was a virtually unavoidable fact of life in Campbell Road. But the tensions of family life – in part materially based – had other effects. There was the rejection of an individual child by a parent, like Walter Spencer by his mother: 'I was the black sheep of the family, unlucky one. Cos I looked like me father.'[42] And there were many other families where parental affection was hard to come by and where loving relationships had to be sought among siblings or elsewhere:

> 'I was always late for school because they used to always find

me sitting on a step cuddling a cat . . . I always wanted
something to cuddle, I think. Those days then . . . you never
used to get a cuddle, you got a cuff. There was no such thing
as love and affection with parents. I can remember my mother
used to give us a bit of affection, she was a nice woman, my
mother. But, you know, you always wanted something that
you could cuddle, sort of thing, and I used to be always
cuddling these cats.'[43]

Exploitative relationships – or, rather, relationships which had
an exploitative component – were also common among parents and
children in Campbell Road. Broadly, exploitation can be gathered
under three headings – emotional, sexual and economic. Emotional
exploitation was, of course, the very opposite of neglect, where a
parent's dependence on a child was at its expense. Whereas neglect
tended to affect children irrespective of gender, emotional exploitation tended to be at the expense of girls rather than boys. An
extraordinary example comes from Jane Munby's experiences at
63 Campbell Road around 1917–19. These are, frankly, blurred
and difficult to reconstruct. But it seems that her mother had
thirteen children, nine of whom died when young, including Jane's
twin. When the First World War broke out, this left Jane (born
1905), an older brother, and two step-sisters, children by Mrs
Munby's second husband. Mrs Munby was a flowerseller at
Covent Garden, and a great drinker. Jane, when young, was kept
on a tight leash, allowed out very little and discouraged from
gambling or mixing with other children. Often, her mother would
not allow her to go to school, and there was much trouble with
the school board man. Around 1917, the elder brother was killed
on the Western Front. From that time until she died, two years or
so later, Mrs Munby took to her bed. She clung desperately to
Jane, the last survivor of ten children by her first husband, who
had left her in favour of a Queensland Road woman. Jane was her
only companion in those last years when the relationship with her
second husband had degenerated to open hatred:

'I never went out. My mother would never allow me out.
That's why I never went to school or anything. My mother
never let me outside the door. I only remember going outside
the door once and that was getting an errand, getting some
bread.'

Unable to read or write, apparently untouched by the school authorities, Jane stayed in her mother's room until she was removed

to hospital, shortly before coming back to die in Campbell Road. Neighbours' children were paid to bring Mrs Munby her beer rather than allow Jane to step outside the door.[44]

Soon after her mother's death, when Jane was just 15, her step-father made a sexual advance to her and she left home, sleeping in doorways for a time. Sexual exploitation – apparently exclusively affecting daughters – had its roots in the compensatory assertions of masculine power and domination, only attainable in the family and in the hierarchies of power within the Bunk; in the crowded living conditions and heavy drinking so much a part of life in Campbell Road; and in the sexually constrained world for men with no money in their pockets and without the means to compete (in terms of appearance, sexual attractiveness, and self-confidence) outside the home:

> 'I was asleep in the bed with me brother, and I woke up and there [my step-father] was, trying to get at me. And so I didn't say a word – I can always remember that – I never said a word, I just sort of got hold of me brother and pulled him over [me] like that. And he left me, me father. I can always remember that. I suppose I was about twelve years old. But I was so quiet about that, I never said a word, I just pulled meself over the other side of the bed. I was terrified.'[45]

Economic exploitation is a less straightforward area. We have already seen the extent of pre-school child labour in Campbell Road, and the need for it to supplement family earnings to something above starvation level. Child labour was not necessarily an evil, for the family or the child. It enabled the child to sustain its own standard of living, to contribute to a mother's housekeeping resources, to nurture pride in achievement and an independent nature. 'It was a steady old plod, yeah,' remembered Jack Duncan's son of the job his father got for him, helping push a coster's barrow from Hornsey Road to Covent Garden at the crack of dawn:

> 'but I don't regard it in the same light as these poor little sods who do it aching in every bone. It was a lark. And I really – I won't say enjoying it, getting up in the morning was a trial, but I didn't regard it in any way as a penance or a torture. And I was glad of the money.'[46]

Nevertheless, there were cases where parents learned to depend on a child's earnings and where the child was kept at work once more at the expense of its development. This could happen impartially to boys or girls, although when children left school gender complications undoubtedly crept in. Nancy Tiverton's mother provides us with an example of schoolchild exploitation on a calculated basis: even here, we can sense the positive side of work for the child herself. When she went to stay with her mother she was 12½:

> 'she said, "You can go out doorstep cleaning, they all do it up here." I said, "All right." I didn't mind, I was glad to do something. And I was earning about four shillings or five shillings. But I didn't half have to work hard on the long steps and that in the cold weather and hot weather and all. The money I got, she asked for it and she never gave me ha'penny out of it. . . . Then when I was 13½, woman in my mum's place turned round and said, "Tiverton," she said, "your daughter can get a job where my girl works." They used to all help one another up there, you know. So she said, "Oo, she's not 14 yet." So she said, "Oh, they don't take birth certificates down there." So she said, "Here, Nancy, down there Monday." Told me, my mother, on the Friday. I was down there Monday starting work. Didn't take a birth certificate, but it was a lovely job. . . . It was a good paying job, about eighteen shillings a week. She had all that.'[47]

Neglect of one or more areas of a child's emotional needs and exploitation of a child's potential in other directions usually went hand in hand with some purposive regulation of behaviour. 'Indiscipline' of children was one of the major characteristics of English slum life according to outsiders,[48] and it is clear why some aspects of materially-based neglect might have looked that way. Unclean skin and clothes, ragged clothing, staying out late, swearing and aggression towards strangers, all might appear as lack of discipline. But even in Campbell Road parents had norms of behaviour and values which they attempted to transmit to their children. Surprisingly, that behaviour and those values were not necessarily in line with the dominant adult code of the Bunk.

In teaching children to stand up for themselves, to fight back, and to think of themselves as no one's servant – apparently universal elements in socialization – parents were clearly true to dearly-held values in the adult world of Campbell Road. But those ideals were hardly at odds with hegemonic morality, even if in the context of the Bunk they could be turned into a refusal to accept the class relations into which children were born. More explicitly oppositional socialization was, however, relatively rare.

Take, for example, attitudes to thefts by children. Cases of
parents instructing children to steal were exceptional. The Barons,
mother and daughter, who connived in thefts as charwomen,
might well have been one example, but by the time of the court
report quoted in the previous chapter the daughter was already
21.[49] A particularly mean case of a father stealing from his 14-year-
old son might serve as instruction by example: the boy ran errands
for a local cleaner's. His father met him in the street and asked
him if he had any money on him. The boy had collected 20s 6d
from a customer and his father told him he had been sent by the
firm to get it from the boy. The 14-year-old and his mother had
to support the father, who 'had done no work for some time', and
five other children. It must have been an awful moment when the
boy had to explain to his employers where the money had gone.[50]
    The only clear-cut case provided by the court reports dates from
1926. Richard Poulson, a costermonger, and his 14-year-old step-
daughter, were charged with stealing a gold ring worth £20 from
the home of a 'foreign correspondent', where the girl did 'odd
jobs' on Sunday mornings. She admitted stealing the ring and
giving it to her step-father: after inquiries, the magistrate
commented 'that there was not the slightest doubt that he had
taught the girl to steal'.[51]
    On the other hand, the bulk of the oral evidence reveals that
parents fought hard to prevent their children stealing. This was
so even where parents had casual criminal careers themselves –
remember Dido James and his two boys, instanced at the end of
the last chapter. And it was not only stealing, with its potentially
serious implications for children and parents, which provoked
parental displeasure. Minor irregular behaviour – all hardly out of
place in Campbell Road – could also be put down by parents
enforcing a moral code which was not their own.
    Take Walter Spencer's mother, for example, who 'used to swear
terrible down the road, out the window. . . . You could hear her
from Paddington Street up to where I lived at 86!' Yet she used
to

> 'stop us from going to different [children] in the Bunk in case
> you got too involved with 'em. . . . You could never swear
> in the house. Not even when we got older. . . . Even like me
> sisters . . . if they come lippy across the table, her hand used
> to come straight over – and they were married and everything.
> She didn't stand for no buck. . . . My father was very strict.
> He didn't like no thieving, nothing like that. . . . If he caught
> you washing in warm water he'd get hold of you under his

arm, run you downstairs, and on the landing you had a tap,
little basin. He'd put you underneath and run the cold
water.'[52]

Telling lies to parents, running errands badly by being too slow
or not getting the right articles or not having the right change,
playing truant from school without parental permission, not doing
household chores, being late for Sunday dinner (usually the one
family meal of the week) were all punishable offences in the
Campbell Road family. In the Purslowes, too, the mother was
the guardian of family morality. Using 'plenty of bad language',
frequently drunk, landlady and moneylender, the code her children
had to obey on pain of a severe beating was very different:

 ' "Don't you ever let me see you go in a pub or else you'll get
the biggest hiding you've ever had.". . . We was never
allowed to swear either, cos if we had've done she was going
to cut our tongue out, and if she ever knew we was going to
thieve – "Don't you let me see you thieving else I'll chop your
hands off!" That was our three rules that we had to keep.'[53]

Bill Dashett, the hard-drinking coster who abandoned his family
from time to time, condoned his daughter's gambling and encouraged her to fight in the street, was also a strict disciplinarian in the
home. Swearing, cheeking, playing truant, not washing frequently
enough, could all call down his wrath.[54]

As in many another case, that wrath could be formidable.
Corporal punishment of children by one or both parents seems to
have been universal in Campbell Road. There was not one respondent who had not been beaten at one time or another. Frequently
these were relatively isolated occurrences. But in a large minority
of cases parental violence could be an oppression.

To his step-son, Pongo Blackman 'was, I would say, brutal, a
very brutal man. . . . I *hated* him, really hated him. He's dead
now. I really hated him. Cos my life was a *misery*, was a misery.'[55]
His step-father would beat him with his fists and kick him. Billy
used to escape to the Lennox Road Mission:

'Anyway, I went to a little singsong one night, and I should
have been looking after the baby or something, and I
remember I come home and I got a *terrific* hiding, *terrific* hiding.
I was still at school then, and I shaped up to him. I said,
"You bastard!", you know then. And I see the look of
amazement come over his face cos I stood up to him. And

anyway, I edged near the door, you know, got near that door,
I run out and I was out all night nearly till I was picked up.
And they took me to Hornsey Road Station. . . . They said,
"Who's your father?" I said, "Pongo Blackman", always
remember the sergeant saying, "Couple of you better go round
there with him." Course they took me back home and said,
"You dare lay into him again!" Soon as they went I got another
hiding! More than I dared do to go down there again, me life
wouldn't have been worth living.'[56]

May Purslowe's mother:

'one night she came in my sister was crying, my Nancy the
younger one next to me; used to be so afraid and I used to
say to her, "You don't wanna be afraid," and she used to cover
her head over. . . . And me mother came in and she was so
drunk and I said to her, "Leave us alone, we don't want you,
you're drunk," and she got hold of the oil lamp and just
threw it at us, threw all the oil and it brought us all up in
blisters, all over. . . . And of course, not having blankets on
the bed, we used to have all old coats and that on us . . . we
just threw the old coats on where it started catching light.'[57]

Mavis Knight's step-father used to punish her for wetting the bed:

'I can remember him flinging me round the room by me hair,
cut me head open on the bed. . . . My brother Billy . . . my
mother was washing him. And we used to have the water carts
come round, believe it or not, to clean the roads. . . . And
of course, kids used to run behind it. My brother Billy, he
heard the water cart coming and he run out. And my father
got hold of him and belted him in the street. He had the buckle
end of the belt, and this buckle went right into his body. And
the people went so mad that they got the Cruelty to Children
on him. And I can remember having to go up – I was only
very young – my brother Billy was only about three or four
then. And I had to go with him up to see this Cruelty to
Children man, we all had to be examined. . . . Billy actually
used to do it in his trousers. . . . And so of course, my father
used to kick him, oh! he used to kick him up the wall. And I
used to hide him sometimes. He never used to come home
till late at night, and he used to go missing. And I used to have
to go out looking for him. And I always remember that – I
used to put him under the bed and everything, but my father

used to get hold of him. Oh he did used to belt him. But
Billy grew very withdrawn, you know. You never saw Billy
laugh. Never.'[58]

It is difficult to compare this sort of behaviour with contemporary working-class childhood from other neighbourhoods. The
NSPCC complained, in 1933–4, of a 'notable and grievous'
increase in cases of brutality against children. In that year 4,208
cases were brought to its notice for the country as a whole; about
1,000 more than thirty years before.[59] But how far complaints to
the society reflected changing patterns of parental behaviour must
remain an open question.

As with levels of violence between men and women, it is the
very lack of evidence – in contemporary sources and subsequent
autobiography from elsewhere – which points to the conclusion
that corporal punishment in Campbell Road was far in excess of
that generally experienced elsewhere. Why should that have been
so? Clearly there were material and cultural elements in Campbell
Road which might have provided some of the immediate stimuli:
the severe overcrowding, for instance, which put great nervous
strains on large families so that normal child-like behaviour must
have stretched parents beyond breaking point on many occasions;[60]
the common consolation of drink, which was a frequent
accompaniment to parental violence in the Bunk and outside;[61] the
culture of public violence in the street; and the traditions of violence
which might seek to impose on children an experience of suffering
similar to the parents' own.[62] Then again, fathers especially were
prone to exact from their children the respect that no one else
would show them. Parents punished children in return for the
punishment society handed out to them:

'My mother had been to the doctor's, and my father had come
in from his endless round of looking for work, and she was
out. . . . And he came in with the hump and slapped us and
put us on the bed and threatened us with death if we moved,
you know.'[63]

But it is clear from examining what contraventions of discipline
might provoke corporal punishment that this public-private
relationship was even more complicated. Parents attempted to
enforce, in many cases, a code of behaviour grotesquely different
from their own. There was a desperate wish that children should
not grow up to be as they were – despised by society outside the
Bunk: and despising themselves as well. We can only wonder at the

degree of self-hatred which moved parents to force their children to do and be something so different from themselves. The rationalising ideologies of independence and egalitarianism and aggressive chauvinism could not withstand the private fears of those who publicly voiced them. Those fears welled up from a deep guilt about the circumstances in which people found themselves, casting inwards the responsibility for worklessness, poverty, poor housing, low public esteem. We have seen already how the contradictions of ideologies in the Bunk frustrated any sort of political synthesis. And we see here the psychic consequences of that frustration.

Parental guilt is likely to have been stronger in women than in men. For at least the men in the Bunk could maintain a compensating self-image of toughness and bravado which might also be transmitted, perhaps through violence itself, to children, especially boys. It could be a powerful self-image for some women, too. But the only self-valorising image for adult women which was acceptable to society at large – that of the competent and caring mother – was virtually unobtainable in the material world of the Bunk. The eternal reciprocity of guilt – mothers exasperated by their apparent inadequacies, children hating themselves for being unloved – added one more painful turn to the screw of social change in Campbell Road.

That screw turned faster and deeper through the intervention of yet one more 'external' agency – the state. Family policing added to the sum of guilt parents might be expected to bear, driving them on to make their children different from themselves. Parents knew, also, that if they failed in that purpose then the state might come in to do the job for them.

State intervention in the family has predominantly revolved around the care of children and has changed remarkably little since the formative Children Act of 1908. That Act stipulated the conditions which might allow the education authorities via the Juvenile Courts to remove a child from its parents until the child was old enough to fend for itself. First came those children and young persons who were Youthful (Juvenile after 1933) Offenders and who had committed an offence punishable in an adult by imprisonment: in London it seems that these offenders had more chance of being sent to an institution than in most other parts of the country.[64] Second were children who needed to be removed from parents for their own physical protection. And third were those whose parents were absent or considered unfit to bring up their children. This crucial category was greatly extended by the Children and Young Persons Act 1933. Until then, children had to fall within quite specific definitions – begging or wandering abroad, criminal or habitually drunken parents, the victims of incest, living in a house of ill-fame, frequenting the company of reputed thieves or prostitutes, chronic truants, destitute and parents in prison, or represented by parents as beyond their control.[65] Many of these were replaced in 1933 by a catch-all summation: 'in need of care and protection' meant children or young persons 'falling into bad associations, or exposed to moral danger, or beyond control'.[66] This change in the law was accompanied by an alteration of institutional care. The old industrial and reformatory schools were replaced by 'approved' schools.

All this reversed the trend away from institutionalising children which had set in after the First World War. For the period 1907–8 to 1913–14, over 1,100 London children a year were sent to industrial or reformatory schools; for 1920–1 to 1932–3, the figure was just over 400; in 1937–8 it climbed to almost 800 a year (see figure 2).[67]

In addition to the law of children, mental health legislation also provided for significant state intervention in family life. The administration of the Mental Deficiency Acts of 1913 and after,[68] allowed for a category of 'moral imbecile' (later 'moral defective') who showed 'mental defect' coupled with 'strong vicious or criminal propensities'. This definition encompassed adults as well as children. But from 1913 to 1929, about half the referrals to the Metropolitan Asylums Board (MAB) under these Acts were made by the LCC Education Department.[69] Continuing concern for the mental capacity of the British 'stock', and a belief in the segregation of the 'defectives' from those they might contaminate genetically, led to an extraordinary increase in investigation and incarceration after 1929, when the Wood Committee's report coincided with a transfer of responsibility for the Acts from the MAB to the LCC. In 1929, under 3,400 persons were detained under the Acts; in 1933 there were over 7,800, and the figure remained generally above 7,000 for the rest of the 1930s (see figure 3).

There are no statistics available for cases from Campbell Road compared with other streets, but it is clear enough that a significant proportion of families were affected by this increasing state intervention in the 'private' life of the Bunk. It would be surprising if that had not been so. We know the street's reputation among official psychologists and sociologists, and of the call for state intervention in streets like it. Campbell Road's label as 'one of the worst streets in London' would have had an amplifying effect on authority's attitude to the people who lived there – in this arena as in others. Around 1922, Charlie Tasker already attended a special

school for 'mental defectives' when he was implicated with other
children from Campbell Road in stealing money from a child in
Finsbury Park. Charlie, and another boy, also a special school child
from the Bunk, were sent to the Manor Institution at Epsom. He
stayed there from the age of 12 to 24.[70] It may be recalled that one
of Mrs Tiverton's daughters was sent to an institution for begging
around 1911 and was never seen by any of the family again; and
an older sister of May Purslowe was sent to Canada as part of
the emigration schemes which lasted into the inter-war period.[71]
Richard Poulson – the man who taught his daughter to steal – had
her taken away from him in return.[72] In 1928, a 16-year-old girl
convicted of stealing from her mother at 36 Campbell Road was
sent to a home.[73] And it was frequently the case that convicted
youths aged 16 to 18 were sent to Boy's Homes for four to six
months and then released on probation, sometimes with an order
not to live at home.[74]

It must not be thought that the tendency to increased institutionalisation by state authorities was placidly accepted by those
it affected.[75] Not everyone, of course, had either the inclination or
the strength of will to struggle against the LCC's Mental Health
or Children's Departments, whose might was righteous even if
not always right. The resources which people drew on were not
those provided by an education lamentably ineffectual in arguing
with 'experts'; or by the purely nominal police court justice which
apparently protected a parent's right to recover a child subject to
a court order. Rather, they drew on the anti-authoritarian and anti-
statist worldviews so much common property in Campbell Road;
and on the fierce individualism stimulated by their economic life
and collective culture. And they waged the struggle with cunning
and tenacity.

In 1933, for instance, Louisa Brown was accused of helping her
daughter Sarah, 26, to escape from the Manor Institution. Sarah,
who had been there for nine years, had been allowed out for a
visit but had then been hidden away by her mother. Despite the
evidence of an LCC doctor that Sarah was 'feeble-minded within
the meaning of the Mental Deficiency Act', Louisa refused to state
where her daughter was now living, except that she was working
for a lady at Finchley and getting 10s a week. 'I would rather go
to prison than Sarah should go back there again. I have been trying
to get her out for years.' Louisa was fined £10 – a heavy sum –
but Sarah apparently did not go back.[76]

Three years later, a similar incident involved George Milton, a
costermonger who has already figured in this narrative for being
arrested for begging in 1924 with his wife and 4-year-old child. In

1936 he was charged with helping his daughter Kate escape from the Belmont Hill Institution, Lewisham, while she was on her second home visit at Christmas 1935. When Kate was 11, in 1923, she had been charged with begging and sent to Belmont until she was 16:

> At the end of five years I tried to get her home. They refused to let me have her. She is 24 years of age now. Do you think it is right that this girl has been caged up – worse than a criminal? It was my fault she was sent there. I was down and out and she was taken away from me. . . . I refuse to allow her to go back. It is not right that she should be caged up all her life.

Milton told the court that Kate was in service with an aunt:

> She was giving every satisfaction and there was nothing the matter with her.
> *Magistrate*: 'If there is nothing the matter with her why don't you do the best thing and let them examine her? . . . Will you tell the authorities where the girl is?'
> *Milton*: 'They would not give me justice if I did.'

He was fined £5, against the Magistrate's inclination, but still refused to tell the LCC where his daughter was living.[77]

In part, these were particularly dramatic instances of a more restrained daily struggle against the external forces impinging on private lives in Campbell Road. There was no end to the number of officials whose job it was to tell people in Campbell Road how they should live. Schoolteachers and the truancy officer (anachronistically known as the school board man), child welfare officers, sanitary inspectors, the relieving officer and the workhouse authorities, and of course, the police, all intervened to a greater or lesser extent in family life. Sometimes, because the object of struggle was perceived as private and personal, the reaction could be violent – in word, if not always in deed. The oral evidence testifies to a number of assaults by parents on schoolteachers for some insult to the family name or some interference in the family economy.[78] At other times, criticism of parental behaviour might be quietly accepted for the sake of peace, while knowing that any change would only be temporary. This was particularly the case where parents kept children, mainly girls, from school to help in the home and with younger children: 'they used to come after her and I used to go for a couple of weeks, and that was that.'[79]

State interventions could be fought against, with varying if generally limited success. The fight was not always for the best of reasons, despite the apparent humanitarianism of George Milton's and Louisa Brown's causes. For the family in Campbell Road was far from being a 'refuge', an idealised 'haven in a heartless world', and many children suffered hard and long in it.[80] The rights of mothers and fathers over their children were frequently abused, as we have seen. Even so, what the state offered, with its industrial and reformatory and approved schools, was not much better.

Family pathology was an important agent of change in Campbell Road. On the one hand, the interminable rows between husband and wife and the negative image of parents for children, especially daughters; the use of violence against children, frequently to excess; the exploitation of children by parents who might ignore their youngsters' needs; the contradictory discipline which reinforced a child's alienation from its parents' mode of life, all built up a centrifugal movement from the Campbell Road family and perhaps from Campbell Road itself. And on the other, state intervention was a machinery of punishment and control, taking children away from home and locking them up for the sins of their parents,[81] regulating behaviour through deprivation or violence, offering the alternative pathology of the institution.[82]

It is not surprising, then, that children should seek their own ways out of the contradictions of family life in Campbell Road. It was not easy to steer a course between family pathology and state coercion, and both would affect the critical years between leaving school and marriage for many youngsters. And the courses chosen depended very much on whether you were a young man or young woman.

6 *Young men: accommodating traditions*

Context

So far, life history has played an important but disjointed part in this analysis of Campbell Bunk. But the last chapter will have demonstrated how the history of a family can illuminate the complexities of change and the social forces leading it on. This chapter and the next will give much more prominence to individual histories at a critical period of the life cycle. Adolescence and early adulthood is a time when seminal steps are taken and decisions reached, frequently committing an individual to a narrowly banded course for the rest of his or her life. In doing so they will affect families and even, if the steps tend to any particular sequence, whole communities. It should be clear that the decisions reached by young men and women in Campbell Road were not randomly ordered, and it should become clear that the patterns which emerged did indeed have pertinent effects on the community there. Those patterns were different for men and women. And there were long-term tendencies over the two inter-war decades which etched some designs deeper than others.

The young men and women of Campbell Road had to construct a life for themselves out of relatively spare and sparse raw material. Their life chances were narrowed by the traditions of rejection from the labour market, the reputation attaching to their home address, the cultural pull of the Bunk and its consolations, the ambitions considered legitimate by their peers – all of which they had been born into or had grown up with. Any of these determining factors might have been enhanced by family pressures or accidental influences inside or outside the street. But the extent to which they were accommodated or challenged defined what sort of change, if any, could be made by young adults. Accommodation reinforced the stability and traditional way of life in Campbell Road, whereas challenge might lead in new directions. It will be argued here that young men's lives tended more to accommodation with the traditions of the Bunk, whereas young women self-consciously challenged its way of life and forced the pace of change in the street; and that this challenge was stronger in the 1930s than the 1920s.

There are two key elements in both accommodation and challenge which need to be discussed briefly before we turn to the life history narratives. Both work opportunities and certain aspects of Bunk culture and contemporary working-class life in and around it were sharply divided by gender. In considering the dynamics of individuals' lives we will need to take account of the context which affected their generation as a whole.

The precise character and extent of juvenile unemployment was a matter for debate in the 1920s and 1930s. Enumeration through the unemployment registers was criticised as an inadequate index, under-representing the actual numbers of juveniles seeking work.[1] Official agencies like the Ministry of Labour and the London Advisory Committee for Juvenile Employment (LACJE) appear studiedly complacent in the face of a little library of serious investigations of youth and unemployment.[2] And although these studies chose particularly to highlight the problems suffered by boys rather than girls, that in itself is no indication that girls were affected less seriously than their brothers.

This subject has received scant scholarly attention since,[3] and in the absence of any authoritative account we have to make what sense we can of the conflicting signposts. It is clear, however, that London was, as ever, a special case. This was the largest market for juvenile labour in the country and by the end of the slump it appears to have been insatiable. It had not always been so. During industrial dislocation caused by returning ex-servicemen in 1918–20, thousands of juveniles, particularly boys, were laid off to make way for demobbed soldiers.[4] By the mid-1920s, the market had returned largely to its pre-war buoyancy.[5] The large majority of school leavers found work easily, and unemployment tended to come in short spells of less than a month between frequent job changes.[6] The worst years of the slump were cushioned by the dramatic fall in the number of school leavers between 1928 and 1932 (down 37 per cent in the LCC area) due to the decline in the wartime London birthrate.[7] And fortunately the effects of the post-war baby boom were absorbed comfortably in the return to prosperity of 1933–5.[8] As early as 1927, LACJE had reported a shortage of 14- to 15-year-olds; by December 1933 there were 2.5 vacancies for every unemployed juvenile; and by 1937 the London shortage was 'urgent' and 'clamant'.[9] This was a markedly more cheerful position than for those youngsters caught in the depressed areas of heavy industry, several thousands of whom were 'transferred' to London from late 1928 to help meet the demand for juvenile labour there.[10]

The picture was, however, more darkly shaded than might first appear. There were quite distinct labour markets for boys and girls. That for boys was severely divided from the adult male labour market and formed a separate internal market of its own, especially for the unskilled. The circulation of labour within it was broken at two points – at 16 and 18 years. Until 1934, 16 was the age employers had to begin paying National Insurance contributions; and 18 was the age most youths sought an adult wage and employers sought cheaper labour. In certain types of work, one or both of these events triggered a period of unemployment; the most critical for future job prospects and the most difficult to recover from was the break at 18.[11]

The jobs which kept this internal circulation in motion were known at the time as 'blind-alley' and were particularly important in the London economy: 'Holloway was extremely limited in its possibilities for really progressive employment, especially for boys.'[12] Blind-alley jobs were densely clustered in the distributive trades – errand and shop boys, van boys, messengers and page boys, newspaper sellers and hawkers, warehouse packers – and the lightest forms of general labouring. In Islington in 1931, 65 per cent of 14-year-old boys were employed in these sectors and 44 per cent of 16- and 17-year-olds.[13] Specifically juvenile work was supplemented by a myriad of temporary or casual jobs stimulated by fluctuating demand in almost any London industry and trade.[14] The London boy labour problem, then, was not in any general sense unemployment, but rather employment in jobs with no future, merely delaying an unavoidable period of unemployment by two or four years, and bearing little on the work available to grown men.[15]

The worst effects of the boy labour market were felt by the children of the unskilled. We have already seen the pressures on youngsters to earn money for their own or their family's subsistence, even before leaving school. We have glimpsed some of the pressures on children which weakened the effectiveness of schooling on a labour market increasingly related to educational achievement.[16] On reaching 14, the children of workless or low-paid or casually employed parents joined the labour market to earn as much as they could; to take the 'biggest shilling'.[17] Another sad symptom of short-run hedonism to middle-class onlookers,[18] to the families and youngsters themselves it was a simple matter of taking the first chance to rise above the poverty line. Individual and family pressures were to take anything that was available, regardless of prospects but mindful of wages; to look locally, rather than incur outgoings on transport and meals;[19] and to take the advice of informal networks of job information, rather than the labour exchange. As for the adult labour market, the quality of labour-power a youngster had to offer was still important in determining just what job he would get and how much money he might earn. It was still the undersized or ugly or slow-thinking youth who found himself unemployed most frequently and for longest:

> One of the standing difficulties . . . is to find work for 14-year-old youngsters who look no more than 10, and are too small to reach the level of the bench or machine in many factories.[20]

And the discrimination affecting men and women looking for work from notorious districts applied perhaps even more forcefully to boys and youths.

Among the unskilled there was not the marked inheritance of employment connecting fathers with sons which characterised skilled manual workers' traditions.[21] Even so, sons tended to follow fathers into the same sort of employment when their four-year induction to the world of work had run its course – into general labour, street selling and so on. Where both were recorded, one in four Campbell Road sons declared the same job title as their fathers on their marriage lines.[22]

Sons followed fathers in other directions as well. Rejection from the labour market and the disappointments of ill-paid, unstimulating work at long hours continued to be an important factor in young men's lives as it had been for their fathers. But the traditional consolations in structures of masculine self-esteem within Campbell Road offered alternatives to status or satisfaction through work. The cultivation of physical strength and its display through aggression; the passion for particular elements in a culture still largely male, although shared and even competed for by many women; the male-dominated underworld on the margins of a lawful subsistence or outside it altogether: all held some attractions for the young men of Campbell Road. Here was a world in which they could compete and value themselves more highly if they won: it was hard to win in the work-dominated world outside. Moreover, this culture of masculinity was, in large degree, validated by the legitimate working-class youth culture taking shape in the 1920s and 1930s.[23] It was thus possible for young men to overcome, to a certain extent, the outcasting problem of life in the

Bunk. It was as if two badly-drawn circles overlapped accidentally: in the common segment the small world of Campbell Road met and merged with the wider society normally outside. For a part, at least, of their lives, young men were able to occupy that common ground, accommodating life in the Bunk and being accommodated by the world outside.

Let us look more closely at how these worlds merged. The importance attached in Campbell Road to masculine strength and aggression, including physical violence, found more than a legitimating echo in the world outside. The 'cult of the body' of the 1920s had been a minority interest, even if it attracted many working-class youths, especially among the unemployed. Even so, the cult had been officially nurtured by the boys' club movement, with its passion for boxing and wrestling and weight-training. Yet 'physical culture' was soon to become a national obsession. The nervous anxiety over the fighting capacity of the British which had given the Edwardian middle classes such a fright re-surfaced in the 1930s. The recreation of male youth of all classes became a matter of state policy as playing fields and 'recs' for working-class youths combined with youth hostelling and hiking for the (literally) better heeled. The Physical Training and Recreation Act of 1937 cast an envious eye at continental youth movements, including Hitler's.[24]

All this overlapped a good deal with sport – especially football and boxing. These were two of the great passions of Campbell Road's young men, especially the former, and both grew in public importance during the inter-war years. The Arsenal were the Bunk's team, their ground at Highbury just a ten-minute walk away. The most famous team in the country during the 1930s, the Arsenal were a tremendous source of pride and confidence for their young supporters. Boys from Campbell Road helped swell the 50,000 gates and were even, apparently, made club mascots from time to time.[25] Young men in the Bunk could earn nicknames from their love of sport – 'Two-Eggs-A-Day' for a man on a training schedule, for example – and the street had its own football team in the 1930s called, for some reason, 'Dundee United'.[26] It would play other similar teams, street- or work-based, on Sundays at Finsbury Park and Hackney Marshes.

The old meaning of 'Keep Fit' had a military connotation – 'For Service' had completed the original invocation. And in the 1930s, the overtones of militarism were far from silent. The drum beat loudly enough in streets like Campbell Road, with its traditions of chauvinism and war sacrifice, and where the army continued to provide an escape route from unemployment or the accidents of life. Army service, the ultimate glorification of and rationalisation for masculine aggression, had attractions in Campbell Road over and above the materialist drive for a secure subsistence.[27]

But there were still wider spheres of overlap between the world of young men in Campbell Road and the world outside. Heavy drinking and drunkenness might have declined, but pubs were becoming more popular among all classes, and the 1920s and 1930s saw a wave of pub building and modernisation (frequently in mock Elizabethan).[28] Gambling, too, found new legitimations – outside street gaming, it is true – but in ways which drew punters from the Bunk as from elsewhere. Greyhound racing, football pools, and one-armed bandits, the ubiquitous gaming machines of working-class cafés where boys and girls spent their spare hours, fuelled the gambling 'craze' of the early 1930s.[29]

Finally, the cinema forged other connections between the male youth of Campbell Road and outside. This was especially true of the American talkies, with their more realistic heroes than the silent era's Valentino, Navarro and Fairbanks. American films offered heroes and heroines who were less hidebound by class than their technically inferior British counterparts. The glamourised male (especially young male) violence of films like *Little Caesar* (with Edward G. Robinson, 1930), *Public Enemy* (with James Cagney, 1931), *Scarface* (with George Raft, 1932) helped working-class youngsters see themselves as heroes rather than bystanders, the subject of life rather than its object. The adopted American accents, dress-styles and mannerisms, which many observers bemoaned as slavish emulation of a new trash culture, can be interpreted quite differently. This borrowed 'style' was a self-conscious identification with a more democratic discourse than anything British society (including its labour movement) had to offer them:

> They acted all the time [reported a journalist who visited 'Islington's most notorious café' in 1934]. Movie mad. . . .
> Clothing, 'the latest worn', ridiculous styles and with a horrible 'cut price' appearance about it. . . . The conversation . . . [was] mostly in American accents. Nearly every girl there was acting a 'hard-boiled Kate' role. Nearly every youth, with a very long overcoat and a round black hat on the rear of his head, was to himself a 'Chicago nut'.[30]

All of these external influences combined with the internal culture of Campbell Road to make life there seem less out of step for young men than it did for young women. Not only were there more consolations and sources of interest in the street for young men: some of those consolations were becoming more respectable, particularly in the 1930s. Even so, the incorporation of male culture in Campbell Road into the dominant culture outside should not be taken too far. For legitimation developed a self-confidence and assertiveness which served to strengthen an important part of the birth-right of young men in Campbell Road: the tendency to seek a resolution of life's contradictions in an individualism blind to the demands of a work-based ordered society outside. One way to control their destinies was to take that tendency as far as it could go – into a professional career in thieving. But that was by no means the only course open to the young men of Campbell Road.

Walter Spencer: The straight and narrow

We have already met Walter Spencer several times and it might help to bring the bits and pieces together before we move into a consecutive narrative.[31] Walter was born just before Christmas 1917 at 86 Campbell Road. He was the second of ten children, two of whom died. His father was a building worker, frequently out of employment. His mother had been born in Campbell Road in 1896. She was the hard-hitting woman who victimised Walter, her second son, for (he thought) looking like his father. He was saved from worse beatings by his maternal grandparents (his grandfather played a concertina in the street for a living), who had a room in the same house and let him sleep with them from time to time. This was a poor and loveless family. 'We wasn't all that close a family. There was no love in the family, like there is when I see other families. No love whatsoever.' Walter had been beaten by his mother for crying when he stabbed his eye on a rusty nail, permanently losing its sight. It was Walter and a brother who suffered that terrible Christmas present of coke and stale bread. Walter's family was one of the most settled in Campbell Road: it was he who could count over 40 relatives in the street by the mid-1930s.

Walter had been a regular attender at school, apart from being kept home on frequent Thursdays to help with chores and younger siblings. But he had not been a truant and he probably had received a standard elementary education, more than many in Campbell Road. He had been a Sunday School boy at the Lennox Road Mission, made to go for the flannelette shirt the children could receive instead of a toy at Christmas. And he was a cub for a time at St Anne's Church, Pooles Park. But he had lost interest by the time he could have graduated into a scout. So when he left school in 1931 he had cut his associations with any local youth organisation.

Like many other lads, he found the Bunk label hard to shake off when he went into the world to seek work:

> 'Now I went after 50 jobs before I got a job. I'd go out all day long. I'd go to every place imaginable. They didn't advertise. "Any chance of having a job in here?" Had to go for 50 jobs. And some places, directly you mentioned Campbell Road: "Sorry, mate." '

He found a job by asking at a coach booking office in Highgate if they needed any help in the office. New proprietors had recently taken over the business and Campbell Road meant nothing to them.

Walter was easy-going, adaptable, and quick to learn. His work record was remarkably stable when compared with other youths from unskilled families at the time. But he was prepared to throw this comfortable number in for the sake of a principled egalitarianism quite at odds with self-interest:

> 'I had that job for about 11 months. And a fella there had been there about, oh so many years before that, I dunno how many years; I thought he told me 11 years. . . . And they said to me one day, "Sonny Jim, can you use a phone?" I said, "No – I could learn." They said, "Well, you'll have to learn, because we're sacking Perry." I said, "Whatever for?" They said, "Well . . . we can't have people going sick." So I said, "I'm very sorry", I said, "but I'm afraid I can't work here no longer. I might be in the same boat as him." Now I was desperate for a job that day, but I couldn't do a thing like that. . . . I turned it right in, there and then.'

He now found alternative work hard to get, only able to take a day here and there when it was offered. One day, the van boy at Nobbs's laundry and dry cleaners in Blackstock Road reported sick and Walter was taken on to replace him. In fact the van boy had landed a job elsewhere and Walter was offered his place, but only after an awkward interview when he reluctantly disclosed his address to Mr Nobbs and begged to be given a chance.

From 1932 to 1940, Walter worked for Nobbs's laundry. Instead of being laid off when he was 17 or 18 and too old for the van, he was taken into the dry cleaning factory. He first learnt the trade by cleaning ladies' gloves and eventually became the assistant to the dry cleaner, learning the mysteries of chemical solvents and their reaction on materials. This was a relatively new skill, and Walter mastered it. By the age of 20 he became the dry cleaner, earning 45s a week.

This was a rare glimpse of prospects for a Bunk boy with such an unpromising background. But perhaps some elements in that background had fitted Walter more aptly for this development than is at first apparent. For all his mother's unloving treatment of Walter, she had always shown a passionate desire for him to keep out of trouble with the police. He had been enjoined, more or less forcibly, not to mix with other boys from the Bunk. This wasn't taken too far, but he could not mix at all with some like the Brittans and the Chines, for example. Walter had a yen for street gaming, but he had to run the risk of his mother's vocal censure if she caught him at one of the gambling schools. When he got mixed up with the police – falsely prosecuted for being involved with other Bunk youths in vandalising a Pullman car at Finsbury Park Station and for biting a policeman's leg – she stoutly defended him at Highgate Juvenile Court and the charge was surprisingly dismissed.

This did not mean that he ignored the influences of Campbell Road entirely. He still cheeked the police as they patrolled the Seven Sisters Road; his brother, at least, was involved in some of the street 'rowdyism' so common a feature of the lower working-class areas of Islington and Holloway in the 1920s and 1930s.[32]

But taking his mother's injunctions to heart, he mixed with boys from Fonthill Road – the son of the rag dealer to whose shop Walter had taken jamjars and old clothes he'd scrounged as a child; another boy from Fonthill Road; and a lad from St Thomas's Road, near the Arsenal, whose home conditions were markedly different from Walter's own:

'Oh Christ, yeah! You take it – when they got electric light and gas, and a gas fire for cooking. And all we had then was a paraffin lamp.'

For some years, these four were inseparable friends, although Walter never dared take them to his home as they took him to theirs, and although he was still friendly on a casual basis with a number of boys from the Bunk. For Walter and his friends outside the street, their favourite activity was cycling in London and the countryside around it. At first Walter had only been able to hire a bike from Drayton Park at sixpence a session. But when he was working he could afford to buy a 'Hercules' for £3 at 2s 6d a week.

The rest of his pocket money – two-thirds of his wages went to his mother for his keep – went on clothes: a suit at £3 from the tallyman, a pair of painted-toe shoes at 5s, and a good shirt for the same money. 'Yeah, always dressed well.'

Relations with girls were relatively asexual, and youthful sexual abstinence in the Bunk was probably the rule rather than the exception, despite the picture of the slum Gomorrah that middle-class observers loved to paint.[33] Taking care to dress well did not necessarily demonstrate concern with sexual attractiveness, even though it clearly related to masculine self-esteem at the time. This was particularly so for *young* men at least:

What about girlfriends?
'It's funny, you know. We didn't take interest in girls, then. They come with us as a gang, like. But regarding that – not like it is today – they just joined you and left you; or we joined them and left them sort of thing. We'll have a chat on the corner with them, or round the corner and that, but that's as far as it went.'
Who was your first girlfriend?
'Well, me first fancy one was me wife. She was about 14 then. But I went with one down at Caledonian Road, a blonde girl down there.'
How did you meet her?
'I used to go out with a boy Dent, another mate from the Bunk. And we'd have a walk round, always walk round the Cally, and I used to go up and talk to any girls those days, just chat with 'em. . . . That's how I met her. But I lost her when she come round my house – she knew where I lived, like, 86 Campbell Road, she found that out. Come round one day, I was out, and my mother evidently told her that she didn't want no effin' blondes in the family! That's how she put it! Cos I don't think she wanted to see me get married, the mother.'
How old were you then?
'I should say I was 17 then.'
Why didn't she want to see you get married?
'Well, she wanted the money, obviously, didn't she.'

But the girl Walter fancied most was Nellie Carrier – originally out of the Bunk but now living next door in Playford Road. He had known her since she was about 14 – 'pretty looking girl she was' – because she used Walters's provision shop on the

Paddington Street corner. She was only tiny when he first knew her, and that suited because he was only a featherweight himself.

In 1940, even though he was 23 and earning good money, Walter was still living at his three-room home, sharing a bed with his brothers aged 25 and 21. Despite his one eye, he was called up. The Army had already come for a brother in the Territorials, and Walter was the second to go. But just two weeks before he went he helped his mother and father move to Pooles Park. The long connection between the Spencer family and Campbell Road had come to a sudden, although incomplete, ending.

An accident while still on training in England left Walter with a leg temporarily in irons and a war cut permanently short. When he returned home in 1942, Walter did not immediately renew contact with Nellie. He'd been ashamed of his lameness and uncertain of its prognosis. But matters were not allowed to rest there:

'Actually, her mother come round to me in Fonthill Road. And she said, "Come and have a drink." See? I said, "Yeah, I'll be round.". . . I never went round. She come round again. "Will you come round home? Have a drink?" "Yeah." Still never went round. So I thought, How can I? Can't go out with a girl with a bloody stick and that. So eventually I did go round. And we had a couple of drinks and that, came up, meet her dad, like, and had a chat with him. And that's how it went on . . . we was married in 1943.'

Nellie, or her mother, found a room near to the Carriers at 4 Playford Road. There they stayed until 1950, when they moved a few streets south of Seven Sisters Road. Walter continued working at the laundry, eventually running the office, until 1964. Apart from war service and six months or so at Western's, he'd been with the one firm for 32 years.

Walter's life experience represents one way in which young men overcame the handicaps of living in Campbell Road without ever rejecting out of hand its traditions. There was his mother's initial push into friendship outside the street; followed, fortuitously, by a job, and then, through his evident talents, regular and reasonably paid work. On the other hand were continuing friendships within the Bunk, propped up by any number of cousins, and the passion for street gambling he shared with his brothers. The balance he was thus able to strike accommodated the world outside without having to relinquish the Bunk. He married outside the street, but only just. The move away from Campbell Road came late and half-hearted, to one or two streets away, and some connections with the Road were maintained for a lifetime. All his life Walter has lived no further than five minutes' walk from Campbell Road.

Billy Tagg: A chapter of accidents

Billy Tagg was born at 52 Campbell Road in 1913.[34] His father, a coffee stall keeper, was one of the Campbell Road men killed on active service during the First World War. His mother subsequently re-married Pongo Blackman, the well-known rag and bone man who was also the Bunk's chief croupier. The family moved to the top end of the Bunk in the process. This was also Pongo's second marriage, and Billy grew up with a sister, step-sister, and three step-brothers. We have already seen the brutality which Pongo imposed on his family and again Billy seems to have got about the worst of it.

Billy had been a regular attender at elementary school – 'I liked school, to keep away from home' – and at the Lennox Road Mission. Even so, his early work days were more unsettled than Walter Spencer's. His poverty provoked a readiness to be involved in little fiddles at work, perhaps also motivated by a wish to help his long-suffering mother. She had less rigorous standards than Mrs Spencer, and she shared in the miserly spoils:

'I started at ten shillings a week in Keith and Blackman's in Holloway Road, engineering. . . . Then I left there – I got a *good* hiding for leaving there – ten shillings a week, I never used to get *nothing* out of that. Then I left there and I got a job riding a trike, taking out tobacco, all round the City, and anywhere, like, with a firm in Holloway Road, Arding and Hobbs, I'll never forget it. Sometimes I used to go with the trike and another time I used to go with a van driver in an old Ford. And we had a little fiddle on and off – well he used to do it cos I was only a youngster. He used to say, "I put some cigarettes in yer pocket, Bill", like. "Yeah, OK". Well I never used to sell 'em, like, but when he was finished, he used to say, "Give us my lot". . . . Well, *my* whack, my mum used to come with me when I finished, like, and we used to go round the streets smoking these different fags. You know what I mean, it was no thieving, it was just to provide 'em, more or less. And one day, he left me coat on the counter, there used to be a big counter going down the . . . warehouse. And he forgot to take me coat into the van and the woman, Mrs Mendoza, she come along and she must have . . . felt these fags. So she had me in there and she said, "I'm not gonna prosecute you", she said, "but you've got the sack." She said, "You've been doing this a long time." So I just took the blame and packed up.'

Billy then had two jobs in quick succession, errand boy for local grocery firms. But it was not work which provided the major source of interest in his life at this time. It was the seductive pull of the Bunk's traditions. Billy developed a passion for gambling. He was one of the most active of the young punters around the late-1920s, and he began to steal to pay for his obsession. The ingenuity he used in devising his fiddles showed considerable talent and worldly cunning in one so young. His victim was his new employer, Mr Elton, a shopkeeper in Cottenham Road:

'I started this with Elton and so I'm getting on a bit now. I still hated him [my step-father], you know, growing up worse, like. Course, my mother had gone away, she went in a mental home cos of the wusname, you know, really boiling up. Anyway, I started with Elton and I used to have to go to Southgate on a trike. You imagine going from Holloway, right over Southgate – I was only a youngster – and the trike used to be loaded up, and I'd go up Southgate, Jolly Butcher's Hill all through the Bourne, about twice a week. So I thought to meself, gotta try and earn meself a few bob here, like. I'm getting a bit wise now, you know. . . . There used to be a lot of gambling down Campbell Road, *hell* of a lot of gambling, *millions* of pound have been on them floors. And I was a bit of a gambler by now. And he used to give me about a pound's worth of change when I went out, in a little shammy. So what I used to do . . . I used to get some bills while I was in the shop, cos I used to serve behind the counter as well, see. And put them in me pocket. Right. When I get there it's all right, but when I come back I used to go indoors first before going back to the shop, see. And of course they'd have all the old dice out. . . . Well out used to come me little bag with *his* money. Anyway, if I lost I had the bills you see. So suppose a woman had eight bob's worth of groceries – I used to copy 'em all out, duplicate 'em see, so I used to give the woman the bill I made out . . . [and] take the *original* bill back that *he'd* made out and say, "Sorry, Mr Elton, she wasn't in. Couldn't get her money, here's the bill." But I'd already signed her as paid on my bill. So it went on and on like that, I kept losing at the old dice, so I'd had two or three hadn't paid.

'Another trick: he used to sell paraffin oil, and they had the gallon cans, see. So I used to take that out, might take out ten, fifteen gallons. Anyway, I always used to go home first before I went to the shop, and have an hour indoors, you know. And I used to [say to myself], Things are bad, like. Say I sold six gallons, it was only about tenpence, shilling a gallon. Right. Well, I'd sold six, I'd sold three. And I used to go under the tap and fill three gallons up with water! . . . So anyway, when I got back, he'd say, "Oh, how many you sold, Bill?" "Only three, Mr Elton," I said. "All right, pour the others back in the tank." He had a big Royal Daylight tank, about 100 gallons – water was going in and all. Well, them days, the old oil lamps was about, you know, no gas or nothing, we never had gas. The old girls used to come in for their pint of oil and a bottle, pint of paraffin. All of a sudden they'd come back and say " 'Ere, that fuckin' oil you sold me – my fuckin' glass has blown up!" and all that, see. "What's the matter with it?" "Oh it *should* be all right.". . . Anyway, he had the Royal Daylight inspector down there. . . . He said, "You're getting water in this tank, Mr Elton!" He said, "How am I getting water?". . . "Well, there's water *in* it!" he said. . . . So I thought to meself, Well, I'll have to ease up on *that* lark for a bit.'

This could not go on for long. Elton, who had been sacked from his previous employment for fiddling and presumably knew some tricks himself, had his suspicions and decided to put Billy to the test. The lad had no one to turn to. His mother was in a mental hospital, his step-father would have beaten him; Mr Speller, who ran the boys' activities of the Lennox Road Mission, had been a true friend to Billy, but they had lost contact. Even he would probably not have been able to do anything about the deep trouble in which Billy had landed himself. In a moment of panic, he turned to a traditional solution to the Bunk boy's problem:

'So anyway, the bills was accumulating but he couldn't dispute it cos he was getting his own bills back, and being a long way away – . . . So, I'll never forget it, one Thursday [his afternoon off] it was. . . . This Thursday afternoon he said, "Bill, would you like to come over to Southgate with me today?" I said, "Southgate? What for?" See, I knew straight away, well I had an idea. So he said, "I'm gonna try and get some of them bills in." So by now I was turned 17 like, but I wasn't 18. And previously my mate had joined the Army,

and he was in the King's Royal Rifles, and I used to try his
hat on, and nice overcoat. I thought to meself, that's the life
for me. But when he said are we going over to Southgate, I
said, "No, I'm going to the pictures, Mr Elton," I said, "I'm
sorry.". . . So he said, "All right.". . . So I thought to meself,
This is it. This is the end of the road. So I go down Eversholt
Street and joined up. I was very small then, you know.
"You're not quite big enough," he said. I *begged* him, you
know, the old colour sergeant. I said, "Take me!" He said,
"Well, stand on yer toes a little bit." Now I'm big enough,
ain't I? So he said, "Where do you want to go?" I said,
"King's Royal Rifles," so he said, "Yeah, OK." From there I
went to the Union Jack Club – I didn't want to go home again,
you see, cos I knew what I was gonna get.'

Other lads from the Bunk took this way out of their problems
– Jack Duncan's son did, as an escape from unemployment, but
he'd moved away from the Bunk by then.[35] But the discipline of
Army life did not suit everyone. Arrests for desertion were fairly
frequent among Campbell Road soldiers, at least in the 1920s:[36] of
the four reported cases without wartime implications, two
concerned 18-year-olds and two of 20 years.[37] But Billy Tagg took
to the life well. From 1930 he trained at Winchester and Tidworth
before being shipped to Calcutta. There he developed the boxing
skills he had first picked up at the Lennox Road Mission, but in
one bout he was cut very badly over one eye. He was transferred
to Belfast where, despite treatment, he lost sight in that eye permanently and was discharged medically unfit.

He returned to Campbell Road in the summer of 1934. He
was disabled, workless, and desperately poor; and he had other
problems as well. Before he had joined the Army, when he was
17, he had got a girlfriend, from 58 Campbell Road, pregnant.
Whether that played any part in the escape to the Army is unclear,
although it probably did not. In any event, he visited Campbell
Road a few times on leave and came back there to live, accepting
that he would have to marry and look after his growing daughter.
He lived for a very short time with his step-father, before
marrying, when he was 21 in September 1934:

'And our wedding day consisted of a cheese sandwich. Cheese
sandwich. That was . . . 1934, September. It cost us seven
and six, the banns, I don't know where I got that money from,
I've no idea. And I had to find a witness. The woman upstairs
was good enough to come with us. And her mother, she came.

I remember – I gave them the fare, the three of them the fare
– three three-ha'pennies, I think it was at the time, and I never
had enough, like, I had to walk to Liverpool Road. That's
not there now, that Registry Office. . . . Anyway, guy in the
office. . . . He said, "Well!" he said, "I wish you – " [holding
his hand out]. I said, "Turn it up, guvnor," I said, "you've
got every ha'penny I had." So he didn't wish me luck! . . .'
Were you out of work at that time?
'Yeah, out of work. I said, "I've gotta walk home!" '

Throughout the 1930s, he continued to be more out of work
than in, taking on casual labouring jobs when they offered, or
taking out a barrow on half profits, even doing 'children's' jobs
like minding cars for the Arsenal football fans:

How long were you out of work?
'Oh, it's hard to say now, you might be out of work a year
or something like that, six months. You never knew when
you was gonna get work. Might be lucky, find one or two
odd jobs, you know, gazumping, bit off the side, you know,
sometimes you had a couple of days' work without the dole
knowing. You'd be glad enough to take it.'

The Bunk continued to offer him consolations. He ran a boxing
club for Mr Speller at the Lennox Road Mission, repaying some
of the friendship he'd been shown there as a boy. There was the
gambling, when he could afford it. There was the rough and
tumble of Bunk life – it was he, remember, who fought Bill Tasker
at the Paddington Street corner on a Sunday morning, egged on
by his bloodthirsty step-father. There were the opportunities for
a little work 'on the side' through Bunk contacts. And there was
the chance of a relatively cheap furnished room for a family who,
for a long time, had nothing. It was for all these reasons that it
never occurred to him to find anywhere else to live outside
Campbell Road, staying there until the 1950s:

'There was no option. No option *but* to stay. I had no money.
I was out of work. I had no option but to stay.'

Harry James and the young thieves of Campbell Bunk

Harry James was born in 1914 at 30 Campbell Road.[38] His father,
Dido, was the travelling knife-grinder with gypsy connections

who had fought Ernie Barnes for the title of 'King of the Pikies': 'he'd fight any man in two shoes.' He was also the part-time receiver of stolen property who mercilessly beat his sons for not keeping straight. Harry's mother was more supportive and protected him from his father. Harry had seven living siblings, only one of whom, a brother, was older.

Harry's schooling at Blackstock Road Elementary was not a happy time: 'I did more wag from school than I did at school', and he was left with severe reading difficulties which stayed with him all his life. There had been one particularly traumatic incident. Harry was a small, underfed, and very poor boy. He carried with him an intense ambition to wipe out, in any way possible, the inequalities bequeathed him at birth. He made up for his short stature by a fierce and fearless aggression, wielding any weapon necessary to make up for his lack of inches and ounces. He would also take whatever he needed – either to live, or to teach someone a lesson for having too much:[39]

'I had one or two good hidings in the school. I thieved a kid's money out of his pocket. He was telling everybody how much money he used to have in his pocket in the cloakroom and all that. I thought, Oh yeah. And he was telling me one day, and I said, "Oh, yeah? yeah?" I crept down and crept into the – where they used to hang all the coats – and I went through all the coats till I found the money. But I got caught. . . . And they had me out in front of all the school and I had six of the best there. Soon as I had six of the best, I made I was going to the toilet like, I was away, you know, I pissed off. I never went to school then for about a fortnight. . . . Till one day the old man was there when the school board bloke come. Ha Ha. That's when he give me – he did go to town on me. He don't only hit you with his hands, he give you the old slipper [i.e. kicked him] and all, you know.'

Harry was also stealing frequently out of school as well. He stole sweets for his schoolfriends from 'old mother Kendall's' shop in Blackstock Road; pies and sausages from the processed meat factory which opened in Campbell Road for a time; bread from Miller's, the German bakers on Paddington Street corner; and meat from Hammett's, the butchers round the corner in Seven Sisters Road. Most of this would end up on the dinner table at home. Harry's mother covered up for him in lying to his father about

the food's origin. This important family support for his thieving
was extended later.

It was in his early teens that thieving began to become a way of
life. Harry began hanging around the Empire Music Hall, stealing
from cars and even from the artistes' dressing rooms and audience
cloakrooms. He began to hawk the swag to likely customers in
Campbell Road, where someone was always looking for articles
on the cheap and no questions asked.

When Harry left school he was barely able to read and write.
Only the dullest and worst-paid work was open to him, and the
alternative sources of excitement and subsistence from thieving left
work with few potential attractions. Nevertheless, he did find a
job labouring in an iron foundry in Holloway Road. He was there
a few months only, until one day a man asked him – because of
his size and evident toughness – if he had ever considered being a
jockey. Harry had grown up with horses at Barnet Fair, the annual
gathering of gypsies north of London every September which his
parents always patronised. The offer was seriously intended and
Harry took it up: 'signed all the papers and all that, just gonna get
on the train, the old mother wouldn't let me go' – perhaps because
of the loss of earnings if he had gone. Whatever the reason, this
was a bitter blow. Harry left home for good:

'Well, then I never done no work after that, I mean, you
couldn't get a job, I mean it's logic, I mean. I left home,
might have been about 15, 16. May have been older than that.
Then I was out thieving all the time, you know.'

But significantly, he stayed in Campbell Road. It is a measure
of the importance of the top end/bottom end divide in the street
that his father – who would have beaten him for his disobedience
in leaving home without permission – did not know where Harry
had gone when he moved in with Rachel Grogan and her son at
the top end of the street. He decided to follow the dominant
tendencies of his life until then by thieving for a living. The
excitement and material rewards of thieving combined with a
means of gaining self-esteem, proving himself a 'man' in this man's
world outside wage labour.[40] He did so at a time when juvenile
crime, yet again, was becoming increasingly a matter of 'public'
concern, and when the police and magistracy would, during the
early 1930s, respond more vigorously than ten years before.[41]

There were three major influences on his choice of career, all
directly related to the advantages of staying in Campbell Road.
Harry James was well placed to become a thief.

First, his elder brother had by this time (1929–30) become an accomplished pickpocket, practising on Harry at home to improve his technique:

'My brother was a thief. He was a good pickpocket. He was the greatest. He used to go down the Zoo and all that, you know. . . . If we see a woman with a purse in her pocket we used to tail on, get up close to her . . . and bop! Slide it out and – . . . He used to do the hoisting. I used to be a cover-up. . . . Me and old Jimmy Copley used to be the cover-up. If we get a purse we'd have it away a bit quick. We always used to know where to meet one another, empty the poke . . . and go round again.'[42]

Second, there were the specific support systems offered by Bunk culture. In the whole of London there were probably only one or two streets of comparable size which could compare with Campbell Road's 'criminal record'. The New Survey of London received from Scotland Yard the address of every person arrested for an indictable offence in 1929. The Queensland Road area, for instance, recorded two; the Rupert Road area five; George's Road seven; Wilmer Gardens, Hoxton, the pre-1914 'worst street in London', locally known as 'Kill-Copper Row' – six; and Essex Street, Hoxton, which carried the title of 'worst street in London' between the wars, seven. In Campbell Road, the figure was twelve – ten men and two women, with ages ranging from 61 to 14½; half were 18 or under.[43] Informal networks for distributing stolen property were strengthened by semi-professional fences – one of the coal-shop keepers for instance. Then the older thieves of Campbell Road might provide advice and practical assistance, and a few bob to someone just released from prison (or 'out of pawn'). For instance, Harry had grown up a close acquaintance of Freddie Creed, born around 1887. Creed ended a long career as a ware-house and shop-breaker at the end of the 1920s, and settled into a less risky business as one of Campbell Road's street bookmakers. He used also to buy some stolen property, occasionally from Harry, until they fell out. Bert Lax, out of Hurlock Street, but who lived in the Bunk for a short time before settling conveniently close in Playford Road, was associated more with Campbell Road than with any other Holloway street. A key figure in the Holloway and Finsbury Park underworld until the Second World War, Lax was born about 1899, fifteen years before Harry James, and was part of an older generation of thieves. But Harry knew him well and drank with him, even though they did not 'graft' together.

There were numerous other examples of older thieves of importance in the underworld locally who either lived in Campbell Road
for a time (even though their families were better-known in other
streets nearby) or who were frequently to be found there, especially
at gambling schools. Sometimes these men went to Campbell
Road for protection, and this was one of the other supports the
street could provide to a young man like Harry. The kip house
under Sonny Smithson's management was one such hiding place,
and we have seen how gamblers were offered sanctuary in a street
where public opinion was more feared than the law.

Third, there was the network of young thieves in Campbell
Road which provided experience to tap, information to use, labour
to exploit, rivals to fight. Between 1929 and 1938, charges against
29 Campbell Road men aged 16 to 25 were reported, for theft or
associated crimes (excluding suspected persons). Virtually all of
these men would have been living in the street at the same time
during the early 1930s at least. Fourteen of them were charged
more than once. Comparable figures for the Rupert Road area,
with a population ('poor and semi-criminal or degraded') twice as
large as Campbell Road's, were twenty young men, of whom six
were charged more than once.[44] Most of these young Campbell
Road men were by no means full-time thieves, even for a short
period. Yet that they could be made into full-time thieves is clear,
both from the internal pressures of Campbell Road and from the
external labelling effects of police propaganda and action, casting
all youth in the same mould. 'This is a very bad neighbourhood',
complained a detective when giving evidence against three young
men from Campbell Road. 'Four out of five of the younger generation are convicted thieves.'[45] And many times evidence against
young men from the street was larded with references to 'associ-
ating with thieves', and keeping 'bad company'. It is difficult to
assess the effect of this amplification in individual cases, but some
careers are suggestive, as well as providing a context for placing
Harry James's experiences.

Take Lenny Chine, for instance, born around 1907. His father
was blind, a match-seller outside Finsbury Park station. Chine's
first court appearance was in early-1929, charged with two other
Campbell Road men with stealing tobacco and cigarettes from a
Fonthill Road café. The other men were a 22-year-old labourer,
on probation as a suspected person; and another 22-year-old
engineer who, a few months later, was to be acquitted of a serious
robbery with violence charge against a Hornsey Road fishmonger.
Chine described himself as a 'wood seller', and Detective Dance
confirmed that he

had done some woodchopping at 66 Campbell Road and he
had been seen pushing a barrow, but lately witness had seen
him at the corner of Playford Road, Fonthill Road, Paddington
Street and Campbell Road, in the company of half a dozen
convicted thieves. If he would but keep from these men he
would be able to work. . . . [But] he will not keep away from
them. He is continually in their company. They never will
work and even if you offered them employment I do not
think they could take it. They cause us no end of trouble with
petty larcenies.

The court missionary had arranged a job out of the area via a
Church Army home. But Chine's mother 'did not want her son
to go away because she would "miss his ha'pence" ', and Chine
himself said, 'I have got to think of my mother. There is no one
to maintain her.' In the event, the job turned out to be in Greece
and the magistrate ordered that he need not go to the home.[46]
Chine stayed in Campbell Road and made up his mind about
the career that offered him most, fastest. Within six months, now
a 'fruit seller', he was back in court, charged with a man not in
custody with stealing car tyres from a garage at Friern Barnet.[47]
A year later he was charged (as a 'labourer') with drunk and
disorderly, fighting with a man in Campbell Road – a 'hostile
crowd' tried to prevent his arrest.[48] There is then a three-year gap
in the court reports which presumably did not reflect a hiatus in
his activities, for in 1933 he was charged (as a 'general dealer' and
giving an address in Queen's Road, Finsbury Park) with breaking
and entering a billiard hall and stealing cigarettes and chocolate,
but he was acquitted.[49] Then, after August Bank Holiday, he was
charged (now a costermonger and back in Campbell Road) with
assaulting the police in a fracas involving two other men and two
young prostitutes.[50] And a few weeks later he was charged with
causing grievous bodily harm to a Wood Green man, but the
evidence was contradictory and Chine was discharged once more.[51]
It was about this time that the police began one of their periodic
campaigns against prostitutes in Finsbury Park. In May 1934,
Chine, car dealer of Campbell Road, and a man giving an address
in Wilberforce Road who was an accomplished house breaker
originally from the Bunk, were charged with living wholly or
partly on immoral earnings, using the Wilberforce Road house as
a brothel. Chine was living with a woman for whom he was
also acting as 'protector' or ponce. Both men were convicted and
received five months' hard labour.[52]
Prison, as so often, failed to 'cure' him. In May 1939, Chine

and two other men were charged with robbery with violence, using a revolver to extort £121 10s from a crooked Whitechapel tobacconist; they had offered him some stolen cigarettes at £2 per thousand in a car at Camden Town. Two days before war broke out, Chine received 12 months at the Old Bailey.[53]

Chine's case is unusual in the diversity of his enterprises, although at least two other Campbell Road thieves also made money from prostitution; one of these, on reliable information, ended up in Soho, driving a Bentley.[54]

More typical were those men like Harry James (for whom Chine was a 'mackerel',[55] generally to be avoided) who kept to fairly narrow patterns of thieving – shop breaking, house breaking and burglary, with an occasional foray into handbag snatching. Harry James almost never worked alone, in any of these enterprises, and when he started out he usually grafted with other young men from Campbell Road. His first jobs, too, tended to be very close to home: shops in Stroud Green Road, Seven Sisters Road, Fonthill Road, even a rag factory in Campbell Road itself.

Harry had a reputation for ready violence if he found himself at all thwarted:

> 'I've known that man to hit somebody on the chin at [the] least look at 'em, going through the tube and somebody he didn't like, bosh, down he went. Now he was *always* looking for someone.'[56]

He kept about him a home-made cosh which he called a 'kennedy,[57] a length of rubber hose filled with lead, which would hurt an opponent without cutting him, thus avoiding a charge of 'wounding'. But he would use whatever weapon was handy – a pair of fire tongs and a cripple's crutch, to take two examples – and was always ready to kick an assailant when he was down: 'putting the old slipper in', he called it, much like his father had done to him when a boy.

It was in this way that Harry fought to establish masculine self-esteem in an ultra-competitive mistrustful world, where his talents were unexceptional for even a petty thief. His criminal career was not impressive.[58] Between 1930 and 1937 he served two lots of three-year borstal, 'the finest finishing-schools for criminals any underworld could wish for'.[59] He was released on licence, probably both times, but once only after two years; he apparently blotted his record by trying to escape from Portland and was sent to Feltham, the institution for 'backward' delinquents. In 1934, between Borstals, he was sent to Pentonville ('a real prison',[60] at the Holloway end of the Caledonian Road) for two months on a 'sus' charge. And from 1937 he was in and out of prison: 'I was never out. The longest I was out was – six weeks – I was back again.' In 1940 he was moved from Pentonville to Lewes after the 'Ville was bombed in an air raid.

We might gain some insight into the local underworld relations of which Campbell Bunk's young men were part by looking closely at Harry's most rewarding job in the 1930s. This was a weekend raid on a Harringay outfitter's which netted him and his two accomplices some £650, the equivalent for each of a year's wages for a London bus driver. By this time, around 1935, Harry was an experienced shop breaker. He was still grafting with some of his earliest acquaintances, like Fatty from Osborne Road, Finsbury Park; Johnny Reader, a café owner from Fonthill Road, in whose back room they'd talk over schemes; George Euesden (no fixed address); Harry Branson from Athelstane Road; and George Stevenson, George Gibbon and another Fatty, all from the Bunk. His days were spent in drinking with these and other pals. Normally he did not get up until 11 or 12 in the morning, but if he was up early or all night he would start drinking in the Covent Garden market pubs and carry on until the afternoon, when he would go back home for 'a couple of hours' kip'. His only passion at this time was clothes, for he, too, was a flashy dresser: 'I had plenty of clothes – might have about two or three dozen shirts. . . . Those times you pay about three or four quid for a pair of shoes, that was a lot of money.' He was also generous with his cash – treating family and friends, and bailing out a fellow thief threatened with eviction, for instance.[61] Women did not 'interest' him:

'. . . they never used to worry me, girls . . . I used to stand and talk to 'em and that, but as for anything else, that was out of the question.'

So, in the evenings, when he emerged from his boozy cocoon he was after only one thing: 'to see what you can get hold of.' It was on one such jaunt that he stumbled across a special piece of luck:

'There was an old woman outside Finsbury Park at that time. She used to sell peanuts and spearmint and all that, you know. I got chatting to her and I said, "I'll have to come round and have a cup of tea one of these nights." So she said, "Yeah." So I said, "I'll help you pack up," like, see. I helped her pack up her little bit of a stall and that – she used to have a big basket. I says to her, "Get in," I said, "I got an old motor, get

in . . . I'll take you home." She said, "It ain't knocked off is
it?" I said, "No, not knocked off, gal, straight one." So I took
her home to Harringay. And when I take her home it's a
fuckin' man's outfitter's. She lived over the top of it. Got
talking to her and that. Three nights running I went there.
Second night I was there I said, "Caw!" I said, "got no fuckin'
fags." I said, "I'll go and get some." She said, "Don't leave
the street door open, will yer?" I said, "No . . . well, give us
a key and I'll let meself in then." So she said, "All right."
Then I had . . . [a] bit of soap – bar of soap. Took an
impression of it and – who cut the fuckin' key? Oh, Johnny
Reader. . . .'
Who did you do the job with?
'Fatty Peters . . . and young Alec Jenner. He used to live in
Playford Road. . . . I told them I had something lined up.
We used to meet in Johnny Reader's caff, in the back room.
How much did you give Johnny Reader for doing the key?
'Nothing! cos we was like – we always used to muck in. . . .
Went in there on a Saturday night, packed all the stuff up
there all night. In there all day Sunday, still packing it all up
and that you know, tying it all up, packing it all up. And get
a load tied up and packed up and that. Put it in the van. Young
Alec Jenner was driving the van. Me and old Fatty was in
there packing it all up and that.'
Where did the van come from?
'Thieved it. Thieved it, put the old ringers on it, dummy plates
on it, you know. . . . We wasn't taking it far. We was only
taking it to Harringay.'
Were you taking it straight to the fence?
'Oh yeah, yeah. . . . He was a boxer. I can't remember what
name he used to fight under. He was a fifteen-rounder . . . I
used to know him as Curly. Some used to call him Texas,
different people used to call him different names, but I used
to know him as Curly. I used to meet him in the Salon Bal,
the old billiard hall [on the corner of West Green Road and
Green Lanes]. All the business was done there. . . .'
Before taking the stuff to Curly, did you fix up a price?
'Well, you'd say, "Well, what do you reckon?" When you go
in a shop, like you buy a pair of socks or a pair of braces,
just to size up and see what it is. . . . Then you say to Curly,
"Well, I reckon about a monkey", five or six hundred quid.
He'd say, "Right. But if there's any more, then you'll have to
wait." So you say that's all right. . . . We wind up getting
about six-fifty, I think it was . . . pound notes.'

How was that shared out? Equal?
'Oh yeah, right to the penny.'[62]

It is possible, without positing any casual relationship between the two, to see how well the ideology and practice of the under-world coincided with the egalitarianism and individualism so prevalent in the Bunk. The Bunk was not only a congenial place for young thieves like Harry James to live in; it was able also to accommodate his state of mind. He was at home there on every level.

Even so, the vagaries of a criminal career meant that he was unable to stay in one place too long. There were strongly countervailing tendencies at work here. On the one hand, the Bunk and Harry James accommodated one another very happily. On the other, as long as he stayed there the police always knew where they could find him if they wanted to. On the one hand, again, Harry could not afford to move out of north-east Holloway without risking taking on the garb of 'stranger' in some other villain's territory.[63] And on the other, magistrates were prone to making place of residence and restricted associations firm clauses in probation and binding orders.

In effect, Harry compromised by renting a furnished room locally, always within ten minutes' walk of Campbell Road; and by spending his time in the Bunk and the nearby haunts he had always used since becoming a man – Johnny Reader's café, the Orange caff in Seven Sisters Road, the Durham pub, and the Pooles Park Tavern:

Where was the share-out done?
'At that time I was living at, I had a furnished room in Victor Road . . . off of Andover. We shared the money out there. . . . I stopped in that house, oh for about three weeks . . . and too many people got to know where I lived, so I thought: Fuck this, I'd better find another rabbit-hutch. From there I moved down to that Isledon Road, Finsbury Park end, yeah. I didn't know like who lived in there until three or four days later. There was Flo Stevenson [a prostitute, originally from Campbell Road] lived in there, and Lennie Beer [her protector] – oh a right fuckin' lot, I'd moved in with a fuckin' load of thieves.'

It was there, about three o'clock one morning, that Harry had a visit from Scotland Yard's 'heavy mob' which led eventually to his second borstal sentence.

During the later 1930s, Harry James teamed up with an older Queensland Road man whom he had met during a short spell at the 'Ville. Talking during exercise periods, they agreed to go 'on the creep' together, burgling occupied houses at night. Their technique, tried and tested by the older burglar, was to use North London's railway lines to gain access to the backs of likely houses. It paid for a time until the inevitable demise, followed by a brief change of tack into another new line.

How many elements of Campbell Road life converge in this young man's life chances and what he was able to make of them. There was the tradition, a family and neighbourhood inheritance both, of rejecting the labour market and the dull demeaning wage relations it offered, in favour of economic individualism. There was acceptance of a dominant communal ideology of egalitarian individualism which left some space at least for action outside society's laws. There was the construction, among men of all ages but especially the young, of a hierarchy of masculine self-esteem based on physical strength, courage and daring rather than on work culture; a masculinity with sympathetic reverberations in a wider popular culture of clubs, sports and cinema. There was the explicitly oppositional element to cultural tradition in the Bunk, with the police as its natural enemy. And there were the amplifying effects of authority's and the wider society's responses, with discrimination by employers, police, social missionaries and magistrates against the young men of Campbell Road: Harry James, for instance, claimed to have been given three years on the evidence of a corrupt and vindictive police inspector.[65]

We have here no pass-key for understanding the vexed etiology of 'juvenile delinquency'. No such simple tool exists, although that will not stop the search going on. Some young men have stolen for a living in every generation: but that does not mean that they have done so for the same reasons, or because of the apparent conjuncture of similar social forces. In the real world of Campbell Road in the years between the wars, certainly until the late 1930s, it was easy, comfortable and logical for a young man to want to become a thief. Dido James and Jack Duncan – whose boy, the potential postal clerk, also became a thief after an abbreviated army career – failed to impose a different order on their sons' lives because so much in the psychic, cultural and economic cosmos of Campbell Bunk pulled in this one direction. Elsewhere the path was not so straight and broad but young men trod it none the less, and for a variety of individual and social reasons. Even in Campbell Road, it was not essential that a young man stole for a living, because many other tendencies could also be accommodated in the

Bunk, as we saw with Walter and Billy. It was merely essential that he was allowed to do so. And in the process he would get encouragement from the minority who had taken the same course with him.

In August 1939 Harry married a girl from Campbell Road whose brother had been his companion in thieving during the early 1930s. She had been away in those years in an industrial or approved school and had not long been back when she married Harry. Immediately, and for the first time, Harry moved away from Campbell Road – to Duncombe Road, just over a mile away in the shadow of the workhouse. Harry's new wife knew all about his means of subsistence and, indeed, he was in prison within two months of being wed. It is unclear whether this move away from Campbell Road was at her instigation or at his: but, in the context of what we know about other young women's aspirations in Campbell Road, this coincidence of marriage and moving away will prove suggestive.

7 Young women and the new world outside

Work, culture and marriage

Boys' and girls' lives in Campbell Road were marked more by their contrasts than by their coincidences. The contrasts were at their sharpest in the years of half-independence from family life, the time when youngsters began to fashion for themselves the template their lives would follow. First, the world of work held very different opportunities for girls than it did for boys. Second, girls (as did boys) took their own material and mental culture from gender-specific sources or from sources which, though shared, held gender-specific meanings. And significantly less of this cultural life was rooted in the Bunk than in the case of young men: Campbell Road held far fewer consolations for girls than it did for their brothers. Third, the alternative life chances of the delinquent career were traditionally more constrained for women than men. And there was one final element which, although common to young men and women both, contained a quite different promise for each: marriage. For girls, marriage was the great fantasy leap out of family and out of Campbell Road. But in making it, there was always a danger that they would re-create the destiny from which they sought escape.

Labour markets, as was remarked in chapter 2, are stratified by more than one social factor, among them gender and age. In the case of women, there were two largely separate labour markets divided less by age than by marriage. Girls and single women had wider job opportunities from which to choose than did married women, whose labour-power was restricted mainly by family considerations and partly by employer prejudice. This division held generally good throughout the inter-war period. Within that basic framework, however, there were important changes which effectively restructured labour opportunities for girls and single women within a generation. And nowhere was that restructuring more radical in its nature and effects than in London.

Before 1914, the dominant employment sectors for girls in

London had been domestic service, shop work, laundries, and factory work in a relatively limited list of trades like dress, food, drink, tobacco, and stationery.[1] The First World War had a growth effect, direct and indirect, on the types of factories in which women worked. Employment increased in the traditional women's trades like food, drink, tobacco and stationery, although employment in dress manufacture and laundries declined sharply. But the wartime introduction of women into the metal-working trades and into other sectors like chemicals, was never to be reversed.[2] When the munitions and gas mask factories switched back to their previous manufactures of saucepans or meters or corsets, women's work, by and large, switched with them. It did not, however go to the same women. Married women were permanently displaced, partly by returning soldiers, mainly by boys and girls. For manufacturing industry had grown increasingly dependent on girls' nimble (and cheap) fingers. The war, which had (for other reasons) created the dependency in the first place, was to be a harbinger of a women's invasion of commodity manufacture in London, especially in new industries, from the early 1920s on.

As early as 1923, the female inspector of factories for the south-east division could report that

> the manufacture of wireless sets and the extension of
> broadcasting has provided employment for a large and
> increasing number of women and girls in processes for which
> women's hands are found particularly suitable. A great deal
> of the work done by the women is skilled or semi-skilled and
> demands accuracy and concentration. In the assembling room
> many very small and delicate wireless and telephone parts are
> put together, and the work calls for care and fineness of
> touch.[3]

To this could be added the manufacture of electrical fittings like lampholders, plug tops, fuse boxes; electrical appliances like vacuum cleaners, gramophones, and neon signs; bulbs, valves, and dry-cell batteries.[4] And then there was the increase in division of labour in the traditional manufacturing trades of London, like furniture making (especially french polishing and upholstery) and box making (tin and cardboard). This helped to bring girls into these factories in large numbers for the first time.[5]

That was certainly the picture for the new industrial suburbs of London, and it is tempting to let it stand for London as a whole. But the scene in Islington was rather less dramatic. Factory employment in the metal trades did increase for women living in the borough, but figures of 1,532 in 1911 and perhaps 2,100 in 1931 are hardly evidence of a revolution.[6] Indeed, the apparent continuities in women's employment locally across the great fracture of the First World War are as distinctive as any changes (see table 18). We will need to look more closely at this picture before we can find clues to understand the changing opportunities for girls in Campbell Road. If we feed in the age variable some of these differences become clearer.

Compared with 1911, employment prospects for girls (aged 17 or under) in 1931 had improved enormously: 80.4 per cent of girls were in work in 1931 against 67.9 per cent before the First World War (see table 19). By far the largest growth sector of girls' employment had not been in manufacturing (which had declined relatively and absolutely) but in commercial occupations (primarily shop work and clerical/typing). The seven-fold increase in this sector was sufficient alone to account for the increase in employment as a whole. On the other hand, the number of indoor domestic servants aged 17 or under declined from 1094 in 1911 to 419 in 1931 (or 14.2 per cent of all occupied girls to 4.9 per cent).

A comparison with the boys' labour market over the same period is illuminating. The proportion of boys occupied stayed much the same at 82.1 per cent in 1911 and 84.7 per cent in 1931. Within that market, the classical 'blind-alley' occupations of van boys and messengers stayed virtually constant at 30.6 per cent of working boys in 1911 and 29.0 per cent in 1931 (comparisons for 'errand boys' are unobtainable). The contrast of a traditional boys' labour market and the dynamic, rapidly changing opportunities for girls is clear.[7]

The expanded commercial sector hardly affected the girls of Campbell Road directly. Typing and clerical jobs were reserved for central school leavers, and few enough Campbell Road girls went from elementary to central school at age 11.[8] These jobs and shop work were most susceptible to employer concern with the socially defined qualities of labour-power – like smartness, good looks, the growing importance of a 'nice' telephone voice.[9]

Before the war, the main work opening for 'rough' girls from the slums had been in laundries or casual domestic service and other cleaning jobs, and the more intermittent, seasonal or noxious forms of factory employment. Factory work was losing its traditional 'rough' reputation in the 1890s and Edwardian period and attracting more girls from respectable working-class families.[10] Clara Collet, in 1893, made clear the status divide among women factory workers:

In trying to give some idea of the life and condition of the factory girl, I must not be understood to refer to all girls in factories. By the 'factory girl' is meant the lower grade of factory workers who may be found in comparatively small numbers in box, brush, and cap factories; who are in the majority in the jam factories, and who hold undisputed sway in the rope and match factories. Girls in factories often earn 11s and upwards; the 'factory girl' generally earns from 7s–11s. . . . I do not refer to the thousands of quiet, respectable, hard-working girls who are also to be found working in factories.[11]

But now the daughters of the respectable working class had set their sights higher, out of the factories and into the offices and superstores. In their wake, factory employment could provide regular, independent and co-operative work for girls from the 'roughest' families, away from the discomfort, drudgery and tyranny of the lowest forms of domestic service and cleaning. The girls from London's poorest families seized their chance with both their 'particularly suitable' hands. Domestic service was left for girls from the provinces, or the transferees from the depressed areas.[12] In the last chapter we noted some continuities between fathers' and sons' occupations in Campbell Road; there was no such continuity between mothers and daughters. Mothers in Campbell Road were charwomen, laundresses, streetsellers; daughters were factory hands above all, with only a minority working in the improved laundries of post-1919 London.[13]

Compared with the prospects for boys from slum streets, factory work was generally regular and contributed greatly to the relatively infrequent and shorter periods of unemployment among girls.[14] Factory work could also have prospects, and some of the poorest girls stuck with work right through marriage and restricted child-bearing, as we shall see in a moment. Factories, too, were changing in these years, with a growing (but not universal) tendency to managerial concern with employee welfare. There was a feeling expressed by some informed observers at the time that factories were attracting a 'better class' of worker, especially among girls.[15] In fact, this reversed cause and effect. Factory work – regular, involving contact with many other girls, in an environment becoming more conscious of cleanliness and wellbeing – actively fostered a concern among workers for socially acceptable standards of dress, behaviour and so on. The factory was becoming a structural element in a new 'feminine' culture.

This was especially so for the girls of Campbell Road, where factory work provided, if the oral evidence is truly indicative, employment for the large majority. But factory girls found themselves in potential competition with smart and fashionable girls employed as shop assistants, Lyons 'nippies', supercinema usherettes, and so on.

> A queue of over 1,000 women and girls was to be seen outside
> the Tottenham Employment Exchange on Friday morning.
> They were waiting to receive their 25s out-of-work bonus. It
> was a well-dressed queue; the musquash and seal coat,
> eloquent of the former munition worker, was not absent, while
> most of the queue-ists appeared to be under 21. . . . On the
> same day the *Herald* advertisement columns contained 187
> advertisements for domestic servants, and about 100 more for
> female assistants for businesses and laundries.[16]

The First World War was only two months buried when those words were written yet they summarised a theme which was to become a truism within a decade: of the factory girl, well turned out, too 'good' for work which had been traditionally done by women like her just a generation before.[17] The key elements were 'femininity' and independence (from parental codes and personal domination by a mistress-employer) and they were to become strongly internalised among working-class girls, and the girls of Campbell Road, during the 1920s and 1930s.

If clothes were important for young men, they were a public (and sometimes a private) obsession for young women. Underpinned by an adaptable mass production industry absorbing technological advances from America and the continent, and by a universal system of credit selling, women's fashions were one of the absorbing interests of the age. They embodied post-war newness as much as any of the growth industries or suburbs or architecture, and were as much a consciously radical transformation of what had gone before: in the changing body shape, for instance, the very reverse of the Edwardian fullness of bust and hips, now replaced by tubular lines, 'the cult of the slim figure' and boyish shape;[18] in the frequent allusions to men's fashions in the tight-fitting hats (even bowlers in 1931), tailored jackets and trousers, imported as beach pyjamas around 1930 but turned into full-blown suits (even with neckties) by 1933; and in the tendencies to reveal more of women's bodies, with the rising skirt hem – six inches above the ankle in 1921, just above the knee by 1928 – and in the fashions of sun-bathing and hiking in the early 1930s.

Clothes were clearly indicative of a dramatic redefinition of femininity at this time. The invasion of previously male domains in fashion suggested ambitions of equality with men – of independence from the oppressions of being female expressed through an identification with male freedoms. At the same time, enormous energy was put into the manufacture of sexual attractiveness with the objective of being 'sought after'[19] by a relative shortfall of available men. 'The London girl', wrote Thomas Burke in 1934, 'is always, of course, under a fire of criticism concerning her behaviour and her dress and her masculine activity.'[20] Significantly, too, clothes were beginning to make women look classless, so that, according to Burke and Orwell, it was difficult to tell the social origins of a young woman by her appearance.[21] In J. B. Priestley's memorable phrase, one of the characteristics of the 'new post-war England' was 'factory girls looking like actresses'.[22] Here was one other way of both building and demonstrating self-confidence for working-class girls, independent (at least in their aspirations) of both gender and class deformities. All this was a very different route to independence and equality than that open to the mothers of Campbell Road, battling it out in the family or with a lady employer.

'The most remarkable outward change of the Twenties was in the looks of women in the towns,' according to Robert Graves and Alan Hodge,[23] and although clothes were a large part of that visual transformation from down-at-heel premature ageing to a modern youthful smartness, they were not the whole story. Makeup – the pre-war property of the prostitute alone – was now in every woman's handbag. It was estimated in 1931 that for every 1,500 lipsticks sold in London just one had been sold in 1921.[24] A skin which was quick to tan was now more fashionable than a pale complexion. Hairstyles changed rapidly with the techniques of permanent waving and curling. Woolworth's rhinestone jewellery looked as good as if it had cost a hundred times as much. And non-visual beauty aids like cheap perfumes and cologne, and a 'proper' (BBC) speaking voice all added to the changing norms of femininity.

These norms were, of course, affected in important details by the passing heroines of fashion and independence popularised by newspapers, girls' and womens' magazines, and most of all by the cinema. Some films had women's fashions as their main or only theme. The emancipated woman or career girl was one of the dominant stereotypes of the 1920s and especially 1930s, with stars like Claudette Colbert and Joan Crawford making their own careers in the role. The *News of the World*, the only newspaper commonly read in Campbell Road, magnified the screen beauty into a paradigm of femininity by relating her off-screen attitudes and behaviour as well as fixing her visual image for study and emulation.[25] It also was a vehicle for the tremendous pressures put on women by advertisers. 'Nothing destroys a woman's charm in the eyes of a man so much as ugly superfluous hair' – or 'Fat', or being 'Bony, Angular, Scraggy', or a 'Shiny Nose', or 'Summer Fag', or 'Grey Hair', or 'Skin Troubles', or 'Yellow-tinged eyes' through 'Constipation'.[26]

The new femininity needed two elements for its full realisation: time and money – to buy clothes, makeup, hairdo's; and to take advantage of occasions when they could be seen – at dances, cinemas (small wonder that usherettes' jobs were so popular among women), cafés and so on. Increasingly, femininity was becoming materially-based, demanding not necessarily high but regular earnings capable of meeting the 5s down and 5s a month for a 'Stylish Costume' or a 9 ct gold 'wristlet watch'. And it needed the sort of leisure time unobtainable from pre-war girls' employment like domestic service.[27] All this was assisted by the ideology of feminism, which helped create a climate of female independence with the vote (1928), and discussions around contraception and abortion.[28] Not all of these influences were to reach very deeply into Campbell Road.[29]

Femininity and independence combined also (in an echo of masculinity and independence) for a minority of young women in crime and prostitution. The delinquent career held far fewer attractions for young women than for young men. In the first instance, factory work and low unemployment relatively easily allowed their material requirements to be met. Second, career security – steady earnings until marriage – offered some peace of mind for the future, avoiding the feeling of fear and hopelessness which accompanied chronic unemployment or blind-alley work for young men. And third, the traditions of female delinquency were not so well established and pervasive as those of working-class youths: in fact, they had weakened since before the First World War in contrast to tendencies in male juvenile delinquency.[30] The prostitute, as we have seen, was much more prone to be an outcast than the thief; and women tended to take to thieving later in life than men.[31] Even so, prostitution or thieving were still viable options for a minority of girls in Campbell Road, and there were many local factors predisposing towards both.

It is impossible to be certain about the dynamics of London prostitution between the wars. Police prosecutions fell during the 1920s but picked up during the 1930s, although they never reached

their pre-war figures.[32] Yet this is likely to reflect police practice
more than the activities of prostitutes; for example, it is clear from
the court reports that there were periodic anti-prostitution drives
by the police around Finsbury Park during 1919–20, 1933–4, and
1936–7. It was probably in the 1930s that Finsbury Park first
gained its reputation as a vice area of London.[33]

The various studies of London prostitution between the First
and Second World Wars, together with autobiographies like 'Sheila
Cousins's' *To Beg I Am Ashamed* (1938), reveal a variety of reasons
for adopting prostitution as a career.[34] But in the changing economic circumstances of young working-class women in post-1919
London it is clear that prostitution, if no longer the only alternative
to destitution,[35] was a sure way of getting faster what other girls
had to wait for: better clothes, decent living quarters, 'varied interests' and money in the post office.[36] It is this which probably
accounts for the large number of prostitutes, even between the
wars, who had previously been domestic servants.[37] 'Sheila
Cousins' apparently earned £20 to £30 a week 'without my having
to make the least effort' around Piccadilly, while living with her
mother in Canonbury and later Finsbury Park around 1929–30.[38]
The contrasts between these girls' lives and those open to friends
or mothers were easily pointed up.

> Why should I give up the profesh. for any job *I* could get?
> [asked a Wardour Street prostitute]. A skivvy! Not on *your*
> life. . . . My mother was one before she married dad. . . . And
> talkin' of marriage, I'd sooner walk the streets till I dropped
> than 'ave to go through what mother did.[39]

When girls were starting with nothing – as they did in Campbell
Road – there were many temptations to catch up as quickly as
they could. And, as for young male thieves, the street (sometimes
even the family) might provide them with exemplars, well-dressed,
looking good, and with money to throw around.

Campbell Road was nearly as notorious for its prostitutes as for
its thieves, As late as 1943 there was said to be '20 known prostitutes' living in Campbell Road.[40] According to a local policeman
they were of three types. The 'less attractive' ones ' "worked" on
Seven Sisters Road between Finsbury Park and Manor House,
using the gardens of houses in the vicinity to perform their services'
at 3s 6d or 5s a go. Then there were those who brought men home
to their room. And finally, 'the smarter ones worked the West
End and could be seen returning home about three or four a.m.'[41]
One of these 'smarter ones' was Flo Stevenson, 'The Queen of

the Prostitutes at Finsbury Park' in the view of another police officer.[42] Born in Campbell Road around 1910 or 1912, she was the daughter of a coalshop keeper. According to her solicitor,

> She had had a very unfortunate life. At the age of 16 she lost her mother. She was turned out by her step-mother. At the age of 18, she had an illegitimate child, whom she now had to keep elsewhere.

At the time of that statement, Stevenson was living in the Isledon Road house which Harry James had moved into after his Harringay robbery. She was sharing a room with her sister: 'Both women were using the room as common prostitutes. . . . On six consecutive days in July [1937] each woman took in three or four men.'[43]

There was a variety of routes into prostitution. One mother reportedly escorted her two teenage daughters on to the Seven Sisters Road and collected their earnings at the end of each night.[44] Some were 'half and half', combining prostitution with working as a waitress or in a laundry, for example.[45] But one contemporary of the Stevensons, not herself a prostitute, thought girls stumbled into it:

> 'But they were nice girls and that. See, nine out of ten girls ended up prostitutes cos that's how they got the money. . . . There was nothing else for them.'[46]

At least – not in the short term. Prostitutes, too, could look on 'the game' as a career, not a life sentence excluding marriage. The Wardour Street prostitute might have held strong views about marriage, but it was a marriage like her mother's she was anxious to avoid. Dolly Thomas, another young prostitute from Campbell Road, 'nice looking girl and all, she was', married Walter Spencer's friend who came from the Bunk and so knew all about her past.[47] A prostitute called Ruth married another man in Campbell Road.[48] And so on.

For many young women in Campbell Road, marriage was the great escape, the fastest route out of Campbell Bunk. That, at least, was the dream. Marriage was probably desired by most young women of that generation. But there is evidence that in Campbell Road the desire was felt more strongly than elsewhere.[49]

There were many reasons why young women should choose marriage as a way out of their predicament. There were strong prejudices against girls living alone or taking a room with another girl. Locally, such a move would have carried the stigma of prosti-

tution, and, in any event, many single girls could not have afforded
the rent of a furnished room. Respectability demanded marriage
for a young woman (not so much in the case of a young man)
before she could create her own household. Marriage was a
strongly normative influence in society as a whole. And when a
woman who had been going steady found herself pregnant – as,
according to the Registrar General in 1938–9, nearly 30 per cent
of first-time wives did – then marriage was the natural next step.[50]

Marriage, consequently, was a young woman's main alternative
to the disadvantages of much family life in Campbell Road: the
overcrowding of bed-living rooms and the primitive washing and
dressing facilities – hardly appropriate for the new-look girl of the
1920s and 1930s; the violent relations between parents and the
physical degradation of mothers; the restrictions on daughters'
independence; and the exploitative relationships between parents
and children. Girls suffered more in this family exploitation, in
obvious ways like being kept home to look after younger
siblings,[51] but also economically. Frequently, mothers felt they had
a right to demand more from their daughters than from their sons,
partly because daughters knew the details of inadequate housekeeping money handed over by fathers, and partly out of a willing-
ness to accept second-best for their sex. But the battles between
mothers and daughters in Campbell Road – not present in every
case but sometimes fiercely fought out – had other, temporal and
poignant origins. Every generation of men and women envies at
least some of the opportunities open to its children.[52] For mothers
whose own childhood was in the London of the 1890s or the early
Edwardian era, the sight of the new world opening up for their
daughters in work, leisure and spending power must have held
bitter regrets as well as satisfactions.

Marriage, too, might be an escape from the inadequacies of
Campbell Bunk outside home and family. Campbell Road's collective culture did not hold the same attractions for the new femininity
as it did for young men and masculine culture. Gambling,
drinking, sport and street theatre were minority interests among
women, especially young ones. It was increasingly to the factory
that young women were looking for stimulation and companion-
ship – frequently shared, of course, with other girls from Campbell
Road but involving extensive outside contacts with other women.
Many elements of the new femininity were frankly out of place in
the Bunk, where smart clothes and a career-girl appearance might
provoke antagonism rather than admiration.[53]

One other component of femininity was at first sight at odds
with the aggressive egalitarianism and independence of the 'new

woman' of the 1920s and 1930s. This was the fetishisation of home
– and woman as home-maker – which was intensified during these
years.[54] This was one of the ideological props to, and consequences
of, the rapid growth of suburban owner-occupation in London as
in the rest of England, and although that was a movement outside
the attainable sphere of young women in Campbell Road it still
had its effect. Romantic love, marriage and building a home
provided much of the substance for novelettes, magazine stories,
popular songs, and English cinema.[55] 'Keeping up with the neighbours' was a laudable ambition and did not yet imply a sneer.[56] A
whole house could be furnished on the never-never – a three-piece
suite for 6s down, a bedroom fitted out for 5s 6d down and 5s 6d
a month. And the key to the door – a wedding ring – could also
be had for a shilling down. How inadequate the homes of
Campbell Road must have seemed when set against these standards: not even gaslight, let alone electricity; one room for a family;
a cold tap in a shared scullery or on the landing; the stench of the
night buckets being emptied each morning. In a survey of working-class Londoners who married between the wars, Eliot Slater
and Moya Woodside could state:

> Marriage and home are synonymous in many people's minds,
> and the equation between the two is a characteristic feature
> of our sample. . . . Wanting a home is the most common
> reason for marriage. . . . Almost the highest praise one spouse
> can give the other is in such phrases as a 'home lover', 'home-
> loving', 'all for the home'.[57]

Table 20 gives details of marriages made by people living in
Campbell Road and Playford Road between 1921 and 1938 at St
Anne's Church, Pooles Park. It reveals very significant differences
in marriage patterns between the two streets. First, men and
women married younger in Campbell Road than Playford. Women
married younger than men in both cases. But in Campbell Road,
over the whole period, 32.4 per cent of women were 20 or younger
at marriage; in Playford Road the proportion was just 8.6 per
cent.[58] The mean age at marriage for spinsters marrying bachelors
in England and Wales in the mid-1930s was 25.0 years; the mean
for Campbell Road was 21.2.[59] This was against the trend to defer
marriage where women's employment prospects were good.[60]
Contrary to the Slater and Woodside survey, which found that
only 'a few' of the marriage partners had known each other as
neighbours,[61] the proportions of marriages with both partners from
the same street (endogamous marriages) seem extraordinarily high.

Even so, there was a marked difference between the 1920s and 1930s, with endogamous marriages at $^2/_3$ to $^3/_4$ of all marriages in the earlier period falling to around half in the 1930s. Endogamous marriages were more common among Campbell Road women than men. There might be a number of reasons for that – prejudice from boys and their families outside, narrower opportunities and reduced social space within which they moved.[62] But I suspect it was more a function of the early age of marriage – in their haste they gave themselves little time to meet boys from outside the street.

There were, of course, striking contradictions in all this. Marriage, the end product of financial independence and a material culture of femininity, was so often the negation of both. A smaller proportion of women worked after marriage between the wars than before 1914, intensifying the domestic role of married women and reducing delegation of household tasks to daughters.[63] And 'home' could become a prison where the needs of young wives were subordinated to those of the breadwinner and the children.[64] Marriage, the escape from an unhappy family background, might yet reproduce the domestic relations from which girls were fleeing.[65] And marriage, the fastest escape from Campbell Road, was more often than not to a young man from the Bunk who had strong tradition-bound attachments to it.[66] These contradictions were well understood, and not only in Campbell Road:

> The willingness to take a chance [in marrying] . . . is a common attitude among women, and is often coupled with hopes of altering undesirable characteristics or circumstances. . . . It may sometimes be put down to the effects of propinquity and the lack of any wide acquaintance for choice. The wish for a home and a hope for security distorts or obscures normal judgment.[67]

We can see now some of the chances taken and judgments made, as well as some of the ways women sought to reconcile the contradictions of marriage as escape.

May Purslowe, Nancy Tiverton, and the struggle with mothers

May Purslowe was born in 1901 at Fonthill Mews, Lennox Road.[68] Before she could walk her family had moved to the bottom end of Campbell Road, where her mother was to stay until the Second World War. Mrs Purslowe, born on the boat from Ireland around 1880, was a rent collector, moneylender, and later a street bookie's runner. She had eleven children by May's father, but only five survived to adulthood and one of those was emigrated to Canada around 1914. Mr Purslowe was mainly a painter and decorator in the Campbell Road tenement houses but he had also been a potman and stallholder at various times. Even before the First World War, this was a relatively (for Campbell Road) well-off family, boasting a piano on which Mr Purslowe entertained parties of neighbours on Saturday nights. But he was killed at Hill 60 in 1917, the piano was sold, and five years later Mrs Purslowe re-married – a son of the organ-hirer from Fonthill Road.

That was around 1923, but by that time May had already married and left home. She had been an irregular attender at school and left while still 13 to work in a factory at Thane Villas making lead soldiers. Like many of the other factory jobs she took on between 1914 and 1922, May first heard of the place through other Campbell Road girls. Onerous work paid by the piece drove her to change jobs and she went, for a time, as tea girl to another toy factory at Riversdale Road, Highbury. She was then 14, and this was the summer of 1915. The demand for female factory labour for munitions and subsidiary war production was beginning to grow beyond all precedent:

'So then somebody else said to me . . . "There's a new factory opened round the corner, in Isledon Road; would you like to come there and work? There's soldering, soldering hand grenade cases." So you know it was no sooner said than done, we'd go there and get a job, they'd only just opened. . . . I think I was earning about 12s a week there. But the solder stuff . . . used to get down your throat. So anyway, we left there and then we says, "Oh well, we'll go try at Turner's; it's a better place there, you get more money. You can go nightwork there" – cos that was a real thing if we could go nightwork. So at 15 I was working at Turner's, drilling and tapping and doing all that sort of thing right up until the end of the war.'

Before long, May had roped in a sister and her mother to work at Turner's, an engineering factory in Blackstock Road which had been a stable for Pickfords before the war. Mrs Purslowe drilled holes in aeroplane wheels, and May did the same for special horse-shoes for the Russian army, or so she was told.

After the war, Turner's tried to shift to domestic commodity production – metal holders for mops, flat iron faces, kettles – but unsuccessfully, and around 1919 the firm closed and May looked for work elsewhere. She tried to work at Ever Ready's in Fonthill Road, but they were apparently more choosy then than later and turned her down because she lived in the Bunk. She soon found work at a sweet factory for two or three weeks, and then Kemps' biscuit bakery in Brewery Road, but 'I got the sack there for taking biscuits home'; then at a pickle factory, also in Brewery Road, but 'the vinegar all got down your throat' so she didn't stay there longer than a morning; then a printer's in New North Road for three or four weeks, but she found the machinery intimidating; then to King's Cross, packing custard powder on piece work, but she and a friend fell out with a strict forelady; then to a mineral water maker's, also in King's Cross, but bottle-washing was dangerous and unpleasant, standing all day on a wet floor, and once more May moved on. This time, though, she found something to suit. A sister had found work at Barrett's sweet factory in Wood Green: 'there was always a queue of people lining up for jobs and if they were short of hands they used to pick one, two, three, in – and tell what room you'd got to work in, and that's it.' May worked at Barrett's for a year or two before marrying in 1922.

May's leisure time was as active as her factory career. She was prominent in the remnants of the 'monkey parade' along Seven Sisters Road, where Campbell Road boys and girls had trouble from the police just after the First World War.[69] She made a nuisance of herself on street corners, singing and shouting 'and have buckets of water thrown over us to clear us off and all that'. She, her sisters and friends hardly ever ate at home, taking meals in cafés in Blackstock Road and around. Three times a week she would go to the pictures, and buy a sixpenny seat at the Empire or when music hall was on at the Marlborough Theatre in Holloway Road. In the summer and at weekends she and her friends would take a boat out on Finsbury Park lake. And on Saturday afternoons they would go to the nearest public baths and then on to Chapel Street, a street-market mecca for the poorest of Islington's fashion-conscious youngsters at the time.

Towards the end of the war, May was earning about £2 10s a week, although this would have reduced by 1920–1. £2 of this she gave to her mother for housekeeping, but no meals other than breakfast were regularly taken at home. Home itself consisted of two rooms, with three girls sharing a double bed in one, and Mrs Purslowe and May's younger brother sharing a double bed in the other; and Mrs Purslowe was spending most of the money on

drink. She had always been a hot-tempered and violent woman –
it was she, it may be remembered, who threw a lighted oil lamp
at her complaining children one night. But the battle intensified
with May over this question of how the 'housekeeping' was to be
used.

May and her mother had always been at loggerheads. May,
according to Mrs Purslowe, 'had got too much of what the cat
licked its arse with.' May became particularly vocal over how she
should be clothed. Mrs Purslowe had taken it on herself to clothe
May out of the money the girl handed over. But her mother's
choice of couturier was restricted to totters' barrows in Campbell
Road and the Fonthill Road rag shop. Clothes became, for mother
and daughter, a fiercely contested symbol of independence:

> 'And this one particular day I said to her, "I'm not giving you
> all my money, I'm gonna buy my own clothes." And we
> went to Chapel Street, Islington market, and I bought a velvet
> skirt and a blouse. And when I came home, washed meself,
> dressed to go out, she says to me, "And where do you think
> *you're* going?" I said, "Well, I'm going out." So she says,
> "Oh are you?" And she did no more, she tore all these clothes
> off me. And of course I cried and went into me aunt's which
> was next door but one, number 31 . . . and I said to her,
> "Mum's tore all my clothes." So she said, "Oh, you better
> stay in here then." And I had to go indoors back again to get
> me old clothes to put on.'

At night, in their double bed, the girls would fantasise about
their future lives away from home:

> 'And us kids used to lay in bed at night crying, my sisters used
> to. And I used to say, "I'm leaving home, I'm not going to
> stay here, I'm not putting up with this any longer." Then my
> sisters used to say to me, "Oh May, don't leave us; don't
> leave us; what we gonna do if *you* leave?" "Oh well, I'll take
> you with me, but I don't know where we're going cos we
> don't earn enough money to pay for a room for any of us."
> And that's how we used to go on every night.'

But a husband could provide a way out. May first met her future
husband, Bob Chelmer, at Turner's. He was on leave from the
army, with a leg wound, and on a visit to his father, who also
worked there, he met May. She went with him – on the second
or third time of asking, she was always hard to please – to the

pictures, and then they started walking out together. After the war, Bob worked as a warehouseman at Houndsditch. He lived at Wood Green, and that was one of the incentives for May to work at Barrett's – she could have her dinner at his mother's home for instance:

> 'when Mr Chelmer first took me home to his house, it was like walking into heaven there. The table was already laid for tea, nice tea and jelly and cakes and all that. I shut me eyes and I thought to meself, Coo, how smashing this could be. She was so nice, you know, was able to talk to her and talk about you and all that sort of thing which we could never do with our mum.'

This was all very different to the reaction Bob Chelmer first received from Mrs Purslowe, perhaps because a potential son-in-law would have been no compensation for the end of May's housekeeping contributions:[70]

> 'First night he took me home I said to him, "You don't want to come down to my door," I said, "because if me mother comes home drunk you'll be sorry." So he said, "Well, that's all right," he said. So of course, home they come from the Duke public house all merry and bright and singing. And when she went to come indoors, there was my husband standing there with me and she says to him, "What the effin' hell are you doing here?" So he said, "Well, I've brought your daughter home." So she said, "Well you can effin' well sling yer 'ook again." So that was that. So I said to him, "Come on, stand up on the corner." She said, "And you don't want to stop up there all night else I'll have a bucket of piss poured over yer!" So that was the wonderful reception he got.'

May had to creep indoors after she had been out with Bob in case her mother caught her staying out late. And once, when dressed in her finest clothes to go with him to the Wood Green Empire, her mother threw a bucket of slops over her because May hadn't done the washing up. But gradually Mrs Purslowe mellowed towards Bob, probably because she was building a relationship for herself with her future husband and was also drinking less.

In 1922, May and Bob were married at Tottenham. Their mutual inclination was to look for a home at Wood Green and this they were able to do – taking rooms over a greengrocer's in St Michael's Road and eventually an LCC house in Risley Avenue. At her

Wood Green homes, May provided a small wedding reception in the years to come for her two sisters, still living with their mother and new step-father in Campbell Road. The sister who had got May the Barrett's job married a greengrocer's son from Wood Green and settled in to the Noel Park Estate, a short walk from where May was living. The other, working as a packer in a Fonthill Road laundry, married a young man from the house opposite in Campbell Road. He maintained strong cultural attachments to the Bunk as one of 'the hounds' or street-corner boys. They took two rooms in Fonthill Road, over a sweetshop, enabling him to keep up his boyhood friendships.

Perhaps that sister had taken less completely to heart promises made in those night-time conversations when the three girls talked about the lives ahead of them:

'We used to say, "God help us. Never let my kids grow up like this." '

Nancy Tiverton felt very much the same.[71] Her story is of particular interest because she was able to fulfill that promise without the advantages of marrying a man who could take her into a new way of life. Nancy was one of the nine children of Ellen Tiverton, the hard-drinking charwoman who left her family at George's Road around 1911 and whose fortunes were briefly described in chapter 5. Nancy was born in 1905 and lived only three or four years with her mother in Campbell Road between 1917 and 1920. We have seen, too, how Nancy was encouraged by her mother to work full-time at factories during the peak years of wartime labour demand, even though she was not yet 14.

The best and last of those jobs had been making cigarette lighters for 18s a week at a factory on the corner of Goswell Road and Compton Street, Finsbury. To get her started there, her mother begged some clothes from better-off cousins at Norwich:

'You ought to see what they sent. They sent me a grey tweed costume; and I'm not telling lies, you know how these men dress in evening clothes with a tail goes down like that? It was a coat like that. And I was only a little dot, you know, and I used to take a hat along, and it was no deeper than that. It stuck on top of my head. I used to have a decent bit of hair then. . . . Oh and me boots. Now I only take fours now, I had very little skinny legs and that. She got a pair of boots from where she worked – you know, them spring sides? Pair

of them. And I could have got me hands right down 'em, like
that. They were as wide as that! I went to work in them. So
of course I couldn't keep me feet in them, so you know what
I done? Put all newspaper down them to keep 'em on me
feet. So they said to me, "Ooh, ain't you got funny boots on?"
So I said, "Yeah, I got bad feet." See, it made me tell lies, I
had to tell lies for me own sake. . . . When I was coming home
to get on the bus, these boys got round me and went like
that and knocked me hat off me head [flicked it off]. Never
forget it, I cried, you know. I knew I was a laughing stock,
a proper laughing stock. What with these boots and the hat
and the costume. Caw dear!'

Apart from threepence a day 'dinner money', Nancy gave all
her 18s a week wages to her mother for precious little in return.
Two elder sisters, both living with Mrs Tiverton at Campbell
Road, worked at the Star Brush factory in Eden Grove, earning
better money than Nancy:

'I thought to meself, I don't know what to do, you know, as
I am now I'll never get a rag on me back. I was a disgrace, I
was, honest. And it wasn't my fault. So I thought to myself,
I know what I'll do. I won't tell mum. I'll go after the
Christmas holiday, go down to Star Brush, see if I can get
on. . . . So I didn't say a word to her. I come out as though
I was coming to work, and down the Star Brush I went, and
got on. Pound and eightpence a week for a fortnight. Then
you got to know how to work that machine, you gotta learn
that in a fortnight. After a fortnight, piece work. . . . So, of
course, you didn't understand the machine in a fortnight but
you had to do it, but I made up my mind. I thought, Right,
I'll bet I'll earn some money here. Cos I wanted some clothes
and I thought that's the only way I could get me clothes. . . .
So anyrate, when I went piece work, oh I did work hard. I
was only piece work about two months, they called me
"Sweater". As soon as the power went up I started, stop there,
put me coat on right till the power went right down. So
within a few months, I'd had a look round the shops up Chapel
Street and that, the clothes. And I thought, Ooh that looks
nice, that costume. Always remember it. I bought a navy blue
gaberdine costume, skirt and a coat, all modern you know;
and a pink crepe blouse with a little Eton collar, very narrow
little bow, black bow there. That was four guineas that
was. . . . But I paid cash for it. How I could save – I didn't
buy no sweets, I was never used to it, never used to buying

fruit, never used to buy books, so every penny I got, well on piece work I was earning the money, not 'arf. . . . So anyrate, she said to me, "How much you pay for that costume?" So I said, "Four guineas." So she said, "Oh. How much them boots?" "Twelve and six." So she said, "Oh." They was down the pawn shop Monday. She asked that so she knew what to ask for, see? Down there Monday.'

This was not the only one of Mrs Tiverton's tricks. Nancy's sister Marjie, four years her elder, was courting a print worker from Walthamstow, well-off indeed in Campbell Road's terms. Each time he visited Marjie he'd give Nancy half a crown. But Mrs Tiverton spotted this the first time it happened and claimed the money as her own thereafter. She cadged, too, from a Campbell Road boy who asked her permission to take Nancy to Finsbury Park Empire: 'So you know what? Before he could take me out my mum say, "Lend us half a crown, Freddie?" ' Nancy had to hide her money in a makeshift moneybelt tied with string round her waist under her clothes; 'I kept that secret. If I'd told her she would have had it she would.'

Marjie left home over her mother's depredations. Mrs Tiverton had pawned one of the rings given her by the Walthamstow fiancé. And Nancy, too, fell unwittingly into a similar trap. Mrs Tiverton provoked a row and told Nancy to go. She gave Nancy a parcel of her clothes – ' "Take that with you, you haven't got to come back no more here for that." ' But the treasured costume and boots were not in the parcel, and Nancy had to go back to her mother for the pawn ticket. It cost her some 15s to redeem her own clothes from the pawnbroker.

Another daughter, Fran, had also drifted back to her father, and it is interesting to contrast briefly the lives of these three sisters outside Campbell Road. Marjie had been uncomfortable in Campbell Road even before the episode of the ring. Her young man presented her with fine clothes as well as jewellery, 'and she felt Campbell Road was too rough for her then.'

'She didn't like Campbell Road, but she couldn't stop with my dad because he wouldn't allow her to go with her chap, see. So in them days you couldn't go into lodgings just as you liked or get a furnished room, so she was obliged to stop with my mum till it suited her, see.'

Fran, on the other hand, picked up with a man from Campbell Road – one of the hounds – and married him when she was 19, in 1922. He turned out to be a drinker and a wife-beater, and eventually she secured a separation order to remove him from their room in George's Road. He returned to Campbell Road to live with his mother, and Fran brought up her children alone.

Nancy, when she was 20, married an Eden Grove man. He had originally come from the Blackfriars area and had notorious cousins around Caledonian Road. In their early years he was only casually employed. Nancy decided she would have to continue working to get the things around her which she had never had in childhood: 'I wanted to better myself, see.' After marriage in 1925, Nancy continued working at the Star Brush until six weeks before her daughter was born, early in 1926. She was quite clear at that time what she wanted from life:

'Now that's the reason I didn't have any more children, see. Cos I thought to meself, Well, it all boiled down – a load of kids, don't it. While you've got a load of children round you, you can't earn. Well, I didn't mind working, work never upset me. . . . I took an oath when I had my girl, I said to him, "I don't want no more children, I want to get something round me." I had it in me that I wanted to get a good home, I never had one and I wanted one.'[72]

She put her name down to start again at Star Brush, but there were no vacancies. In the interim she worked for a week washing bottles at a factory at Grays Inn Road, against her husband's wishes. But when her baby was nearly a year, a vacancy arose at Star Brush and she went back to her old job. She was there, in all, twenty-two years.

When she was 28, in 1933, she was made a chargehand, with paid holidays, just about the time her husband found regular work at the Electric Light:

'We went on a week's holiday that year. I thought, Right, we've got the chance. I paid for every penny of that myself, the lodging money, beer money, food out, coach fare and everything.'

Her job was to check the quality of work turned out by the women under her charge, to repair the machines when they went wrong, and to make punches for the machines as necessary. Unlike her husband, she was a skilled worker:

'You know what money he used to earn in the war years?

Three pound five a week round the Electric Light. And I was earning five pound eighteen a week, nearly twice as much as him.'

Most of her earnings went into the home. All the household's strategic decisions over where they should live were made by her. Originally, she had set up home in one room a few doors from her father in George's Road. She fitted it out with new furniture, but at first they had only enough to fill the single room. In a couple of years, her mother-in-law told her that in her house in Eden Grove two rooms had fallen vacant through the death of a tenant. There they stayed for eight or nine years, until about 1935. Then,

'I'd been at work and had no more children, and I was saving up, and I thought to myself, Well, here goes, I'm gonna get some stuff round me. From there I went to Lesly Street. Now, if you know anything about Lesly Street it was very select round there years ago, and it took me nearly three months to get round there. References here, references there.'[73]

A few years later, Nancy took the tenancy of a seven-roomed house at Lough Road, subletting to help pay the rent of 30s a week. That was around 1938.

The difference in Nancy Tiverton's condition between the end of the First World War and the beginning of the next was a rags-to-comfort story of determination and single-mindedness. The contrast with her mother could hardly have been more pointed. Mrs Tiverton never visited any of her daughter's homes. She stayed on at Campbell Road until the end of the Second World War when, too old and sick to go on charing, she moved in with another daughter and died within a year.

Jane Munby and the delinquent solution

Jane Munby was born in the Islington workhouse in 1905. Her mother, a flower seller originally from the George's Road area, was living with her second husband (a coal heaver at the Finsbury Park rail yards) at the bottom end of Campbell Road. Jane was the girl who had been kept away from school by her mother when her last surviving brother was killed in the First World War. When her mother died in 1920, Jane was 15. Her step-father made sexual advances to her, and when they were rejected threw her out.[74]

The details of Jane's story are elusive and frequently contradictory, but some basic information is clear enough. Her childhood
had been lonely, virtually reclusive in the last years before her
mother died. She was unable to read or write and was subjected
to few of the influences felt by other girls of her time and place,
most notably the world of work. She had none of the connections
which were so important to young women getting factory work
from Campbell Road.

When she was kicked out by her step-father, Jane stayed for a
time with 'a half-aunt' in Campbell Road, probably not a relation
but a friend of her mother's. She was there a few months, but it
was just somewhere to sleep rather than a home – 'I was on me
own all day.' For some reason she left that family and then slept
rough for a considerable period (in doorways and passages in
Campbell Road; in the women's lodging house at George's Road;
in stables, even barns on Wanstead Flats and in the open air on
Hampstead Heath). She carried her possessions, little more than a
change of underclothes, in a paper carrier bag and kept clean by
using Hornsey Road and other public baths. It was to Campbell
Road that she would turn for shelter most frequently, and it was on
one such visit that she was befriended by Mrs Harper, a neighbour
bringing up two children on her own, who offered her a home in
return for housekeeping and childminding.

During a period of about two years, between the ages of 15 and
17, Jane lived on her wits. It was during the time with her half-
aunt that she took up with another girl from the Bunk – Daisy
Farnold. Daisy was a rough and ready type, one of two daughters
of a prostitute. The Farnolds had two rooms but Jane never stayed
there – 'cos her mother was a prostitute. . . . But thank Gawd I
was a good clean woman; thank Gawd for that!'

Daisy was a thief, and Jane became one too. According to Jane,
it was Daisy who instructed her in the skills of shoplifting (mainly
clothing from women's outfitters) and who adopted her as a junior
partner: 'she was what I called the guvnor . . . mind you, she
couldn't do as she liked with me, but she was the guvnor in
everything.' They would travel all over North London. It was
Jane's role mainly to distract the shop assistant while Daisy helped
herself:

'Well, there'd be just picking up things and looking at 'em,
like they do now, they'd say they like this or I'd say I liked
that, and blah blah blah that's that, and they'd got it. She had
it and I didn't know she had it.'

Daisy carried most of the loot and was responsible for disposing of it and paying Jane her share:

'She had what they used to call years ago, their clients. . . . If she'd got a client anywhere it could have been from her mother. See, cos she used to take a lot of stuff to her mother. . . . I never used to be with her when she was doing any of that. We'd done our work, as I used to say it! – and I wouldn't see her no more. She wasn't a girl that I [liked being with all the time].

This life lasted until Jane settled in with Mrs Harper. Her needs were small and were easily satisfied by Mrs Harper's arrangement of board and lodging in return for looking after her children while she was at work. By the time she moved in, around 1922, Jane was already courting her future husband, Harry Cranton. He was from a poor family out of Hornsey Road, close to Queensland Road. He lived in 'two rooms and a little attic' with his parents and a deaf-and-dumb sister. Harry had been courting another girl in Campbell Road but they broke up and he switched his attentions to Jane the same evening.

They married in 1923, when Jane was 18½ and three or four months pregnant. At first they had no home and Jane continued living separately with Mrs Harper. It was Harry's mother who eventually found a place for them, a furnished first floor back in Queensland Road for 10s a week.

Jane and Harry found it desperately hard to make ends meet. Harry was a handy man but the most casual of labourers, frequently unemployed and with no fixed trade. He had taken out a barrow from time to time and sold favours at the Coronation; he decorated rooms, shifted scenery at Olympia and the Agricultural Hall, upholstered a suite for a neighbour, and so on. Jane was forced on to out-relief and the relieving officer was a frequent visitor. Small wonder that 'My husband was never a one for a posh home. We never had a posh home.'

Home, as in the case of Nancy Tiverton, shifted from place to place, but largely due to circumstances outside Jane's control. The first Queensland Road home did not last long as the landlady objected to babies – and there was an additional problem over a blanket which Jane had pawned for food. They then moved to George's Road but were displaced by the LCC clearance scheme to Sutton Dwellings, Upper Street. They were there a few months only – the demand for regular rent would have been a problem for a family on casual earnings – before moving to a basement at

Donegal Street, a poor turning north of Pentonville Road. They were there from about 1929 to 1939, when they moved up the hill to White Lion Street.

Jane, who had been told by her mother that she was a Catholic, was effectively prevented from working – even if the inclination had taken her – by a large family quite out of step with her generation. She had thirteen children, two more than her mother. The first, a son born in 1924, entered at an early age into a world of economic relations which would have been clearly recognisable in Campbell Road:

> 'My eldest son, he's been working since he was a kiddie of five years old. Right from when he was five, he was a forager. He'd go and earn a few coppers here, he'd go to the train station and carry [bags] and get a few coppers. He was always coming in and say " 'Ere you are, mum. Tomorrow's dinner." '

Jane Munby's testimony reminds us that the experiences of young women were not universally shared: not everyone left behind the social relationships and expectations of their mother's generation. It has been argued elsewhere that experience of work, especially in factories, was vital in widening horizons for women even if they stopped work on marriage; and that work and its potential availability was an important factor in encouraging women to restrict the size of their own families.[75] Jane's life bears that out, especially in the dramatic contrast with Nancy Tiverton, whose origins were just as inauspicious. Ironically, it was Nancy's mother and her urgent desire for money to spend on drink which drove her daughters into factory labour and into a chain reaction of expanding consequences. But the pressures from Jane's mother had been in the opposite direction – overprotective, home-centred and isolated.

Jane, Nancy and May were all close contemporaries. The shadow of women's lives before the First World War hung dark over their early years of independence around 1919–23. The rupture between mothers and daughters in Campbell Road could be hard-fought and painful in those years. But by the 1930s, the new world opening out for women had become a widely accepted fact of life. The struggles with mothers were no longer so intense for the daughters of Campbell Road. And the forces behind the chain reaction were becoming irresistible.

Mavis Knight, Olive Tasker, and a new world for women

Mavis Knight was born in 1917 at the City Road Lying-In Hospital.[76] Her father was a serving soldier, who appears never to have lived with her mother (although she took his surname), and Mavis never knew him. Ada, her mother, set up home with William Childers, a cockney-Irish casual dock labourer, at the top end of Campbell Road around 1920. Ada, a street seller of salads, had nine children by William between about 1922 and 1937. Of her ten children, nine survived to adulthood, but at the drastic expense of her own health. Several times she was admitted to hospital with malnutrition and related illnesses. Childers was also a sick man, eventually dying of a nasal cancer: it may be remembered that he was particularly violent towards his children. The family was very poor, living in desperate overcrowding (ten in two rooms in 1936), and had seen the inside of the workhouse two or three times.

Mavis's life was to be very different to her mother's. Although there was some tension between these women (Ada used to pawn Mavis's coat from time to time) there were not the battles which had marked the earlier period. Mavis had been a regular attender at school, and when she left Upper Hornsey Road Elementary in 1931 she found work by asking for it at the Golden Ring Jam Factory in Durham Road, where she filled bottles with ginger beer for 10s a week. She then had 'all sorts of jobs', including one at a sweet factory in Blackstock Road, before being taken on as tea girl in Stephen's Ink factory in Drayton Park. She worked there from about 1933, when she was 16, to the outbreak of war and evacuation.

It was after Mavis started work that she began to take an interest in her appearance and to be struck by her effect on boys in Campbell Road and outside. She owned hardly any clothes at first,

> 'but as I went along I managed to get meself something off the tallyman, sort of thing, and pay him sixpence a week or something like that, you know. But gradually I was beginning to sort of dress meself. I was always trying to make meself look nice.'

She could not afford much makeup and did not know how to apply it properly when she had it:

> 'my mum said to me once, "You look like a bloody clown!

Take that muck off your face!'' But I never used to – not that
I'm bumming myself up, but I never used to need makeup,
cos I was always very brown, very tanned. . . . I used to have
quite a lot of the boys after me down in Campbell Road –
because, let's face it, you were so ignorant you never knew
the assets you had. I mean, you never realised that your figure,
or whatever you had that was good, someone was looking at
it and liking it. . . . But I can remember that all of a sudden I
started taking an interest in meself and thinking that, you
know, I could look good, you know. But it was a thing that
you didn't realise that you had the assets you did have.
But you would have gone to the pictures as a young girl, so you
would have known what the stereotypes of desirable women were?
'Oh yeah, oh yeah. But when you see Carol Lombard and you
used to see the blonde girl – what was her name – the It Girl
. . . Jean Harlow. . . . You saw Ronald Coleman. My
favourite was the little fella . . . James Cagney. Oh I *loved*
him. He was my heart-throb, he was. And then there was
Clark Gable – oh I used to drool over him, really drool.'

When it came to dating boys, Mavis found her address a social
embarrassment. At a 'flannel dance', an informal gathering for the
Stephen's Ink workers, she met the son of one employee who lived
in a turning off Blackstock Road:

'And he took a liking to me and he started taking me out. And
then, I went to the home. Then after that he said, "I can't go
out with you any more. . . . If you didn't live in Campbell
Bunk it would be all right." So that was that, you see.'

It was plainly easier in those circumstances to date boys from
Campbell Road. And around 1935, when she was 18, Mavis started
going steady with Willie Knowles. He had been born in Campbell
Road in 1914, his father a tinker and his mother a costermonger,
and he was from one of the oldest-established families in the street;
'We was both slummie, the pair of us.' They would call at each
other's homes from time to time and would see each other nearly
every evening. They might go to the Astoria if they were lucky,
'and if he had sixpence to spare we'd have sausage and chips in
the [Orange] Caff.' But generally it was the smaller picture palaces
or just out for a walk: 'there was nowhere to go, actually, as far
as money was concerned, cos we couldn't afford it.' They never
went to the West End or to any of the 'tea dances' for more
fashionable working-class youth.

In 1936 they were married, when Mavis was 19 and Willie 22. They could not afford an engagement ring and so 'just got married' one Saturday at St Anne's Church, Pooles Park. They had a 'one-tier wedding cake . . . some ham sandwiches and a few bottles of beer and that was it', back at her mother's home. Mavis was married in a brown coat and brown and pink dress – 'couldn't afford white' because whatever she wore had to do service again for best. Willie had a new suit – both his and hers were bought through the tallyman. Both sets of parents came to the service, together with some of Mavis's friends from the ink factory, but the small reception was family only. They all walked to the church and back. That evening, 'we had a shilling left, and we got a tuppenny and a pennorth [of fish and chips] each.' When that was finished they left for the new home which Mavis had set up for them at Benwell Road.

Setting up home was the quite explicit rationale for their marriage:

> *Of all the motives for getting married, what was the most important as far [as you were concerned]?*
> 'The home, having the home. And having each other, I suppose, as well. You didn't realise that part until you were together. To get a home you had to have each other, didn't you.'

Work was instrumental in fixing in Mavis's mind what a decent working-class home should be like. She had visited a workmate's home in Benwell Road and saw 'how her home was, how nice her mother used to keep it and how clean it was'. Work also helped directly provide her with a place of her own:

> 'Where I worked in Stephen's Ink factory was some very nice people, and they used to help me. And they got me this flat in Benwell Road, cos we was talking about getting married. And I had two rooms and an attic. *I* got it all furnished. . . . I worked – I saved and schemed and scraped and everything else. I got all my home on hire purchase, for which I paid 15 bob a week. . . . I had a bed, and I had a dressing table and a wardrobe . . . and I had lino on the floor, if you please, lino! . . . Then in the kitchen I had two fireside chairs and I had a gas stove. And I had quite a nice little home, actually. . . . So I had everything that I had never had before – the comforts, you know. And that was why you got married, because you wanted to get out of the Bunk.'

When you told your mum you were getting married, did you tell her you were going to leave Campbell Road as well?
'No, no. . . . She knew I wanted to get married to get out of the Bunk. And no way was I going to live in the Bunk when I got married.'

To achieve her ambition, Mavis remained at work until 1938, when she had her first daughter; and then went back to work nine months later, leaving the baby with a neighbour. Willie worked regularly as a labourer at Bellchamber's glass factory in Ronalds Road, but his earnings were low – not much more than her own 30s a week, Mavis thought.

Setting up and maintaining home meant working. And working meant restricting child-bearing. This, again, was something Mavis felt clear about, against the trend for the wives of the unskilled nationally, but indicating that the circumstances of Campbell Road provoked a stronger reaction than elsewhere against large families for this generation of mothers.[77] But she was entirely ignorant about contraception and sex, having been told nothing by her mother and having little contact with the mother and baby clinics recently set up.[78] Under those circumstances, family restriction took its toll of a marriage whose primary purpose anyway had not been the fulfillment of romantic love but rather an escape from home and neighbourhood:

'We didn't want to have a big family for the fact that what we'd seen with ourselves. I mean, his mother had a big family, she had about ten kids, too. And with the way we'd lived as youngsters, as kids, I was determined I wasn't gonna have a big family. But there was only one way of avoiding children those days, and that was using a sheath or whatever it was, you know. Or the withdrawal method. . . .
You used withdrawal rather than the sheath?
'Yes, lots of times, yeah. That's what caused a lot of the – what shall I say – you missed out on love, sort of thing. Where you should have sort of loved one another, you didn't know it *meant* anything.'

Mavis, like Nancy Tiverton and May Purslowe, saw her own early days in terms of a struggle to better her life chances and escape from the destiny she had been born into. She saw it, too, as a lonely struggle, in contrast to those content to inherit the parental backroom and the orange boxes and the bucket for night-soil. In explaining her desire to leave home and Campbell Road,

Mavis distanced herself from any motivation of social climbing. But she sought only for an individualist theory of how she had been able to escape and found it in a putative genetic birthright from the father she had never known:

> 'But I always, from a kid – I dunno why – I always wanted something nice, I always felt that I should live in something – there's something better. I don't know why – see, I never knew my father, I might have had a bit of something that *he* had in him, you don't know do you? But I always wanted to better meself, even from a kid. I used to be different – I used to *feel* different, somehow, to all the other – not a snob or anything – but I used to feel that I was different to all the other kids that lived the way they brought up in that [turning]. And lots of people used to say, "You wouldn't think she come from Campbell Road, would you?" '

But by the mid-1930s, Mavis's experience, far from being the exception, was becoming the rule.

Olive Tasker was born in 1926 at St Pancras Workhouse.[79] Her father, who had been gassed in the First World War, was chronically unemployed, and died in 1938, when Olive was 12. Her mother, who came from around the King's Cross Road, suffered from rheumatoid arthritis and was eventually confined to a wheelchair. Olive was one of seven children, one of whom had been admitted to a mental institution through a trivial offence in which he had been involved. By the time Olive left school, in 1940, two older children had married – a brother lived in Campbell Road and a sister lived in Playford Road. Olive's small wages, together with what little public assistance the family was allowed, had to support her mother and two sisters still at school. It was she, too, who had to make the strategic decisions about whether or not to change the family home. In all these things, the tough independence of a girl's upbringing in Campbell Road was to serve her well.

Olive's first job on leaving school was at the Itonia Battery Co., Lennox Mews, just a few yards from the top of the Bunk. Her wages were 10s at the beginning for work in 'the black room', where the carbon cores were tied together. It was dangerous work, even for young fingers, and very dirty: 'I used to come home like a sweep. I was black.'

Many of the girls at the Itonia were from Campbell Road – or Whadcoat Street as it was by now – and in Olive's experience, other home conditions were similar to her own. Olive's two-roomed home was poor enough, but it was the road it was in which gave her the itch to get away. This was 1941; Olive was 15 and old enough to think for herself, and places were easy to come by:

> 'And it was I that went down to Isledon Road, and there was an agent there – like a sort of a landlord he was, he used to have rooms. And he had – I forget how I got to know about the two rooms in Yonge Park now, but anyway we got these two rooms. . . . And the rooms were bigger. Although you had two rooms, they were bigger rooms, and plus the fact that you had an inside toilet, which was in the hall. So it was kind of better than what we had in Campbell Road, you know.'
>
> *You say you wanted to get away. Was there any incident that sparked that off or was it a general feeling or – ?*
> 'No, it was just a general feeling, I think. I think there were so many – I think possibly the fact there was so many people saying about the street then, you know, and I was getting sort of that age: I thought, "Ooh I'd never want to marry someone from down the street," you know . . . I knew 'em all, kinda thing, you know, I mean they'd never done me any harm, I just thought I wanted something better, you know, you do don't you when you're that age.'

The quality of their home changed little in the process. They moved everything they had on a barrow to Yonge Park and bought nothing new. It was not until the younger sisters began to earn that Olive's mother began to get more and newer furniture around her.

Olive married when she was 17 – just a month before her 18th birthday. By then she had already been two years out of the Bunk, but even so marriage for her was an escape from poverty and home responsibilities.

By a strange irony, her husband had been born and bred in Campbell Road, although there was a significant age difference and they had never known each other as children. Tom Garnett was 23 years old, the son of a jobbing builder and decorator father and a charwoman mother. He had had an extraordinary career by Campbell Road standards, because although he came from a poor family he had been able by chance to secure a trade for himself. As a boy, out late at night, he had been fascinated by the tailoring classes at the LCC Day Continuation school in Hornsey Road.

The instructor had taken him under his wing and Tom had become a skilled presser in the West End bespoke. By the time of his marriage he was earning £16 a week. He 'didn't see the point of Olive working' and she gave up the Itonia on marriage. Although she 'did a job for a while, couple of times', her working days were over. Olive had no children of her own but adopted one and also had the responsibility of bringing up Tom's brother's four children.

May Purslowe's working life began at the end of one war and Olive Tasker's at the beginning of the next. The difference between them was a generation of change in Campbell Road within which young women had played a continuous and escalating role. May Purslowe had waited till marriage before moving out of Campbell Road at the age of 21; Olive Tasker, for much the same reasons, had been 15 when she organised the move of her whole family away from the street, nineteen years later. May left at a time of relative stability within Campbell Road; Olive left when the movement away from the street had turned into a neap tide. For the tendencies which had hardened and deepened in the inter-war years were crystallised irreversibly by the Second World War itself.

8 The fall of Campbell Bunk

Moving out

'I joined the army meself, I went to Malaya and I was over there at the time of the outbreak of war. I never used to get this home-sickness – "Wish I was back in London with the lamplights gleaming on the pavements in the wet" – phaw, you must be potty, cos this was lovely. There you were living really the life of Riley in the Far East although you *were* a very subordinated creature being a buckshee soldier. But the point about coming back – always at the back of my nut – I'd think, Wonder how that old Bunk's getting on. It sort of left its poison, its venom there! . . . And when I did come back [and spoke to someone] – "Yer wouldn't know it! It's gawn dahn!" '[1]

Harry Duncan, Jack's son, had joined the army in 1935. By then he had been away from the Bunk four years – his parents had moved above a fish shop in Hornsey Road. The complaints of the remaining 'Bunkites' refer particularly to the war years – for reasons to be made clear in a moment – but they would have rung true in the late 1930s as well. For from a number of angles the Bunk had indeed 'gone down', even by 1939.

Some of the indicators of decline have to remain speculative. But it would be surprising if the Bunk had not experienced some of those changes in norms and behaviour common to working-class London as a whole which might be characterised as a reduction in 'rough' behaviour. We should expect there to have been less drunkenness in the 1930s than the 1920s, fewer assaults on police, fewer rows between neighbours, less domestic violence, quieter Bank Holiday or Guy Fawkes Night revels. And what limited evidence there is from the court reports in the local press eloquently supports this common-sense speculation (see table 12).

But perception of decline is perhaps at its sharpest when it seems as though people no longer want to go on living in a place. Streets need people to keep them lively. The most telling evidence of

decline would be to show that Campbell Road was losing population faster than people were coming in to make good the loss.

Clearly we must be careful here, for to show a reduction in
population in Campbell Road would do no more than confirm a
dominant demographic trend of the time. Islington and other parts
of inner London were all growing 'quieter', more law-abiding,
more private. Both cause and expression of this change was the
shift of population away from older crowded areas and even from
the outer ring within the county boundary. But if the net rate of
population decline in Campbell Road were faster than elsewhere
then that would be evidence that the street was losing its function
as a place of refuge and community life.

In the absence of manuscript Census data the evidence here
cannot be cast iron but it is surely hard enough. Table 21 shows
an analysis of the electoral registers for Campbell Road and Playford Road at certain dates between 1930 and 1946. Between 1931
and 1938, the population of Islington was estimated to have fallen
by 9.2 per cent.[2] The number of individuals registered on the
voters' list at Playford Road between 1930 and 1938 dropped by
7.5 per cent. In Campbell Road, the fall was 29.0 per cent. In
1938, Campbell Road was occupied by 1,088 persons, 396 (or 26.7
per cent) fewer than in 1909.[3] In that earlier year 1 house was
unoccupied: in 1938, 9 (out of 104) were vacant or turned over
wholly to commercial users. In Playford Road in 1938, all 107
houses were residentially occupied.[4]

Not all of the changes to which Campbell Road was subject
during the inter-war years led ineluctably to an exodus from the
street. But some bore that tendency very strongly. And it is worth
recapping those elements of change, met with in previous chapters,
which contributed to this significant movement out.

Some of these factors were external to the street; others evolved
from within. Perhaps the biggest external influence was the cluster
of economic factors which set the 1930s off from the 1920s, in
Campbell Road as in the rest of London. For those in work,
average earnings more than kept pace with the cost of living and
real wages rose consistently through the 1930s, especially from
1936.[5] There was a dramatic fall in London unemployment from
early 1933. Trends towards decasualising labour supply intensified
in local authority services, dock labour and road haulage, and we
have seen how men might become regulars in the 1930s when they
had been casuals in the 1920s. For large families with children
leaving school, opportunities to earn in the juvenile labour market
of the 1930s had never been better, especially for girls. Reducing

competition among street sellers and street finders meant richer pickings for those who clung on. And expansion of the commodity market gave greater opportunities to the shop breaker, shoplifter and crooked dealer. Income support from the LCC Public Assistance Committee was not generous but, especially after Labour control in 1934, it was better than under the guardians and was emerging from the shadow of the workhouse.[6] And those who were not poor had more surplus – especially second-hand clothing – for charities to dispense to the needy.

The rising standard of living was most noticeable to the poor, who could count their good fortune in ha'pennies and pennies. A reduction in poverty signified a loss of function for Campbell Road. Its advantages were needed less. There were fewer families requiring furnished rooms, where unrestricted rents were a liability at a time of cheap second-hand furniture and credit purchase of new.[7] Its landlords' traditional tolerance of overcrowding continued to be a boon but internal support networks, built out of the constant danger of desperate need, were probably patronised less enthusiastically as the 1930s moved on.

There was a second cluster of changes around the cultural life of Campbell Road and its relation to the world outside. The mutual consolations of people in the street were becoming even more minoritarian and isolated in the 1930s. Street gaming pitches were fewer through slum clearance (in Brand Street and George's Road) and through police suppression of 'socially undesirable' uses of the street (see table 12, section 5). Campbell Road's name for drunkenness, domestic violence, inter-neighbour rows might have been less deserved in the 1930s then the 1920s but the difference went unremarked by its neighbours. In 1937, as part of the LCC's periodic review of London's street names, Campbell Road was renamed Whadcoat Street (and when the road is referred to after that date it will be called by the new name). But the old nickname and reputation still held good, standing out even more luridly against a backdrop of ever quieter shades. And the stigma of living in the Bunk grew more marked in consequence.

This cultural shift could only have weakened the self-confidence of youngsters growing up in the street in the 1930s. Even young men, able more easily to fit in with the Bunk's traditional way of life, were increasingly vulnerable to this labelling process. Discrimination by employers, the police and magistrates, even the parents of friends outside, affected all to some degree and must have been one factor to weigh in deciding to move or stay. For young women, though, it was only one among many, as we have just seen.

Then there was the dynamic of decline itself. Once the process had begun it was irreversible with a tendency to accelerate. The sense of wanting to escape from the street became very powerful. Table 21 shows the reduction in individuals on the electoral register in the four years between October 1930 and October 1934 as 11.8 per cent; in the next four years it was to be 19.4 per cent. We can guess how this dynamic might have operated, even for young men. Take the substantial group of young male thieves in Campbell Road in the early 1930s. By the late 1930s, after 1937, those who appear in the court reports are almost invariably living elsewhere. The first moves away were probably prompted more by prosperity than police suppression. But this would have weakened support and comradeship for those remaining, cutting the ties that kept them there. There became few reasons to stay, not enough to outweigh the ease with which the police could find them.

The quality of housing and home life attainable in Campbell Road compared with that outside was clearly one important reason to leave. The housing market was both a source of change within Campbell Road, and the medium through which change worked. It would be hard to exaggerate its importance in accounting for the fall of Campbell Bunk

There were a number of influences at play here. Housing standards are always relative. And to understand the decline of Campbell Road we must try to situate it in the changing working-class housing market of Holloway between the wars.

The most significant variation was in the expanding opportunities for larger and better-equipped housing for working-class families in Islington and the rest of London. Access to this housing was, of course, rationed by price. But skilled workers on regular incomes could explore two new avenues more or less firmly shut to their fathers and mothers. The first led to owner occupation, usually in new dwellings bought on mortgage. The second was renting from a local authority.

Owner occupation was not a realistic choice for most working-class families before the 1950s. Even so, houses could be bought on working-class incomes and the costs and benefits of owner occupation were brought home to everyone by advertisers, newspaper articles, imaginative sales gimmicks, cinema newsreels and feature films. After interest rates fell in the early 1930s, even the *News of the World* carried advertisements for freehold houses in West London at £545 or weekly repayments of 13s 10d, aimed at workers earning about £4 per week.[8] Deposits might be as little as £5. And not a few families relying on blue-collar wages took the bait.[9] It was these houses, too, which tended to be the subject of the ideology of 'home', aimed especially at women and fostering consumerism and competitiveness.

A more realistically attainable option – as we saw in the case of May Purslowe – was to rent from the council, especially the LCC. This was the best working-class housing to be had through renting and it became more available – in Islington and outside – as the 1930s wore on. By 1939, Islington Council had built over 1,300 flats and houses, mainly in Highbury and Upper Holloway. Around 3,100 LCC dwellings had also been provided in the Borough by that time, all but 500 of them built after 1919. To this relatively small public sector stock of 4,400 (about 10 per cent of Islington's dwelling stock) should be added the LCC's overspill estates, built for Londoners in housing need who could afford to pay the rents. The LCC's cottage estates had comprised just under 3,500 dwellings before 1914; before the Second World War there were around 63,000. The most important estates from Islington's point of view were White Hart Lane (Tottenham) and Watling (Edgware), but substantial numbers also made the trek east to Becontree.[10] These three out-county estates together contained over 32,000 houses and flats by 1938.

Now these were all just pinpricks in the vast corpus of London housing, but their influence was felt well beyond the point of impact. The rents might well have been nearly as much as a mortgage and affordable only by skilled workers, or the families of unskilled workers with several earners;[11] the estates might have been a long way from employment prospects, with high transport costs to and from work; the people who lived there might have been un-neighbourly and stand-offish and worse: but the LCC cottage estates made flesh an idyllic ideal of the family house with a garden and all mod. cons. And they put that dream within the potential grasp of large sections of the London working class. People in Campbell Road were directly affected by all this only rarely. But their sons, and especially their daughters, worked with people for whom one of the 'council places' was a realisable ambition.

Council housing and owner occupation helped fuel the centrifugal movement of population away from the middle of London. The inner districts of Shoreditch, Finsbury, Holborn and so on lost people fastest, but even the less crowded outer ring within the county boundary was affected, especially from the late 1930s. Islington lost an estimated 32,300 people (10.0 per cent) between mid-1932 and mid-1938; the decline between the ten years 1921 and 1931 was only 2.7 per cent. For those who left – or even those who stayed on in the new council blocks – housing conditions might change drastically for the better.

Most council homes in the mid- to late 1930s were being built with electric lighting and power points, gas fires in living rooms, instantaneous gas water heaters serving kitchen sink and bath in a separate bathroom; most flats were of three, four or five rooms with a private balcony to the living room.[12] Even in the traditional London tenement house, gas was all but universal by the early 1930s, frequently with electricity as well.[13] Overcrowding, too, declined during the 1930s in response to the movement of population to the out-county districts easing the pressure on house room: in 1935 there were 6,757 'overcrowded' households in Islington, in 1938 just 3,534.[14]

All this was some indication of rising standards, and expectations followed and drove them upwards. But back in Campbell Road, housing conditions seemed a millennium behind the times: one or two rooms to live in, three if you were lucky; sharing an outside WC with two or three other families, sometimes more than 20 people; no gas until 1937 or 1938, lighting rooms with oil lamps and cooking meals on a worn-out range or taking them to the baker's; battling with bed bugs and rat infestations from the broken drains; dragging coal up four flights of stairs and trying to keep warm around a broken fireplace with a bad draw; getting water from a shared tap in the scullery or over a triangular stone sink on a half-landing; collecting slops and urine in buckets and emptying them morning and evening in the outside closet.

All this felt so outdated not only because of new working-class housing but because much of the very worst was being pulled down. Housing conditions in Campbell Road had been among the worst in Islington since the 1890s, more through overcrowding and the sharing of facilities than through the state of repair or intrinsic unhealthiness. But slum clearance after 1919, and especially after 1930, was removing the worst of the early nineteenth-century outworn buildings – tiny houses with shared taps, gulleys and closets in a common yard, or pitch-black basements with ceilings just above street level. Slum housing accommodating about 7,000 people was cleared in Islington between the wars. By the late 1930s, Campbell Road was among the worst left standing. The public authorities were powerless to improve matters. Between 1906 and 1909, the Islington sanitary inspectors were making 1,700 visits in Campbell Road each year: 'fully half the time of one Inspector is spent in this road.'[15] In 1919 the Ministry of Health made Compulsory Purchase Orders on three empty houses there to return them to housing use,[16] but the Orders were not proceeded with. The Housing Act 1930, better known for its slum clearance provisions, gave the LCC the power to declare Improvement Areas, at the request of a Metropolitan Borough. Housing conditions had to be 'dangerous or injurious to health' through disrepair or sanitary defects and overcrowding or bad arrangement, but wholesale demolition was not required.[17] As part of its five-year housing plan, Islington requested the LCC to declare Campbell Road an Improvement Area in 1935. But the LCC only declared four Improvement Areas in London before the power was repealed by the Housing Act 1935, and none was in Islington.[18] The early 1930s saw a half-hearted campaign by the borough's minority Labour councillors to get Campbell Road represented as an unhealthy area under the 1930 Act and demolished as a slum by the LCC or Islington.[19] But when the Labour Party took power in 1934 it found more pressing slum clearance priorities in the narrow streets of the old Islington village around Upper Street and Essex Road. The Housing Act 1935 gave councils power to deal with one of Campbell Road's biggest problems – overcrowding. But due to the size of the problem, Islington's appointed day, after which the new legal standard could be enforced, was delayed until 1 April 1938.[20] And lack of rehousing accommodation, but most especially the war, made the Act a dead letter. As late as 1938, Whadcoat Street was still probably the most overcrowded road in Islington.

The drift away from Campbell Road was, therefore, unaffected by state action. It was, however, assisted by the mechanics of its own internal housing market. It will be remembered that finding alternative housing while living in the Bunk was not always easy. One response to this, probably from the earliest years, had been to make the move in short steps – shifting to nearby streets like Playford and Fonthill Roads or Pooles Park.[21] This was aided by Campbell Road's own rentiers, who expanded their property holdings into nearby streets. The Neals owned 80, 82 and 84 Playford Road and 49 Pooles Park as well as properties in the Rupert Road area by 1938, for instance, and it is possible that one of the Steeds had expanded in this way, too.[22]

The late 1930s saw the move away of several individuals or families who have figured so far in these pages, and their experiences make this local connection clear enough. Harry James and Mavis Knight were joined by Sylvie Dashett (to Berriman Road, 1938), the Harper family (to Playford Road, 1939), Billy and Ronnie Drover, separately on marriage (each to Playford Road, around 1935); Walters, the shopkeepers, around 1935; the last of the Steeds, shopkeepers and landlords in Campbell Road since the

1860s, moved to Canvey Island and elsewhere between 1934 and 1938.[23] And the electoral register for Playford Road in 1938 reveals many other familiar names from the Bunk.

In the context of British housing policy between the wars, slum clearance was the only effective means of improving poor housing. But bureaucratic niceties restricted its use to only certain categories of dwelling, and Campbell Road/Whadcoat Street slipped through the net until the 1950s. Had it not been for the war, however, there is little doubt that it would have been dealt with ten years earlier. But while retarding state action and the clearance of Whadcoat Street, the war accelerated dramatically the tendencies to decline which had been developing from the early 1930s on.

The war

The war started nothing but changed everything. There was not one fact of life in Whadcoat Street which remained the same in the six years after 3 September 1939. To all intents and purposes, these years saw the real end of Campbell Bunk. By the time the war was over, 37 houses, one in three, were empty or turned over to commercial use.[24] Many were derelict. In 1946, the electoral register of Playford Road recorded 457 individuals, just 25 (or 5.2 per cent) fewer than in 1938, and not one house seems to have been vacant. In Whadcoat Street, only 263 individuals were on the list, 50.8 per cent down on 1938: of the 311 households recorded on the electors' roll in 1938, 214 (or 68.8 per cent) had moved out of the street by 1946 and only 71 new households had moved in to replace them (see table 21).

Among those who moved away during these years were many familiar names: the Spencers and some of the Taskers as we have seen, in 1940 and 1941 respectively; Mavis Knight's mother (her step-father had died) to Hornsey during the Blitz; the Shorts, whose boy Tommy had such a range of street enterprises in the early 1930s, in 1943 to Fonthill Road; Mr and Mrs Dunn, he to Fonthill Road and she to Playford Road, around 1942; Mrs Best, the shopkeeper at the bottom end, around 1942; the Chines, the Grogans, the Stevensons, Mrs Tiverton, even the Catchpoles, chimney-sweeps in Campbell Road since 1882.[25]

Why did this process of moving out, well established by 1939, reach such dramatic proportions during the war years? The answer lies both in the war's special effects (evacuation, enemy action, and army experience) and in the wartime accentuation of significant trends already taking place in the late 1930s (full employment, opportunities for profitable enterprise, the extension of welfare, and the altered housing market).

Between 1 and 3 September 1939, 659,000 Londoners, 37 per cent of those eligible, left the capital for various destinations in provincial towns and villages all over southern England. The large majority were children but probably 70,000 were mothers or pregnant women. These were just the official evacuees. At least as many again joined the private exodus to friends or relatives or expensive havens in the countryside.[26] Among the volunteers for the government scheme were Whadcoat Street children and mothers – Olive Tasker and her sister, to a farm at Hitchin, for example.[27] But like many others, within eight weeks they were back, lulled by the phoney war which lasted until May 1940. And although there were flurries of evacuation that summer of the invasion scare, mass evacuation did not begin again until the night bombing of London started on 7 September 1940. By November, about 120,000 mothers and children, mainly from the East End, had been evacuated to safe areas once more.[28] Countless more shifted to safer areas of London, away from primary targets or areas thought likely to become them: significantly for Whadcoat Street, proximity to a railway station was commonly taken as a danger sign. The drift back to London from this second movement was slower and more uneven. And people returned to a London badly disorganised by bombing and to a housing market in chaos. The flow into London this time was not necessarily back to the old family home.

The major effects of evacuation on working-class Londoners were two-fold. First, it dislocated temporarily many neighbourhoods, even those which did not suffer directly from enemy action.[29] No bomb exploded in Whadcoat Street, although a land mine or parachute bomb dropped in Pongo Blackman's back yard – he reportedly charged an entrance fee to view it. 'It was safely dismantled and all the locals claimed that Hitler could not destroy the "Bunk".'[30] But there was more than one way to kill a street, and evacuation in the face of enemy action played its part. Usually, evacuees were women and children. On their return they might have a number of reasons for finding a different home – as, indeed, had the men they left behind. Opportunities to take a house with more room, or with better shelter arrangements, or with a bit of garden to grow your own food, were mounting daily as families packed up their valuables and moved out of the danger areas. There were advantages, too, in moving from furnished rooms: it must have been tempting to move a furnished home wholesale to unfurnished rooms at a lower rent, secure that in the general chaos landlords would be helpless to recover their property.

Second, evacuation bolstered expectations of what a home should be like among women or young girls like Olive Tasker, whose experience might hitherto have been confined to the London tenement house.[31] 'In many ways, evacuation spelt a compulsory levelling-up in standards,'[32] as foster-parents clothed and fed and housed their needy charges to the standards expected by their own children. In 1943 it was said of the Whadcoat Street area that 'A large proportion of the children are of low moral standards, but a number of those who have been evacuated show a marked improvement.'[33] Coming back to the Bunk could be just too much of a come-down for some of these.

Evacuation dislocated women's lives in particular and had an effect on their consciousness and expectations. Army service, on the other hand, mainly affected men, even though London women joined the WRACs and other units in large numbers. The army provided men with the opportunity, most of all, to meet women with no local ties, an opportunity not easily come by in the inward-looking world of the Bunk. Walter Spencer, it may be remembered, was conscripted despite having only one eye: 'I thought, That's a bit of luck, cos everybody in the Bunk wanted to get away in the army.'[34] While there, Walter took up for a time with a girl from Southampton before settling down with Nellie Carrier. But his younger brother, also a conscript, married a girl from Berkhamsted whom he'd met while in khaki.[35]

These, then, were elements of change inserted into life in Whadcoat Street directly by the war. But they overlaid more fundamental but no less visible movements in labour supply and demand, economic opportunities, welfare, and the housing market, all of which affected Whadcoat Street and the people who lived there – or who might have lived there.

First, the traditional reserve army of labour disappeared from mid-1943. Even from early 1941, when the UK unemployment rate was still 6.6 per cent, there were labour shortages of unskilled men across a range of industries despite a growth in the labour force on pre-war figures of 2,306,000 (or 10.5 per cent).[36] It was at this time that Essential Work Orders (EWOs), restricting the freedom of employers to dismiss workers, and of workers to leave a job, were applied to the building industry, which had carried the largest pre-war labour surplus in London. The supply was to get so short that Ernest Bevin, the Minister of Labour, attempted without success to move 'designated craftsmen' to labouring work of national importance.[37] The 'unemployables' evaporated in the

The fall of Campbell Bunk   229

frantic quest for labour-power. In May 1940 there were 200,000 on the Unemployment Assistance Board's 'dead men's' register; by December 1943 there were 18,000. Between July 1941 and September 1945, the Ministry of Labour found employment or training for 93 per cent of the 426,000 disabled men and women it had interviewed.[38] New reserves had to be drawn in outside the ranks of the casuals, the disabled and the elderly by conscripting unmarried women from December 1941. By June 1943, 7.25 million women were working in the services or in industry, 2.16 million (or 42.4 per cent) up on June 1939.[39] The war years were a time, also, for strengthening the organisation of workers in trade unions with the proportion of unionised men rising from 38.9 per cent in 1939 to 45.5 per cent in 1943; for women the rise was from 16.0 per cent to 29.5 per cent.[40]

The opportunities for Whadcoat Street's men and women of regular, well-paid employment had never been so good. This was the surest route to relative prosperity, greatly expanding the already wider horizons of the later 1930s. Demands for unskilled male labour outstripped supply – in building and demolition work, in road-mending and pipe-laying and on the railways, all making good bomb damage; in road haulage, especially office and domestic removals for the millions of house-moves made by Londoners in these troubled years;[41] in civil defence and air raid precautions, a natural haven, it was said at the time, for those in fringe jobs whose peacetime opportunities had disappeared – like bookies' touts or dog-track labourers;[42] in the ancillary manual services of the local authorities, shorn of their fittest men for war service; and in the traditional areas of employment like coal heaving, portering at goods yards and markets, van and lorry driving, where any male labour-power was at a premium from 1941. Even Mr Dunn, gassed in the First World War, who had done no work since 1926, was drafted into firewatching ; his son, who did little enough work before the war and hardly any after, joined the ARP and did removals and building work in his spare time.[43]

All women were offered an expansion of the opportunities mainly open to single women and girls before the war. As between 1914 and 1918, the growth of factory production in war-related activities provided employment for married women outside the traditional sectors of charing, laundry work and so on: 'The war accomplished a great winkling out of skivvies, chars and slaveys.'[44] The percentage of working women who were married rose from 16 per cent in 1931 to 43 per cent in 1943.[45] This increase in the availability of work for women was accompanied by more choice and better jobs, in terms of both pay and conditions. Women's labour raised many household earnings above the poverty line. Sylvie Dashett changed her job at Western's laundry to work at a rag factory at Falkland Road, Harringay, 'government work' subject to an EWO. Mavis Knight joined the WAAFs. Nancy Tiverton was tempted away from her job at Star Brush – after 22½ years – for a job at an army clothing factory on less skilled work but much better money at £5 18s a week. And the Itonia battery works seems to have become colonised almost entirely by women from Whadcoat Street.[46] It was said in 1943 of the Whadcoat Street area that

> A great many mothers go out to work, relying on the older children being provided with school dinners, and leaving the babies in the care of Day Nurseries or Granny.[47]

There were opportunities, too, for richer pickings from economic enterprise, both inside and outside the law. Fresh fruit and vegetables, the staple fare of street entrepreneurs, were never rationed and although shortages occurred from time to time there was always something to sell. Availability of alternative earnings also reduced competition among costers. Men and women who had pushed a barrow before the war now found a regular and profitable market pitch, rented from the council, easier to obtain. Bill Dashett 'had the allocation' to sell flowers at the Wells Terrace entrance to Finsbury Park tube during the war years, for example.[48] Even Harry James around this time sold hot chestnuts in the winter outside the Duke of Clarence: he took £32 in one night, 'and they never cost me a farthing'.[49] Some former street sellers even moved into shops, made cheap by plummetting rental values in areas vulnerable to air attack.

Scavenging was turned from being the most untouchable of pre-war livelihoods into a national duty. Recycling waste materials, especially metals, paper, glass and rags, was an urgent object of the war effort. Bomb-damaged and abandoned houses and factories gave many opportunities for salvaging saleable materials and most totters probably had a good war.[50] As before 1939, scavenging could slide imperceptibly into thieving and the opportunities from theft during the war years increased for those left to take them. It was during the war that Harry Duncan, whom Jack had tried to recruit into the post office, while still in khaki began a long career as a burglar around Finsbury Park. Harry James took advantage of the blackout (and an under-strength police force) to escape detection while entering shops and to escape arrest when coming out.[51] And doors left unlocked by occupiers hurrying to shelters made thieving almost too easy: 'Air raids', according to Wally Thompson, an Islington thief, '. . . were the best ally London's crooks ever had.'[52]

But Harry James also dabbled on the margins of the greatest source of illicit profit during the war years – the black market. 'Some day someone should write a treatise on Britain's war-time black market. It was the most fantastic side of civil life in war-time,' remembered Billy Hill, the Camden Town racketeer,[53] and many a Whadcoat Street entrepreneur or 'hound' would have agreed. Billy Hill made a fortune dealing in whisky; Harry James, like a cheap imitation, sold bottles of cold tea as whisky to gullible American soldiers in the Durham pub.[54]

Musher Gates, born in Campbell Road but properly out of Queensland Road, followed an instructive career during these prosperous years. He had already been a relatively successful street trader before the war, accumulating capital on the half-profits system and re-investing it in barrows and a coal lorry. But the black market helped realise his full business potential. He worked in demolition and coaling in the winter and in food in the summer: 'I was in the egg game, tomato game, everything I was.' He used to load his lorry at a village in Hertfordshire with eggs, pork, tomatoes and butter, and sell them in the West End, or exchange them for sexual favours from 'French tarts'. At the end of the war he had saved £8,000 in cash, owned two freehold houses in Waltham Cross, ran coal and fruit businesses, and made a little name for himself in Soho, the Eldorado of the London underworld.[55]

Now these men were not Stanley Settys[56] – although Albert Quinn, the Caledonian Road thief who stayed for a time at Campbell Road, did work for a man he called 'The Cockney Millionnaire': he apparently made his fortune selling American army lorries.[57] The local black market was mostly small-time. It attracted to it a casual fringe of army deserters without official papers who could not work for wages but had to live on their wits, as well as the more established thieves and confidence tricksters of the pre-war local underworld.[58] Even so, competition for black market gleanings was not that stiff. Many underworld characters had been called up.[59] And the crop was ripe enough for even the largest appetite. The war gave opportunities for individual profit-taking far in advance of anything which had gone before or anything these men were likely to see again in their lifetimes.

This tide of prosperity was helped on its way by a powerful inshore breeze – welfare for all. The horrors, real and imagined, revealed by evacuation provoked a consciousness of sin and neglect among the English middle classes which had not been experienced since the 1880s. The reports of town children – verminous, bedwetting, foul-mouthed, eating their food with their fingers – filled newspapers, sociological investigations, even novels and plays.[60] This shock to middle-class sensibility helped swell the movement towards a 'new democracy' which was so much a feature of the intellectual life of the war years. Discussion of ideas, especially round what the country should look like after the war, probably reached more strata than ever before. It was pushed deepest by the furore surrounding publication of the Beveridge Report in November 1942, but was kept alive for the next three years in both service life and civvy street.

But the new welfare had action as well as talk. Never before had so much provision been made for the poor in big cities, whether it be feeding (especially of children), ante- and post-natal support, health care in clinics and hospitals, nurseries and education generally, housing for the homeless, and income support. Most of these wartime reforms directly benefited women and were able to make flesh some of the ambitions and expectations they had built up during the 1930s. School meals and free milk were available to all children and for the poorest meals were free: 'In place of a relief measure, tainted with the Poor Law, it became a social service.'[61] The national milk scheme provided cheap or free milk to mothers and children out of school. The vitamin welfare scheme provided free fruit juice and cod liver oil for all infants and pregnant women. The hospital service improved drastically so that for expectant mothers there were 50 per cent more maternity beds in 1945 than in 1938. The elderly received higher pensions and supplementary allowances. Seven million children were immunised against diphtheria. And so on.[62] And there is evidence that these benefits were reaching even into Whadcoat Street during the war years.[63]

Improvements in the material benefits of welfare were matched by a re-orientation of social policy. The despairing ideology of 'the social problem group', the bottom 10 per cent of the population which had seemed to call for some genetic intervention rather than social improvement, gave way to concern with 'the problem family'. This discovery of the war years, especially of the period of evacuation, led to a policy of intensive family therapy. Whatever its ideological overlays and practical shortcomings, the rhetoric of problem families was at least more hopeful of change than that of the social problem group. When the problem family had been identified – always a difficult task because no satisfactory definition could ever be agreed upon – the recipe was support and supervision, or 'rehabilitation' in the jargon of the time. Pacifist

Service Units bolstered the welfare resources of the local state in teaching families to be clean, better mannered, less aggressive, to manage more competently on a low budget, and so on. The Church of England Temperance Society set up a residential settlement in Whadcoat Street around 1943 where 'a Warden and a small team of social workers' could 'establish friendly contact with their neighbours and . . . provide for them a centre to which they can turn for help and guidance of all kinds.'[64]

But even for the non-problem family in receipt of relief, it was not merely the quality and quantity of welfare provision in the war years which affected their lives: it was the way in which welfare was dispensed. Claimants were less subjected to surly and parsimonious investigation and the household means test was abandoned.[65] Not only, then, was poverty decreasing: but those who remained poor were less stigmatised than they had been before the war.

All of these fundamental social changes had major implications for the housing market. The reduction in poverty gave people a chance to afford better housing and further weakened the relevance of Whadcoat Street's special functions. The ideology of home-based consumerism was defended from wartime rigours by the production of utility furniture after mid-1942. Temporarily effaced social distinctions meant that the psychic support obtained from living with others similarly placed was now not so important. And people wanting to move away were faced with less discrimination by potential landlords or local authorities. These hardening reasons to move coincided with expanded opportunities to do so. Masked by all the comings and goings, London was losing permanently a substantial proportion of its pre-war households. The centrifugal movement which had been an old established feature of London life was quickened by the war. Every borough within the county boundary except Hampstead lost population during the war, and Islington's population is estimated to have fallen by 19.4 per cent between 1938 and 1951.[66] The war caused tremendous damage to the quality of housing in Islington. But because of the population decline overcrowding decreased and house room available for each household expanded.[67] For the people of Whadcoat Street, larger dwellings in better repair and with more facilities were readily available in neighbouring streets. Although the council was unable to build during the war there was more chance of becoming a council tenant because of incidental vacancies and requisitioning. And the continued overcrowding within the street gave residents high priority when council vacancies arose. An enquiry carried out in 1943 in the Whadcoat Street area – Whadcoat Street was 'Exe

Street' – stated that 'Many families from ["Exe"] street have been
moved to new Municipal flats in other parts of the Borough.'[68]

The extent of the movement away from the Bunk hastened the
process of dereliction, already advanced through generations of
landlord neglect and the abuses of over-occupation:

> The appearance of 'Exe' Street suggests that it has suffered
> badly from blast: actually the damage to empty houses is
> caused by the bursting capacity of boys, not bombs. First the
> windows are systematically smashed: then the frames are
> levered out and sold as fire wood. The door panels follow in
> company with anything else that may be portable, or that
> ingenuity can render portable.[69]

Slum clearance

In 1946, Whadcoat Street was but a faint reflection of Campbell
Road. But that does not mean to say that it was unrecognisable.
Remnants of the old Bunk lived on. There were still nearly 100
households who had lived there before the war, including some of
the most famous, even if they were on their last legs: Pongo
Blackman, Harry James's parents, the Dashetts, the Nesbitts, the
Pentons, Tubby Nicholls, the Neals, the Gibbons whose boy had
been killed in the coal yard tragedy, and Bucknell the coal shop
owner. Some of the Bunk's traditions had lived on with them.
Street gaming, for example, had been carried on with fewer
punters at weekends throughout the war, and it was even said that
in Whadcoat Street, 'During the blitz gambling on the pavements
seemed particularly popular, probably because it brought relief
from the nightly strain.'[70] After the war, gaming continued until
the end, but only at Bank Holidays and public festivals.
Bonfire Night continued, too, as a big event in the street's
calendar.

Connections with the old pre-war way of life were also maintained by those who had left but who felt drawn back. They
returned for visits to relatives or to see how old friends were
getting on or just to watch the street's last years of decline. Walter
Spencer, for instance, took his young child to the Bunk's Bonfire
Night celebrations:

> 'And Bonfire Nights you'd find some of the old people who'd
> moved out come back there to see how you were getting on.
> Their sort of meeting place there. . . . Oh yeah, you go round

there you'd see people you hadn't seen for some time. Course, during the war you lost interest in [touch with] a lot of people, you don't know where they've gone or anything.'[71]

These return visits were probably more common among men than women. But even Olive Tasker 'used to get curious. I used to go through there sometimes you know, and look.'[72]

It is likely, too, that the street's tradition as a refuge for the very poor was continued by at least some of the new arrivals who came to the street during the war or soon after. Certainly some came because they were homeless and could find nowhere else. Liz Francis, an abortionist in the street in the 1940s and 1950s, moved into the Bunk around 1941. She took four rooms above an empty shop: she and her children and her mother were the sole occupants. Liz, originally from Camberwell, had been evacuated from rooms in Cross Street, Islington, to Leicester. But when she returned to London, she had nowhere to live and was accommodated in a council reception centre at the Round Church, Drayton Park. While waiting for the council to find her a home she heard that there were plenty of rooms in Whadcoat Street and moved herself in. Liz Francis's own poor background fitted her well for life in the Bunk: she totted for old rags, went hop-picking with other families from the street, enjoyed the annual coach beanos and the 1953 Coronation shindig, as well as performing illegal operations for women locally.[73]

Some small part of Campbell Bunk thus continued in an abbreviated form until the demolition of Whadcoat Street, kept alive by the families who had clung on through two decades of great change. Around 1946, some 37 of Whadcoat Street's 104 houses (36 per cent) appear to have been empty. Eighteen of these were derelict and would never be used for housing again. The rest were a mixture of buildings turned over to commercial uses – sheet metal works, plastic moulders, motor engineers, upholsterers, children's wear manufacturers and more by the early 1950s – and a very few were probably repaired and re-occupied during the late 1940s. The number of households registered on the electoral roll in 1946 was slightly more than half the number registered in 1938.

Decay had gone too far for the old buildings to be improved by landlords or the municipal authorities. The first priority of the post-war council had been to salvage housing worth repairing, to clear bomb sites and build new homes to meet the shortage of modern accommodation. Their second priority was to clear slums, and Whadcoat Street was top of that list. The council made demolition orders on some houses at the top end in the early 1950s. At the same time they negotiated with the LCC over who should take responsibility for clearing the whole street. Eventually, Islington Council began the clearance process early in 1952. It was to take five years.

On 21 March 1952, the Metropolitan Borough of Islington resolved to declare a clearance area at the top end of Whadcoat Street and to buy the land for redevelopment. All of the street north of the Paddington Street (after 1937, Biggerstaff Street) junction was to be taken. Of the 54 buildings, 14 had been demolished, 7 were derelict and a further 2 were vacant or turned over to commercial use. Eight houses had been abandoned by their owners and rents collected by the council in lieu of rates and taxes. The southern part of the street was dealt with in two separate orders resolved on 18 February 1955. Of the 50 buildings, just 27 were occupied. At the time of council action therefore, 50 out of 104 houses were no longer used for living accommodation; the population had declined to 154 households, 504 persons. This was just under half the pre-war population. All the houses in the clearance areas had settled and bulged walls, all roofs leaked generally or in part, floors were springy, fireplaces broken, outside WCs defective, and all ground floor walls suffered rising dampness. The orders were confirmed by Harold Macmillan and Duncan Sandys, Ministers of Housing and Local Government, and demolition took place between 1953 and 1957.[74] Any trace of the old Campbell Road was all but obliterated by the housing estate which the council built on the site. Today, the turning into Seven Sisters Road and 20 feet of roadway hold out the promise of a street; but it is quickly dashed by an iron fence and a ragged bit of lawn.

Epitaph

For insiders as well as outsiders, the demise of Campbell Road and others like it over the past thirty years has been watched with ambivalent emotions. As we might expect, many of those brought up there, especially men, lament the passing of the good things which even a blighted childhood had in plenty. But oddly enough, Campbell Bunk is missed by people who never set foot in it, were fearful of it when it was there, and who would warn their children away from it if it were there today. 'Everybody smiles when I mention it', a puzzled North London magistrate said of Campbell Road in 1928, and those who knew it by experience or repute still do. The smile reminds us that the reputation of Campbell Bunk was envied as well as despised. The Bunk was an urban subconscious, an abandoned but liberated other self, the Hyde lurking in every respectable street of Jekylls. And with its passing, the cement which bonds us more and more firmly to our masters was felt, ever so slightly, to harden.

We have not seen its like since. The post-war world restructured many of the social components which had helped produce the phenomenon of Campbell Bunk. The reserve army of labour has been entirely reconstructed by the importation of labour-power, adding new racial dimensions to class relations, especially in determining how the lumpen class position comes actually to be filled. The old free market in inner city housing has effectively been replaced by state provision for the poor and individual ownership for the rest: the opportunities for communities like that in Campbell Road to develop and reproduce their own traditions have become intensely more difficult. Probably they have become less necessary as the wartime welfare arrangements extended into the post-war years, carrying with them an even more pervasive policing of family life.

Even so, capitalist class relations continue to produce a lumpen class position, filled by people who are of no current usefulness to capital and who tend to be parasitic on it and on the working class. A dependent class or an underclass is rediscovered at irregular but frequent intervals by social investigators who claim it as a new social force. The play remains the same: only the cast list changes.

It is, though, more difficult for the actors to get together, and we should not expect to find today the precisely delineated spatial 'community' we found in Campbell Road. But as the post-war transition works itself out we can expect lumpen communities to recur. They will take many forms. In London there can already be seen, in a combination of chronic structural unemployment among young blacks and disillusionment with approved means of achieving society's rewards, that rejected and rejecting relationship which characterised the pre-war lumpenproletariat of Campbell Bunk. The means of expression and traditions draw on different cultures than those found in the old Bunk,[75] but they are likely only to widen the separation from dominant society's norms and legitimations. And relations between the new lumpenproletariat and the state (which is in a much more aggressive mood now than fifty years ago) have already reached a guerrilla warfare of spasmodic ferocity which puts the 'golden age' of Campbell Bunk profoundly in the shade.

Figures and tables

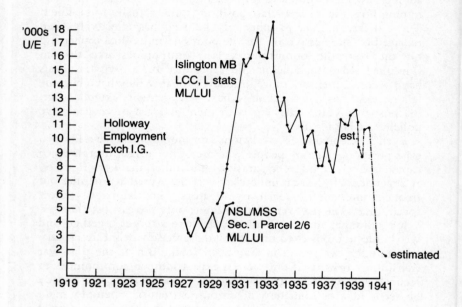

Figure 1   Unemployed in Islington and Holloway

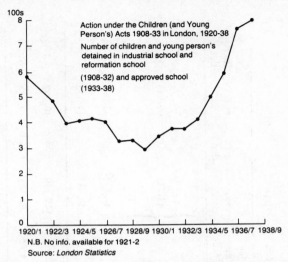

Figure 2   Action under the Children (and Young Persons) Acts 1908–33 in London, 1920–38. Numbers of children and young persons detained in industrial school and reformatory school (1908–32) and approved school (1933–8)

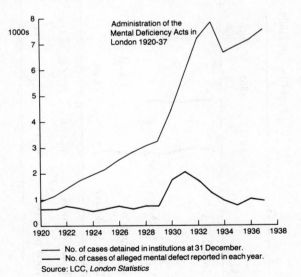

Figure 3   Administration of the Mental Deficiency Acts in London 1920–37

TABLE I

Population of Holloway and Islington 1851–1951

Area	1851	1861	% inc/ dec	1871	% inc/ dec	1881	% inc/ dec	1891	% inc/ dec
Tufnell Park									
Upper Holloway ward	7,604²	7,286		22,330		43,735		60,913	
Tollington ward		6,873¹		22,897²		42,169²		43,601²	
Lower Holloway	7,178	17,406		26,135		34,235		42,453	
Total Holloway	14,782	31,565	+113.5	71,362		120,139	+68.4	146,967	+22.3
Total Islington	95,329	155,341	+63.0	213,325	+37.3	282,865	+32.6	319,143	+12.8

TABLE I *continued*

Area	1901	% inc/dec	1911	% inc/dec	1921	% inc/dec	1931	% inc/dec	1951	% inc/dec
Tufnell Park	31,995		33,526		33,750		33,409		N/A	
Upper Holloway ward	33,978		37,116		35,721		32,874		N/A	
Tollington ward	33,922[1]		30,609[1]		30,832[1]		31,005[1]		N/A	
Lower Holloway	41,424		39,352		40,139		38,327		N/A	
Total Holloway	141,319	+5.0	140,603	−0.5	140,442	NC	135,615	−3.4	99,270[1]	
Total Islington	334,991		327,403	−2.3	330,737	+1.0	321,795	−2.7	235,632	−26.8

Notes

Figures underlined are estimates.

1 Excludes Queensland Road/Brand Street areas, which were located in Highbury Ward.

2 Includes Queensland Road/Brand Street areas by incorporating St Barnabas Parish, formed 1861.

Sources: Published Census vols 1851–1951.

242 Figures and tables

TABLE 2   Campbell Road and Palmerston Road 1881:
Occupational class, males and females

	Campbell Road Number	%	Palmerston Road Number	%
Males				
1 Building craftsmen	70	19.8	70	24.6
2 Manufacture (inc. metals)	44	12.4	49	17.3
3 Uniformed WC (ex. railway porters and clerks)	11	3.1	14	4.9
4 Printers	5	1.4	2	–
5 Clerks	6	1.7	28	10.0
6 Shop work (inc. errand boy)	18	5.1	26	9.2
7 Misc. service	21	5.9	13	4.6
8 Misc. distribution	9	2.5	20	7.0
9 Carmen and horsekeepers	25	7.1	16	5.6
10 Labourers (inc. building, general and others)	107	30.2	21	7.4
11 Sweeps, dealers, carters, unemployed	18	5.1	6	2.1
12 Porters	20	5.6	14	4.9
13 Teacher and professional	–	–	5	1.8
Total	354	to 100	284	to 100
Females				
1 Laundress	21	21.0	13	19.1
2 Washerwoman, charwoman	35	35.0	4	5.9
3 Domestic service	19	19.0	14	20.6
4 Dress manufacture	10	10.0	26	38.2
5 Miscellaneous	14	14.0	11	16.2
Total	99	to 100	68	100

Source: 1881 Census, Enumerators' Record Books, RG.11–259/60.

TABLE 3   Campbell Road and Palmerston Road 1881:
Place of birth of head of household and spouse, boarders and lodgers

	Campbell Road No.	%	Palmerston Road No.	%
Islington	111	20.9	32	7.5
Rest of London county	162	30.5	117	27.5
Home Counties	127	23.9	91	21.4
East Anglia	42	7.9	66	15.5
Rest of England	73	13.7	90	21.1
Rest of Great Britain	15	2.8	25	5.9
Rest of world	2	0.4	5	1.2
Total	532	100.1	426	100.1

Source: 1881 Census, Enumerators' Record Books RG.11.259/260.

TABLE 4   Common lodging houses in Holloway, 1895–1938

	1895			1909			1933			1938	
No.	Address	Beds	No.	Address	Beds	No.	Address	Beds	No.	Address	Beds
11	Gordon Place/ Highgate Hill	127	8	Gordon Place	62M	8	Gordon Place	53M	8	Gordon Place	53M
1	87 Highgate Hill	23		87 Highgate Hill	16M						
1	8 Flowers Mews	65		8 Flowers Mews	72M	1	8 Flowers Mews	62M	1	8 Flowers Mews	30M
1	26 Campbell Road	33									
1	27 Campbell Road	28									
3	35–9 Campbell Road	100	3	35–9 Campbell Road [closed c. 1919]	27W, 61M						
1	47A Campbell Road	90	1	47A Campbell Road [closed 1913]	71M						
4	4–10 Queensland Road	84	4	4–10 Queensland Road	34M, 18MC						

TABLE 4 continued

	1895			1909			1933			1938	
No.	Address	Beds	No.	Address	Beds	No.	Address	Beds	No.	Address	Beds
2	23–5 Queensland Road	16	2	23–5 Queensland Road	28W						
2	1–3 Eden Grove	112	2	1–3 Eden Grove	107M						
1	10 Milton Place	22	1	10 Milton Place	22M						
1	162 Hornsey Road	6									
2	160–2 St James's Road	81	2	160–2 St James's Road	76M						
			2	10–12 Campbell Road [1901]	52M	2	10–12 Campbell Road [closed 1934]	45M			
			3	102–6 George's Road [1897]	51W	2	104–6 George's Road [closed 1938]	34M			
			1	68 George's Road [1900]	38W						
			1	29 Hornsey Road [1897]	88M	1	29 Hornsey Road [closed 1933]	76M			
			1	8A Hornsey Street	48M	1	8A Hornsey Street [closed 1934]	48M			
31		787	33		871	15		318	9		83

Note: There was also a Church Army 'Labour' House in Holloway Road from at least 1898 to 1934.
Sources: Islington MOH Annual Reports.

TABLE 5

Campbell Road common lodging houses – dates of first registration

Address	Lodgers	Date of registration	Keeper
47a	90	30.10.1880	John King
26	33	24.11.1887	John Thorn
35	32	14.02.1889	Arthur Norris
37	45	14.02.1889	Arthur Norris
27	28	28.08.1889	John Thorn
39	23	18.04.1890	Arthur Norris
10 & 12	49	02.08.1901	Hugh Hersey
8 houses	300		

Sources: LCC/PH/REG/1/9 & 10. Islington MOH Report 1901, p. 209.

TABLE 6

Campbell Road 1880–1930: Admissions during selected years to the workhouse (or infirmary via the workhouse)

		1880	1890	1900	1910	1920	1930
Admissions from Campbell Road	No.	32	168	184	255	57	37
	1880 = 100	100	525	575	796.9	178.1	115.6
Number in Islington Workhouse and Infirmary on last day in last week of December	No.	1245	1778	2727	3668	2054	2036
	1880 = 100	100	142.8	219	294.6	165	163.5

Sources: ISBG 281/8–9, 15, 23–4, 32, 41–2, 57–8.
        ISBG 360/1–23.

TABLE 7   Occupational class (I): Campbell Road and 'black' areas, 1919–39

Men	1919–29 Campbell Road No.	%	'Black' areas[1] No.	%	1930–9 Campbell Road No.	%	'Black' areas[1] No.	%
1 Building crafts	14	7.8	19	6.9	5	6.6	6	4.7
2 Manufacture (inc. metals)	17	9.5	27	9.9	5	6.6	11	8.5
3 Uniformed WC			9	3.3			5	3.9
4 Printers	1						2	1.6
5 Clerks[2]	3	1.7	3	1.1			3	2.3
6 Shop work	4	2.2	10	3.6	7	9.2	4	3.1
7 Misc. service	4	2.2	9	3.3	2	2.6	5	3.9
8 Misc. distribution	2	1.1	5	1.8	2	2.6	3	2.3
9 (a) Carmen	13	7.3	29	10.5	2	2.6	7	5.4
(b) Motor driver	1				3	4.0	1	
10 Labourers	59	33.0	73	26.5	20	26.3	27	20.9
11 (a) Street sellers	25	14.0	47	17.0	13	17.1	33	25.6
(b) Street entertainers	6	3.4	1		1	1.3		
(c) Street dealers	12	6.7	12	4.4	8	10.5	2	1.6
(d) Street services	5	2.8	7	2.5	1	1.3		
(e) Road sweeper/dustman			3	1.1			3	2.3
(f) Unemployed	1		3	1.1	1	1.3	1	
12 Porters	11	6.2	19	6.9	3	4.0	16	12.4
13 Teacher and professional								
14 Lodging-house keeper	1				1	1.3		
Total	179	to 100	276	to 100	74	to 100	129	to 100

(Bracketed group totals for street sellers/entertainers/dealers/services: 1919–29 Campbell Road 26.9; 'Black' areas 23.9; 1930–9 Campbell Road 30.2; 'Black' areas 27.2)

TABLE 7 *continued*

Occupational class (I): Campbell Road and 'black' areas, 1919–39

Women	1919–29				1930–9			
	Campbell Road		'Black' areas[1]		Campbell Road		'Black' areas[1]	
	No.	%	No.	%	No.	%	No.	%
1 Laundress	3	10.4	7	10.6	2		1	
2 Charwoman	8	28.6	17	25.8	1		2	
3 Domestic servant	1	3.6	5	7.8	1		1	
4 Dress manufacture	1	3.6	6	9.1				
5 (a) Misc. service	5	13.9	10	15.2	2		1	
(b) Misc.	3	10.7	6	9.1	2		4	
6 Street sellers, entertainers	7	25.0	13	19.7	4		3	
7 Shop workers			1	1.5				
8 Other			1	1.5	1			
Total	28		66		13		12	

Notes
1 The George's Road, Queensland Road, and Rupert Road areas, population 1938 = 3,320; the population of Campbell Road, 1938 = 1,088.
2 Probably bookmakers' clerks.
Source: *Islington Gazette* and *Islington and Holloway Press* 1919–39. ISBG 64.

TABLE 8   Occupational class (II): Campbell Road 1919–40

Men	No.	%	Women	No.	%
Building craftsmen			*Laundry work*		
Painter and decorator	4		Laundress	4	
Bricklayer	1		Packer	2	
Builder	2			6	10.7
Builder (employer)	2		*Factory hands*		
Glazier	1		Sweet makers	3	
	10	9.0	Brush makers	3	
Uniformed working class			Battery makers	4	
Railway workers	4		Others	6	
Busman	1			16	28.6
Postman	1		*Service*		
	6	5.4	Domestics (indoor)	2	
Other regular employment			Charwomen (and office		
Slaughterer	1		cleaners, etc.)	11	
Laundryman	2		Washerwomen	2	
Cinema commissionaire	1		Waitress	2	
Shoemaker	1			17	30.4
Meat porter	1				
Tailor's presser	1		*Street sellers, etc.*		
French polisher	1		Costermongers (inc.		
	8	7.2	flower sellers)	13	
Factory hands			Totter	1	
Glassworkers	4			14	25.0
Metal polishers	3		*Shopkeepers*	2	3.6
	7	6.3			
General labour					
Bricklaying labourers	3		Total	55	to 100
Casual labourers	6				
Roadmaker	1				
Carman	1				
Dustmen	6				
Coal heavers/coalmen	6				
	23	20.7			
Street sellers, etc.					
General dealers, totters, etc.	12				
Costermongers	13				
Other street sellers	9				
Street services	5				
Street entertainers/ musicians	9				
Shopkeepers	48	42.9			
	10	9.0			
Total	112 to	100			

Source: Transcripts of oral testimony.

TABLE 9   Occupational class (III): Campbell Road 1929

Men	No.	Women	No.
Uniformed working class		Charwoman	1
LCC tram conductor	1	Laundress	1
		Hawker	1
General labour		Factory hands	2
Carman	1	Pastry cook	1
Labourer, iron foundry	1		
Casual labourers	4		
Meat porter (casual)	1		
Railway carriage cleaner	1		
Street sellers, etc.			
Wire basket maker and seller	1		
Rag and bone merchant	1		
Jobbing sign-writer	1		
Knife grinder	1		
Total	13		6

Source: NSL/MSS, House Sample Survey Cards, Islington.

TABLE 10
Occupational groups 1931: Great Britain, London county, Islington

	Gt Britain %	County of London %	Metropolitan Borough of Islington %
1 *Employers and proprietors*	6.7	6.5	5.5
2 *White-collar workers*			
(a) Management and administrative	3.7		
(b) Higher professionals	1.1	0.9	0.5
(c) Lower professionals and technicians	3.5	6.5	4.7
(d) Foremen and inspectors	1.5	1.0	1.1
(e) Clerks	6.7	12.2	12.6
(f) Salesmen and shop assistants	6.5	8.0	8.1
3 *Manual workers*			
(a) Skilled	26.7		
	(55.4)	46.0	48.5
(b) Semi-skilled	28.7		
(c) Unskilled	14.8	19.0	19.0
	99.9	100.1	100.0

Source: Census 1931. Halsey, A. H., 1972, p. 113. Routh, G., 1965, pp. 4–5.

TABLE II

Selected occupations: Islington 1931

	Men		Women	
	No.	%	No.	%
All occupied	109,450	100	61,329	100
General labour				
General labourers (so described)	2,995	2.7	24	
Labourers (so described)	940	0.9	9	
Builders' labourers	1,411	1.3		
Domestic service				
Charwomen, office cleaners	156	0.1	3,235	5.3
Street sellers, etc.				
Costermongers and hawkers	1,142	1.0	217	0.4
Newsvendors	267	0.2	10	
Total	6,911	6.2	3,495	5.7

Source: 1931 Census.

TABLE 12

Reports of persons living in Campbell Road and the 'black' areas against whom charges were brought, 1919–39[a] (Figures are for Men with Women in brackets)

	Campbell Road				'Black' areas[b]			
	1919–29 Persons		1930–9 Persons		1919–29 Persons		1930–9 Persons	
	No.	%	No.	%	No.	%	No.	%
1 Crimes against property								
Robbery with violence	1				1		3	
Attempted robbery with violence	3							
Burglary	1							
Breaking and entering	16		10		14		17(1)	
Attempted breaking and entering			1		1		3	
Theft	38(19)		24(3)		53(29)		36(8)	
Theft by means of a trick	2		1					
Obtaining money by false pretences					4			
Embezzlement	1				2		2	
Incitement to rob			1				1	
Fare dodging	1							
Coining/uttering	1				1			
Receiving stolen property					3			
Criminal damage	6		1		3(3)		3	
Suspected person	10		9		15(2)		17	
Section 7 Prevention of Crimes Act	1				1			
	81(19)	37(32.2)	47(3)	41.6(10)	98(34)	27.7(27.4)	82(9)	41.8(45)

TABLE 12 *continued*

| | Campbell Road | | | | 'Black' areas[b] | | | |
	1919–29 Persons No.	%	1930–9 Persons No.	%	1919–29 Persons No.	%	1930–9 Persons No.	%
2 Crimes of violence								
Murder (infant)								
Manslaughter					(1)		(1)	
Grievous bodily harm	3(1)		1		1		2(1)	
Wounding	3				9			
Assault (domestic)	10		2		5(1)		2	
Assault (neighbour)	14(10)		1(1)		12		5(1)	
Assault (other)	9		3(1)		19(15)		3	
Attempted suicide	1				19(2)			
Unlawful threats			2		3			
Child assault/neglect/abandon	3(3)				1(3)		1	
Unlawful possession of firearm					1			
Cruelty to animals	2		3		4		4	
	45(14)	20.6(23.7)	12(2)	8.8(6.7)	74(21)	20.3(16.9)	17(3)	8.7(15)
3 Crimes against authority								
Assault on police	10		3(1)		19(5)		6	
Obstructing police	5(1)		1(1)		4		3	
Assisting escape from public institution								
Harbouring subject of adoption order					(1)			
Refusing to have child vaccinated					2			

TABLE 12 *continued*

	Campbell Road				'Black' areas[b]			
	1919–29 Persons No.	%	1930–9 Persons No.	%	1919–29 Persons No.	%	1930–9 Persons No.	%
3 *Continued*								
Desertion from army	5				3		1	
Breaking terms of probation order					(2)			
Unlawfully obtaining unemployment benefit/relief	1		3		13		4	
	21(1)	9.6(1.7)	7(2)	6.1(6.7)	41(8)	11.6(6.5)	14	7.1
4 *Crimes against sexual code*								
Keeping a brothel					(3)		(0)	
Living on immoral earnings			1					
Soliciting	(4)		(4)		(2)			
Bigamy	1(2)				1(1)			
Failure to maintain wife/child	7		6		1		2	
	8(6)	3.7(10.2)	7(4)	6.2(13.3)	2(6)	(4.8)	2	1.0
5 *Crimes against cultural code*								
Drunk and disorderly/incapable, etc.	13(12)		11(10)		33(36)		20(2)	
Insulting/obscene words/behaviour	7		5(1)		12(8)		9(4)	
Gaming in street	13		3		10		4	
Suffering gaming in refreshment house					2(1)		1	

TABLE 12 continued

	Campbell Road				'Black' areas[b]			
	1919–29 Persons No.	%	1930–9 Persons No.	%	1919–29 Persons No.	%	1930–9 Persons No.	%
5 Continued								
Discharging fireworks/making bonfires/playing cricket/football in streets			4		1		10	
Street betting	7				20			
Keeping betting house			3(2)		1(2)		4(I)	
Frequenting betting house					2		I	
	40(12)	18.3(18.6)	26(13)	23.0(43.3)	81(47)	22.9(37.9)	50(7)	25.5(35)
6 Offences committed while earning a living in streets								
Trading without a licence	1(1)						1(I)	
Obstructing street with barrow	3(1)		3(1)					
Causing child to sell in streets	1(1)		4		53(5)		25	
Shouting street cries					1			
Selling short weight	2							
Begging	14(4)		5(2)		1(2)		2	
Procuring child for begging	(1)							
Allowing child used for begging	1(1)		(1)		1(1)			
Wandering without visible means of support	1		1(1)				I	
	23(9)	10.5(15.3)	13(5)	11.5(16.7)	56(8)	16.4(6.5)	29(1)	14.8

TABLE 12 continued

| | Campbell Road | | | | 'Black' areas[b] | | | |
| | 1919–29 Persons | | 1930–9 Persons | | 1919–29 Persons | | 1930–9 Persons | |
	No.	%	No.	%	No.	%	No.	%
7 *Other*								
Cycling/driving dangerously	1		1		2		2	
Road Traffic Act offences			3					
	1		4	3.5	2		2	1.0
Total	219(60)		116(29)		354(124)		196(20)	

Notes

(a) The table counts individuals against whom specific charges were brought rather than the number of charges. A second charge brought for the same crime during either of the two periods against the same person has not been counted. E.g., during 1921–9, there were reports of 38 men living in Campbell Road and charged with theft; 16 men were also charged with breaking and entering. Some men might be counted in both categories; some men charged with theft during the period might also appear if reported as charged with theft during 1930–9.

(b) The 'black' areas are the same as for table 7.

Sources: *Islington Gazette; Islington and Holloway Press;* 1919–39.

TABLE 13

Ages of persons admitted to the Islington Workhouse from Campbell Road, 1920 and 1930

Age	Men	Women	Total	Total as %age of age cohorts in Islington population (1921)
0–11	9	9	18	90
12–19	1	5	6	44
20–24	–	4	4	50
25–34	2	7	9	58
35–44	4	13	17	126
45–54	6	9	15	130
55–59	4	5	9	225
60–64	4	2	6	200
65–69	4	2	6	240
70+	3	2	5	143
Total	37	58	95	

Note: A population of 95 distributed proportionately among the age cohorts pertaining in Islington in 1921 would produce 8 persons aged 20–24; the number here is 4, or 50%. A figure of 100 in column 5 would represent a normal distribution for that age cohort compared with the Islington population as a whole.
Sources: ISBG 281/41–2; 281/57–8.
    Census 1921.

TABLE 14   Household characteristics and housing space 1938: I Campbell Road

Persons in H/H	Rooms occupied						Total H/Hs	% all H/Hs	Persons	%
	1	2	3	4	5	6				
1	61	8	1				70	23.8	70	6.4
2	32	21	4	1			57	19.4 ⎫	114	10.5
3	1	23	5				30	10.2 ⎬ 42.2	90	8.3
4	2	24	9	4		2	37	12.6 ⎭	148	13.6
5	1	20	5	2	1		31	10.5	155	14.2
6		12	9	1	3		26	8.8	156	14.3
7		5	9	1			15	5.1 ⎫	105	9.7 ⎫
8		6	7				14	4.8	112	10.3
9			7				7	2.4 ⎬ 14.7	63	5.8
10		1	3				4	1.4	40	3.7 ⎬ 32.7
11				1			1	0.3	11	1.0
12					1	1	2	0.7 ⎭	24	2.2 ⎭
Total dwellings	97	120	59	10	5	3	294		1,088	
% all dwellings	33.0 ⎫	40.8 ⎬ 93.9	20.1 ⎭	3.4	1.7	1.0				

Source: IS/OC.

TABLE 15 Household characteristics and housing space 1938 II 'Black' streets of Holloway, exc. Campbell Road[1]

Persons in H/H	Rooms occupied							Total H/Hs	% all H/Hs	Total persons	% all persons
	1	2	3	4	5	6	7				
1	91	38	12	2				143	15.4	143	4.3
2	35	92	41	17	4	1		190	20.4	380	11.4
3	7	71	49	24	6	4		161	17.3	483	14.5
4	1	59	47	31	6	4		148	15.9	592	17.8
5		32	45	33	11	5	1	127	13.6	635	19.1
6		17	29	24	6	5	1	72	7.7	432	13.0
7		3	11	12	6	2		34	3.7	238	7.2
8			4	9	5	5		23	2.5	184	5.5
9			3	6	3	1	1	14	1.5	126	3.8
10			1	1				2	0.2	20	0.6
11				1	1			2	0.2	22	0.7
12			1	1				2	0.2	24	0.7
13				2				2	0.2	26	0.8
14											
15			1					1	0.1	15	0.5
Total dwellings	134	312	244	163	48	27	3	931		3,320	
% all dwellings	14.4	33.5	26.2	17.5	5.2	2.9	0.3				

(Bracketed groupings shown in table: % all dwellings for rooms 1–3 = 74.1; % all H/Hs for persons 2–4 = 53.6; % all H/Hs for persons 7–15 = 8.6; % all persons for persons 7–15 = 19.8)

Note
1 Rupert Road area: Rupert Road, Hampden Road, Cromwell Road, Milton Grove.
Queensland Road area: Queensland Road, Queensland Place, Queens Square, Instow Place, Emily Place.
George's Road.

TABLE 16   Household size and housing space III Three 'unskilled above poverty line' streets of Holloway[1]

Persons in H/H	Rooms occupied							Total H/Hs	%	Total persons	%
	1	2	3	4	5	6	7				
1	52	20	6					78	16.6	78	5.2
2	12	39	42	4	4	4		105	22.3	210	13.9
3	2	27	52	16	7			104	22.1	312	20.7
4		13	34	27	10	3		87	18.5	348	23.1
5		5	16	16	7	8		53	11.3	265	17.6
6		1	8	6	3	3		21	4.5	126	8.4
7		1	1	1	5	2	2	12	2.6	84	5.6
8		1		2	2	1		6	1.7	48	3.2
9					1	1	1	3	0.6	27	1.8
10					1			1	0.2	10	0.7
Total of dwellings	66	107	159	72	40	22	3	470		1,508	
% of all dwellings	14.0	22.8	33.8	15.3	8.5	4.7	0.6				

(Bracket groupings: columns 1–3 of % of all dwellings = 70.6; Total H/Hs % rows 2–4 = 62.9, rows 7–8 = 5.1; Total persons % = 11.3)

Note
1 Ashburton Grove, Playford Road, Pooles Park.

TABLE 17

Family and household characteristics Campbell Road, 'black' streets and 'unskilled' streets 1938

	Campbell Road N = 294	% all households 'Black' streets[1] N = 931	'Unskilled'[2] streets N = 470	Islington (1931)
1 adult[3]	24.2	15.4	16.6	
2 adults	18.0	18.8	21.9	
One-person family[4]	1.0	1.1	0.4	
Young family[5]	26.2	27.9	25.3	
Large young family[6]	13.6	7.6	1.7	
Adult household[7]	16.0	27.9	31.2	
Large adult household[8]	1.0	1.3	3.0	
Total	100.0	100.0	100.0	
Average size of household (persons)	3.7	3.7	3.2	3.3

Notes
1 See notes to table 15.
2 See notes to table 16.
3 Person 14 years or over.
4 1 adult with child/ren under 10 years.
5 2 adults with 1–4 child/ren under 10 years.
6 7 or more persons, including 1 or more child/ren under 10 years.
7 3–6 adults.
8 7 or more adults.

Source: IS/OC. NSL, vol. VI p. 44 for average size of Islington household.

TABLE 18   Women's employment, Islington 1911 and 1931

	1911	% occ.	1931	% occ.
Manufacture (all metals)	1,532	2.9	2,129	3.5
Manufacture (dress)	13,273	24.8	10,140	16.5
Manufacture (food, drink, tobacco)	1,189	2.2	1,617	2.6
Manufacture (paper, printing, etc.)	3,184	6.0	3,161	5.2
Manufacture (other)	3,154	5.9	4,275	7.0
Total manufacture	22,332	41.8	21,322	34.8
Commercial (inc. shop work, clerks and typists)	7,958	14.8	14,641	23.9
Personal service (inc. hotels, institutions, etc.)	17,812	33.2	17,182	28.0
Other	5,491	10.3	8,184	13.3
Total	53,593 (41.8% of all women)	100.0	61,329 (44.9% of all women)	100.0

Note: Figures underlined are estimates. The 1931 Census groups 'other workers' in separate classes into one general 'other and undefined workers' category. The 1921 Census has 'other workers' enumerated under the class of employment in which they worked. I have applied the proportions of 1921 categories to the 1931 figures for manufacture.
Source: Census 1911, 1921, 1931.

TABLE 19   Girls'[1] employment, Islington 1911 and 1931

	1911	% occ.	1931	% occ.
Manufacture (all)	4,450	57.8	3,798[2]	44.6
Commercial	450	5.9	3,154	37.0
Personal service	1,850	24.1	1,108	13.0
Other	940	12.2	459	5.4
Total	7,690 (67.9% of all girls)	100.0	8,519 (80.4% of all girls)	100.0

Notes
1 A 'girl' is under 18.
2 Figures underlined are estimates (see table 18).

TABLE 20   Age of marriage at St Anne's church: Campbell Road and Playford Road 1921–38

| | 1921–29 | | | | 1930–8 | | | |
	Campbell Road	%	Playford Road	%	Campbell Road	%	Playford Road	%
Marriages in[1]	60	75	38	69.1	17	54.8	24	57.2
Woman marrying out	7	8.8	7	12.7	2	6.5	9	21.4
Man marrying out	13	16.2	10	18.2	12	38.7	9	21.4
Total marriages	80	100.0	55	100.0	31	100.0	42	100.0
One partner[2] under 21	14	17.5	8	14.6	9	29.0	4	9.5
Both partners under 21	12	15.0	–	–	3	9.7	–	–
Both partners over 21	54	67.5	47	85.4	19	61.3	38	90.5
Total marriages	80	100.0	55	100.0	31	100.0	42	100.0
Women under 21[3]	23	31.5[4]	4	8.3	10	34.5	3	9.1
Men under 21	13	19.4	1	2.2	3	15.8	–	–
Total under 21	36	50.9	5	10.5	13	50.3	3	9.1
Mean age of woman, first marriage	23.1		25.3		22.0		23.2	
Mean age of man, first marriage	25.7		26.6		24.9		25.9	

Notes
1 Marriages where both partners give an address in the same street.
2 This section includes partners who are not living in Campbell Road or Playford Road.
3 This section only includes partners living in Campbell Road or Playford Road.
4 Percentages in this section are of all partners living in Campbell or Playford Roads.
Source: Register of Marriages, St Anne's, Pooles Park.

TABLE 21   Household mobility, Campbell Road and Playford Road 1930–46

	1930–1934		Change %	1934–1938		Change %	1938–1946		Change %
	No.	%		No.	%		No.	%	
Campbell Road									
Static households	172	41.4		144	38.1		51[a]	16.4	
Mobile households	243	58.6		234	61.9		260	83.6	
Total households	415	100.0	−8.9	378	100.0	−17.7	311	100.0	−46.0
Static individuals	277	36.8		246	37.0		79	14.8	
Mobile individuals	476	63.2		418	63.0		456	85.2	
Total individuals	753	100.0	−11.8	664	100.0	−19.4	535	100.0	−50.8
Playford Road									
Static households	140	53.0		111	41.1		69	28.4	
Mobile households	124	47.0		159	58.9		174	71.6	
Total households	264	100.0	+2.3	270	100.0	−10.0	243	100.0	−12.4
Static individuals	258	49.5		212	39.8		127	26.3	
Mobile individuals	263	50.5		320	60.2		355	73.7	
Total individuals	521	100.0	+2.1	532	100.0	−9.4	482	100.0	−5.2

Notes
'Household' is identified by common surname.
'Static' means a household or individual living at the same house at both dates.
'Mobile' means a household or individual not living at the same house at both dates.
[a] 97 households on the register in 1938 still had members living in the street (not necessarily at the same house) in 1946.
Sources: IS/ER 1930, 1934, 1938, 1946 (October list in each case).

Notes

1 The rise of Campbell Bunk

1 Holloway here means that part of the Metropolitan (now London) Borough of Islington north of Highbury Corner but excluding Highbury. From the York Road (now Way) border with St Pancras in the west, the southern boundary runs east along the LMS Railway to Highbury Corner; north up Holloway Road; east along Drayton Park; and north along the railway line from Drayton Park station to Stroud Green Road, the border with Hornsey. It includes the whole of the N7 (Holloway) and N19 (Upper Holloway) postal districts, most of N4 (Finsbury Park) in Islington, and nothing else.

2 The local vicar on Campbell Road, 1897, quoted in Booth, C. (1902), Series 3, vol. 1, p. 138.

3 Coull, T. (1864), p. 57. See also Cromwell, T. (1835), pp. 152 ff.

4 Lewis, S. (1842), pp. 48–9. Lewis was referring to Islington as a whole but the land rises to the north.

5 Knight, C. (1841–4), vol. 1, p. 243.

6 Holloway (1924), p. 6.

7 Cromwell, T. (1835), pp. 383–4.

8 Lees, L. H. (1979), pp. 207, 210, 229.

9 IS/D 3547, abstract of title of the freeholders of the Seven Sisters Estate.

10 See Dyos, H. J. (1961), pp. 114–18. For the politics of the Societies, see Gauldie, E. (1974), pp. 208–13.

11 IS/D 3504–3524.

12 The Islington Vestry Surveyor records 4 houses in 1865, 7 in 1866, and 13 in the St Pancras's part of Campbell Road in 1867. ISV/SDP, Books, 11, 12, 13, 15, 21, 22, 28, 29, 43.

13 Information from the Ordnance Survey map, 1869.

14 ISV/SDP, books as in n. 12.

15 Hornsey Road (1921), pp. 9–10.

16 Census MSS, 1871, Enumerators' Record Books, RG 10 305.

17 Booth, C. (1902), Series 3, vol. 1, p. 138. In 1872, the Vestry Sanitary Committee prosecuted the owner of vacant land in Campbell Road to remove a nuisance from 'stagnant water' on the site: ISV/SC vol. 3, 4 March 1872, p. 89.

18 Booth MSS, Group B, vol. 207, pp. 169–72 (punctuation corrected).

19 LCC PH/REG/1/9, ref. 5286. See also refs 5172, 5173.

20 According to one strand of Campbell Road folklore it might have been responsible for the street's nickname, referring to the lodging house bunks (Mr P, CB36, 21.1). Other explanations favour corruption of the 'Bung', the name supposedly given to Campbell Road's beer shop. But apart from Bung being a common slang term for brewers and tap rooms, I am unable to verify this. I favour the connotations of hiding place and sanctuary, as in 'do a bunk'.

21 Ross, E. (1983), pp. 6–7, found 21 per cent in Old Nichol Street in 1871 and 8 per cent in a respectable street near Victoria Park.

22 All data from Census MSS, 1881, Enumerators' Record Books, RG 11 259–60.

23 See LCC/PH/REG/1/13.

24 Samuel, R. (1973), passim.

25 Calculated from ISBG 281/15.

26 ISBG 253.

27 ISBG 253, vol. 11, 20 Aug. 1889.

28 ISBG 253, vol. 11, 15 Oct. 1889.

29 ISBG 253, vol. 11, 24 Dec. 1889.

30 Islington MOH (1895), pp. 176–8.

31 Islington MOH (1909), p. 251.

32 ISBG 253, vol. 11, 30 Sept. 1889.

33 ISBG 253, vol. 11, 8 Oct. 1889.

34 ISBG 253, vol. 11, 28 Jan. 1890.

35 Booth MSS, Group B, vol. 208, p. 85.

36 ISBG 253, vol. 11, 1 July 1890.

37 ISBG 253, vol. 11, 16 Oct. 1889.

38 ISBG 253, vol. 11, 20 and 21 June 1890 (Julia Mills).

39 ISBG 253, vol. 11, 1 July 1890.

40 In the George's Road area, for example, Booth's investigators were told of 'a great deal of changing from house to house within this narrow radius'. Booth MSS, Group B, vol. 349, p. 125.

41 ISMB/PHC 1908–9, 4 Jan. 1909, pp. 167–8. Inspector Ward's report is dated 30 Dec. 1908.

42 Mrs B, CB25, 18.5.

43 Islington MOH (1895), pp. 176–8.

44 ISBG 253, vol. 11, 16 Oct. 1889 (Louisa Rowlett); 4 Nov. 1889. (George Game); 11 March 1890 (Kate Moss); 29 April 1890 (Louisa Frost).

45 Booth, C. (1902), Series 3, vol. 1, p. 138. Booth MSS, Group A, vol. 36, pp. 26–7 and Group B, vol. 207, p. 145 and vol. 349, pp. 31–3.

46 Booth MSS, Group A, vol. 37, pp. 69–70; Islington MOH (1895, 4th Quarter), p. 28.

47 Booth, C. (1902), Series 3, vol. 2, p. 111.

48 Mr A, biographical details.

49 There were gypsies just to the north of Campbell Road in the 1870s, according to an alderman's reminiscences; IG, 8 Oct. 1926.

50 Islington's location quotient for male transport workers as a whole was 1.09 in 1911; for road transport workers it was 1.33. Calculated

from Census (1911). In this instance, a location quotient is designed to demonstrate concentrations of a workforce resident in one locality compared with the overall density in the area as a whole. It is calculated as follows: (No. of men employed in road transport in Islington as percentage of men employed in road transport in the County of London) ÷ (No. of occupied men in Islington as percentage of occupied men in the County of London). See Hall, P. G. (1962), pp. 16–17.

51 Men from Campbell Road worked in these coal yards from the earliest years. See Heaven, E. F. (1934), p. 20.

52 Booth, C. (1902), Series 3, vol. 1, p. 151.

53 Calculated from Census (1911). For Great Britain see Halsey, A. H. (1972), p. 118.

54 Booth MSS, Group B, vol. 349, p. 175.

55 Gissing, G. (1886), p. 401; and (1891), pp. 116–17.

56 Booth, C. (1902), Series 1, vol. 2, Appendix (Maps) and Series 3, vol. 1, pp. 164–5. See also Booth MSS, Group B, vol. 348, pp. 231–41 and vol. 349, pp. 1–203 passim.

57 Islington MOH (1909), pp. 233–8.

58 IS/DIR 1874. IG, 2 Sept. 1922.

59 IG, 2 Sept. 1922, letter from 'A British Legionite'.

60 Information from Kelly's Directory and IS/DIR.

61 Oral evidence from Mr I, Mrs A, and Mr Tom Gamby.

62 Booth MSS, Group B, vol. 206, p. 93.

63 Information from IS/DIR and IS/RB.

64 Booth MSS, Group B, vol. 206, p. 84.

65 Booth, C. (1902), Series 3, vol. 1, pp. 138–41.

66 Booth, C. (1902), Series 3, vol. 1, p. 141.

67 Booth MSS, Group B, vol. 208, pp. 13–14.

68 Booth MSS, Group B, vol. 207, p. 173.

69 Booth MSS, Group B, vol. 208, p. 85.

70 Islington MOH (1896), pp. 74–80.

71 IG, 2 April 1909; ISMB/PHC 1908–9, 4 Jan. 1909, pp. 167–8; Islington MOH (1909), p. 233 ff.

72 ISMB/PHC 1908–9, 4 Jan. 1909, pp. 167–8.

73 NCC/MS, 1875, p. 16; 1880, pp. 18–19; 1885, p. 22.

74 The decline in Islington as a whole over the period was about 46 per cent.

2 The dynamics of class

1 NSL MSS, House Sample Survey Cards 21/295, 296, 429; 22/873, 885, 981; 23/1997.

2 NSL MSS, House Sample Survey Cards, as in n. 1 plus 21/670, 673; 22/1108, 1178, 1482, 1494, 1536; 23/1838. There is no hard information for the number of households in Campbell Road in 1929. The NSL MSS gives 15 households in 3 houses. The IS/OC survey of 1938 gives 10 households for the same 3. This dramatic reduction

would give a total of 441 households in 1929 compared with 294 in 1938. But the reduction was very uneven between individual houses: 25 Campbell Road had 26 people living there in 1929, 12 in 1938; 90 had 11 in both years. I estimate the reduction in Islington's population between 1929 and 1938 as 9.7 per cent; increasing the 1938 figure for households by that proportion gives the number of households in 1929 as 323. In the absence of anything better I have chosen the midpoint between that and the 1929 estimate of 441 – 382.

3 NSL/PNL.
4 *NSL*, vol. 3, p. 259.
5 Marx, K, (1852), p. 442.
6 See, e.g., the analysis of Eugène Sue's *The Mysteries of Paris* in Marx, K. and Engels, F. (1844), pp. 192 ff and 198 ff; and Engels, F. (1845), p. 126. For subsequent polemic see Marx, K. (1850) and Engels, F. (1870), p. 163.
7 Ollman, B. (1971), p. 120 ff.
8 Marx, K. (1867), vol. 1, p. 602.
9 Marx, K. and Engels, F. (1846), pp. 70–4; Engels, F. (1845), pp. 123–33, 157.
10 Marx, K. (1852) and (1850) throughout.
11 In the following discussion on class I have found the work of several Marxist theorists helpful, especially Wright, E. O. (1978) and (1979), the work of Nicos Poulantzas (especially 1974), Cohen, G. A. (1978) and Thompson, E. P. (1963) and (1978).
12 Marx, K. (1867), vol. 1, p. 621.
13 Marx, K. (1844), p. 274. See also Sennett, R. and Cobb, J. (1972), pp. 34–5, 93 ff.
14 Hall, P. G. (1962) and Smith, D. H. (1933).
15 HMFI (1925), pp. 4–5; (1935), p. 10. On the growing industries, all well represented in London, see Beveridge, W. (1944), pp. 316–20. On the place of London within the national economy, see Pollard, S. (1962), p. 125 ff.
16 From HMFI (1920) and (1938).
17 Thornhill, J. F. P. (1935), pp. 101–2.
18 Hall, P. G. (1962), p. 161.
19 Richardson, H. W. and Aldcroft, D. H. (1968), pp. 288–91.
20 Priestley, J. B. (1934), p. 4.
21 Islington MOH (1922), p. 41; Warnes, A. M. in Evans, A. and Eversley, D. (eds) (1980), p. 34.
22 Forshaw, J. H. and Abercrombie, P. (1943), p. 93.
23 From Kelly's Directories. But see the comments on this source in Hall, P. G. (1962), p. 18. For confirmation of the trend see Forshaw, J. H. and Abercrombie, P. (1943), p. 87.
24 See Beveridge, W. (1930), p. 358 and (1944), p. 67; and Stevenson, J. and Cook, C. (1977), p. 286.
25 LCC/LS.
26 LCC/LS; Wilkinson, E. (1939), p. 259.
27 Colin Clark, *National Income and Outlay*, quoted in Pilgrim Trust,

(1938), pp. 25–6. See also Bakke, E. W. (1933), p. 49; Sinfield, A. (1981), pp. 18–19; Showler, B. and Sinfield, A. (1981), pp. 9–10.

28 Beveridge, W. (1944), p. 67.

29 Sinfield, A. (1968), p. 27; Pilgrim Trust (1938), pp. 7–10.

30 Pilgrim Trust (1938), pp. 31, 59; NSL, vol. 3, p. 167. For numbers of able-bodied unemployed on relief in Islington see PP Unemployed on Relief 1927 (Cd 3006); 1928–9 (Cd 3218); 1929–30 (Cd 3433), pp. 8–9 in each case.

31 Hill, P. (1940), pp. 27 ff; Bakke, E. W. (1933), p. 51; Brockway, F. (1932); Marx, K. (1867), vol. 1, pp. 167–8.

32 Pilgrim Trust (1938), pp. 143 ff; Bakke, E. W. (1933), pp. 62 ff; Jahoda, M. et al. (1933); NSL, vol. 3, p. 163; Beales, H. and Lambert, R. S. (1934), pp. 26 ff.

33 Bakke, E. W. (1933), p. 50; Pilgrim Trust (1938), p. 12.

34 Pilgrim Trust (1938), p. 132 ff.

35 See Edwards, I. (1947), p. 78, but see also pp. 22, 76, 89; and MacGill, P. (1914), p. 183.

36 ISMB/UE, 4 Dec. 1925, pp. 323–4, report of the Borough Engineer.

37 Hancock, W. K. and Gowing, M. M. (1949), pp. 142–3; and Fig. 1.

38 NSL, vol. 3, p. 163.

39 Mrs F, CB38, 4.2.

40 Mr H, CB39, 7.3.

41 IG, 13 Sept. 1929.

42 I&HP, 6 Dec. 1932.

43 Mr B, CB09 and CB10, 1.1–20.8. This troupe idea, not uncommon among the less inhibited elements of the unemployed, was taken up by the Lennox Road Mission in 1932. They formed the 'Black Diamond Troupe' of unemployed lads from Campbell Road who earned money in the suburbs for the Mission. See Heaven, E. F. (1934), p. 30.

44 I&HP, 2 March 1935.

45 NSL, vol. 1, p. 33; Davison, R. C. (1929), pp. 180–1; Pilgrim Trust (1938), p. 56; Stedman Jones, G. (1971), p. 336; Whiteside, N. (1979), pp. 516–17.

46 I&HP, 12 Feb. 1938.

47 E.g. Mrs J, CB41, 7.3, 12.6.

48 See Richardson, H. W. and Aldcroft, D. H. (1968), pp. 37, 70, 127; NSL, vol. 2, pp. 68, 69, 88, 110; Cole, G. D. H. (1945), pp. 128–34. For the extent of the London building boom between the wars see Jackson, A. (1973), pp. 100, 111–12.

49 NSL, vol. 2, p. 120.

50 I&HP, 30 July 1932.

51 Mrs E, CB29, 55.3.

52 NSL, vol. 1, p. 27. On the importance of small firms in the building industry see Richardson, H. W. and Aldcroft, D. H. (1968), pp. 33–5, 122; and Cole, G. D. H. (1945), pp. 125–7.

53 Mr I, CB16, 9.3.

54 Mr P, CB36, 3.2.

55 Kuczynski, J. (1938), p. 70; Cole, G. D. H. (1945), p. 131; Richardson, H. W. and Aldcroft, D. H. (1968), p. 123.
56 *NSL*, vol. 2, pp. 60, 110.
57 In 1931, the location quotient for male road transport workers in Islington, as against the County of London, was 1.23. For location quotients see ch. 1, n. 50.
58 For the casual fringe among drivers and conductors see Healey, B. (1980), p. 55.
59 PP Committee on Motor Transport, 1937 (Cd 5440), p. 2. See also Bullock, A. (1960), pp. 250–1.
60 *NSL*, vol. 8, p. 50 and vol. 5, pp. 347–8.
61 Mr H, CB39, 21.1; Mr M, CB12, 4.7.
62 Bullock, A. (1960), pp. 250–1, 460, 544–6, 618–19.
63 *NSL*, vol. 8, pp. 38–40, 45, 51–2.
64 *NSL*, vol. 8, pp. 51–2.
65 Mr B, CB09, 6.2; CB10, 20.6.
66 *IG*, 21 Jan. 1920. See also Tiley, G. (1975), p. 20.
67 *NSL*, vol. 5, pp. 117–27; PP Committee on Wholesale Food Markets, 1920–1 (Cd 1341), p. 9. Morse-Boycott, D. (1931), pp. 140–1.
68 Brown, J. (1946), pp. 37–8, 45, 68, 216.
69 I am grateful to Bob Branton for this reference.
70 NCM, Feb. 1929, p. 22.
71 Mrs D, CB19, 20.3; Mr M, CB12, 5.2; Mr C, CB07, 5.3; Burke, T. (1922), p. 77; Rodaway, A. (1960), p. 99.
72 Jones, J. A. (1934), p. 55; see also Tiley, G. (1975), p. 17.
73 Decasualisation was begun by Islington's first Labour council in 1921, under pressure from the Municipal Employees' Association, but the Municipal Reformers probably put the brake on until mechanisation of dust removal and some street cleaning. See ISMB/CC, vol. 19, 20 April 1921, pp. 147–8. For the daily hirings see *IG*, 12 Aug. 1921, letter from 'A Casual'.
74 *NSL*, vol. 8, pp. 253–4.
75 *NSL*, vol. 2, pp. 429–30.
76 NCM, Feb. 1929, p. 22.
77 Mrs E, CB27, 15.1. According to *NSL*, vol. 2, p. 453, the going rate (presumably without a meal) was 5s a day.
78 Mr J, CB06, 19.1.
79 Mrs A, CB04, 18.4.
80 Mr B, CB09, 7.5. See also Bullock, A. (1960), p. 462.
81 Mr H, CB39, 10.3; Mr B, CB09, 8.2.
82 Mr P, CB36, 29.2.
83 Beveridge, W. (1909), p. 108.
84 Out of a sample of 210 economically active heads of households in NSL/PNL, 32 (15.2 per cent) paid no national insurance. The figures for Campbell Road were 13 and 5 (38.5 per cent).
85 Pilgrim Trust (1938), p. 58.
86 Mrs G, CB35, 5.3–6.3.
87 Mrs F, CB38, 9.2.

88 *I&HP*, 29 April 1933.
89 ISBG 64, 24 July 1929, p. 2.
90 Mr J, CB11, 31.2.
91 *NSL*, vol. 6, pp. 351–5, 358–9.
92 NSL MSS, Section 1, Parcel 5/5, p. 3. Dr Shrubsall was a member of the Wood Committee (see n. 122 below, and ch. 4).
93 Calder, A. (1969), p. 447.
94 Pilgrim Trust (1938), p. 177.
95 Marx, K. (1867), vol. 1, pp. 305–7.
96 Mrs L. CB34, 1.1, 18.4.
97 Mrs J, CB41, 4.2.
98 Mrs J, CB44, 38.3.
99 Mr H, CB39, 24.1–2.
100 Mr J, CB06, 28.2.
101 Mr B, CB09, 3.6.
102 *IG*, 11 July 1919.
103 Beales, H. L. and Lambert, R. S. (1934), pp. 225–6. See also the moving letter from a disabled Londoner in Brockway, F. (1932), pp. 217 ff.
104 Pailthorpe, G. W. (1932), pp. 113–16.
105 See Gillain, L. (1954), pp. 65 ff. *IG*, 2 April 1919, 1 May 1919.
106 Hirst, F. W. (1934), pp. 297–9.
107 *IG*, 2 Jan. 1917. A letter in *IG*, 2 Sept. 1922 gave the figure of 400 men joining up from Campbell Road.
108 ISBG 64, 24 July 1929, p. 23.
109 *IG*, 20 Aug. 1932. See also *IG*, 27 July 1927.
110 *TEHW*, 17 Oct. 1919.
111 *IG*, 29 March 1921.
112 Calculated from IS/OC. On the use of this source see White, J. (1977).
113 See, e.g., Islington MOH (1936), map facing p. 28.
114 Mrs B, CB25, 35.1.
115 In 1934, the *NSL* (vol. 6, p. 187) claimed that 'Practically all houses – even the very poorest' were supplied with gas or electricity, and often with both'.
116 That was how Robert Young, the local Labour MP, described Campbell Road in 1930 (*I&HP*, 11 Jan. 1930).
117 *IG*, 21 July 1921.
118 Mr I, CB16, 7.1.
119 See, e.g., a report of a baby scalded to death at 52 Campbell Road (*IG*, 23 Sept. 1920); and of a fatal fire at 25 Campbell Road in Mr B, CB10, 12.1.
120 Wood Committee (1929), Pt IV, p. 201.
121 Blacker, C. P. (ed.) (1937), p. 13.
122 See, e.g., the Wood Committee (1929), especially Dr Lewis's report, and the PP Committee on Sterilisation of the 'Unfit'.
123 Graves, R. and Hodge, A. (1941), p. 27.
124 Blacker, C. P. (ed.) (1937), pp. 176–8.

125 Mrs J, CB44, 38.3; numbers verified by IS/OC (Mrs J had moved
    out in 1936 but a new baby had replaced her by 1938).
126 Mr H, CB39, biographical details.
127 *IG*, 7 March 1919, 11 Nov. 1919.
128 *I&HP*, 15 June 1929, 20 July 1929.
129 Mrs E, CB27 and CB28, 1.1–88.1, throughout.
130 NSL MSS, Sec. 1, Parcel 5/7, np. For the tribulations of a nervous
    and educationally backward Islington youth from this period see the
    unjustly neglected Gillain, L. (1954).
131 Mullins, C. (1943), pp. 134–6.
132 Mountain, T. W. (1930), pp. 64 ff.
133 PP Employment of Prisoners, 1935 (Cd 4897), pp. 16–17.
134 Gordon, J. W. (1932), p. 214; Davis, V. (1937), p. 245; Morris, N.
    (1951), p. 306; Fletcher, J. W. (1972), p. 11.
135 For a useful exposition of labelling or social reaction theory see
    Taylor, I. *et al.*, (1973), pp. 139–71.
136 Mrs B, CB25, 22.2.
137 *IG*, 2 Sept. 1922.
138 *IG*, 5 Sept. 1922.
139 Mr J, CB06, 6.1; CB11, 36.3. See also Tucker, J. (1966), pp. 63–4
    for similar ploys in a Bristol housing estate with a bad reputation.
140 *IG*, 28 Aug. 1924.
141 Crossick, G. (1978), pp. 47, 59.
142 Zweig, F. (1949), pp. 8–9.
143 Pilgrim Trust (1938), p. 156.
144 *NSL*, vol. 3, p. 307.
145 See Bakke, E. W. (1933), p. 83.
146 Thompson, B. (1933), p. 211.
147 Thompson, B. (1933), p. 110. Willis, P. (1977), p. 102 makes very
    similar points.
148 Worby, J. (1939), pp. 206–8; see also (1937).
149 But they existed none the less: see Williamson, B. (1982), pp. 44,
    128, 210, 225. And for other examples of 'penny capitalism' among
    the skilled working class see Benson, J. (1983).
150 Children's economic enterprise rates hardly a mention in Opie, I. and
    P. (1959), apart from calendar festivals like Guy Fawkes and St James'
    Day grottoes.
151 Mr L. CB01, throughout.
152 Mr I, CB16, 24.2.
153 In Mr B, CB10, 12.1.
154 Mrs J, CB41, 3.4, 13.2.
155 Mayhew, H. (1861–2), vol. 1, p. 7.
156 Mrs J, CB41, 31.2, 34.5.
157 Mrs D, CB18, 8.2.
158 Letter from ex-PS Stan Costin, Feb. 1979, to author.
159 Booth, C. (1902), vol. 3, pp. 151–2.
160 Borrow, G. (1874), pp. 207–40.
161 Samuel, R. (1973), pp. 129–30.

162 *IG*, 8 Oct. 1926; Samuel, R. (1973), p. 130.
163 See Mr G, CB02, throughout.
164 *NSL*, vol. 3, p. 291.
165 In Islington, the number of licensed street traders fell from its highest point of 558 in 1933 to 323 in 1938. See Islington MOH (1933), p. 79, and (1938), p. 78.
166 See Edwin Pugh in Adcock, St J. A. (1928); Gillain, L. (1954); Orwell, G. (1933), pp. 143–59; Thompson, B. (1933); Greenwood, W. (1937), pp. 102 ff; Allingham, P. (1934); Goodwin, J. (1925) and (1936); Jones, J. A. (1934); Jennings, F. L. (1926); Common, J. (1938) (Simon Blumenfeld in).
167 In Islington, the number of rag-and-bone men known to the sanitary authority had reduced from 37 in 1933 to 21 in 1938: Islington MOH (1933), p. 67; (1938), p. 47.
168 Tebbutt, M. (1983), p. 157.
169 *IG*, 25 April 1921, 26 Sept. 1922, 7 May 1923 for examples (flowers from Covent Garden, a barrow from Hornsey Road, scales from the Caledonian Road market).
170 *I&HP*, 20 Aug. 1932 (14 days); 5 Aug. 1933 (3 months); 22 Sept. 1934 (3 months) after already receiving a brief sentence in August 1934.
171 *I&HP*, 5 Aug. 1933. Oral evidence from Mrs C, CB37, throughout.
172 *IG*, 14 July 1926.
173 Mr F, CB03, 15.1 and throughout.
174 Mr F, CB03, 8.2.
175 *I&HP*, 11 May 1929 (oven doors and stove plates from an empty house); 14 Sept. 1933 (iron railings). For earnings from totting see Morse-Boycott, D. (1931), pp. 164–5.
176 Jennings, F. L. (1926), p. 95; for the potential earnings of street singing – 13*s* 7*d* in one afternoon in Chapel Market – see Worby, J. (1937), p. 163.
177 Mr J, CB06, 13.2.
178 Mr J, CB06, 22.3. Allingham, P. (1934), p. 317 ff gives 'Funkum' as meaning perfume. The word is not in Partridge, E. (1972).
179 *IG*, 24 Oct. 1924, 1 Nov. 1924.
180 *IG*, 27 July 1927; *I&HP*, 13 Dec. 1930, 20 Aug. 1932.
181 *I&HP*, 2 May 1936, 2 Jan. 1937, 16 April 1938, 1 Oct. 1938.
182 See, e.g., Worby, J. (1937), pp. 227–8.
183 Mr I, CB15, 4.2.
184 *IG*, 17 Sept. 1922, 27 Sept. 1922.
185 See, e.g., Durant, R. (1939), pp. 3 ff, 121.
186 Evans, A. and Eversley, D. (eds) (1980), p. 34.
187 Hill, P. (1940), pp. 27–39.
188 See Davies, A. E. (1937), pp. 28–9; Barker, B. (1946), pp. 134–51; Gibbon, G. and Bell (1939), pp. 320–43.
189 IS/LP (1937), pp. 5–6.
190 Gibbon, G. and Bell, R. W. (1939), pp. 410 ff.
191 Mr M, CB12, 1.1, 10.6.

192 Mr P, CB36, 29.3, 34.3.
193 Mayhew, H. (1861–2), vol. 1, p. 33.
194 Mr A, CB21, 30.3.
195 Mr A, CB22, 51.1.
196 *IG*, 13 July 1926.
197 *IG*, 9 Jan. 1929.
198 *IG*, 30 Jan. 1922.
199 *I&HP*, 12 Nov. 1932.
200 *IG*, 26 Oct. 1922.
201 According to the *NSL* (vol. 6, pp. 117, 137–8, 143, 411), 'the poor'
     were fairly widely dispersed in the Western Survey Area, only about
     25 per cent living in streets marked blue or with a blue line. Given
     that the *NSL*'s category was mainly made up of the elderly, widows
     and sick wage earners, this is hardly surprising.
202 IS/OC. For the movement from common lodging house to furnished
     room see Gordon, J. W. (1932), p. 222.
203 Cole, G. D. H. and M. (1923), pp. 17–18, 21, 89.
204 Calculated from NSL/PNL.
205 There were very few common lodging house beds for women after
     the First World War, as in London as a whole. See Chesterton, Mrs
     C. (1926).
206 Calculated from NSL/PNL.
207 See White, J. (1977).
208 White, J. (1977) and IS/OC. See also *NSL*, vol. 3, p. 224.
209 Rowntree, B. S. (1901), pp. 136 ff.
210 *NSL*, vol. 4, Map 1 (unskilled above the poverty line).
211 Mr H, CB39, 1.1–2, 1.4, 14.2, 20.2.
212 *I&HP*, 18 June 1927, 25 June 1927, 2 July 1927.
213 Mrs L, CB34, 13.1.
214 Mr H, CB39, biographical details; IS/OC, 14 Whadcoat Street.
215 Mrs L, CB34, 8.4 and biographical details; IS/OC 82 Whadcoat
     Street.
216 Mrs B (3 addresses), Mrs G (5), Mrs J (3), Mr F (3), Mr M (2), Mr
     L (3), Mr P (2), Mr E (4); 69 per cent of Campbell Road households
     (defined by surname) were no longer listed on the electoral roll for
     the same house in 1938 as had been there in 1933: some of this change
     would have comprised movement within the street. The comparable
     figure for Playford Road was 65 per cent. I am grateful to John
     Chanin for help with this analysis. For evidence of similar mobility
     in Shoreditch see Scott, L. P. (1938), p. 13.

3 Collective identities

1 *IG*, 12 Dec. 1919.
2 *IG*, 3 Feb. 1925.
3 *I&HP*, 6 Feb. 1932.
4 *I&HP*, 6 May 1933.

5 Mr B, CB10, 17.4; Mrs H, CB10, 18.2.
6 Mrs J, CB41, 11.3.
7 Mr F, CB03, 21.3; Mr N, CB04, 6.1; Mr L, CB01, 7.2.
8 Mr L, CB01, 8.1.
9 Mrs E, CB27, 18.1–2.
10 Mr I, CB16, 9.1.
11 Mr I, CB16, 9.2.
12 *IG*, 31 Aug. 1922.
13 *I&HP*, 25 Aug. 1928.
14 On this point see also Ross, E. (1983). For examples of women's
   support networks in inter-war London see Ring, E. (1975), pp. 9–10,
   27–8.
15 Mr M, CB12, 2.2; Mrs C, CB37, 30.4; Mr L, CB01, 23.1; Mrs F,
   CB38, 7.1.
16 Mr I, CB15, 2.1; CB16, 7.4.
17 Mrs B, CB25, 8.1, 8.3, 9.4; Mr I, CB16, 18.6 and CB17, 26.4; Mr
   M, CB15, 13.1–2.
18 Mrs I, CB24, pp. 2–3.
19 Mr I, CB17, 33.2.
20 Mr P, CB36, 11.2.
21 Mrs B, CB25, 40.4–5, 41.1; Mrs I, CB24, 1.5. *NSL*, vol. 3, p. 330.
22 Mr H, CB39, 3.2. The Lennox Road Mission capitalised on these
   arrangements with their Vernon Help-One-Another Society (formed
   1899) which depended on Campbell Road women subscribing 3*d* a
   week, paying out sickness benefit of 5*s* p.w. for 13 weeks. See
   Heaven, E. F. (1934), p. 13. As everywhere, these home-grown
   'diddlum clubs' were vulnerable to fiddles; see Mrs I, CB24, 2.1.
23 Mrs B, CB25, 11.2–12.1.
24 Mrs J, CB41, 11.4–12.1.
25 Mr I, CB15, 1.5.
26 Tebbutt, M. (1983), esp. pp. 54–5.
27 Mrs J, CB41, 34.5; Mrs C, CB37, 7.1.
28 Mrs B, CB25, 23.7, 24.6; Mrs E, CB27, 11.2.
29 Mr G, CB02, 24.2.
30 Mrs B, CB25, 31.4.
31 Mrs J, CB41, 22.3, 37.1.
32 Mr I, CB16, 10.2.
33 Mrs B, CB25, 28.7, 11.2.
34 Mrs F, CB38, 13.2; Mr I, CB16, 10.2.
35 Mr G, CB02, 7.3; CB05, 42.3; CB08, 57.3.
36 Mrs A, CB04, 8.2, 9.1.
37 Mr P, CB36, 1.1–3.
38 Mr D, CB43, 4.2.
39 Mr P, CB36, 35.1.
40 Mr H, CB39, 17.2. See also *I&HP*, 12 Dec. 1936, where a moneylender (male) sueing a man for £15, claimed to have 100 customers
   among the men at the Holloway Bus Garage; and Fox, R. M. (1937),
   pp. 81–2.

41 Mr P, CB36, 15.1; Mr B, CB09, 8.3.
42 Mr G, CB05, 31.4, 40.2.
43 *I&HP*, 18 June 1927.
44 Gillain, L. (1954), pp. 53 ff. The lodging house described was 29 Hornsey Road, *c.* 1932 (info. from author). See also Hilton, J. (1935), p. 50; Orwell, G. (1933), pp. 119, 127, 136, 150.
45 Mrs L, CB42, 49.4.
46 Mrs E, CB29, 68.2.
47 Mr P, CB36, 12.2.
48 Information from Kelly's Directories and IS/DR.
49 Mr I, CB16, 19.5.
50 Mrs N, CB37, 31.3.
51 Mr I, CB16, 20.1.
52 For London between the wars see, e.g. Bailey, D. (1981), p. 6; for Leeds see Hoggart, R. (1957), pp. 52–3; for wartime London see Paneth, M. (1944), p. 55. For comparable examples of loyalty to threatened neighbours see Willmott, P. (1966), p. 151.
53 Mrs L, CB34, 19.1; Mrs J, CB41, 23.4.
54 Mr M, CB12, 3.7; Mrs N, CB37, 32.4. Variations on this popular boasting rhyme were current all over Britain until at least the 1960s, and perhaps still are, although examples from a *street* as against a district or school appear to have been rare. See the correspondence in *History Workshop*, 10, autumn 1980, p. 214 and 11, spring 1981, pp. 196–7; Opie, I. and P. (1959), p. 355; Hewins, A. (1981), p. 135.
55 For a similar reaction against a stranger in a fairly tough East End street see Massingham, H. (1936), pp. 75 ff; and for other outsiders' reactions see Jephcott, A. P. and Carter, M. P. (1954), p. 88; Paneth, M. (1944), pp. 13–14, 123, 124–5; Spinley, B. M. (1953), p. 23. For the way in which these events fit the labelling process see Taylor, I., Walton, P. and Young, J. (1973), ch. 5.
56 Information from Mr Fred Brewster.
57 Mr N, CB04, 14.3.
58 Mr N, CB04, 16.1.
59 Mr G, CB02, 25.3.
60 Mr N, CB04, 15.3.
61 *The Times*, 4, 7, 16 and 29 Jan. 1930. See also *IG* and *I&HP* for the same period.
62 *IG*, 10 Jan. 1930.
63 *IG*, 14 Jan. 1930.
64 *I&HP*, 18 Jan. 1930.
65 Morse-Boycott, D. (1931), p. viii: 'in a slum one cannot be serious for very long, or else one would go mad.'
66 A similar point is made by R. D. Storch in Storch, R. D. (ed.) (1982), p. 9. See also the discussion in Williams, R. (1980), pp. 40–2 on 'residual cultural forms'.
67 See also Bailey, P. (1978), p. 88.
68 Information in letter to author from ex-PC Jones. See also Pegg, M. (1983), pp. 58 ff.

69 In Sept. 1937, 9 people were charged with drunk and disorderly at the North London police court. 'There have not been so many for a number of years.' *I&HP*, 11 Sept. 1937. See also Mannheim, H. (1940), p. 165; *NSL*, vol. 9, pp. 246 ff; Meakin, W. (1931), pp. 156 ff. Even so, Rowntree, B. S. (1941) p. 368, estimated the average working-class consumption of drink at 7s per week per family, or 10 per cent of total income. In Campbell Road, such a sum would have been about 14 per cent of total income.

70 See MacGill, P. (1914), p. 120.

71 Mrs B, CB25, 10.5.

72 Mrs E, CB27, 22.3.

73 Mrs G, CB35, 10.2–3.

74 Mr M, CB12, 3.4.

75 Mrs N, CB37, 25.3.

76 Rowntree, B. S. (1941), p. 368.

77 See *NSL*, vol. 9, pp. 270 ff.

78 Mr C, CB07, 10.8; Westerby, R. (1937), pp. 147 ff.

79 *I&HP*, 7 July 1934, 3 Nov. 1934, 14 Dec. 1935, 25 July 1936. For women and street betting see Massingham, H. (1936), p. 57.

80 See Morgan, A. E. (1939), pp. 256 ff; Mannheim, H. (1940), pp. 216–7; Hoggart, R. (1957), pp. 114–16.

81 See Carnelly, J. B. in Booth MSS, Group B, vol. 207, pp. 169–77; and *Our Street* (1943).

82 Mr F, CB03, 5.2. *NSL* (vol. 6, p. 184) mentions gambling on the roofs of 'rough' tenement blocks.

83 See Jackson, T. A. (1953), p. 137 on a Leeds coster, *c*. 1918.

84 Mr F, CB03, 17.1.

85 Mr F, CB03, 17.2.

86 Mr B, CB09, 2.5 and 3.2.

87 Mr F, CB03, 11.2.

88 Mr A, CB23, 54.7.

89 Mrs L, CB42, 43.3.

90 Mrs A, CB04, 3.2, 4.1.

91 Mrs A, CB04, 2.6, 3.4.

92 Mrs A, CB04, 2.6.

93 Mrs C, CB37, 25.6.

94 Mr F, CB03, 23.1; Mr B, CB09, 3.4.

95 For this light-hearted relationship between 'straight' and mentally handicapped residents of Geel, the Belgian town with a 600-year tradition of caring for mentally abnormal within the community, see Sedgwick, P. (1982), pp. 254–5. And as evidence that we viewed these things differently then: in 1922 the Disabled Society invited applications for a London boxing competition 'entirely for men who have lost a limb'; *IG*, 2 Oct. 1922.

96 Mr J, CB13, 44.1. This is reminiscent of some factory initiation rites of the time: see Willis, T. (1970), pp. 21–2; Pollitt, H. (1940), p. 28.

97 Mr L, CB01, 1.2. Contrast Jackson, B. (1968), pp. 82–4, for victimisation of 'simple' workers in factories.

98 Hatton, S. F. (1931), p. 26.
99 Heaven, E. F. (1934), p. 2.
100 Mr I, CB15, 3.7.
101 Mr I, CB17, 32.4.
102 *IG*, 10 April 1923: 19 May 1925.
103 Mr M, CB15, 13.6.
104 *I&HP*, 15 Oct. 1927. For the relative wealth of moneylenders see *Our Towns* (1943), p. 18; Ring, E. (1975), p. 140. For the tensions, both class and gender, of the moneylender/client relationship, see Tebbutt, M. (1983), pp. 50–5.
105 Mr H, CB39, 6.1.
106 Mr J, CB14, 56.4.
107 Mr M, CB12, 6.7; CB15, 13.3.
108 Mr M, CB15, 13.3.
109 Segal, C. S. (1939), pp. 23–4; Barltrop, R. and Wolveridge, J. (1980), pp. 91–2. See also Ring, E. (1975), p. 70.
110 Letter to author from ex-PS S. C. Caplen, 5 Feb. 1979.
111 *I&HP*, 5 March 1932.
112 Mr A, CB22, 37.3, 39.1–2.
113 *IG*, 2 April 1921. *I&HP*, 26 June 1937.
114 Mrs D, CB18, 1.1.
115 Mrs B, CB25, 35.3.
116 Mrs J, CB41, 17.1.
117 Mr I, CB17, 30.3.
118 Mr P, CB36, 5.2, 35.1. For a similar reaction see attitudes to 'Mrs Morgan' in Massingham, H. (1936); and Orwell, G. (1944), pp. 25–6: 'almost no one in England approves of prostitution.'
119 Mrs H, CB10, 20.4.
120 *IG*, 10 June 1924.
121 *IG*, 24 July 1929; 31 July 1929.
122 *IG*, 2 April 1919.
123 'My wife is right when she said it affects me *as a man*: it isn't the money so much as the feeling men have': an ex-unemployed man in Sinfield, A. (1981), p. 41. There is considerable similar evidence from the inter-war years, usually not so directly expressed. See Beales, H. and Lambert, R. S. (1934), pp. 75–6, 88, 103, 105, 172, 174, 180, 277; Newsom, J. (1936), p. 46; Pilgrim Trust (1938), pp. 147, 150, 195.
124 Durant, H. (1938), pp. 99–100.
125 Edwards, I. (1947), pp. 18, 25–6; Beales, H. and Lambert, R. S. (1934), pp. 79, 209; Pilgrim Trust (1938), pp. 342–3.
126 See MacGill, P. (1914), pp. 209, 255–6, who expresses well the oppositional pride of the 'fighting man'. For an interesting study of violent men, placing psychology in a social context, see Toch, H. (1969).
127 Mr N, CB04, 11.2. See Willmott, P. (1966), pp. 150 ff for similar manifestations of the cult of toughness'.
128 Mr C, CB07, 10.5. *I&HP*, 8 Jan. 1938, 15 Jan. 1938.
129 Mrs B, CB25, 28.4.

130 Mr G, CB08, 58.2. Contrast the domestic role of women in mining areas where the male role of breadwinner is rarely challenged, in Macintyre, S. (1980), p. 143.

131 Mr N, CB04, 16.1. See also McVicar, J. (1974), pp. 145–6.

132 Mr J, CB13, 43.5.

133 Mrs K, CB37, 12.2. For instruction between generations in the 'subculture of violence' in Toch, H. (1969), pp. 233 ff.

134 Mr I, CB16, 21.1. For the relative rarity of street fights in London by the late-1920s see Davies, W. H. in Adcock, St J. A. (1928), p. 970; Heren, L. (1973), pp. 194 ff; Margrie, W. (1934), pp. 6, 38.

135 IG, 14 Sept. 1920.

136 IG, 9 June 1920.

137 IG, 16 Aug. 1929.

138 I&HP, 30 June 1928; 7 July 1928.

139 IG, 8 Aug. 1922.

140 I&HP, 29 May 1926.

141 IG, 11 Aug. 1925.

142 I&HP, 9 Feb. 1929. For the use of iron railings in street fights see Massingham, H. (1936), p. 53.

143 I&HP, 4 July 1931.

144 IG, 1 June 1920, 8 June 1920, 17 June 1920.

145 Mr I, CB16, 20.4; Mr G, CB05, 31.2 ff.

146 Frankenberg, R. (1966), p. 238: 'In a community even conflict may be a form of cooperation.'

147 See Williams, R. (1980), pp. 91–2, who makes the same point.

148 Mr J, CB11, 39.4 (speaking of Bert Lax).

149 See also Morse-Boycott, D. (1930), p. 55.

150 Barltrop, R. and Wolveridge, J. (1980), pp. 54–5.

151 IG, 22 Jan. 1929.

152 I&HP, 13 April 1929, 20 April 1929.

153 IG, 7 Jan. 1927.

154 I&HP, 25 Aug. 1928.

4 Ideology, politics and forms of struggle

1 Mr J, CB11, 37.6.

2 Mrs N, CB37, 8.1; Mrs J, CB41, 20.7, 22.1.

3 Mr I, CB17, 33.1.

4 Mrs K, CB37, 11.3.

5 On 'rough and ready' see Mrs A, CB04, 14.2; Mrs D, CB19, 17.3. On 'do as you please' see Leeson, B. (1930), p. 62 (Dorset Street, Spitalfields).

6 Mr M, CB12, 10.3, 11.3.

7 Mr M, CB12, 11.3.

8 Mr N, CB04, 9.2; Mr F, CB03, 13.1.

9 Mr A, CB20, 10.1.

10 On this point see Orwell, G. (1941), pp. 84–5.

11 I do not know the origin of this slogan but it was of wide provenance in London between the wars, mainly on banners during street celebrations of national festivities. It was also used as a nom-de-plume by an ex-serviceman writing to *TEHW*, 4 July 1919, p. 7.

12 Orwell, G. (1944), p. 33 thought the slogan 'rather servile', but that, I think, is an outsider's view.

13 On this point see Nairn, T. (1981), p. 100.

14 Mr H, CB39, 20.1.

15 Mr P, CB36, 17.3.

16 Mrs L, CB 34, 24.2.

17 Orwell, G. (1944), p. 37. For examples of labour movement hostility, see McShane, H. and Smith, J. (1978), pp. 157–8; Coombes, B. L. (1939), p. 187; Macintyre, S. (1980), pp. 88, 91–2; Bell, T. (1941), p. 263, 279–80; Copeman, F. (1948), p. 61.

18 North Islington elected its first Labour MP in 1929 and regained the seat from the National Conservatives at a by-election in 1937. South and West Islington had both voted Labour from 1923.

19 *IG*, 18 March 1922.

20 *I&HP*, 27 Dec. 1930; 25 July 1931.

21 Mr I, CB45, 63.1.

22 *IG*, 6 Nov. 1934, and letter from A. L. Morton in *History Workshop*, 10, autumn 1980, p. 214. Of the 6 Communist Party candidates contesting Tollington Ward in 1934, 4 were railwaymen, 1 was a journalist and 1 a vehicle builder (*Daily Worker*, 18 Oct. 1934).

23 There was already considerable feeling against the Welsh within many English working-class communities: see Bakke, E. W. (1933), pp. 7–8.

24 Mrs J, CB41, 23.3.

25 Mr P, CB36, 18.3.

26 See, e.g., the fascinating letter from 'A Casual' complaining of union interference in the 'equal' distribution of casual labour at the Islington dust depot; *IG*, 12 Aug. 1921.

27 *IG*, 14 July 1926.

28 *I&HP*, 18 June 1927.

29 Mr A, CB21, 24.6, 29.3; CB22, 50.1. For the Sabini Mob see Samuel, R. (1981), and pp. 267–8 for similar examples. Meltzer, A. (1976), p. 11, however, recalls a 'Tramps' Union' in mid-1930s London.

30 Mrs G, CB35, 14.1.

31 Mrs K, CB37, 8.1.

32 Mr I, CB16, 18.3. For a very similar expression of working-class Toryism, from Finsbury around 1930, see Ring, E. (1975), p. 93.

33 See Rawnsley, S. in Lunn, K. and Thurlow, R. C. (1980).

34 In fact, at least one person from Campbell Road with unusually strong pro-Jewish sympathies could never stomach the BUF's anti-semitism: Mr P, CB36, 18.1.

35 Reay, W. T. (1920), pp. 164–5.

36 Mr M, CB12, 11.4. There was also an anti-Mussolini song current in Campbell Road after 1935: Mrs K, CB37, 32.3.

37 See Rawnsley, S. in Lunn, K. and Thurlow, R. C. (1980).
38 Mr A, CB21, 31.2–3.
39 Mrs I, CB24, 2.1.
40 Mr I, CB17, 31.2.
41 *NSL*, vol. 6, p. 359.
42 Wood Committee (1929), pp. 79–80.
43 Wood Committee (1929), pp. 81, 84–5.
44 Committee on Sterilization (1933), p. 37.
45 *NSL*, vol. 6, ch. XIII; Jones, D. C. (1934), vol. 3, pp. 477 ff; Carr-Saunders, A. and Jones, D. C. (1937), chs XIX and XX.
46 See especially Burt, C. (1925) and (1937); for an excellent recent commentary see Gould, S. (1982), ch. 6.
47 On criminal justice see Calvert, E. R. and T. (1933), pp. 46–9. On sanitary administration see Martin, C. R. A. (1935). On moral reform see Blacker, C. B. (ed.) (1937).
48 Mullins, C. (1943), pp. 124 ff; (1945), ch. 1.
49 *NSL*, vol. 6, pp. 358, 411.
50 Philp, A. F. and Timms, N. (1957), pp. v, vii.
51 See, e.g., Chapman, C. (1925), throughout.
52 Letter to author from ex-PC Jones (letter 1).
53 Mr I, CB15, 3.7.
54 Mr I, CB17, 32.6.
55 Mr M, CB15, 13.6.
56 Mr J, CB11, 38.5.
57 Mr J, CB14, 51.1.
58 Mr I, CB15, 3.5.
59 Mr G, CB02, 9.1.
60 For allegations of false charges see Mr J, CB13, 45.4; Mr G, CB05, 43.1 and CB08, 50.1; *I&HP*, 25 April 1931 for an allegation by Bert Lax. For illegal detention see Mr B, CB09, 1.4; Mr A, CB21, 9.5. For assaults by the police see Mr G, CB08, 50.1; Mr A, CB21, 23.1, 24.1; *IG*, 24 Aug. 1928, 10 July, 1931; Morse-Boycott, D. (1931), pp. 18–19; Chapman, C. (1925), pp. 149 ff; Rentoul, G. (1940), p. 83.
61 Letter to author from ex-PS S. C. Caplen, 5 Feb. 1979. An ex-PC remembered Campbell Road as the last night double patrol in London.
62 This urban myth pops up in other places, too, like Wilmer Gardens ('Kill Copper Row'), Hoxton. Police shared in the tradition and the myth had currency in Hornsey Road police station (information from ex-PC Jones). For a rural example see Samuel R. (1975), p. 151, where a policeman is tipped down a well.
63 *IG*, 15 Feb. 1926.
64 Letter from ex-PC G. M. Hoyle, received by author on 19 Feb. 1979.
65 *IG* 3 April 1913.
66 Letter from ex-PC Hoyle.
67 *IG* 29 June 1920.
68 RC on Police Powers, 1929, (Cd. 6312), pp. 79–80.
69 Letter from ex-PC Hoyle.

70 For a Campbell Road man doing this in Vorley Road see *I&HP* 5 May 1928.
71 *I&HP* 18 June 1927.
72 *IG* 24 Aug. 1928, 28 Aug. 1928.
73 Letter from ex-PC Hoyle.
74 Letter 1 from ex-PC Jones.
75 Letter 1 from ex-PC Jones.
76 Letter, 5 Feb. 1979, from ex-PS S. C. Caplen.
77 Chapman, C. (1925), p. 153.
78 *IG*, 10 Feb. 1920.
79 See White, J. (1983).
80 For the services see NCM April 1924, p. 40; May 1924, p. 50; they continued until 1929 at least. For the good-humoured reception see Mrs L, CB42, 47.1. Earlier reactions to the Salvation Army's street meetings had not been so tolerant, one older resident remembering them being pelted with winkle shells: Mrs B, CB25, 32.8.
81 Mr N, CB04, 20.1.
82 Mr L, CB01, 2.2.
83 *IG*, 30 Aug. 1927.
84 Mr L, CB01, 19.4.
85 For physical attacks on boys' clubs see Munthe, M. (1961), pp. 33, 103–5 (the Tarn Street area of Southwark, *c.* 1932); Paneth, M. (1944), pp. 102–4 (Notting Hill, *c.* 1942, boys and girls).
86 *I&HP*, 1 July 1933, 8 July 1933, 22 July 1933, 11 Nov. 1933.
87 On the nature of the struggle see Englander, D. (1983), ch. 3.
88 Mrs B, CB25, 8.2; Mrs C, CB37, 24.5; Mr J, CB11, 32.2.
89 *I&HP*, 6 Aug. 1938. See also Mrs B, CB25, 8.2.
90 Report of Sanitary Inspector Wm Ward on Campbell Road in ISMB/PHC, 1908–9, 4 Jan. 1909, pp. 167–8.
91 Mr I, CB17, 32.8; Mr B, CB09, 1.5. For similar post-war allegations see *NLP*, 22 Aug. 1952.
92 *IG*, 30 Dec. 1920. See also *IG*, 18 Oct. 1920 for a similar assault by a Campbell Road labourer; and Mrs H, CB10, 19.2.
93 Mr M, CB15, 13.7.
94 Mrs D, CB19, 16.2.
95 Mrs K, CB37, 4.5; Mrs C, CB37, 5.1.
96 Smithson, G. (1930), p. 14. See also Ingram, G. (1930), pp. 13 ff; Spencer, W. (1932), pp. 65–6.
97 Mr N, CB04, 20.2.
98 Letter 2 from ex-PC Jones.
99 *IG*, 16 Jan. 1929, 23 Jan. 1929.
100 *IG*, 18 June 1929.
101 For a similar thought see Hewins, A. (1981), p. 96; Worby, J. (1939), p. 20.
102 Mr I, CB16, 13.3, 25.6. For other examples see Humphries, S. (1981), pp. 145–6.
103 Mr A, CB20, 10.3.

104 Jephcott, P. and Carter, M. P. (1954), p. 68; Jasper, A. (1969), pp. 8–9.
105 *IG*, 17 Dec. 1919.
106 *IG*, 14 Feb. 1928, for example.
107 *NSL*, vol. 7, map 8.
108 *IG*, 24 Oct. 1923, 29 Oct. 1923: she was given probation and bound over.
109 *NSL*, vol. 14, map 3.
110 *IG*, 28 Aug. 1924; 4 Sept. 1924; 11 Sept. 1924.
111 *IG*, 13 March 1926; 19 Aug. 1927.
112 For corroboration see Jephcott, A. P. and Carter, M. P. (1954), p. 67.
113 Mr D, CB43, 15.2.
114 Beales, H. L. and Lambert, R. S. (1934), p. 253; Parker, T. and Allerton, R. (1962), pp. 41, 43.
115 See, e.g., *I&HP*, 11 May 1929; 14 Sept. 1933.
116 Mr G, CB02, 7.2, 9.1.
117 *IG*, 3 Feb. 1925. See also *IG*, 18 Sept. 1924.
118 *IG*, 17 April 1925.
119 *IG*, 17 Dec. 1926.
120 *IG*, 20 Aug. 1925. For Cumberland Street, one of the few Holloway streets with a black line in the poverty maps, see *NSL*, vol. 7, map 8.
121 *IG*, 27 March 1924; *I&HP*, 18 Feb. 1928; *IG*, 22 Jan. 1929.
122 *I&HP*, 8 Oct. 1925.
123 Mr F, CB03, 19.4; Mr L, CB01, 15.1; Mr B, CB09, 9.2.
124 *I&HP*, 5 Nov. 1927; 17 Sept. 1938.
125 *IG*, 30 July 1926; *I&HP*, 6 Feb. 1932.
126 Mr J, CB14, 52.1–2, 53.1.
127 Mr J, CB06, 26.2; CB13, 42.3. ISBG 64, 7 March 1929, p. 5.
128 Mr J, CB11, 41.1.
129 Mr G, CB02, 7.1.

5 The family and social change

1 Stedman Jones, G. (1983), pp. 217–18.
2 IS/OC. The comparable figures in the unskilled working-class streets of Playford Road, Pooles Park, and Ashburton Grove combined were 2.0 and 1.1.
3 For similar comments on lower working-class areas of London in the mid-nineteenth century in respect of domestic violence see Tomes, N. (1978), pp. 328–9.
4 Donzelot, J. (1977), p. 43 has noted the frequency of letting to lodgers, which makes the working-class 'family space a social space as well'.
5 For an assertion that the separation between public and private cannot be taken for granted in discussing the family see Barrett, M. and McIntosh, M. (1982), pp. 89–90.
6 See Mrs E, CB27–9, 1.1–88.1.

7 Mrs K and Mrs M, CB37, 16.3–5.
8 Mrs K, CB37, 1.6, 2.3, 4.1. On infant mortality and the unskilled see Titmuss, R. M. (1943), pp. 57–8.
9 Mr F, CB03, 3.1, 9.1.
10 Mrs D, CB18, 1.4.
11 Mrs F, CB38, 1.1.
12 IG, 17 Feb. 1920, 18 May 1920, 12 Dec. 1920, 4 Oct. 1921.
13 IG, 1 Jan. 1924.
14 IG, 19 May 1925.
15 I&HP, 2 July 1927.
16 On this general point see Godelier, M. (1981), p. 17; Tomes, N. (1978), pp. 333, 341.
17 Mrs B, CB25, 8.1; Mrs K, CB37, 11.1; Mr H, CB39, 18.1; Mr G, CB02, 24.2.
18 Mrs B, CB25, 32.5.
19 Mrs B, CB25, 9.5.
20 Mrs D, CB18, 8.1.
21 Chapman, C. (1925), pp. 58–9; see also 'Corder, R. E.' (1925), p. 69 and Cancellor, H. L. (1930), pp. 137 ff. For prevalence of domestic violence among the unskilled see Lewis, E. L. (1924), p. 54.
22 Mr F, CB03, 23.3.
23 Jahoda, M. et al. (1933), pp. 85–6; Beales, H. L. and Lambert, R. S. (1934), pp. 73–4, 82, 93, 171 ff; Pilgrim Trust (1938), pp. 146–7.
24 Beales, H. L. and Lambert, R. S. (1934), p. 277.
25 Beales, H. L. and Lambert, R. S. (1934), p. 275.
26 See Tomes, N. (1978), p. 341.
27 See the discussion in Barrett, M. (1980), pp. 19–29. For a similar point, differently expressed, see Tomes, N. (1978), p. 334.
28 Beales, H. L. and Lambert, R. S. (1934), p. 74.
29 Mr H, CB39, 22.1.
30 Compare Ross, E. (1983), p. 8.
31 On the relationship between drink and assault see NSL, vol. 1, p. 401; Mannheim, H. (1940), pp. 177–8.
32 I&HP, 16 Feb. 1935, 2 March 1935.
33 Mr P, CB36, 6.1, 19.3; Mrs J, CB41, 35.1.
34 Letter from ex-PC Jones (punctuation amended).
35 Mrs H, CB10, 17.3.
36 Mr P, CB36, 19.3–20.1. For other evidence on money as the major source of rows between husband and wife see Tebbutt, M. (1983), p. 38; Tomes, N. (1978), p. 331. Gervaise Rentoul, an experienced London magistrate, wrote that 'in my experience want of means is the greatest single cause of marital unhappiness' (1940), p. 177. Dobash, R. and R., found sexual jealousy the most frequent cause of domestic violence (in Whitelegg, E. et al. (1982), p. 190) but in a more affluent time and place: see also Whitehead, A. (1976), p. 189.
37 Our Street (1943), p. 13.
38 Mr L, CB01, 14.1; Mr P, CB36, 13.2; Mr F, CB04, 5.2. McIntosh, M. in Brunt, R. and Rowan, C. (1982), p. 124.

39 Mrs E, CB27, 8.4.
40 *IG*, 28 Nov. 1919.
41 *IG*, 19 May 1920.
42 Mr I, CB16, 9.3.
43 Mrs J, CB41, 24.4.
44 Mrs D, CB18–19, 1.1–22.3.
45 Mrs J, CB41, 19.1.
46 Mr J, CB11, 40.2.
47 Mrs E, CB27, 8.4, 11.2, 12.1.
48 See, e.g., Spinley, B. (1953), p. 59 and throughout; Paneth, M. (1944), p. 46.
49 *IG*, 28 Aug. 1924.
50 *IG*, 17 April 1925.
51 *IG*, 13 and 20 March 1926.
52 Mr I, CB45, 36.1–59.1.
53 Mrs B, CB26, 51.5–52.2.
54 Mrs K, CB37, 8.4–14.5.
55 Mr F, CB03, 2.2, 3.1.
56 Mr F, CB03, 16.2.
57 Mr B, CB25, 10.5, 11.1.
58 Mrs J, CB41, 18.3, 22.3.
59 Mannheim, H. (1940), p. 78; Behlmer, G. (1982), p. 239.
60 See Thompson, P. *et al.* (1983), p. 339 and Thompson, P. (1975), p. 174 for greater frequency of corporal punishment in large families.
61 Mannheim, H. (1940), pp. 178–9.
62 Thompson, P. *et al.* (1983), pp. 216–17.
63 Mr P, CB36, 6.1.
64 According to Elkin, W. A. (1938), p. 132, the average proportion of juveniles found guilty of indictable offences and sent to institutions was 9–10 per cent for the period 1925–35. In London, the figure for 1930 was 16 per cent: LCC/LS, vol. 36, p. 207.
65 Children Act 1908, 8 Edw. 7, c67, sec. 58.
66 Children and Young Persons Act 1933, 24 & 25 Geo. 5, c12, sec. 61. There were more precise additional categories but in general the specificity of language in the 1908 Act had been dispensed with.
67 On the increase in committals following the Children and Young Persons Act 1933 see Elkin, W. A. (1938), p. 207.
68 I.e., excluding action taken under the Lunacy and Mental Treatment Acts 1890–1930.
69 LCC/LS, vol. 36, p. 157.
70 Mrs L, CB34, 21.2; CB42, 55.6.
71 Mrs E, CB27, 4.3; Mrs B, CB25, 2.2. General Booth's Migration Scheme for Boys was still sending Islington children to New Zealand in 1926: *IG*, 17 Sept. 1926.
72 *IG*, 20 March 1926.
73 *I&HP*, 1 Sept. 1928.
74 See, e.g., *I&HP*, 11 Nov. 1933 and 23 Dec. 1933.

75 For the struggles in reformatories and other institutions see Humphries, S. (1981), pp. 213 ff.
76 *I&HP*, 7 and 21 Jan. 1933, 18 Feb. 1933.
77 *I&HP*, 7 March 1936, 21 March 1936. For a similar case involving a Rupert Road woman see *I&HP*, 29 Aug. 1931. See also 'Corder, R. E. ' (1925), p. 75, where an Islington councillor was harassed in the street by a woman who blamed him for having her child taken from her by the authorities.
78 See Mrs K, CB37, 9.2; Mrs B, CB26, 64.3; Mr L, CB01, 10.1. For a case of a Queensland Road woman assaulting a teacher see *IG*, 21 Oct. 1927. For evidence that these assaults were not confined to the 'rough' elements see Humphries, S. (1981), pp. 82–3.
79 Mrs K, CB37, 17.2.
80 See Mary McIntosh's criticisms of Lasch and Humphries in Brunt, R. and Rowan, C. (1982), pp. 123–4.
81 Meyer, P. (1977), p. 37.
82 On industrial, reformatory and approved schools in general see Elkin, W. A. (1938), ch. VIII; Benney, M. (1936); Gillain, L. (1954); Humphries, S. (1981), ch. 8. For a more positive view of approved schools see Maxwell, R. P. (1956), ch. III.

6 Young men: accommodating traditions

1 Eager, W. McG. and Secretan, H. A. (1925), pp. 28–33; Jewkes, J. and Winterbottom, A. (1933), pp. 18, 22.
2 Jewkes, J. and Winterbottom, A. (1933); Eagar, W. McG. and Secretan, H. A. (1925); PEP (1935); Gollan, J. (1937); Jewkes, J. and S. (1938).
3 But see Garside, W. R. (1977).
4 Garside, W. R. (1977), p. 324; Davison, R. C. (1929), pp. 172–3.
5 LACJE (1924), p. 17; HMFI (1926), p. 58.
6 ML (1926), p. 10; Secretan, H. A. (1931), p. 53.
7 PP Juvenile Labour, 1928, (Cd 3327), pp. 3–4.
8 PEP (1935), pp. 32–3.
9 LACJE (1927), p. 6; (1932–3), p. 9; LRACJE (1937), p. 4; (1938), p. 9. See also HMFI (1937), p. 16. The local press reported a surplus of vacancies over registered unemployed juveniles in Islington in 1936: *I&HP*, 10 Oct. 1936.
10 Jewkes, J. and S. (1938), throughout. About 4000 'transferees' came to London between late 1928 and the end of 1933: LACJE (1932–3), p. 10.
11 Gollan, J. (1937), pp. 156 ff; Secretan, H. A. (1931), p. 55; Morgan, A. E. (1939), pp. 42–53.
12 *IG*, 12 June 1925.
13 Calculated from Census (1931), pp. 616–17 (Table 18).
14 NSL/PNL recorded 49 categories of employment for 80 sons, not all of whom would have been juveniles.

15 Eagar, W. and Secretan, H. A. (1925); Butterworth, J. (1932), pp. 40, 54; LACJE (1925), p. 5; LRACJE (1935), p. 4; Gollan, J. (1937), p. 240.

16 'As to the GPO', reported the Holloway LACJE in 1925, 'only those boys should think of applying to become messengers who could pass the examinations': *IG*, 12 June 1925.

17 Eagar, W. McG. and Secretan, H. A. (1925), p. 11.

18 Kerr, M. (1958), p. 68.

19 Scott, L. P. (1938), in a survey of 180 Shoreditch boys and girls, found 81 per cent of boys worked within 15 minutes of home (p. 24).

20 Eagar, W. McG. and Secretan, H. A. (1925), p. 55. See also Lewis, E. L. (1924), pp. 34–6; Gillain, L. (1954), pp. 26–7.

21 See Crossick, G. (1978), pp. 116–17.

22 Calc. from St Anne's/RM 1921–38: the total number, however, is very small (12 out of 46). See also Lewis, E. L. (1924), p. 95.

23 Brake, M. (1980), p. vii, makes a similar point for the 1970s.

24 See Clarke, J. J. (1946), pp. 139–40; Morgan, A. E. (1939), pp. 387 ff. For the physical side of boys' clubs see Russell, C. E. B. and Russell, L. M. (1932), pp. 85–116. For the 1930s fashion of Keep Fit see Graves, R. and Hodge, A. (1941), pp. 381–2.

25 Mr L, CB01, 5.1.

26 Mr I, CB45, 39.3. Could Dundee have been a joking Scottish reference to Campbell?

27 Orwell, G. (1941), p. 79: 'In peace time, even when there are 2 million unemployed, it is difficult to fill the ranks of the tiny standing army, which is . . . manned by farm labourers and slum proletarians.'

28 See, e.g., Burke, T. (1936), p. 83.

29 *NSL*, vol. 9, ch. X.

30 *I&HP*, 7 April 1934. For other comment on the Americanisation of London youth see Burke, T. (1934), pp. 30–1; Hatton, S. F. (1931), pp. 40–1; Secretan, H. A. (1931), pp. 85, 87. For similar influences from American detective fiction see Worpoe, K. (1983), ch. 2.

31 The following is taken from Mr I, CB15, 16, 17 and 45, 1.1–65.2.

32 See *IG*, 29 Sept. 1926: letter from 'Fairplay' complaining of 'rowdyism' around Liverpool Buildings; 8 Oct. 1926, letter from 'Sufferer', with similar complaints about Beaconsfield Buildings; 6 Sept. 1927 and *I& HP*, 23 June 1928, about 'disgusting behaviour' by youths at Highbury Corner. *I&HP*, 7 April 1934 ran a story of 'outrages' by youths against St Joseph's RC Church at Highgate Hill; and 5 Dec. 1936 for trouble around a coffee stall in Hornsey Road.

33 See, e.g., Conquest, J. (1933); *Our Street* (1943).

34 The following comes from Mr F, CB03, 1.1–26.1

35 Mr J, CB06, 5.2, 16.3. See also Cook, G. A. (1983), p. 6 for the boys of a poor family joining the army.

36 See *IG*, 12 July 1920, 16 Nov. 1923, 16 April 1925, 20 April 1925, 4 July 1925.

37 For army misfits in the Second World War see Trenaman, J. (1952).

38 The following comes from Mr G, CB02, 05, and 08, 1.1–59.3.

39 According to Jephcott, A. P. and Carter, M. P. (1954), p. 67, this was a common-enough attitude to theft.

40 Compare Beales, H. L. and Lambert, R. S. (1934), pp. 253–4: 'I feel I am *somebody*, and I certainly never felt that during my 2 years of honest idleness.' See also McVicar, J. (1974), pp. 132–3; Benney, M. (1936), p. 141.

41 In 1930 in Greater London, 1,274 juveniles were proceeded against in the juvenile courts for indictable offences; in 1935, the figure was 4,854 (LCC/LS). Mannheim, H. (1940), p. 130, noted a similar tendency for the ages of offenders to fall between 1929 and 1938. Elkin, W. A. (1938), p. vii, wrote of the increase in young offenders brought before the courts, especially since the CYPA 1933. See also Bagot, J. H. (1941), pp. 35–6; Carr-Saunders, A. M. *et al.* (1943), p. vii; BYPA (1937), p. 27. For an example of respectable fears see the publisher's note to Humphreys, C. and Dummett, R. E. (1933), p. 5.

42 For the importance of these family influences see Hill, B. (1955), pp. 16–17; East, W. N. (1942), p. 39; Parker, T. and Allerton, R. (1962), pp. 21, 27. Poke = purse. Hoisting = picking pockets.

43 NSL/MSS, Sec. 1, parcels 10, 11.

44 Information from court reports in *IG* and *I&HP*, 1929–39. Within London, Islington did not display an especially high proportion of juvenile delinquency; the 'worst' areas were Finsbury, Holborn and Shoreditch. See Burt, C. (1925), pp. 70–3; Wallis, C. P. and Maliphant, R. (1967), p. 252.

45 *I&HP*, 23 Feb. 1929.

46 *I&HP*, 23 Feb. 1929, 9 March 1929.

47 *IG*, 10 Sept. 1929.

48 *I&HP*, 14 June 1930.

49 *I&HP*, 28 Jan. 1933.

50 *I&HP*, 12 Aug. 1933.

51 *I&HP*, 16 Sept. 1933.

52 *I&HP*, 26 May 1934, 2 June 1934, 9 June 1934.

53 *I&HP*, 20 May 1939, 1 Sept. 1939.

54 Letter from ex-PC G. M. Hoyle.

55 Both scavenger and 'maquereau' or pimp. On status consciousness in the underworld see Ingram, G. (1930), pp. 45–6; Biron, C. (1936), p. 247. And on the unpopularity of 'ponces' see Allen, T. (1936), pp. 170–1.

56 Mr N, CB04, 17.2.

57 See Partridge, E. (1972).

58 Even the 'Boss of Britain's Underworld' made mistakes: he did 15 spells of imprisonment, totalling 17 years (Hill, B. (1955), p. 2).

59 Hill, B. (1955), p. 20. See also (for Portland in the 1930s) Fletcher, J. W. (1972), p. 47; Benney, M. (1936), pp. 237–8.

60 Crew, A. (1933), p. 169.

61 Generosity was admired in the underworld: see Hill, B. (1955), pp. 46–7; Gordon, C. G. (1925), pp. 88, 99–100; Allen, T. (1936), pp. 55–6.

62 These share-outs were frequently verified by mutual searches: Thompson, W. (1956), p. 25.
63 On the parochialism of the London underworld see Hill, B. (1955), pp. 6–7.
64 For evidence of police corruption and abuse of power see White J. (1983).

7 Young women and the new world outside

1 *NSL*, vol. 1, p. 329.
2 *NSL*, vol. 1, p. 335.
3 HMFI (1923), pp. 46–7.
4 *NSL*, vol. 2, ch. III; Gollan, J. (1937), pp. 73–5.
5 *NSL*, vol. 2, ch. IV.
6 Calculated from Census (1911) and (1931).
7 Calculated from Census (1911), (1921), and (1931).
8 Some did: see Mrs H. Hewitt, CB40, throughout.
9 See Gamble, R. (1979), pp. 130–2; Forrester, H. (1979), p. 74.
10 Meacham, S. (1977), pp. 181–5; Tottenham History Workshop (1982), pp. 64–70.
11 Booth, C. (1902), Series 1, vol. 4, pp. 322–3.
12 Graves, R. and Hodge, A. (1941), p. 45; *NSL*, vol. 2, p. 467. On the continuation of domestic service among girls from unskilled families outside London see Lewis, E. L. (1924), p. 73.
13 *NSL*, vol. 5, p. 363 and ch. VIII.
14 LACJE (1932–3), p. 8 and throughout; BYPA (1937), p. 22.
15 HMFI (1928), p. 7.
16 *TEWH*, 17 Jan. 1919.
17 Graves, R. and Hodge, A. (1941), p. 45.
18 Odhams (1933), p. 600.
19 Advertisement for *Daily Mirror* Beauty Week in *NoW*, 16 June 1935, . p. 17.
20 Burke, T. (1934), p. 64.
21 Burke, T. (1934), pp. 65–6; Orwell, G. (1941), pp. 97–8 and (1944), pp. 38–9.
22 Priestley, J. B. (1934), p. 401.
23 Graves, R. and Hodge, A. (1941), p. 175.
24 Graves, R. and Hodge, A. (1941), p. 278.
25 This is true at least for the 1930s.
26 Advertisements in *NoW*, 14 June 1925; 16 June 1935.
27 See the script of a 'working-class woman's' radio talk in 1934, given in Marwick, A. (1980), p. 161; and Durant, H. (1938), p. 78.
28 Rowbotham, S. (1977); Branson, N. (1975), pp. 203 ff.
29 On the ignorance of birth control among unskilled labourers' wives see Gittins, D. (1982), pp. 165 ff and 184.
30 Mannheim, H. (1940), pp. 346 ff.
31 Mannheim, H. (1940), pp. 336–7.

32 Mannheim, H. (1940), p. 352.
33 In the 'Lenny Chine' living on immoral earnings case quoted in ch. VI, the prosecuting counsel claimed that Wilberforce Road was 'infested with prostitutes' (I&HP, 2 June 1934); whereas the NSL poverty map gives it as mainly middle-class or wealthy with a touch of skilled working class (1929).
34 Royden, A. M. (ed.) (1916); Stringer, H. (1925); Chesterton, Mrs C. (1928); Hall, G. M. (1933); Cousins, S. (1938); Scott, G. R. (1936).
35 Hall, G. M. (1933), pp. 84 ff.
36 Scott, G. R. (1936), pp. 26–7; Chesterton, Mrs C. (1928), p. 155.
37 NSL, vol. 9, p. 302.
38 Cousins, S. (1938), p. 148.
39 Scott, G. R. (1936), p. 27.
40 Our Street (1943), p. 13.
41 Letter 1 from ex-PC Jones.
42 Letter from ex-PS S. Costin, Feb. 1979.
43 I&HP, 31 July 1937; see also 6 March 1937.
44 Letter 1 from ex-PC Jones.
45 Mrs D, CB18, 1.1; I&HP, 19 June 1937.
46 Mrs J. CB41, 17.1, 29.4.
47 Mr I, CB17, 30.4.
48 Mr F, CB03, 1.2.
49 For the ideology of marriage among working-class women in late nineteenth-century London see Stedman Jones, G. (1983), pp. 226–7; and Orwell, G. (1939), p. 133 for similar attitudes in 'the poverty-stricken officer class'.
50 Slater, E. and Woodside, M. (1951), p. 111.
51 Lewis, E. L. (1924), p. 81.
52 But see Whitehead, A. (1976), p. 198 for an interesting contra-insight.
53 For a similar example from Bethnal Green see Doris Bailey's fine memoir (1981, pp. 100–2).
54 See Gittins, D. (1982), pp. 57–8, 176, 183.
55 See, e.g., 'Turned Out Nice Again' (1941) starring George Formby.
56 'I couldn't keep up with the neighbours', a depressed young housewife complains to her friend: 'I try so hard to keep the house looking as nice as the neighbours', Violet . . .': Rinso advert, NoW, 16 June 1935.
57 Slater, E. and Woodside, M. (1951), pp. 117–18. The research for this book was carried out between 1943 and 1946, but its major evidence comes from the late-1920s and 1930s.
58 Calculated from St Anne's/RM, 1921–38 inclusive.
59 Slater, E. and Woodside, M. (1951), p. 288. In the Campbell Road sample of 28 first marriages I have deducted one couple, both aged 46, who would have been too old for the Slater and Woodside survey. Compare Gittins, D. (1982), p. 73, whose sample of 28 women from Essex, Lancs, and S. Wales gave a mean of 24.7 years for factory girls, 22.4 for office/shop girls, and 20.8 for girls in service/at home. Lewis, E. L. (1924), p. 81 also notes early marriages among the unskilled in Glasgow and Middlesborough.

60 Gittins, D. (1982), p. 72.
61 Slater, E. and Woodside, M. (1951), pp. 94–5.
62 See Ross, E. (1983), p. 5.
63 Gittins, D. (1982), ch. 4.
64 Gavron, H. (1966); Slater, E. and Woodside, M. (1951), chs 5 and 9.
65 According to Slater, E. and Woodside, M. (1951), p. 41, 28 per cent of people in the survey came from 'unhappy' family backgrounds.
66 For evidence of friction between girls and boyfriends who kept links with street gangs while courting see Humphries, S. (1981), p. 179.
67 Slater, E. and Woodside, M. (1951), p. 122.
68 The following comes from Mrs B, CB25 and 26, 1.1–69.6.
69 IG, 15 July 1919.
70 Gittins, D. (1982), p. 72.
71 The following comes from Mrs E, CB27–9, 1.1–88.1.
72 This decision to restrict family size was, of course, in tune with the climate of the times: see Gittins, D. (1982), throughout.
73 NSL, vol. 7, map 8 gives Lesly Street only as 'unskilled labourers' above the poverty line.
74 The following comes from Mrs D, CB18–19, 1.1–22.2.
75 Gittins, D. (1982), p. 182.
76 The following comes from Mrs J, CB41 and 44, 1.1–56.2.
77 Compare Gittins, D. (1982), pp. 171–2.
78 On the ignorance of contraception among wives of unskilled men see Gittins, D. (1982), pp. 165 ff. Coitus interruptus was the favourite method of contraception (29.4 per cent against 25.2 per cent using the sheath) in Slater and Woodside's study of inter-war London marriages: (1951), p. 294.
79 The following comes from Mrs L, CB34 and 42, 1.1–57.1.

8 The fall of Campbell Bunk

1 Mr J, CB06, 5.2.
2 1931: 321,795; 1938: 292,300 (Registrar General's estimate in Islington MOH (1938), p. 2.
3 See Table 14 and Islington MOH (1909), p. 236.
4 Information from IS/OC and IS/ER 1938.
5 See Routh, G. (1965), p. 110; Halsey, A. H. (1972), pp. 121–2. Real wages in the 1920s appear to have fallen after 1921.
6 For details see LLP (1936), pp. 12–13; Gibbon, G. and Bell, R. W. (1939), pp. 410 ff.
7 On the high-rent abuses in furnished tenancies see Cole, G. D. H. and M. (1923), pp. 17–21.
8 NoW, 16 June 1935, p. 19.
9 See, e.g., Jackson, A. (1973), pp. 166, 190–1, 196; Foakes, G. (1975), p. 59.
10 Young, T. (1934), p. 315. For Watling see Durant, R. (1939), p. 121.
11 Durant, R. (1939), pp. 3–4.

12 See Flats (1938), throughout.
13 *NSL*, vol. 6, p. 187.
14 Islington MOH (1938), p. 72.
15 Islington MOH (1909), pp. 236–7.
16 *IG*, 21 Oct. 1919.
17 Housing Act 1930, 20 and 21 Geo. V, c39, sec. 7.
18 On Islington's 5-year plan (which does not specify the improvement areas) see Islington MOH (1933), pp. 68–9. On the LCC's action see LCC (1937), p. 10. See also ISMB/SPC, vol. 6, pp. 103–4, 108 and 141–2.
19 Speeches in the council chamber reported in *IG*, 27 Dec. 1930; *I&HP*, 27 July 1931.
20 On the local effects of the Housing Act 1935 see Islington MOH (1936–8) throughout.
21 See *Our Street*, (1943), pp. 4–5.
22 Information from IS/OC.
23 Evidence from oral sources and street lists.
24 Estimated from IS/ER.
25 Evidence from oral sources, street lists and IS/ER 1938 and 1946.
26 Titmuss, R. M. (1950), ch. 7 and app. 4.
27 Mrs L, CB42, 32.2.
28 Titmuss, R. M. (1950), ch. 18.
29 See Calder, A. (1969), pp. 255–6.
30 Letter 1 from ex-PC Jones. Mr B, CB09, 7.4.
31 See Idle, D. E. (1943), p. 94.
32 Titmuss, R. M. (1950), p. 119.
33 *Our Street* (1943), p. 10.
34 Mr I, CB16, 22.1.
35 Mr I, CB45, 56.1.
36 Hancock, W. K. and Gowing, M. M. (1949), p. 351; Beveridge, W. H. (1944), pt III.
37 Bullock, A. (1967), pp. 56–8, 158–61.
38 Bullock, A. (1967), pp. 288, 290.
39 Hancock, W. K. and Gowing, M. M. (1949), p. 351.
40 Halsey, A. H. (ed.) (1972), p. 124.
41 Calder, A. (1969), p. 364.
42 Calder, A. (1969), p. 227, citing Barbara Nixon, *Raiders Overhead*, (1943).
43 Mr H, CB39, 3.3, 18.3, 21.1.
44 Calder, A. (1971), p. 462.
45 Summerfield, P. (1984), p. 31.
46 Mrs K, CB37, 21.4; Mrs J, CB44, 52.4; Mrs E, CB29, 85.2; Mr H, CB39, 26.3–4.
47 *Our Street* (1943), p. 8.
48 Mrs K, CB37, 5.2.
49 Mr G, CB08, 57.4.
50 See Gillain, L. (1954), p. 165.
51 See also Hill, B. (1955), p. 76.

52 Thompson, W. (1956), p. 140.
53 Hill, B. (1955), p. 73.
54 Hill, B. (1955), p. 74; Mr G, CB02, 17.1.
55 Mr A, CB23, 58.6.
56 See Hughes, D. in Sissons, M. and French, P. (1963).
57 Mr D, CB43, 11.1–13.2.
58 On army deserters in Campbell Road see Mr I, CB16, 17.1, 25.2; for elsewhere see Mullins, C. (1948), p. 73; Grafton, P. (1981), pp. 38–9.
59 See Burke, S. (1966), pp. 41–2.
60 See, e.g., *Our Towns* (1943); Joan Temple's *No Room at the Inn* (quoted in Osborne, J. (1981), p. 173); Marwick, A. (1980), p. 218; Dark, S. (1943), pp. 41–2; Isaacs, S. (1941); Calder, A. (1969), chs 2 and 4.
61 Titmuss, R. M. (1950), p. 510.
62 See Titmuss, R. M. (1950), throughout; Ferguson, S. and Fitzgerald, H. (1954), throughout.
63 *Our Street* (1943), p. 8.
64 *Our Street* (1943), p. 15. For 'problem families' see Stephens, T. (1945); Blacker, C. P. (ed.) (1952); Philp, A. F. and Timms, N. (1957), which listed 153 works on the subject since 1943.
65 Titmuss, R. M. (1950), pp. 515–16.
66 For the effects of the war on London's demography see LCC (1951).
67 In 1935, 41.6 per cent of Islington households lived in dwellings with permitted numbers of 3 or under (equivalent to 2 rooms or less): Islington MOH (1936), pp. 54–5. In 1951, sub-division IIIA (inc. N. Islington) had 24.0 per cent of households living in 1 or 2 rooms: Census (1951), p. 22.
68 *Our Street* (1943), p. 7.
69 *Our Street* (1943), pp. 9–10.
70 *Our Street* (1943), p. 12.
71 Mr I, CB45, 51.1.
72 Mrs L, CB42, 37.1.
73 See Mrs I, CB24, pp. 1–3.
74 Information from public local inquiry documents in possession of the author, and *IG*, 22 Aug. 1952.
75 But for some similarities see *The Brixton Disorders: Report of an Inquiry by the Rt. Hon. The Lord Scarman, OBE* (1981), Cd 8427.

Bibliography

1 Oral sources
2 Unpublished documents
3 Small-circulation publications
4 Official publications
5 Newspapers
6 Published sources (primary and secondary)

Abbreviations (libraries and other archives)

GL   Guildhall Library
GLRO   Greater London Record Office
IBE   Islington Borough Engineer's Dept
ICL   Islington Central Library
ITH   Islington Town Hall
LSE   British Library of Political and Economic Science at the London
        School of Economics
PNL   Polytechnic of North London

Note: Bibliography lists only authorities cited in the text or footnotes. References are to first editions of published works except where otherwise specified.

2 Unpublished documents

Booth MSS: Booth Manuscripts (LSE)
Census MSS: Census Enumerators' Record Books, 1871, 1881
ISBG: Records of the Islington Board of Guardians (GLRO)
ISBG/64: Minutes of the Board
ISBG/68–71: Arrears, Maintenance and Prosecution Committee (4 vols)
ISBG/253: Registers of Rough Examinations as to Settlement (11 vols)
ISBG/281: St John's Road Workhouse Weekly Admissions Orders (59 vols)
ISBG/360: Weekly Statements of Relief (Form A) (23 vols)
IS/D: Deeds held at ICL
IS/ER: Metropolitan Borough of Islington: Registers of Electors (ICL)
IS/RB: Vestry of St Mary Islington/Metropolitan Borough of Islington: Rate Books (ICL)

1 Oral sources

Code	Pseudonym	Yr. of birth	Yrs resident Campbell Road	Main occupation	Father's occupation	Mother's occupation	Relationship to other respondents
Mrs A	Mrs Steel	1893	c.1895–c.1910 c.1919–c.41	Costermonger	Painter/decorator	Laundress	Mother of Mr N
Mrs B	May Purslowe	1901	1902–22	Factory work (various)	Painter/decorator	Moneylender/landlady	
Mrs C	Ada Dashett	1902	1930–c.52	Costermonger	Navvy	None	Mother of Mrs K, Mrs M, Mrs N
Mrs D	Jane Munby	1905	1905–20	None (casual thief)	(SF) Coal heaver	Costermonger	
Mrs E	Nancy Tiverton	1905	1917–20	Factory work (brushes)	Unemployed	Charwoman	
Mrs F	Emmie Froud	1905	1905–28	Factory work (boxes)	Unemployed	Laundress	
Mrs G	– Boycott	1910	1912–c.27	Factory work (sweets)	French polisher	None	
Mrs H	Marjie Drover	1910	c.1914–c.35	Factory work (batteries)	Signwriter	None	Sister of Mr B and Mr C
Mrs I	Liz Francis	1911	c.1941–c.55	Factory work (kettles)/abortionist	Unknown	Unknown	
Mrs J	Mavis Knight	1917	c.1920–36	Factory work (ink)	(SF) Dock labourer	Costermonger	
Mrs K	Sylvie Dashett	1924	1924–38	Laundry shop hand	Costermonger	Costermonger	Daughter of Mrs C, sister of Mrs M, Mrs N
Mrs L	Olive Tasker	1926	1929–41	Factory work (batteries)	Unemployed	None	Wife of Mr K
Mrs M	–	1932	1932–47	Factory work (bottle tops)	Costermonger	Costermonger	Daughter of Mrs C, sister of Mrs K, Mrs N
Mrs N	–	1942	1942–c.52	Unknown	Costermonger	Costermonger	Daughter of Mrs C, sister of Mrs K, Mrs M

Mr A	Musher Gates	1902	1902–c.5	Costermonger/coal dealer	Painter/costermonger	Charwoman	
Mr B	Ronny Drover	1902	c.1914–c.35	Labourer	Signwriter	None	Brother of Mrs H and Mr C
Mr C	Billy Drover	1911	c.1914–c.35	Painter/decorator	Signwriter	None	Brother of Mrs H and Mr B
Mr D	Albert Quinn	1912	c.1933–c.4	Thief	Carman	None	
Mr E	–	1912	1912–c.32	Unknown	Sack maker	Unknown	
Mr F	Billy Tagg	1913	1913–c.55	Labourer	(SF) Totter	None	
Mr G	Harry James	1914	1914–c.35	Thief	Tinker	Unknown	
Mr H	Jimmy Dunn	1916	1926–52	Labourer	Unemployed	Costermonger	
Mr I	Walter Spencer	1917	1917–43	Laundry work	Bricklayer	None	
Mr J	Harry Duncan	1917	c.1920–31	Labourer	Street singer	Charwoman/factory work (radios)	
Mr K	Tom Garnett	1920	1922–42	Tailor's presser	Builder/decorator (d. c.1922)	Charwoman	Husband of Mrs L
Mr L	Tommy Short	1920	1920–c.43	Butcher	Dustman	Charwoman (d. 1927)	
Mr M	Tom Nesbitt	1922	1922–c.53	Labourer	Street musician	Costermonger	
Mr N	– Steel	1924	1924–c.41	Labourer	Builder/decorator	Charwoman	Son of Mrs A
Mr P	– Harper	1928	1928–39	Builder			

Note: (SF) = stepfather

ISMB/CC: Metropolitan Borough of Islington: Cleansing Committee, Minutes (ITH)

ISMB/PHC: Metropolitan Borough of Islington: Public Health Committee, Minutes (ITH)

ISMB/SPC: Metropolitan Borough of Islington: Special Committee, Minutes (including Housing and Public Health (Slum Areas) Joint Sub-Committee) (ITH)

ISMB/UE: Metropolitan Borough of Islington: Special Committee re Unemployment, Minutes (ITH)

IS/OC: Metropolitan Borough of Islington: Overcrowding Survey 1938, House Survey Cards (to be deposited at ICL)

ISV/SC: Vestry of St Mary Islington: Sanitary Committee, Minutes (ITH)

ISV/SDP: Vestry of St Mary Islington: Surveyor's Drainage Plans, Books 11–2, 13, 15, 21–2, 28–9, 43 (IBE)

LCC/PH/REG/1: Registers of Common Lodging Houses, vols 5–10, 13–14 (GLRO)

NSL MSS: New Survey of London Life and Labour, Manuscript Records (LSE)

NSL/PNL: Computer-based analysis of 263 household survey cards from NSL MSS, representing unskilled heads of households in Holloway (PNL)

ST ANNE'S/RM: St Anne's Church, Tollington Park, Register of Marriages (at the Vicarage, Moray Road)

Tiley, GL (1975): George Leslie Tiley: 'Memories of Islington Between the Years 1899 and the 1930s' (MS in the possession of Mrs Sheila Leslie)

3 Small-circulation publications

Heaven, E. F. (1934): *Lennox Road Mission Hall 1874–1934: Diamond Jubilee Celebration Souvenir.* (GL)

Holloway (1924): SUPERINTENDENT OF HOLLOWAY FREE MISSION: *One Hundred Years Ago in Holloway, 1825–1925.* (GL)

Hornsey Road (1921): ANON: *One Hundred Years in Hornsey Road, 1821–1921: A Centenary Souvenir of Hornsey Road Wesleyan Mission.* (GL)

IS/DIR: *The Islington Directory* (1863–1905). (ICL)

IS/KELLY: *Kelly's Highbury, Holloway and Tufnell Park Directory* (1909–16). (ICL)

IS/LP (1937): ISLINGTON LABOUR PARTY: *What Labour Has Done for Islington.* (Bishopsgate Institute)

Islington MOH: *Medical Officer of Health's Annual [and Quarterly] Reports on the Health and Sanitary Condition of the Parish of St Mary, Islington* (1856–99).
Medical Officer of Health's Annual [some Quarterly] Reports on the Health and Sanitary Condition of the Metropolitan Borough of Islington (1900–38).

Kelly's: *The Post Office London Directory, County Suburbs* (1919–23). *The Post Office London Directory* (1924–57).
LLP (1936): LONDON LABOUR PARTY: *What Labour Has Done for London.*
NCCM: *New Court Congregational Magazine.* (GLRO)
NCC/MS: New Court Chapel, Tollington Park: *Manual* (1892–1944). (GLRO)
NCM: *New Court Magazine* (1924–39). (GLRO)
Our Street (1943): [CHURCH OF ENGLAND TEMPERANCE SOCIETY]: *Our Street. (ICL)*

4 Official sources

Census (1911): Census of England and Wales 1911: County of London.
Census (1921): Census of England and Wales 1921: County of London.
Census (1931): Census of England and Wales 1931: County of London. Census of England and Wales: Occupation Tables.
Census (1951): Census 1951 England and Wales: Report on Greater London and Five Other Conurbations.
Census 1951 England and Wales: Occupation Tables.
HMFI: Annual Reports of the Chief Inspector of Factories and Workshops.
LACJE: The Annual Reports of the Advisory Council for Juvenile Employment.
LRACJE: The Annual Reports of the London Regional Advisory Council for Juvenile Employment.
ML (1924): MINISTRY OF LABOUR: *Report on an Investigation into the Personal Circumstances and Industrial History of 10,000 Claimants to Unemployment Benefit, Nov. 5th to 10th, 1923.*
ML (1926): MINISTRY OF LABOUR: *Report on an Enquiry into the Personal Circumstances and Industrial History of 3331 Boys and 2701 Girls Registered for Employment at Employment Exchanges and Juvenile Employment Bureaux, June and July, 1925.*
ML (1928): MINISTRY OF LABOUR: *Report on an Investigation into the Personal Circumstances and Industrial History of 9748 Claimants to Unemployment Benefit, April 4th to 9th, 1927.*
ML/LUI: MINISTRY OF LABOUR: *Local Unemployment Index.*
PP CTTEE ON MOTOR TRANSPORT: *Report of a Committee on the Regulation of Wages and Conditions in the Road Motor Transport Industry (Goods),* 1936–7, Cd 5440.
PP CTTEE ON STERILISATION: *Report of the Committee on Sterilisation,* 1933–4, Cd 4485.
PP CTTEE ON WHOLESALE FOOD MARKETS: *Ministry of Food Departmental Committee on Wholesale Food Markets,* 4th Report, 1921, Cd 1341.
PP EMPLOYMENT OF PRISONERS: *Report of the Departmental*

Committee on the Employment of Prisoners: Part II Employment on Discharge, 1934–5, Cd 4897.
PP JUVENILE LABOUR: Memorandum on the Shortage, Surplus and Redistribution of Juvenile Labour based on the views of Local Juvenile Employment Committees, 1928–9, Cd 3327.
PP STREET TRADING: Report of the Committee Appointed to Consider the Question of the Regulation of Street Trading in the Metropolitan Police District, 1922, Cd 1624.
PP UNEMPLOYED ON RELIEF: Unemployed Persons in Receipt of Domiciliary Poor Law Relief. 1927, Cd 3006. 1928–9, Cd 3218. 1929–30, Cd 3433.
RC ON POLICE POWERS: Report of the Royal Commission on Police Powers and Procedure, 1928–9, Cd 6312.
WOOD COMMITTEE (1929): Report of the Committee on Mental Deficiency, being a Joint Committee of the Board of Education and the Board of Control.

5 Newspapers

IG: Islington Gazette
I&HP: Islington and Holloway Press
NLP: North London Press
NoW: The News of the World
TEWH: Tottenham and Edmonton Weekly Herald
The Times

6 Published sources

ABRAMS, M. (1945): The Condition of the British People, 1911–1945.
ADCOCK, St John (ed.) (1928): Wonderful London (3 vols).
ALLEN, Mary S. (1925): The Pioneer Policewoman.
ALLEN, Trevor (1936): Underworld: The Biography of Charles Brooks, Criminal.
ALLINGHAM, Philip (1934): Cheapjack.
BAGOT, J. H. (1941): Juvenile Delinquency: A Comparative Study of the Position in Liverpool and England and Wales.
BAILEY, Doris M. (1981): Children of the Green: A True Story of Childhood in Bethnal Green, 1922–1937.
BAILEY, Peter (1978): Leisure and Class in Victorian England: Rational Recreation and the Contest for Control, 1830–1885.
BAKKE, E. Wight (1933): The Unemployed Man: A Social Study.
BARKER, Brian (1946): Labour in London: A Study in Municipal Achievement.
BARKER, Diana Leonard and ALLEN, Sheila (eds) (1976): Dependence and Exploitation in Work and Marriage.
BARLTROP, Robert (1975): The Monument: The Story of the Socialist Party of Great Britian.

BARLTROP, Robert and WOLVERIDGE, Jim (1980): *The Muvver Tongue*.

BARRETT, Michele (1980): *Women's Oppression Today*.

BARRETT, Michele and McINTOSH, Mary (1982): *The Anti-Social Family*.

BEALES, H. L. and LAMBERT, R. S. (eds) (1934): *Memoirs of the Unemployed*.

BEAUCHAMP, Joan (1937): *Women Who Work*.

BEHLMER, George K. (1982): *Child Abuse and Moral Reform in England, 1870–1908*.

BENEDETTA, Mary (1936): *The Street Markets of London*.

BELL, Thomas (1941): *Pioneering Days*.

BENNEY, Mark (1936): *Low Company: Describing the Evolution of a Burglar*.

BENSON, John (1983): 'Working-Class Capitalism in Great Britain and Canada 1867–1914', *Labour/Le Travailleur*, vol. 12, autumn 1983, pp. 145–54.

BEVERIDGE, W. H. (1909): *Unemployment, A Problem of Industry* (2nd edn, 1910).

BEVERIDGE, W. H. (1930): *Unemployment, A Problem of Industry* (1909 and 1930).

BEVERIDGE, W. H. (1944): *Full Employment in a Free Society*.

BEVERIDGE, W. H. and Others (1932): *Changes in Family Life*.

BINDER, Pearl (1935): *Odd Jobs*.

BIRON, Sir Chartres (1936): *Without Prejudice: Impressions of Life and Law*.

BLACKER, C. P. (ed.) (1937): *A Social Problem Group?*

BLACKER, C. P. (ed.) (1952): *Problem Families: Five Inquiries*.

BOOTH, Charles (1902): *Life and Labour of the People in London* (17 vols).

BORROW, George (1874): *Romano Lavo-Lil: Word-Book of the Romany or, English Gypsy Language* (1923 edn).

BRAKE, Mike (1980): *The Sociology of Youth Culture and Youth Subcultures: Sex and Drugs and Rock'n'Roll?*.

BRANSON, Noreen (1975): *Britain in the Nineteen Twenties*.

BROCKWAY, A. Fenner (1932): *Hungry England*.

BROWN, Jane (1946): *I Had a Pitch on the Stones*.

BRUNT, Rosaline and ROWAN, Caroline (eds) (1982): *Feminism, Culture and Politics*.

BULLOCK, Alan (1960): *The Life and Times of Ernest Bevin. Vol. 1 Trade Union Leader, 1881–1940*.

BULLOCK, Alan (1967): *The Life and Times of Ernest Bevin. Vol. 2 Minister of Labour, 1940–1945*.

BURKE, Shifty (1966): *Peterman: Memoirs of a Safe-Breaker*.

BURKE, Thomas (1922): *The London Spy: A Book of Town Travels*.

BURKE, Thomas (1934): *London in My Time*.

BURKE, Thomas (1936): *Will Someone Lead Me to a Pub?*

BURT, Cyril (1925): *The Young Delinquent* (4th edn, 1944).

BURT, Cyril (1937): *The Backward Child* (4th edn, 1958).

BUTTERWORTH, James (1932): *Clubland* (2nd edn, 1933).

BYPA (1937): BRITISH YOUTH PEACE ASSEMBLY: *Youth in Britain Today*.

CALDER, Angus (1969): *The People's War. Britain 1939–45* (1971 edn).

CALVERT, E. Roy and Theodora (1933): *The Lawbreaker: A Critical Study of the Modern Treatment of Crime*.

CANCELLOR, H. L. (?1930): *The Life of a London Beak*.

CARR-SAUNDERS, A. M. and JONES, D. Caradog (1937): *A Survey of the Social Structure of England and Wales: as illustrated by statistics*.

CARR-SAUNDERS, A. M., MANNHEIM, H. and RHODES, E. C. (1943): *Young Offenders: an Enquiry into Juvenile Delinquency*.

CHAPMAN, Cecil (1925): *The Poor Man's Court of Justice: 25 Years as a Metropolitan Magistrate*.

CHESTERTON, Mrs Cecil (1926): *In Darkest London* (2nd edn, 1930).

CHESTERTON, Mrs Cecil (1928): *Women of the Underworld*.

CHESTERTON, Mrs Cecil (1936): *I Lived in a Slum* (1st paper-covered edn, c. 1937).

CLARKE, John J. (1946): *Social Administration, including the Poor Laws* (4th edn).

COHEN, G. A. (1978): *Karl Marx's Theory of History – A Defence*.

COHEN, Max (1945): *I was One of the Unemployed*.

COHEN, Phil (1979): 'Policing the working-class city', in NATIONAL DEVIANCY CONFERENCE/CONFERENCE OF SOCIALIST ECONOMISTS: *Capitalism and the Rule of Law: from Deviancy Theory to Marxism*, pp. 118–36.

COLE, G. D. H. (1945): *Building and Planning*.

COLE, G. D. H. and Margaret (1923): *Rents, Rings and Houses*.

COLE, G. D. H. and Margaret (1937): *The Condition of Britain*.

COMMON, Jack (ed.) (1938): *Seven Shifts*.

CONQUEST, Joan (1933): *The Naked Truth: Shocking Revelations about the Slums*.

COOK, George A. (1983): *A Hackney Memory Chest*.

COOMBES, B. L. (1939): *These Poor Hands: the Autobiography of a Miner Working in South Wales*.

COPEMAN, Fred (1948): *Reason in Revolt*.

'CORDER, R. E.' (1925): *Tales Told to the Magistrate*.

COULL, Thomas (1864): *The History and Traditions of Islington*.

COUSINS, Sheila (1938): *To Beg I Am Ashamed: the Authentic Autobiography of a London Prostitute*.

CREW, Albert (1933): *London Prisons of Today and Yesterday: Plain Facts and Coloured Impressions*.

CROMWELL, Thomas (1835): *Walks Through Islington. . . .*

CROSSICK, Geoffrey (1978): *An Artisan Elite In Victorian Society: Kentish London 1840–1880*.

DARK, Sidney (1943): *If Christ Came to London*.

DAVIES, A. Emil (1937): *The London County Council 1889–1937: A Historical Sketch*.

DAVIES, W. H. (1909): *The Autobiography of a Super-Tramp* (1942 edn).

DAVIS, Val (c. 1937): *Gentlemen of the Broad Arrows*.

DAVISON, Ronald C. (1929): *The Unemployed: Old Policies and New*.
DONZELOT, Jacques (1977): *The Policing of Families*.
DURANT, Henry (1938): *The Problem of Leisure*.
DURANT, Ruth (1939): *Watling: A Survey of Social Life on a New Housing Estate*.
DYOS, H. J. (1961): *Victorian Suburb: A Study of the Growth of Camberwell* (1973 edn).
EAGAR, W. McG. and SECRETAN, H. A. (1925): *Unemployment Among Boys*.
EAST, W. Norwood (1942): *The Adolescent Criminal: A Medico-Sociological Study of 4000 Male Adolescents*.
EDWARDS, Ifan (1947): *No Gold on my Shovel*.
ELKIN, Winifred A. (1938): *English Juvenile Courts*.
ENGELS, Frederick (1845): *The Condition of the Working-Class in England. From Personal Observation and Authentic Sources* (1973 Moscow edn).
ENGELS, Frederick (1870): Preface to 'The Peasant War in Germany', 2nd edn, in MARX, Karl and ENGELS, Frederick: *Selected Works in 3 Volumes* (Moscow, 1973), vol. 2, pp. 158–71.
ENGLANDER, David (1983): *Landlord and Tenant in Urban Britain, 1838–1918*.
EVANS, Alan and EVERSLY, David (eds) (1980): *The Inner City: Employment and Industry*.
FERGUSON, Sheila and FITZGERALD, Hilde (1954): *Studies in the Social Services*.
FLATS (1938): ASCOT GAS WATER HEATERS Ltd: *Flats: Municipal and Private Enterprise*.
FLETCHER, John William (1972): *A Menace to Society: My 35 Years in Prison – for Stealing £40*.
FOAKES, Grace (1975): *My Life With Reuben*.
FORRESTER, Helen (1979): *Liverpool Miss* (1982 edn).
FORSHAW, J. H. and ABERCROMBIE, Patrick (1943): *County of London Plan*.
FOX, R. M. (1937): *Smoky Crusade*.
FRANKENBERG, Ronald (1966): *Communities in Britain: Social Life in Town and Country* (1969 edn).
GAMBLE, Rose (1979): *Chelsea Child*.
GARSIDE, W. R. (1977): 'Juvenile Unemployment and Public Policy Between the Wars', *Economic History Review*, XXX, 2, pp. 322–39.
GAULDIE, Enid (1974): *Cruel Habitations. A History of Working-Class Housing 1780–1918*.
GAVRON, Hannah (1966): *The Captive Wife: Conflicts of Housebound Mothers* (1983 edn).
GIBBON, Sir Gwilym and BELL, Reginald W. (1939): *History of the London County Council 1889–1939*.
GIDDENS, Anthony (1973): *The Class Structures of the Advanced Societies*.
GILLAIN, Louis E. (1954): *The Pavement my Pillow*.
GISSING, George (1886): *Demos. A Story of English Socialism*.
GISSING, George (1891): *New Grub Street*.

GITTINS, Diana (1982): *Fair Sex. Family Size and Structure, 1900–39.*

GODELIER, Maurice (1981): 'The Origins of Male Domination', *New Left Review*, 127, May–June 1981, pp. 3–17.

GOLLAN, John (1937): *Youth in British Industry: A Survey of Labour Conditions Today.*

GOODWIN, John C. (1925): *Queer Fish.*

GOODWIN, John C. (1936): *One of the Crowd.*

GORDON, Charles George (1925?): *Crooks of the Underworld.*

GORDON, J. W. (1932): *Borstalians.*

GOULD, Stephen Jay (1982): *The Mismeasure of Man.*

GRAFTON, Pete (1981): *You, You and You! The People Out of Step with World War II.*

GRAVES, Robert and HODGE, Alan (1941): *The Long Week-end. A Social History of Great Britain 1918–1939.*

GRAY, Frank (1931): *The Tramp: His Meaning and Being.*

GREENWOOD, George A. (1922): *England To-Day. A Social Study of Our Time.*

GREENWOOD, Walter (1937?): *How the Other Man Lives.*

HALL, Gladys Mary (1933): *Prostitution: A Survey and a Challenge.*

HALL, P. G. (1962): *The Industries of London Since 1861.*

HALSEY, A. H. (1972): *Trends in British Society Since 1900. A Guide to the Changing Social Structure of Britain.*

HANCOCK, W. K. and GOWING, M. M. (1949): *British War Economy.*

HATTON, S. F. (1931): *London's Bad Boys.*

HEALEY, Bert (1980): *Hard Times and Easy Terms, and other tales by a Queens Park Cockney.*

HEREN, Louis (1973): *Growing Up Poor in London.*

HEWINS, Angela (1981): *The Dillen. Memories of a Man of Stratford-upon-Avon.*

HILL, Billy (1955): *Boss of Britain's Underworld.*

HILL, Polly (1940): *The Unemployment Services. A Report Prepared for the Fabian Society.*

HILTON, Jack (1935): *Caliban Shrieks.*

HIRST, Francis W. (1934): *The Consequences of the War to Great Britain.*

HOGGART, Richard (1957): *The Uses of Literacy.*

HUMPHREYS, Christmas and DUMMETT, R. E. (1933): *The Menace in Our Midst.*

HUMPHRIES, Stephen (1981): *Hooligans or Rebels? An Oral History of Working-Class Childhood and Youth 1889–1939.*

HUTT, Allen (1933): *The Condition of the Working Class in Britain.*

IDLE, E. Doreen (1943): *War Over West Ham: A Study of Community Adjustment.*

INGRAM, George and MACKENZIE, De Witt (1930): *Hell's Kitchen. The Story of London's Underworld as Related by the Notorious Ex-Burglar George Ingram to De Witt Mackenzie.*

ISAACS, Susan (ed.) (1941): *The Cambridge Evacuation Survey. A Wartime Study in Social Welfare and Education.*

JACKSON, Alan A. (1973): *Semi-Detached London: Suburban Development, Life and Transport, 1900–39.*

JACKSON, Brian (1968): *Working-Class Community.*

JACKSON, T. A. (1935): *Solo Trumpet. Some Memories of Socialist Agitation and Propaganda.*

JAHODA, Marie, LAZARSFELD, Paul F., ZEISEL, Hans (1933): *Marienthal. The Sociography of an Unemployed Community* (1974 edn).

JASPER, A. S. (1969): *A Hoxton Childhood.*

JENNINGS, Rev. Frank L. (1926): *In London's Shadows.*

JEPHCOTT, A. Pearl and CARTER, M. P. (1954): *The Social Background of Delinquency.*

JEWKES, John and Sylvia (1938): *The Juvenile Labour Market.*

JEWKES, John and WINTERBOTTOM, Allan (1933): *Juvenile Unemployment..*

JONES, D. Caradog (ed.) (1934): *The Social Survey of Merseyside* (3 vols).

JONES, D. Caradog (ed.) (1945): *The Social Problem Group. Poverty and Abnormality of Intelligence.*

JONES, James A. (1934): *Wonderful London Today.*

KERR, Madeline (1958): *The People of Ship Street.*

KIDD, Ronald (1940): *British Liberty in Danger. An Introduction to the Study of Civil Rights.*

KLEIN, Josephine (1965): *Samples from English Cultures* (2 vols).

KNIGHT, Charles (ed.) (1841–4): *London* (6 vols).

KUCZYNSKI, Jurgen (1938): *Hunger and Work. Statistical Studies.*

LCC (1928): *Housing. With Particular Reference to Post-War Housing Schemes.*

LCC (1937): *London Housing.*

LCC (1939): LCC PUBLIC ASSISTANCE DEPT: *'The House'. London's Public Assistance Institutions.*

LCC (1951): *Administrative County of London Development Plan 1951: Analysis.*

LCC/LS: *London Statistics* (annual vols).

LEES, Lynn Hollen (1979): *Exiles of Erin. Irish Migrants in Victorian London.*

LEESON, B. (1930): *Lost London. The Memoirs of an East End Detective.*

LEWIS, E. Llewellyn (1924): *The Children of the Unskilled. An Economic and Social Study.*

LEWIS, Samuel Jnr (1842): *The History and Topography of the Parish of St Mary, Islington, in the County of Middlesex.*

LIDBETTER, E. J. (1933): *Heredity and the Social Problem Group.*

LUNN, Kenneth and THURLOW, Richard C. (eds) (1980): *British Fascism. Essays on the Radical Right in Inter-War Britain.*

MACGILL, Patrick (1914): *Children of the Dead End. The Autobiography of a Navvy.*

MACINTYRE, Stuart (1980): *Little Moscows. Communism and Working-Class Militancy in Inter-War Britain.*

McSHANE, Harry and SMITH, Joan (1978): *Harry McShane: No Mean Fighter.*

McVICAR, John (1974): *McVicar, By Himself* (1979 edn).

MANNHEIM, Hermann (1940): *Social Aspects of Crime in England Between the Wars.*

MARGRIE, William (1934): *The Diary of a London Explorer. Forty Years of Vital London Life.*

MARTIN, C. R. A. (1935): *Slums and Slummers. A Sociological Treatise on the Housing Problem.*

MARWICK, Arthur (1980): *Class. Image and Reality in Britain, France and the USA since 1930.*

MARX, Karl (1844): *The Economic and Philosophic Manuscripts of 1844* (in MARX, Karl and ENGELS, Frederick: *Collected Works*, vol. 3, Moscow 1975, pp. 229–346).

MARX, Karl (1850): 'The Class Struggles in France, 1848 to 1850', in MARX, Karl and ENGELS, Frederick: *Selected Works in 3 Volumes,* Moscow 1973, vol. 1, pp. 186–299.

MARX, Karl (1852): 'The Eighteenth Brumaire of Louis Bonaparte', in *Selected Works*, vol. 1, pp. 394–487.

MARX, Karl (1867): *Capital*, vol. 1 (1974 edn).

MARX, Karl and ENGELS, Frederick (1844): *The Holy Family, or Critique of Critical Criticism* (1975 Moscow edn).

MARX, Karl and ENGELS, Frederick (1846): *The German Ideology, Part 1* (1974 edn).

MASSINGHAM, Hugh (1936): *I Took Off My Tie.*

MAUGHAN, Cuthbert (1931): *Markets of London.*

MAXWELL, Richard P. (1956): *Borstal and Better. A Life Story.*

MAYHEW, Henry (1861–2): *London Labour and the London Poor* (4 vols).

MEACHAM, Standish (1977): *A Life Apart. The English Working Class, 1890–1914.*

MEAKIN, Walter (ed.) (1931): *The Social and Economic Aspects of the Drink Problem.*

MELTZER, Albert (1976): *The Anarchists in London 1935–1955: A Personal Memoir.*

MEYER, Phillipe (1977): *The Child and the State. The Intervention of the State in Family Life* (1st English edn, 1983).

M.-O. (1939): MASS-OBSERVATION: *Britain.*

MORGAN, A. E. (1939): *The Needs of Youth. A Report Made to King George's Jubilee Trust Fund.*

MORRIS, Norval (1951): *The Habitual Criminal.*

MORSE-BOYCOTT, Rev. Desmond (1930?): *Ten Years in a London Slum.*

MORSE-BOYCOTT, Rev. Desmond (1931): *We Do See Life!*

MOUNTAIN, T. Whyte (1930): *Life in London's Great Prisons.*

MULLINS, Claud (1943): *Crime and Psychology.*

MULLINS, Claud (1945): *Why Crime? Some causes and remedies from the psychological standpoint.*

MULLINS, Claud (1948): *Fifteen Years' Hard Labour.*

MUNTHE, Malcolm (1961): *The Bunty Boys.*

NAIRN, Tom (1981): 'The House of Windsor', *New Left Review*, 127, May–June 1981, pp. 96–100.

NEWSOM, John (1936): *Out of the Pit. A Challenge to the Comfortable.*

NSL (1930–35): SMITH, Sir Hubert Llewellyn (ed.): *The New Survey of London Life and Labour* (9 vols).

ODHAMS (1933): ODHAMS PRESS LTD: *The Pageant of the Century.*

OLLMAN, Bertell (1971): *Alienation. Marx's Conception of Man in a Capitalist Society* (2nd edn, 1976).

OPIE, Iona and Peter (1959): *The Lore and Language of Schoolchildren.*

ORWELL, George (1933): *Down and Out in Paris and London* (1966 edn).

ORWELL, George (1939): *Coming Up For Air* (1983 edn).

ORWELL, George (1941): *The Lion and the Unicorn* (in ORWELL, Sonia and ANGUS, Ian: *The Collected Essays, Journalism and Letters of George Orwell*, vol. 2, 1970 edn, pp. 74–134).

ORWELL, George (1944): *The English People* (in *Collected Works*, vol. 3, pp. 15–55).

OSBORNE, John (1981): *A Better Class of Person. An Autobiography, 1929–1956* (1982 edn).

OUR TOWNS (1943): *Our Towns: A Close-Up.*

PAILTHORPE, G. W. (1932): *What We Put in Prison, and in Preventive and Rescue Homes.*

PANETH, Marie (1944): *Branch Street: A Sociological Study.*

PARKER, Tony and ALLERTON, Robert (1962): *The Courage of His Convictions.*

PARTRIDGE, Eric (1972): *A Dictionary of Historical Slang.*

PASSINGHAM, W. J. (1934): *London's Markets: Their Origin and History.*

PEGG, Mark (1983): *Broadcasting and Society, 1918–1939.*

PEP (1935): POLITICAL AND ECONOMIC PLANNING: *The Entrance to Industry.*

PHILP, A. F. and TIMMS, Noel (1957): *The Problem of the 'Problem Family'.*

PILGRIM TRUST (1938): *Men Without Work: A Report Made to the Pilgrim Trust.*

POLLARD, Sidney (1962): *The Development of the British Economy, 1914–1950.*

POLLITT, Harry (1940): *Serving My Time.*

POULANTZAS, Nicos (1974): *Classes in Contemporary Capitalism* (1978 edn).

PRIESTLEY, J. B. (1934): *English Journey* (1949 edn).

QUIGLEY, Hugh and GOLDIE, Ismay (1934): *Housing and Slum Clearance in London.*

REAY, W. T. (1920): *The Specials – How They Served London. The Story of the Metropolitan Special Constabulary.*

RENTOUL, Sir Gervais (1940): *Sometimes I Think. Random Reflections and Recollections.*

RICE, Margery Spring (1939): *Working-Class Wives. Their Health and Condition.*

RICHARDSON, Harry W. and ALDCROFT, Derek H. (1968): *Building in the British Economy Between the Wars.*

RING, Elizabeth (1975): *Up The Cockneys!*

RODAWAY, Angela (1960): *A London Childhood.*

ROSS, Ellen (1983): 'Survival Networks: Women's Neighbourhood Sharing in London Before World War I', *History Workshop*, 15, spring 1983, pp. 4–27.

ROUTH, Guy (1965): *Occupation and Pay in Great Britain 1906–60.*

ROWBOTHAM, Sheila (1977): *A New World For Women. Stella Browne: Socialist Feminist.*

ROWNTREE, B. Seebohm (1901): *Poverty. A Study of Town Life* (1903 edn).

ROWNTREE, B. Seebohm (1941): *Poverty and Progress. A Second Social Survey of York.*

ROYDEN, A. Maude (ed.) (1916): *Downward Paths. An Inquiry into the Causes which Contribute to the Making of the Prostitute.*

RUSSELL, Charles E. B. and Lilian M. (1932): *Lads' Clubs. Their History, Organisation and Management.*

SAMUEL, Raphael (1973): 'Comers and Goers' (in DYOS, H. J. and WOLFF, Michael (eds): *The Victorian City: Images and Realities*, 1977 edn, vol. 1, pp. 123–60).

SAMUEL, Raphael (ed.) (1975): *Village Life and Labour.*

SAMUEL, Raphael (1981): *East End Underworld: Chapters in the Life of Arthur Harding.*

SCF (1933): SAVE THE CHILDREN FUND: *Unemployment and the Child.*

SCOTT, George Ryley (1936): *A History of Prostitution: from Antiquity to the Present Day.*

SCOTT, L. P. (1938): *Growing Up in Shoreditch.*

SECRETAN, H. A. (1931): *London Below Bridges. Its Boys and Its Future.*

SEDGWICK, Peter (1982): *Psycho Politics.*

SEGAL, Charles S. (1939): *Penn'orth of Chips. Backward Children in the Making.*

SENNETT, Richard and COBB, Jonathan (1972): *The Hidden Injuries of Class.*

SHOWLER, Brian and SINFIELD, Adrian (eds) (1981): *The Workless State. Studies in Unemployment.*

SINCLAIR, Robert (1937): *Metropolitan Man. The Future of the English.*

SINFIELD, Adrian (1968): *The Long-Term Unemployed. A Comparative Survey.*

SINFIELD, Adrian (1981): *What Unemployment Means.*

SISSONS, Michael and FRENCH, Philip (eds) (1963): *Age of Austerity 1945–51* (1964 edn).

SLATER, Eliot and WOODSIDE, Moya (1951): *Patterns of Marriage. A Study of Relationships in the Urban Working Classes.*

SMITH, Douglas H. (1933): *The Industries of Greater London.*

SMITHSON, George (1930?): *Raffles in Real Life. The Confessions of George Smithson, alias 'Gentleman George'.*

SOUTHGATE, Walter (1982): *That's The Way It Was. A Working-class Autobiography 1890–1950*.

SPENCER, Walter (1932): *The Glory in the Garret* (1933 edn).

SPINLEY, B. M. (1953): *The Deprived and the Privileged. Personality Development in English Society*.

STEDMAN JONES, Gareth (1971): *Outcast London. A Study in the Relationship Between Classes in Victorian Society*.

STEDMAN JONES, Gareth (1983): *Languages of Class. Studies in English Working-Class History 1832–1982*.

STEPHENS, Tom (1945): *Problem Families. An Experiment in Social Rehabilitation*.

STEVENSON, John and COOK, Chris (1977): *The Slump*.

STORCH, Robert D. (ed.) (1982): *Popular Culture and Custom in Nineteenth-Century England*.

STRINGER, Hubert (1925): *Moral Evil in London*.

SUMMERFIELD, Penny (1984): *Women Workers in the Second World War. Production and Patriarchy in Conflict*.

TAYLOR, Ian, WALTON, Paul, YOUNG, Jock (eds) (1973): *The New Criminology. For a Social Theory of Deviance*.

TAYLOR, Ian, WALTON, Paul, YOUNG, Jock (eds) (1975): *Critical Criminology*.

TEBBUTT, Melanie (1983): *Making Ends Meet. Pawnbroking and Working-Class Credit*.

THOMPSON, Bonar, (1933): *Hyde Park Orator* (1936 edn).

THOMPSON, E. P. (1963): *The Making of the English Working Class*.

THOMPSON, E. P. (1978): *The Poverty of Theory, and Other Essays*.

THOMPSON, Paul (1975): *The Edwardians. The Remaking of British Society*.

THOMPSON, Paul with WAILEY, Tony and LUMMIS, Trevor (1983): *Living the Fishing*.

THOMPSON, Wally (1956): *Time Off My Life*.

THORNHILL, J. F. P. (1935): *Greater London: A Social Geography*.

TITMUSS, Richard M. (1943): *Birth, Poverty and Wealth. A Study of Infant Mortality*.

TITMUSS, Richard M. (1950): *Problems of Social Policy*.

TOCH, H. (1969): *Violent Men. An Inquiry into the Psychology of Violence* (1972 edn).

TOMES, Nancy (1978): 'A "Torrent of Abuse": Crimes of Violence Between Working-Class Men and Women in London, 1840–1875', *Journal of Social History*, vol. 2, no. 2, 1978, pp. 328–45.

TOTTENHAM HISTORY WORKSHOP (1982): *How Things Were. Growing up in Tottenham, 1890–1920*.

TRENAMAN, Joseph (1952): *Out of Step. A Study of Young Delinquent Soldiers in Wartime. . . .*

TUCKER, James (1966): *Honourable Estates*.

WALLIS, C. P. and MALIPHANT, R. (1967): 'Delinquent Areas in the County of London: Ecological Factors', *British Journal of Criminology*, vol. 7, no. 3, July 1967, pp. 250–84.

WESTERBY, Robert (1937): *Wide Boys Never Work.*

WHITE, Jerry (1977): 'When Every Room was Measured: the Over-crowding Survey of 1935–6 and its Aftermath', *History Workshop*, 4, autumn 1977, pp. 86–94.

WHITE, Jerry (1979): 'Campbell Bunk: A Lumpen Community in London Between the Wars', *History Workshop*, 8, autumn 1979, pp. 1–49.

WHITE, Jerry (1983): 'Police and People in London in the 1930s', *Oral History*, vol. 11, no. 2, autumn 1983, pp. 34–41.

WHITEHEAD, Ann (1976): 'Sexual Antagonism in Herefordshire' (in BARKER, D. L. and ALLEN, S. (eds) (1976), pp. 169–203).

WHITELEGG, Elizabeth *et al.* (eds) (1982): *The Changing Experience of Women.*

WHITESIDE, Noelle (1979): 'Welfare Insurance and Casual Labour . . . 1906–26', *Economic History Review*, XXXII, 4, Nov. 1979.

WILKINSON, Ellen (1939): *The Town That Was Murdered. The Life-Story of Jarrow.*

WILLIAMS, Raymond (1980): *Problems in Materialism and Culture: Selected Essays.*

WILLIAMSON, Bill (1982): *Class, Culture, and Community. A Biographical Study of Social Change in Mining.*

WILLIS, Paul E. (1977): *Learning To Labour. How Working-class Kids get Working-class Jobs.*

WILLIS, Ted (1970): *Whatever Happened to Tom Mix?*

WILLMOTT, Peter (1966): *Adolescent Boys of East London* (1969 edn).

WORBY, John (1937): *The Other Half. The Autobiography of a Spiv.*

WORBY, John (1939): *Spiv's Progress.*

WORPOLE, Ken (1983): *Dockers and Detectives. Popular Reading: Popular Writing.*

WRIGHT, Erik Olin (1978): *Class, Crisis and the State* (1979 edn).

WRIGHT, Erik Olin (1979): *Class Structure and Income Determination.*

YOUNG, Terence (1934): *Becontree and Dagenham. A Report Made for the Pilgrim Trust.*

ZWEIG, F. (1949): *Labour, Life and Poverty* (1975 edn).

Index

abortion, 73, 194, 235
adoption, 137–8
American influence, 166
army, 47–8, 59, 165–6, 174–5, 186, 219, 228
Arsenal Football Club, 40, 54, 83, 109, 165

begging, 31, 48, 61–2, 68, 77, 114, 135, 158–9
bigamy, 68
blacks, 47, 105
Bonfire Night, 89, 120–1, 234–5
bookmakers, see gambling
borstal, 182, 185
Brock Committee (1933), 113

cafés, 83, 116, 183, 185, 201, 213
Caledonian Market, 20, 42
Campbell Road: development, 11ff; moving in, 13–18, 60, 67–9, 136; moving out, 12, 14, 134–5, 138, 160, 171–2, 187, 203–4, 206–7, 208, 214–16, 216–17, 220–36; moving within, 17, 69; name change (to Whadcoat Street), 221; population, 14, 22, 25, 29, 220, 222, 226, 235–6; as refuge, 75–6, 118, 134, 180, 209, 235; reputation, 23–5, 51, 72–3, 79–80, 89, 113, 116, 117, 124, 127, 129, 157, 168, 213, 221; top end/bottom end, 13, 78–9, 178
Canvey Island, 92, 226
capital accumulation, 64–5, 95, 231

casual labour, see labour markets
child labour, 53–5, 150–1, 169, 211
child neglect, 71–2, 75, 148–9
cinema, 40, 83, 166, 193–4, 213, 222
class, 31ff; see also lumpenproletariat
clothing, 71, 104, 148, 166, 170, 183, 192–3, 202, 204–6, 212, 214
clubs, 23, 25, 95, 108, 122–3, 167
common lodging houses, 13, 14–16, 18, 24, 25, 47, 60, 66, 76–7, 99, 129, 180, 209
contraception, 194, 215
costermongers, see street enterprises
crime, 23, 24, 28, 33, 39, 50–1, 53, 56, 65, 71, 122, 123–30, 152, 221; communal ventures, 125–6, 129, 178, 180, 182; professional thieves, 64, 89, 128, 132–3, 176–87, 209–10, 230–1; theft between neighbours, 47, 100–1; theft from employers, 51, 126–8, 172–4; theft within the family, 144–5, 152, 158
Cypriots, 105

disability (mental and physical), 25, 38–9, 45–50, 67, 68, 71–2, 89, 92–3, 98, 146–7, 157–9, 167, 175, 180, 210, 216, 228–9
discipline, 104–5, 151–3, 175
drunkenness, 16, 49, 82, 84–5, 89, 143, 154

emigration, 158

evacuation, 227–8
eugenics, 112–13

factory work, 21, 36, 43, 50, 51,
   168–9, 172, 178, 189–92, 197,
   200–1, 204, 205, 207, 212,
   216–17, 229–30
family life: family size, 13, 14, 24,
   27, 66, 67, 137, 191, 207, 211,
   215, 218; feuds, 99–100;
   relations between husband and
   wife, 74, 75, 91, 96–7, 132,
   139–46; relations between
   parents and children, 71–2, 75,
   140–1, 145, 146–7, 147–60,
   164, 169, 170, 172, 177–8, 181,
   191, 196, 197, 202, 203, 206,
   211; see also violence
femininity, 166, 191–4, 197–8,
   212–13
Finsbury Park coal yard tragedy,
   81–2
First World War, 40, 46, 47–8, 49,
   88, 106, 110–11, 124, 138, 149,
   162, 172, 189, 192, 200, 212

gambling, 13, 23, 26, 76–7, 80,
   85–6, 89–90, 103–4, 115,
   118–20, 148, 166, 171, 173, 176,
   179, 180, 234
General Strike, 108–9
George's Road, 9, 18, 29, 55, 67,
   77–8, 81, 135–6, 179, 204, 207,
   208, 209
gypsies, 19, 55–6, 60, 99, 176–7,
   178

Holloway: geography, 8, 264n1;
   history, 9–11; economy, 19–22,
   36–7, 163
home, idealization of, 197–8,
   207–8, 214–15, 222–3
hop-picking, 73, 235
household formation, 135–7,
   138–9, 143, 146
housing conditions, 48–9, 63, 71,
   92–3, 169, 198, 201, 224; see also
   overcrowding

housing market, 12, 14–19, 25,
   66–7, 69, 176, 185, 207,
   210–11, 217, 221, 222–5, 227–8,
   233–4
housing policy, 113, 224–6; see also
   slum clearance
Hoxton, 19, 64, 76, 179

infant mortality, 137, 138–9, 148,
   149, 167
Irish, 10, 67, 105, 107, 212
Islington: economy, 36–7, 41,
   189–90; social structure, 30,
   220; see also Holloway
Islington Communist Party, 108
Islington Labour Party, 63, 107–8,
   225

Jews, 54, 105

kinship, 22, 73

labour markets: casual (men),
   19–20, 30, 33, 34, 39–44, 176,
   207, 210, 220, 228–9; for boys,
   162–4, 168–9, 172–3, 178, 190;
   for girls, 51, 75, 162–3, 188–92,
   200–1, 204, 205, 212, 220; for
   women, 14, 20–1, 30, 40, 43–4,
   74, 127–8, 188, 207, 229–30
landlords, 17–18, 22–3, 41, 69, 74,
   89–90, 91, 104, 107–8, 123–4,
   225, 228, 236
language, 56, 59, 60, 61–2, 179
Lennox Road Mission, 25, 43,
   121–2, 153, 167, 172, 174, 175,
   176
literacy, 107, 108, 130–1, 149, 177,
   178, 193–4
London: economy, 36, 37, 162–3,
   188–9; image of, in 1930s, 36
London County Council (LCC),
   45, 53, 54, 63, 81, 89, 113, 134,
   157–9, 203, 210, 217, 221, 223,
   225
lumpenproletariat, 31ff, 62, 65,
   128, 142

marriage, 171–2, 175–6, 187, 188,